Also by Elisabeth Bumiller

MAY YOU BE THE MOTHER OF A HUNDRED SONS

THE SECRETS OF MARIKO

FOR WOMEN ONLY
(with Jennifer Berman, M.D., and Laura Berman, Ph.D.)

CONDOLEEZZA RICE
AN AMERICAN LIFE

Elisabeth Bumiller

RANDOM HOUSE
NEW YORK

CONDOLEEZZA RICE

AN · AMERICAN · LIFE

A BIOGRAPHY

Published in the United States by Random House, an imprint of
The Random House Publishing Group, a division of Random House, Inc., New York.

RANDOM HOUSE and colophon are registered trademarks of Random House, Inc.

Library of Congress Cataloging-in-Publication Data

Bumiller, Elisabeth.
Condoleezza Rice : an American life : a biography / Elisabeth Bumiller.
p. cm.
Includes bibliographical references.
ISBN 978-1-4000-6590-5
1. Rice, Condoleezza, 1954– 2. Stateswomen—United States—Biography.
3. Cabinet officers—United States—Biography. 4. Women cabinet officers—United States—Biography. 5. African Americans—Biography. 6. Bush, George W. (George Walker), 1946– —Friends and associates. 7. United States—Foreign relations—2001– 8. National Security Council (U.S.)—Biography. 9. Stanford University—Officials and employees—Biography. I. Title.
E840.8.R48.B86 2007
355'.033073092—dc22
[B] 2007031981

Printed in the United States of America on acid-free paper

www.atrandom.com

2 4 6 8 9 7 5 3 1

First Edition

Book design by Carol Malcolm Russo

Title-page photograph: Reuters/Matt Dunham

FOR STEVE

CONTENTS

INTRODUCTION

September 11, 2001, dawned brilliant and clear in Washington, a gorgeous late summer day. Condoleezza Rice, eight months into her job as national security adviser to President George W. Bush, was in her office as usual around 6 A.M., happy to have some breathing space with the president away. Bush was on an overnight trip to Florida to visit a Sarasota elementary school and to push for an education bill that was languishing in Congress. It was all so minor—"just a little trip to Florida," Rice recalled[1]—that neither she nor her deputy, Stephen Hadley, had bothered to accompany him. One of them was usually along on presidential trips to handle whatever national security questions might come up, but in this case they sent Deborah Loewer, a Navy captain who was the director of the White House Situation Room.[2]

Rice was standing at her desk shortly before 9 A.M. when her assistant came in to tell her that a plane had hit the World Trade Center. Rice thought it was odd, but she assumed that a small plane had veered out of control. Within moments her assistant came back to say that the plane was in fact a commercial airliner. Rice thought that was unusually odd. "So I called the president and he'd just heard, and he said, 'That's a really strange accident,' " Rice recalled. "And I said,

'Yeah, it really is.' " She told Bush she would get back to him when she knew more.[3]

Minutes later, Rice was in a meeting of her top aides in the conference area of the Situation Room when her assistant handed her a note saying that a second plane had struck the World Trade Center. Andrew H. Card, Jr., the White House chief of staff, had just whispered the same thing into Bush's ear in the Florida classroom, adding, as if he already knew that he was speaking for history, that "America is under attack."[4] Rice, like everyone else at the White House, knew immediately it was terrorism. "I have to go," she abruptly told her staff.[5]

Rice, the first African-American woman to become national security adviser and later secretary of state, headed from the conference area into the Situation Room's operations center, where her first thought was to assemble a crisis meeting of the administration's national security team. But she couldn't find Donald Rumsfeld, the secretary of defense.[6] Colin Powell, the secretary of state, was in Peru, and Rice was unable to get a call through to George Tenet, the director of the Central Intelligence Agency.[7] All around her was chaos. Richard Clarke, the National Security Council's counterterrorism chief, who had just raced to the Situation Room from a conference three blocks away, was living through his worst nightmare as he tried to convene a videoconference of his top aides. Bush's motorcade was heading toward Air Force One in Florida, but it was a convoy that did not know where it was ultimately headed. Neither the president nor the Secret Service had decided where Bush should go after his plane took off, and so far the only goal was to get the president up in the air as fast and as high as possible.[8] Franklin Miller, the NSC's senior director for defense, who had joined the group in the Situation Room, recommended to Rice that fighter jet escorts be dispatched to protect Bush's 747. "Make it happen," Rice said, as Miller recalled.[9]

Upstairs, where Vice President Dick Cheney remained in his office, the Secret Service had just learned from a tower supervisor at Reagan National Airport that a plane whose pilot refused to communicate appeared to be heading toward the White House. The agents did not know then that the plane was American 77, flown by a Saudi hijacker, Hani Hanjour (and assisted by two Al Qaeda terrorists the CIA had failed to put on a watch list), but the news was dire enough for the Secret Service to order the immediate evacuation of the vice president.[10] Agents propelled Cheney out of his chair and into the tunnel leading underneath the White House to the specially designated bunker, officially the Presidential Emergency Operations Center, which had been built below the East Wing as a shelter for Franklin D. Roosevelt during World War II.[11]

At the moment Cheney entered the tunnel, 9:37 A.M., American 77 crashed into the Pentagon.[12] Rice, who was still in the Situation Room trying to reach Rumsfeld, looked up and saw the wreckage on television. Within minutes the Secret Service ordered her to the bunker, too. Rice thought to call her closest living relatives, her uncle and aunt in Birmingham, to tell them that she was okay and to spread the word among the family. Then she was instantly whisked away.[13]

Rice got to the bunker around 10 A.M. and took a seat next to the vice president. The next hours would be the most harrowing of her life. They were filled with snap decisions, fragmentary information, reports of impending attacks that proved false, mixed signals, tense phone calls, and nearly unbearable anxiety and confusion. Minutes after arriving, Rice watched the television in disbelief as the South Tower of the World Trade Center collapsed in a massive cloud of dust and debris, killing thousands. "There was a groan in the room that I won't forget, ever," one witness later said.[14] Then suddenly Rice was whipsawed by reports that yet another inbound aircraft—presumably hijacked—was heading toward Washington. The Air Force was trying to set up a combat air patrol of fighter jets over the nation's capital, a CAP in military parlance, and Cheney wanted to establish the rules of engagement—in short, whether the pilots should be authorized to take the extraordinary step of shooting down a commercial airliner loaded with passengers.[15] The president was now aloft on Air Force One, and Rice remembered hearing Cheney inform the president in a phone call to the plane, "Sir, the CAPs are up. Sir, they're going to want to know what to do." Rice then recalled hearing Cheney say, "Yes, sir."[16] Rice remembered the phone call as occurring within a few minutes, perhaps five, after she arrived in the bunker.[17] As she later recounted it, "The Pentagon was asking, 'What shall we do if . . . ?' And the vice president talked to the president and conveyed that, in fact, they should, if necessary, shoot it down."[18]

Within moments, a military aide informed the vice president that the aircraft now heading toward Washington—United 93—was eighty miles out. The aide asked for authority to engage, and Cheney said yes.[19] I. Lewis "Scooter" Libby, the vice president's chief of staff, who was with the group, later described Cheney's decision as quick and decisive, "in about the time it takes a batter to decide to swing."[20] The aide returned a few minutes later to say that the plane was now sixty miles out and, no doubt wanting to make sure that he had absolutely clear instructions for the ghastly event that he thought was about to occur, repeated his request to engage. Cheney again said yes. Joshua Bolten, the White House deputy chief of staff, who was unaware of any previous discussion about shooting down airplanes, had what he later recalled as a "quiet moment." He then suggested that the vice president get in touch with the president to confirm the engage order. Cheney did so. On Air Force One, Ari Fleischer, the White House press secretary, who was taking notes, recorded at 10:20 A.M. that the president had told him—Fleischer—that he had authorized a shoot-down.[21] Back in the bunker, word soon arrived of an aircraft down in Pennsylvania. Rice recalled the sudden horror in the room at what they believed the American fighter jets had done.[22]

"We thought we'd shot down a plane," Rice said. "Because the plane that crashed in Pennsylvania, we didn't understand what had happened to it, and so I just remember the vice president saying to the Pentagon, 'You must know whether or not we engaged, whether or not a fighter engaged a civilian aircraft. You *have* to know the answer to that.' Because they kept saying, 'Sir, we're trying to find out.' And then I would get on the phone and say, 'Come on, you've got to tell us. *Did we engage a civilian aircraft?*' "[23]

Within minutes Rice was focused on a new catastrophe: reports of another hijacked plane heading toward Washington, this one only five to ten miles out. Believing there was only a minute or two before impact, Cheney once again authorized that it be attacked.[24] Steve Hadley had by now joined the group, and in a conference call with the Pentagon he conveyed the understated terror of the moment. "I need to get word to Dick Myers that our reports are there's an inbound aircraft flying low five miles out," Hadley said, referring to Richard Myers, the chairman of the Joint Chiefs of Staff. "The vice president's guidance was we need to take them out."[25] Those in the bunker held their breath, but nothing happened. Eventually Rice and the others learned that the hijacked plane was in fact a medevac helicopter.[26] They also learned that the plane they thought had been shot down had actually crashed on its own in Pennsylvania, the result of passengers' attempts to overpower the hijackers, which sent the plane to the ground before it reached either the U.S. Capitol Building or the White House, its possible intended targets.

Above ground, the streets of downtown Washington were bedlam, then silent. The entire White House had been ordered evacuated by the time Rice arrived in the bunker, so she did not see the fleeing kitchen staff in white aprons or the women running barefoot with their high heels in hand. "Incoming, incoming, get out of here!" one stunned tourist heard a guard shout as workers spilled from the White House gates.[27] On the horizon across the Potomac River, a pall of white and orange smoke rose from the supposedly impregnable Pentagon.[28] Bureaucrats collected on the sidewalks, unsure of what to do or where to go, but most soon joined the exodus in the traffic jams out of town. By afternoon, anyone who called the White House switchboard, a famously efficient Washington institution, would hear a brief recording saying to hold for an operator and then the line would go dead.[29]

Rice spent some of the rest of her time in the bunker trying to track aircraft with Norman Mineta, the transportation secretary, who had joined the group. Although the Federal Aviation Administration had grounded every plane in the sky, some were still in the air and unaccounted for. It was a strange thing for the national security adviser to be doing, but to her it seemed critical to the job of assuring that the threat of terrorists on hijacked planes was contained. "There were false reports of planes, unidentified planes, squawking all over the place," Rice said. "We were doing many, many things, but we would write down on a yellow pad that these numbers are still out there."[30]

Rice also called the Russians and spoke directly to President Vladimir Putin, who was trying without success to reach Bush on Air

Force One. She informed Putin of the nature of the attacks as the Americans understood them and that the military response was nothing that should cause concern in Moscow. "I said, 'Our forces are going to go on alert,' and he said, 'I know, and we're standing down so there'll be no confusion,' " Rice recalled.[31] For Rice, a student of the Cold War, Putin's comment that he would not put his own military on alert in response to the Americans was a terse but profound reminder of how far the world had been transformed in the decade since she had been a midlevel foreign policy aide in the first Bush administration and the end of the Soviet Union in 1991. In an instant, a new order dawned that drew Russia and the United States as allies against a twenty-first-century threat.

Around the same time, Rice asked Hadley to call Richard Armitage, Powell's deputy at the State Department, to urge him to send a cable to all overseas posts with the message that "the United States of America is functioning" because otherwise, she later recalled, "they'll think we've been decapitated."[32] In retrospect, Rice realized that her experience in war games—from a part-time job at a military contractor in Denver to classroom simulations as a political science professor at Stanford University—must have kicked in, even though this was not the war she had prepared for. "It was almost as if my nuclear war training propelled me to do certain things," she said.[33]

While Rice worked feverishly in the bunker, a bizarre spectacle unfolded as the president went on a day-long odyssey across the United States. Cheney had told Bush it was too unsafe to return to Washington, as had the Secret Service,[34] so after taking off from Florida, Air Force One went on a zigzag course, east from Sarasota to the Atlantic, then north, then west.[35] The 747 finally landed midday at Barksdale Air Force Base near Shreveport, Louisiana, where it was surrounded on the ground by Air Force personnel in full combat gear with M-16s.[36] Bush, looking shell-shocked, made a brief, halting statement to the nation, was told by the Secret Service it was still unsafe to return to Washington, and so reluctantly flew on to Offutt Air Force Base in Omaha, one of the most secure military installations in the United States.[37] From Offutt, Bush conducted an improvised National Security Council meeting by videophone with Rice, Cheney, and Rumsfeld in Washington. When it was over, a frustrated Bush told the Secret Service he was overruling them and heading back to the White House.[38]

Rice caught up with Bush shortly after he returned, about 7 P.M., and consulted with him on the draft of a speech he was to give that night to the nation. The president's chief speechwriter, Michael Gerson, had written that the United States would make no distinction between those who planned the acts and those who tolerated or encouraged the terrorists, but Bush thought "tolerated" and "encouraged" were too vague and instead proposed the word "harbor."[39] He asked Rice what she thought. "You can say it now or you'll have other opportunities to say it," she told him.[40] In those early days, Rice was reluctant to give her opinion to the president unless he pressed, but since he had asked, she told him she favored using "harbor."[41] In an 8:30 P.M. nationally televised speech from the Oval Office, as Rice watched nearby, Bush made it official: "We will make no distinction between the terrorists who committed these acts and those who harbor them," the president said.[42] The White House would grandly call the president's declaration the centerpiece of a new Bush Doctrine.

Rice was back in the bunker at 9:30 P.M. for a meeting with the president and the senior national security team, including Cheney, Rumsfeld, and Powell, who had just arrived back from Peru. She returned to her office after the meeting and was still there talking to Hadley and Card when the Secret Service burst in a little after 11 P.M. The three had to get to the bunker, the agents said, because another plane was headed for the White House.[43] Rice was now in an exhausted fog, and when she got downstairs the scene she encountered struck her as almost comic. The first person she saw was the president's brother Neil, who had been visiting and was now sitting on the floor.[44] Next she saw the president, who had been rousted from bed by the Secret Service and was in his shorts and T-shirt. The first lady was in a nightgown and a robe and struggling to see without her contact lenses. One of the household maids—Rice knew her as Maria—was there, too, as were the president's dogs, Barney and Spot.

The Secret Service told the president that he would have to spend the night in the bunker. "They opened up this mangy-looking sofa bed that I don't think had been opened up since like 1958," Rice recalled. "And the president just looked at them and said, 'I'm not staying here.' And the whole gang kind of walked back up the hallway."[45] By then, the agents had learned that the plane was another false alarm, but they told Rice that it was still too dangerous for the national security adviser to spend the night at home and that she would have to stay at the White House. Rice thought she would sleep in her office, but Bush insisted that she take one of the guest bedrooms upstairs.[46]

An assistant was sent over to Rice's apartment at the Watergate to fetch a change of clothes, and by 1 A.M. Rice was in bed on the third floor of the White House residence, too overwhelmed by the day's events to sleep. She turned on the television and stared dully at the screen for a while. "I was watching the news but I wasn't really watching the news, you know?" she said. "I was just sort of watching the commentary."[47] She felt almost as if she were in a state of shock.[48] When she looked back on the day, she remembered it as a hazy stream of events, "like a series of reels, you know, in a movie." Finally Rice turned out the light but tossed and turned. "The only thing I remember thinking was you have to concentrate on what you have to do tomorrow, and concentrate on what the president needs to do tomorrow," she recalled. As for blaming herself for anything that had happened, "I wasn't—not yet."[49]

At 4 A.M., Rice finally gave up on any real sleep and got dressed and headed down to her office.[50] The West Wing was dark and silent, but it was mid-morning in Europe, and Rice had a message to call Nicholas Burns, her old deputy from the Bush I days who was now the U.S. ambassador to NATO. Rice reached Burns in Brussels, and he told her that NATO was set to vote on invoking Article 5, the mutual defense clause in the organization's founding treaty that held that an armed attack against any of the NATO allies in Europe or North America "shall be considered an attack against them all." As Rice had known since graduate school, the article had been meant to express American solidarity with Europe in the event of an attack by the Soviet Union. Now here was Europe ready to invoke Article 5 in a way that had never been intended, or even contemplated, as the supreme declaration that an attack upon the United States was an attack upon the entire Western alliance. All alone in her office, exhausted and overwhelmed, Rice found herself choking up with emotion over the sheer audacity and generosity of the European gesture. "For all these years NATO existed, it never had to do that," she said. "It felt very comforting to have friends."[51] The practical implication of invoking Article 5 was that NATO would join in the war in Afghanistan that was soon to begin.

Over the next days, as it became clear that Osama bin Laden had masterminded the attacks, Rice tried to regain her footing. She was sleeping very little and was consumed by back-to-back crisis sessions and the relentless feeling that she needed to get things under better control. "We had to create everything on the fly," she recalled.[52] The day after the attacks, there had been an unwieldy meeting in the Cabinet Room with everyone from Tenet to the treasury secretary weighing in with their separate agendas and game plans, and she realized it had been so unfocused as to be useless. "I remember thinking this is a very inefficient way to do this because some people are only really concerned about things like the financial system and some people were concerned about were nuclear power plants tied down and some people were worried about how to get the airports up and running," she said.[53]

After the first two or three days, Rice began to ask herself what she said she had not thought about during her sleepless night at the White House: Could anything have been done to stop the attacks? She insisted years later that she never thought for a minute that she had erred in not paying enough heed to Richard Clarke, the counterterrorism chief, who had warned her repeatedly in 2001 about the possibility of a terrorist attack. Still, she said, "you lose three thousand Americans and you think, 'Is there anything I should have done that I didn't do?' "[54] Whatever Rice might have allowed herself to think in private, her public answer would always be no. "I've asked myself a thousand times what more we could have done," Rice would later tell the 9/11 Commission that investigated the terrorist attacks. "I know that had we thought that there was an attack coming in Washington or New York, we would have moved heaven and earth to try and stop it. And I know that there was no single thing that might have prevented that attack."[55]

But it was a question that Americans would soon start asking themselves, and it would dog Condoleezza Rice, as national security adviser and as secretary of state, for the rest of her time in office.

Less than two months later, on the morning of October 29, 2001, Bush and his senior advisers were bombarded with a new wave of intelligence reporting, much of it deemed credible, that suggested that terrorists were likely to strike the United States again the following week.[56] The reporting indicated that terrorists might use conventional explosives to disperse radioactive material, perhaps in Washington or New York, or that Al Qaeda would use a hijacked airplane to attack a nuclear power plant.[57]

George Tenet presented the grim scenario to the president in the Oval Office at the 8 A.M. national security briefing, and Cheney announced that he was leaving immediately for his "undisclosed location"—typically Camp David, the presidential retreat miles from the White House in Maryland's Catoctin Mountains[58]—which assured that if Bush were killed in an attack on Washington, there would be a survivor to lead the government through the crises.

Rice, who was still shell-shocked by the attacks on the World Trade Center and Pentagon, reacted with alarm. She had an enormous emotional attachment to the president that had only intensified since September 11. At forty-seven, Rice had never married or had children, and George and Laura Bush had become family to her. Now, worried about the president's safety, she asked Bush if he thought he needed to go to an undisclosed location, too.[59]

"Those bastards are going to find me right here," Bush shot back, in Rice's recollection.[60] It was the kind of macho bravado that had marked the president's speech since September 11. "Me, too," Rice quickly responded, but with none of Bush's swagger.[61]

For Rice, it was a chilling moment. Every morning she saw a thick stack of classified documents, the daily "threat assessment," which compiled in terrifying detail what U.S. intelligence agencies had picked up about potential terrorist attacks against the United States. "It changes your psychology," Rice later said.[62] Bush's words now brought home to her that she was spending sixteen hours a day in a potential Ground Zero.[63] As a minister's daughter she believed in an afterlife and felt that she had long ago made peace with death, but she had not bargained on coming to work every morning thinking that she might not survive. Still, Rice knew without hesitation that she would stay by the president's side. If the bastards were going to find him in the Oval Office, they would find her there, too.

The moment was a crucial bonding experience in the extraordinary American story of Condoleezza Rice, the first African-American woman in a job first held by Thomas Jefferson and a partner to a president who has driven some of the most cataclysmic events of our time. Rice's fifty-four years are both a personal voyage of a young black woman out of the segregated American South and a public journey through the great challenges and debates of the late twentieth and early twenty-first centuries in the United States: national security, the rise of terrorism, the polarization of presidential politics, and the role of race and women.

Born at the dawn of the civil rights movement, Rice grew up under Bull Connor's reign of terror in Birmingham, where she knew one of the girls killed in the Sixteenth Street Baptist Church bombing in 1963. Four decades later she had risen to become the government's leading proponent of American values overseas. In between these bookends of her life, she studied the Soviet Union under Josef Korbel, Madeleine Albright's father, and came to a far different view of the world from the only other woman secretary of state. Rice was a protégée of Brent Scowcroft, the national security adviser in the White House of the first President Bush, and later a controversial provost of Stanford University. As national security adviser in the first term, she missed vital clues to the September 11 attacks, enabled the hawks to go to war with Iraq, and aggressively promoted the threat of a "mushroom cloud" from weapons of mass destruction that did not exist.

As secretary of state in the second term, she has tried to salvage stability from the ruins of the Iraq policy that she helped create and to revive a classical American diplomacy. So far she has had mixed success. She has reached an early agreement with North Korea that could lead to that country giving up its nuclear weapons, and she has rallied the world's major powers toward isolating and pressuring Iran to do the same. But Rice's stepped-up involvement in the Middle East has so far borne little fruit. Iraq, the nation on which her patron gambled his presidency, has descended into civil war.

In recent years, Rice's life story has taken on elements of myth, promoted in part by Rice herself. The official narrative is one of a precocious child, nurtured by adoring, ambitious parents, who threw off the yoke of her forebears and marched from one triumph to the next. Like most myths, this one contains elements of truth, but it is far from the real story. Rice, like everyone else, had moments of doubt, disappointment, and real crisis. She was not an academically brilliant student. She liked parties, dated football players, and spent part of her college years floundering. As provost at Stanford, she so antagonized the faculty that the Department of Labor began an investigation, still ongoing, into discrimination at the university against women. The investigation has since broadened to include discrimination on the basis of race. Throughout her life, Rice has experienced failure as well as success. Iraq, her friends say, is likely to be her greatest failure of all.

Rice is a cool and controlled presence in public, but her life has been extraordinarily turbulent underneath. Her years at the White House and State Department have been marked by battles over policy and ideology, not only with Donald Rumsfeld, the former defense secretary who was her well-known nemesis, but with the powerful and secretive Cheney, a far more formidable adversary. In the very first days of the administration, Rice had to go to Bush to stop Cheney from grabbing a major part of her job, running National Security Council meetings in the president's absence, as Cheney had proposed to Bush that he do.[64] Rice told the president that it was her responsibility by tradition and right, and Bush sided with her.[65] Later, Rice went to Bush to tell him that Cheney had to be pulled back after the vice president gave a bellicose speech in August 2002 that effectively threatened war with Iraq and alarmed much of the world.[66] Bush gave Rice the go-ahead to call Cheney and rein him in herself.[67]

In more recent years, Rice and Cheney have argued over the administration's treatment and incarceration of terrorism suspects at secret CIA prisons in Europe and at Guantánamo Bay, Cuba. In an unusual face-off in front of the president at a National Security

Council meeting in August 2006, Rice argued that the CIA prisons should be closed and Cheney argued that they should not.[68] Rice won—Bush effectively closed the prisons weeks later—but so far the president has rejected her arguments to shut down Guantánamo, which Cheney has said should stay open.[69]

Well into 2007, Rice and Cheney were on opposite ends of the administration's attempt to stop the nuclear threat from Iran. Rice was the chief advocate of diplomacy and Cheney the chief skeptic, and by June a furious debate had broken out between Rice and her deputies and Cheney's staff, who went public with warnings that the United States would eventually have to consider air strikes against Iran.[70] Rice was dismissive of the saber rattling. "I'm not going to try to account for the vice president's staff," she said coolly in an interview in June 2007. "I don't spend a moment thinking about what the vice president's staff might think. Not even a moment. I spend a lot of time thinking about what the vice president might think."[71]

With Cheney, Rice added, "we're probably a lot closer than people think on these issues." As for herself and her approach to Iran, "I am skeptical one day and optimistic the next. I probably have more confidence in diplomacy than some people, but it's not that anybody's saying, 'I have no confidence in diplomacy, therefore we ought to do something else.' "[72]

Rice's battles with Rumsfeld were far more territorial and personal. From the beginning, the defense secretary viewed Rice as in over her head and treated her so dismissively that Rice bit back at him in meetings, forcing Andrew Card, then the White House chief of staff, to assume the role of mediator and try to smooth things over after the flare-ups.[73] The squabbling took a more serious turn in the run-up to the Iraq War in 2002 and 2003, when Rumsfeld held back so much vital war planning information from the national security adviser that Rice had to deploy three full-time people on her staff to ferret out the information she needed from the Pentagon. Her spies scoured the classified Pentagon Web site and called old contacts for information,[74] and one even put on his military uniform and pretended to be visiting friends at the Pentagon in order to spirit away documents for Rice.[75] But the relationship between Rice and Rumsfeld became more equal when Rice joined the cabinet as secretary of state. "Don Rumsfeld has to pay attention to her!" Bush told former secretary of state George Shultz, as Shultz recalled it.[76] Later, Rice had an indirect but crucial hand in Rumsfeld's ouster when she pushed Bush to consider replacing him with her old friend Robert Gates, who got the job.[77]

On one major issue, Rice, Cheney, and Rumsfeld were in total agreement—the war in Iraq. Rice helped conceive it and was one of its chief advocates, and when the president finally asked her, point-blank in the Oval Office in December 2002, if he should take the country to war, she said yes.[78] There is no evidence that Rice raised major objections to the war or serious questions about the false intelligence that justified it. As a result, she failed in a basic part of her job as national security adviser, which was presenting the president with all the options, particularly dissenting opinions. "The dog that did not bark in the case of Iraq's W.M.D. program, quite frankly, in my view, is the National Security Council," David Kay, the administration's onetime weapons hunter, told Congress in remarks aimed at Rice in 2004.[79]

Although Rice presided over foreign policy at the White House, she inserted herself, with the president's blessing, into domestic policy as well. "She wouldn't stay in her lane," said Andrew Card.[80] Rice irritated some members of the White House staff when she took it upon herself in the first term to attend domestic policy meetings, feeling that she was an expert on, for example, health care, since she had overseen Stanford Hospital as the university's provost.[81] She also once told Card, only half jokingly, that the job she really wanted was secretary of health and human services.[82]

Rice weighed in on race discrimination at critical moments. When the White House was considering what position to take in a pair of friend-of-the-court briefs on two cases before the Supreme Court that challenged the University of Michigan's affirmative action programs, Rice told the president that universities should be able to use race as one factor in admissions policies[83]—a view she said positively influenced the administration's eventual position, which supported diversity as a goal in college admissions.[84] But Rice was appalled by the administration's response to Hurricane Katrina, even though she herself had to be chased back to Washington after she was spotted laughing at a Broadway show and buying expensive shoes on Fifth Avenue at the height of the crisis. "You have a race problem," she told the president, then insisted that she tour devastated areas in her home state of Alabama to try to placate blacks who felt Bush had turned his back on the impoverished African-Americans hit hardest by Katrina.[85] Blacks welcomed her visit, but many African-Americans across the country remain skeptical of her because of her allegiance to an administration that has such a poor record on race relations.

Rice is famously driven and disciplined, with an enormous capacity for hard work, and like the president is an exercise fanatic. But when she lets down her guard, Rice is not the starchy schoolteacher she often appears to be in public, and in private can be irreverent, vulnerable, and human. Despite her glamour, she has only a modest social life. She attends Presbyterian services in the suburban reaches of northwest Washington on most Sunday mornings that she is in town, and often practices afterward with an amateur chamber music group—Rice trained to be a concert pianist—in her Watergate apartment. Rice goes to hear symphonies and opera at the nearby Kennedy Center with a small but loyal group of women friends, and since becoming secretary of state has become part of another group of black professional women who gather in each other's homes for drinks and talk. Among them are Donna Brazile, the Democratic political strategist and commentator, and Eleanor Holmes Norton, a Democrat who is the District of Columbia's delegate to Congress. Rice cooked for the group in her apartment one evening in January 2007. "She's really a good colored girl at heart," Brazile said. "You don't see that publicly. She can drink wine and fry some chicken."[86] On other evenings, Rice relaxes with popular television shows like *American Idol*, reads little for pleasure, and has lately taken up golf. But hers is overall a work-centered life.

She comes from a line of tough-minded and well-educated Southern women who married late or not at all, and who raised few if any children. Rice had plans to marry a football player for the Denver Broncos when she was a graduate student in the 1970s, and she has had a twenty-five-year on-again, off-again relationship with a former player for the San Francisco 49ers, Gene Washington, who is her escort for White House state dinners, visits her on weekends in Washington, and spent Thanksgiving 2006 with her and family and friends at Camp David. Some of Rice's best friends are gay, and her longtime single status has led to speculation in the press that she is, too. "I'm not," Rice said simply in an interview in 2007. "I quite like men."[87] She shrugged off the talk. "I think if you're a single woman, I sometimes see people saying, 'Well, there must be an explanation for that.' Well, my explanation is I just haven't actually ever found anyone I wanted to be married to."[88]

One of Rice's most marked characteristics is her loyalty—to George Bush and, before him, to a succession of other powerful bosses and mentors, from former national security adviser Brent Scowcroft to former secretary of state George Shultz to Gerhard Casper, the president of Stanford who plucked the young Rice from the university's professorial ranks to make her provost. But Rice's allegiance to Casper went only so far after her loyalties had switched elsewhere. In 2005, when the German-born Casper spoke to a White House intermediary about becoming the United States ambassador to Germany, Bush seemed receptive.[89] But Rice, by then the secretary of state and thus in charge of the U.S. diplomatic corps, would not go along because Casper had become a vocal critic of the Iraq War.[90] Casper had in any case decided that his disagreements with the administration were too profound to accept the job.[91]

Although her friends marvel at how much she has remained the same over fifty-four years, Rice's story is one of continued reinvention: Democrat turned Republican, concert pianist turned political scientist, foreign policy realist turned idealist turned realist again. Her biggest transformation has been the most recent, from the weak national security adviser she was in the first term to the more forceful and self-confident secretary of state she has been in the second. But shedding so many skins raises the question of what she really stands for. Rice would say "transformational diplomacy," her Bush-inspired vision of spreading democracy around the world. But in reality—and by instinct, training, and experience—she is a pragmatist who for four overwhelming years got swept away by her devotion to the president and the hawks who held the power.

It is important to remember that Rice had only two years of mid-level White House experience when George Bush made her his national security adviser in charge of coordinating the elephants in the room—Cheney, Rumsfeld, and Powell. Rice quickly saw that the main source of her power was her closeness to the president. Her realization came at a time when she herself was emotionally bereft. Rice's beloved father had died, leaving her parentless, nine days before she arrived in Washington to be national security adviser. Rice quickly became Bush's confidante, friend, soother, and protector—a relationship almost unique in modern history that did not serve the best interests of the nation. At the same time, White House advisers came to see that Bush, because of his affection for Rice, did not make more demands on her and push her to do the job he needed.

"The president loved Condi, but I don't want you to take that as sexual or emotional," Andrew Card said, speaking carefully.[92] Other senior White House staff members saw much the same thing. "It's just an extraordinary emotional bond between the two of them," said a former White House staff member who was close to Rice. "It expressed itself in policy and all the rest, but it just expresses itself. There's a pureness to it. This has to be said carefully, but I think they love each other in some familial sense."[93]

Rice and Bush are remarkably alike. Both are products of American elites—Bush from Northeastern WASPs, Rice from aspiring Southern black patricians—who are supremely self-confident on the surface but harbor resentments underneath. Rice, like Bush, has been underestimated her entire life, as a black, as a woman, and often as the youngest person in the room. Both have practical streaks overshadowed by ideology, and both are highly political—a little known fact about Rice, who talked about running for the United States Senate from Colorado while she was still a graduate student in the 1970s.[94] On election night of 2004, rather than remaining home alone in her quiet Watergate apartment, Rice sat in the White House "war room" literally at the side of Karl Rove, the president's powerful political adviser, and served as an impromptu aide helping to sift through election returns.[95]

In more recent years, Rice has toyed with the idea of a race for governor of California, and her staff has said she would be interested in running when Arnold Schwarzenegger's term expires in 2011. In this election cycle, she has adamantly rejected any talk of running for president, but she has never ruled out accepting a spot as the vice presidential candidate on the Republican ticket. Her staff members have pushed her hard in that direction, and remain amazed at how relatively little—at this point—she has been tarred with the fiasco in Iraq. Polls show that Rice still has the highest approval ratings in the administration.[96] But when she is talked about as a possibility on the GOP ticket, as she certainly will be, the discussions will inevitably focus on her role in committing the United States to a disastrous war—and whether that will make her too big a target for the Republicans in 2008.

In reporting and writing this book, I interviewed more than 150 people in Washington, Birmingham, Palo Alto, Denver, and New York. I drew from eight one-hour interviews with Rice at the State Department in 2006 and 2007 for the purposes of this book, and from two other lengthy interviews with her at the White House in late 2003 for a *New York Times* article about her relationship with the president. Although I am grateful for Rice's cooperation, this is not an "authorized" biography but an independent work of journalism. Rice will see it for the first time when it is published.

History may well judge Rice's most important accomplishment to be her diplomacy with North Korea and Iran, which will serve as a foundation for the next administration, whether Democrat or Republican. But she will be better remembered for her influence on the president during some of the most terrifying and troubling years in the United States. Rice, the student of power, evolved in her mastery of it with George Bush. Understanding her is crucial to understanding the forty-third presidency, a period when Rice brought to the making of history her own history, one of the great narratives in American life.

—August 2007

CONDOLEEZZA RICE
AN AMERICAN LIFE

CHAPTER 1

Twice as Good

Alabama, 1892–1962

The story of Condoleezza Rice begins at the close of the nineteenth century on a cotton plantation in southeastern Alabama, near the flourishing little town of Union Springs. The area was on the edge of Alabama's Black Belt, named for the rich soil and slave labor essential for cotton, the state's number one cash crop. By the early 1890s the slaves had been free for more than a generation, but so many remained as sharecroppers on the masters' plantations that planters still controlled the lifeblood of the land.[1] New railroads that intersected in Union Springs had only made the planters richer, as their grand Victorian and Greek Revival homes attested. Now they could send their cotton to the markets in Montgomery in hours instead of the days it had taken by mule.[2]

In 1892, according to the census records of the surrounding Bullock County, Condoleezza Rice's grandfather, Albert Robinson Ray III, was born.[3] His father was a plantation field hand. But Albert's grandfather, at least according to Rice family lore, was the white owner of the plantation, and his mother was a favored black servant in the plantation household. The family has no written record of Alto, and there are no clues in the 1890 or 1900 Bullock County census records.[4] Rice knows little about Alto—her great-great grandfather—or the nature of his relationship to her great-great-grandmother beyond the apparent one of sexual exploitation of servant by master common to this place and time. "I know that Alto, who was white, was either Italian-born in Italy and made it here somehow, or his parents made it here somehow," she recalled in an interview years later.[5]

Rice also knew that one of her great-aunts, Nancy Ray, had sandy-colored hair and blue eyes. That was clear from the photographs of Nancy that Rice saw as a child, and from the recollections of her parents and grandparents.[6] White ancestry was common to other middle-class black families in Birmingham, and across the South—one of Rice's black friends claims a Jewish judge in her bloodline[7]—and, while not something discussed casually with outsiders, was no cause for shame. Many black household servants were taught to read, were exposed to fine things like "silver and china and linen," and came to learn "about how advantaged Americans lived," said Rice's friend Freeman Hrabowski, a Birmingham native who is now the president of the University of Maryland, Baltimore County. (Hrabowski says his great-great-grandfather was a white slave owner from a plantation near Selma.)[8] One of Rice's friends has recalled jokingly discussing with her whose white ancestors were more aristocratic.[9] "It was just sort of part of the landscape," Rice said.[10]

Whatever the specifics of Rice's ancestry—the family says there were white landowners, favored household servants, and education going back generations on her father's side as well—the important point is that it powerfully shaped her view of herself as a black patrician. Any serious look at her life must begin here, in an intermingling of the races and two separate strands of American history. Rice grew up seeing herself as part of the nation's founding culture. At the least, her ancestry was a crucial part of the self-confidence that fueled her rise. She never considered herself an outsider or called herself an "African-American"—to her ears an immigrant designation she has always rejected.

"We have a racial birth defect that we've never quite dealt with," Rice said. "Which is that, really, there were two founding races—Europeans and Africans. They came here together, there was miscegenation. We founded and built this country together, and we are more intertwined and intertangled than we would like to think."[11] She has long said that the shock over Thomas Jefferson's relationship with the slave Sally Hemings was misplaced and naive, although she acknowledges the legacy of rape that produced so many mixed-race children in the South at the time. "It's a legacy that was basically not one of choice and volition but of violence and oppression," she said. "And so I think that's why people have trouble admitting it and talking about it and understanding it."[12]

In Rice's family, the Italian ancestry appears to have been a source of pride, or at least was valued enough to make the family pass Italian names down through succeeding generations. Albert Robinson Ray III's brother was named Alto, and later, Albert would name one of his own sons Alto—Alto Ray, Condoleezza Rice's uncle. Two of the other children of Albert—Angelena and Genoa—also had Italian names.[13]

Condoleezza is of course an Italian name, too, made up by Rice's mother from the Italian musical notation "con dolcezza," which means "with sweetness." The family story has always been that Rice's mother picked the name because she was a classically trained musician and loved Italian opera. But in an interview in late 2006 Rice suggested that her name was in part inspired by the man she believes to be her Italian ancestor. "Alto, as you can tell, is an Italian name," Rice said, adding, "as is Condoleezza."[14]

In Union Springs in the 1890s, little is known of Albert Robinson Ray III, Condoleezza Rice's grandfather, other than his likely labor in the cotton fields. Rice family lore picks him up again at the age of eleven, around 1904, when a white man is said to have assaulted his sister. Albert responded to the attack by beating up the white man, a crime so severe for a black youth that he fled Union Springs, terrified that he would be lynched.[15] His fears were not unfounded: Like much of the South, Bullock County experienced a sharp erosion of black civil rights after Reconstruction ended in 1877. Between 1889 and 1921 in Bullock County there were seven documented lynchings.[16]

As the Rice family tells it, Albert ended up at a Birmingham train station at 3 A.M. Somehow—the family has few details—Albert met a white family, the Wheelers, who owned a coal mine and took him in. Albert lived with the Wheelers and worked in their mine until well into his twenties.[17]

Albert Ray may have been fleeing, but in 1904 he was also following the well-beaten path of black field laborers to "The Magic City," the name given to Birmingham only three decades after its birth. The city had been incorporated in 1871 by ten investors who formed the Elyton Land Company in what was then the town of Elyton and bought 4,457 acres of mineral-rich property at a point where two major railroads were expected to intersect.[18] By the start of the twentieth century, Birmingham was a booming postwar manufacturing city, named for the gritty industrial center in England, and was said to be the only place on earth where the essential ingredients of iron- and steel-making—coal, iron ore, and limestone—existed in one spot.[19] Birmingham was heavily dependent on poor black laborers like Albert Ray, who helped fuel a growth so phenomenal that in 1904, the same year he arrived in town, the city's boosters chose Vulcan, the Roman god of fire and the forge, as the symbol to promote Birmingham worldwide. The city sent a giant statue of Vulcan as its exhibit to the 1904 St. Louis World's Fair, where it won the Grand Prize.[20] Still the largest cast iron statue in the world, today Vulcan overlooks Birmingham from the top of Red Mountain. He has had a more recent and direct role in Condoleezza Rice's life: During George W. Bush's 2000 presidential campaign, Bush's foreign policy advisers—Rice was their coordinator—nicknamed themselves the Vulcans, after the statue in Rice's hometown. At first the name was an inside joke, but the advisers began to use it publicly because it captured the image of power, toughness, and durability they sought to portray.[21]

In 1918, Albert Ray was still working in the Wheelers' mine when he married, at the age of twenty-eight, Mattie Lula Parham, a classically trained pianist and a graduate of St. Mark's Academy in Birmingham, an institution Condoleezza Rice later recalled as a "finishing school."[22] Parham's father, Rice said, had been "somebody high up in the African Methodist Episcopal Church."[23] The family does not know how Albert and Mattie Lula met, but Rice does know that they settled in Hooper City, a rural area north of Birmingham. Between the years 1923 and 1936 they had five children—another Albert, another Mattie, Angelena, Alto, and Genoa.[24] Mattie, with her classical training, gave piano lessons to the children in the neighborhood, for 25 cents a lesson, and Albert, with no education, branched out from coal-mining to a blacksmith business and then construction. He built the house the family lived in, at 3708 Fourth Street West. As he prospered, he added on, expanding from five rooms to ten. He also dug the well, kept cows and pigs, and owned a car. The Rays were the third or fourth family in Hooper City, upwardly mobile for the time, and proud.[25]

"I guess we might have been poor, but we never knew we were poor," Genoa McPhatter, the youngest child, said. "I can remember we always got practically everything that we wanted."[26] The family dressed well—"Mother shopped at expensive stores for us, so consequently we grew up into clothes," McPhatter said—and had an ease with white people. "My daddy had a lot of white friends," McPhatter said, recalling how whites would come in for horseshoes to her father's blacksmith shop. "To be perfectly frank, we didn't even realize when they would come that it was segregation, because they had such a good relationship there together."[27]

Albert and Mattie Lula sent all five children to black colleges in the South: Tuskegee in Alabama, Spelman in Atlanta, Johnson C. Smith in Charlotte.[28] Angelena, Condoleezza Rice's mother and the middle of the five children, stayed home and graduated from Miles College in Birmingham. In the family, she stood out for her musical abilities—she played the piano like her mother—and for her sharp tongue. "She was a very sweet, kind child, but don't say anything to her," McPhatter recalled of her older sister. "If she didn't agree with what you were saying, if she felt like it was wrong, she could really lash out."[29]

Angelena went on to teach music and science southwest of Birmingham at Fairfield Industrial High School, in a black working-class community of the same name that overlooked the massive U.S. Steel mills. Angelena was a refined presence in the scruffy town—beautiful, light-skinned, with an insistence on standard English. "The thing I remember most is she drilled us in writing," recalled Richard Arrington, Jr., Birmingham's first black mayor, who was one of Angelena's students. She taught him, he recalled, to say "had gone" instead of "had went." "Nobody had ever told me that," Arrington said. "My parents had come out of the Black Belt and we spoke black dialect in our home."[30] One of Angelena's other students was Willie Mays, a source of family pride, which Condoleezza Rice made sure to mention in an early meeting with George W. Bush, a lover of baseball and the former managing partner of the Texas Rangers.[31]

It was at Fairfield High that Angelena met a fellow teacher, John Wesley Rice, Jr.[32] He was a big man, charismatic and outgoing. On Sundays he preached in Birmingham at Westminster Presbyterian, a position he had inherited from his father. The preaching job was part-time, as was common in those days. From Monday to Friday Rice taught gym and served as Fairfield's head basketball coach and assistant football coach. Although he did not have the property of the Rays, there was education and white ancestry in his family, too.

John Rice's grandmother was Julia Head, the mixed-race daughter of a white plantation owner—Condoleezza Rice's great-great-grandfather—and another favored black house slave from Greene County, in western Alabama. As the family lore has it, when Union soldiers ransacked the neighboring plantations at the end of the Civil War, Julia, under instructions from her white father, hid the horses from the Northern invaders—an act of loyalty, or at least of obedience, that the family cites today.[33]

Julia could read and write, as could the man she married, a former slave from South Carolina named John Wesley Rice, Condoleezza Rice's great-grandfather.[34] After the Civil War, Julia and John Rice settled as tenant farmers in Greene County, where they raised a son, also named John Wesley Rice, Condoleezza Rice's grandfather. John Wesley Rice eventually graduated from Stillman College, the historically black school in Tuscaloosa, an accomplishment of such note in the Rice family that Condoleezza Rice made it a centerpiece of a speech she gave at the 2000 Republican National Convention. In what was effectively her introduction of herself to the nation, Rice told the delegates in Philadelphia the story of "Granddaddy Rice." Her narrative, which made clear that she was from a black educational elite, set out the themes of self-reliance and godliness much admired by her Republican audience.

"George W. Bush would have liked Granddaddy Rice," Rice told the delegates. "He was the son of a farmer in rural Alabama, but he recognized the importance of education. Around 1918, he decided he was going to get book-learning. And so, he asked, in the language of the day, where a colored man could go to college."[35]

Granddaddy Rice was told of Stillman, where he enrolled but ran out of cotton to pay for tuition after his first year. What was he to do? "Praise be, as he often does, God gave him an answer," Condoleezza Rice told the crowd. "My grandfather asked how those other boys were staying in school, and he was told that they had what was called a scholarship. And they said, 'If you wanted to be a Presbyterian minister, then you can have one, too.' Granddaddy Rice said, 'That's just what I had in mind.' "

Rice drove home her point: "And my family has been Presbyterian and college-educated ever since."[36]

Granddaddy Rice's education encompassed literature as well. In a story that Condoleezza Rice has often told, her grandfather spent the astonishing sum of $90 during the Depression on seven leather-bound, gold-embossed books, including the works of Dumas, Shakespeare, and Hugo. When Rice's wife objected, he told her not to worry, he would pay for them over time. (In later years his niece, Theresa Love, Condoleezza Rice's aunt, would go to the University of Wisconsin and get a Ph.D. in Victorian literature.)[37]

Granddaddy Rice's first congregation was in Baton Rouge, but the church soon dispatched him to start schools and Presbyterian congregations all over the South. By 1943, he had settled in with his last congregation, a small mission in Birmingham that became Westminster Presbyterian. In 1951, after the church had completed a new building on Sixth Avenue South, he turned over the pulpit to his son, John Wesley Rice, Jr., the gym teacher and high school coach who had earned a divinity degree, as his family expected, from Johnson C. Smith University in North Carolina.

Three years later, on Valentine's Day 1954, John Rice, Jr., and Angelena Ray were married by Granddaddy Rice in Angelena's mother's music room in the family house in Hooper City. The wedding was tiny—and held exactly nine months to the day before the couple's first and only child was born. "My mother said it was a good thing I wasn't early," Rice recalled.[38]

The birth occurred on November 14, 1954, a Sunday, at 11:48 A.M., while John Rice was still in the pulpit. Angelena had gone home to Hooper City to stay with her mother for the last six weeks of her pregnancy, and delivered her daughter at the segregated Holy Family Hospital nearby. When John Rice stepped down from the pulpit, he found his mother waiting for him in his office. "You have a little girl," she told him.[39]

Angelena's choice of the name Condoleezza reflected not only her baby's musical and Italian heritage but a mother's fierce ambitions for her daughter. To Angelena's ears, "Condoleezza" was melodious and elegant and sang of worlds beyond Birmingham. To others it sounded like a classic African-American name, and as a teenager at her first integrated school in Denver, Rice would shorten it to "Condi," the name she prefers to be called as an adult. But at home and in Birmingham she was always "Condoleezza," even though not everyone in the family found the name as romantic as Angelena did. "My God, why are you going to name her Condoleezza?" Genoa McPhatter asked her sister, incredulous. "She'll never learn how to spell it!"[40]

After the baby was born, Angelena left her job as a schoolteacher and settled into a life lived literally within the church. The parsonage in those days was a collection of five dark rooms at the back of the sanctuary—a bedroom, a living room, an office for the minister, a bath, and kitchen. Today there is still a vent in the ceiling from the old wooden stove.[41] The modest surroundings reflected Westminster's position as a minor congregation in the hierarchy of powerhouse black churches in Birmingham, where Sixteenth Street Baptist and Sixth Avenue Baptist were dominant. There were very few black Presbyterians in the South or in Birmingham, and Westminster rarely had more than a hundred people in the pews on Sundays.[42] But the members of Westminster considered themselves a cut above other black congregations[43]—they owned their homes, they were teachers in the schools, they brought their babies to services in beautiful clothes. Condoleezza's dresses alone were a sight to behold.

"She had Condoleezza coming in like on a platter with all the little ruffles around," remembered Annye Marie Downing, a longtime friend of the Rice family. "She'd come after the service had started because she had to get her little doll all dressed up."[44] Angelena always took care over her daughter's appearance, Downing recalled. "I remember to this day her by the ironing board, and she'd have the little panties, ironing the little ruffles around them," Downing said. "Oh, she just did it with so much pride."[45] Within the family, Angelena was known as an intense, devoted mother. "Condoleezza was her world, and she didn't care who knew it," said Lativia Alston, Condoleezza's first cousin.[46] Angelena rarely let anyone even hold her baby. "She just didn't want to share Condoleezza," McPhatter said. "She didn't want anybody breathing on her, I guess."[47]

By 1958, the church had built a separate parsonage eight blocks away, at 929 Center Way SW, where the Rices moved that spring, when Condoleezza was three. The house, a bungalow with dark green siding, was a step up from the quarters at the back of the church. There were two bedrooms, a bath, a living room, and a kitchen. The house today looks run-down, but in the early 1960s, it was among the best that existed for black families in Birmingham.

Center Way was in the heart of Titusville, one of a handful of middle-class black neighborhoods in Birmingham at the time. It had been founded in the 1860s on the site of the original Elyton by freed slaves[48] and was once called "Tiddlesville," perhaps after a William A. Tiddles who lived nearby.[49] After World War II, large tracts of farmland in the area—locals still remember hills covered with pecan, peach, and cherry trees—were sold off to returning black veterans and a small but growing number of African-Americans with college degrees.[50] The new area was called South Titusville. The Rices' neighborhood, in the western part of South Titusville and just two miles southwest of Birmingham's downtown, was shaded by crepe myrtle, magnolia, and dogwood and given the bucolic name of Honeysuckle Circle. Locals estimated that there were three thousand to four thousand middle-class households in Titusville at the time, representing some fifteen thousand people, and making it one of the larger middle-class black communities in the South.[51] In more recent years, the population has decreased to about five thousand, and today many of the black residents are working-class and poor.[52]

Titusville was not as fashionable as nearby Smithfield, a more elite black community that had a greater concentration of professionals and was home to some of the most well-known African-Americans in town. Arthur Shores, the city's most prominent black attorney, lived in Smithfield, as did R. C. Johnson, the principal of the all-black Parker High School and the father of Alma Powell, who would become the wife of another secretary of state, Colin Powell. The black militant Angela Davis, the daughter of college-educated parents, lived in Smithfield until 1958, when she left at the age of fifteen to attend school in New York City.[53]

If Smithfield was tonier than Titusville, it was also more dangerous. Titusville had always been entirely black, but parts of Smithfield had been white, and the change in its racial makeup was the flash point in the civil rights conflagration that marked Condoleezza Rice's childhood. After World War II, blacks squeezed by a city housing shortage began moving into the all-white northern section of Smithfield, in open defiance of unconstitutional zoning laws that restricted black access to such neighborhoods.[54] White vigilantes responded by bombing so many black-owned properties in Smithfield that the area became known locally as "Dynamite Hill." Nationally, the city became known as "Bombingham" for the close to fifty bombings that occurred in Birmingham between 1947 and 1966.[55]

The homes in Titusville were new ranches and split-levels, about 1,300 square feet, usually of brick, with basements and attached garages. George Hunter, an architect who lived across the street from the Rices, had built many of them, not least because they represented one of the few opportunities to him for work. No white firm in town would hire him, so Hunter drew his designs only for black people, who were living, effectively, under an American apartheid.

Outside Titusville, there were whites-only schools, churches, restaurants, drinking fountains, lunch counters, dressing rooms, and public bathrooms. Blacks had to sit in the back of city buses, and were barred completely from Kiddieland, the local amusement park. Inside Titusville there was a parallel universe of black schools, churches, social clubs, youth groups, dance classes. Black maids cleaned white homes and black waiters served at the whites-only country clubs, but for the most part the races never mixed. Condoleezza Rice, like everyone else in Titusville, lived her life entirely among her own kind. "She didn't know any white people," Jack Straw, the former British foreign secretary, recalled with amazement of his visit with Rice to

Birmingham in October 2005, when he met her family, childhood friends, and teachers.[56]

At the time that the Rices moved to Titusville, there had been some agitation for an end to segregation. In 1956, Arthur Shores had accompanied his client, Autherine Lucy, when she tried to enroll as the first black student at the all-white University of Alabama. That same year Fred Shuttlesworth, the fiery black minister of Birmingham's Bethel Baptist Church and one of the founders of the Southern Christian Leadership Conference, was nearly killed when his home was blown up on Christmas. The following year Shuttlesworth was beaten by a mob with bicycle chains and baseball bats when he tried to enroll his daughters at the all-white Phillips High School.[57]

But the middle-class blacks of Titusville generally viewed the confrontational tactics, and Shuttlesworth in particular, with alarm. "Black people thought he was moving too fast," recalled James T. Montgomery, Shuttlesworth's physician, a friend of Martin Luther King, and a prominent black doctor in Titusville who knew the Rices. "Any movement at all for them was too fast. That's the truth, actually. And those of us who thought that he needed to be vocally supported, openly supported, were small in number."[58]

Birmingham's black bourgeoisie conformed largely to the worldview of Booker T. Washington, the founder of Tuskegee Institute and an advocate of economic self-help and gradualism. Washington's view was also the view of Rice's parents, who dealt with the apartheid by ignoring it, to the extent that was possible. Above all, their goal was to protect their daughter from the knowledge that she was considered a second-class citizen by white Birmingham. Within the insulated world of Honeysuckle Circle, that was for a time possible.

Mothers taught each other's children in classes at Center Street School and at Ullman High. The fathers were teachers, too, or preachers, or local milkmen, or steelworkers who brought home good wages. Church was the religious and social center of life. There were Girl Scout troops, Boy Scout troops, and baseball teams. "Everybody knew everybody," recalled Celeste Mitchell King, a childhood friend of Rice from Titusville and a former member of Westminster Presbyterian. "We couldn't act up because everyone knew our parents."[59]

The Rices owned a car, so they did not have to take seats in the back of Birmingham's buses. For years they had shunned the dirty "colored only" drinking fountains and public bathrooms. "We avoided even being associated with that," Genoa McPhatter recalled. "We never used the bathrooms out, because Mother said that rather than go to another bathroom, we would always come home and go to the bathroom. So we knew that we did not go with white people, but we really didn't feel the effects, I guess, of segregation."[60] Alto Ray, McPhatter's older brother, had similar memories. "Daddy told us, 'Wait till you get home to drink. Wait till you get home to go to the bathroom.' If you had to go in the back door, we just wouldn't go," Ray said. "As a matter of fact, I never got on a bus, a segregated bus, in my life."[61]

In the catchphrase of the neighborhood, Condoleezza Rice would be "twice as good" as the white daughters of the industrialists in Mountain Brook, and be more than ready to take them on when segregation ended, as the Rices felt it inevitably would. "It was like if you're really going to compete, you have to be ten times better," recalled Deborah Cheatham Carson, a childhood friend who went on to work for one of Bill Clinton's presidential campaigns and became reacquainted with Rice when both were living as adults in Palo Alto. "Mother said, it has to be so obvious that you're the best, and then you get considered."[62] Assimilation was the goal, and teachers were tough about manners and dress. When girls went on school field trips to the symphony, they were told to wear white anklets and skirts that were not too short. "They used to call us in there right before we went, and if you weren't dressed a certain way, you didn't get to go," Carson recalled. "That was getting you ready for the big world out there."[63]

John and Angelena poured their hearts into the project of their lives: the teaching, molding, and polishing of Condoleezza. Each brought distinct characteristics to her upbringing. John Rice was the extrovert, the gregarious preacher, a big man in a small community, the high school football coach who took his daughter to all the games. He had a booming voice and his daughter unreservedly adored him. When she was four, he started a Thanksgiving tradition, the Rice Bowl, when he ran plays with her in the backyard.[64] "She'd say, 'When I get grown, I'm going to marry me a professional football player,' " recalled Carolyn Hunter, the wife of George Hunter across the street.[65]

Angelena, in contrast, was more of an introvert, in charge of Condoleezza's musical career, etiquette, and clothes. Neighbors in Titusville referred to her as elegant, lovely, and a "real Southern lady," but people who knew her better heard the sharp tongue of her youth. "What Angelena said, Angelena meant," recalled Eva Carter, a member of John Rice's youth group, one of his students at Ullman High, and now the wife of the current minister at Westminster Presbyterian. Carter often got rides with the Rices to and from church and, from her spot in the backseat, heard Angelena hold forth. "She did not dress it up," Carter said. "She was not like Reverend Rice, who never raised his voice. Angelena could speak her mind. Angelena had an air, she really did."[66]

Rice described her mother as "very tough-minded" and "pepperlike"[67] and told friends that she had a temper. "She said her mother could scream, just like anybody else's mother," recalled Deborah Carson.[68] Rice characterized her mother as a "patrician" from the side of the family that understood culture. "She cared a lot about fine things," Rice said. "She dressed very well. We shopped a lot."[69]

Angelena dressed particularly well when she led her high school musical performances—*Aida*, *Porgy and Bess*, and a Liszt retrospective, to name a few. McPhatter remembered one time when her sister was particularly well turned out in stylish high heels for an operetta performance. "Mrs. Simmons, one of the teachers, who was a friend of hers from school, they had on shoes that were similar," McPhatter said. "So she says, 'Oh, Angelena, we have on shoes alike!' " She looked down and she said, " 'No, we don't have on shoes alike. You got your shoes from Baker's, and I got my shoes from Blach's.' "[70] Years later, McPhatter still recalled her astonishment at her sister's proud mention of her purchase at one of Birmingham's most exclusive stores. "If the ground had opened, I would have gone through it," McPhatter said. "She was like that. She was very outspoken."[71]

Rice's mother always had a clear view of what she considered class, and white people did not necessarily measure up. "Her mother thought Jimmy and Rosalynn Carter were a national embarrassment," said Coit "Chip" Blacker, the director of the Freeman Spogli

Institute for International Studies at Stanford and a longtime friend of Rice, recalling his conversations with Angelena in the early 1980s. The reason, Blacker said, is that "she thought they were hicks." Angelena was a Democrat, he said, but "this is this thing, you know, this status-class thing."[72]

Rice had a more polite version. "I remember that she was sort of put off by the down-home nature of the inaugural, and all that," Rice said, adding that Angelena thought it "caricatured the South a bit."[73]

The education of Condoleezza began with music. When Rice was three, her mother went back to work as a teacher at Western Olin High School in Ensley, a community in the heart of one of the old steel mill areas. John Rice had by then moved up from coaching at Fairfield High to become the guidance counselor at Ullman High School near the center of town. For day care, they dropped off their daughter at Angelena's mother's house in Hooper City, where Condoleezza listened enthralled, or so the family lore has it, to the piano lessons that her grandmother would give to her students.

"I would go and bang at the piano when the students left," Rice recalled. "And soon I started asking her, 'Well, let me take music home.' Because I wanted to pretend I was like the students. And she would give me music. And finally I was taking all the music away, and so she gave me a book one day to take home instead. And I said, 'This isn't music.' And she said to my mother, 'You know, let me try to teach her to play. She clearly wants to learn.' My mother said, 'She's three.' But that's how I learned to play."[74]

Condoleezza was soon receiving further instruction from her mother, who felt her child was exceptionally gifted. To confirm her view, she and John took Condoleezza for psychological testing at Southern University in Baton Rouge. "I knew my baby was a genius!" Angelena exclaimed afterward.[75] The first song Condoleezza learned was "What a Friend We Have in Jesus," and by the age of four she had given her first recital.

Condoleezza had in the meantime learned to read, at age three, and was so ahead of her peers that Angelena tried to enroll her in first grade at the age of five. When the school deemed Condoleezza too young and refused, Angelena, undeterred, took a year off from teaching and schooled her daughter at home. Neighbors recall that Angelena kept her daughter on a tight regimen—early morning classes, lunch, then classes again. "When we were going to school, before eight, Condoleezza would be out playing," said Vanessa Hunter, one of Rice's childhood friends, who was a daughter in the Hunter family across the street. "Her mother would ring the bell and Condoleezza would come in."[76] Rice's parents later piled up so many books by her bedside table that she stopped reading for pleasure, and does not to this day. "I grew up in a family in which my parents put me into every book club," Rice once said. "So I never developed the fine art of recreational reading."[77]

Condoleezza finally entered the Brunetta C. Hill School in September 1961, two months shy of her seventh birthday, as a second grader. Chubby-cheeked, with her hair neatly braided by her mother, Rice wore plaid skirts and white Peter Pan collars. Her parents continued their close watch over her education, and at one point bought new textbooks for their daughter's entire class because they felt the ones handed down from the white schools—the practice at the time—were old and outdated.[78] By sixth grade, Condoleezza was working as an assistant in the school's administrative office, where her duties included helping the secretary write reports required by the Board of Education. "She was my second registrar, let's put it like that," said Parnell Jones, the school principal. "She was always forward, she wanted to be something."[79]

Condoleezza's piano practicing was at the same time intensifying under Angelena's tutelage. Even during summer vacations, friends would find themselves listening to Condoleezza practice Mozart and Beethoven before she was allowed to join in the neighborhood stickball games. "We would sit outside her house for hours on end waiting for her," recalled Carole Smitherman, a playmate who became president of the Birmingham City Council.[80] Rice, knowing that her friends were there, would "open the window and she would serenade our whole street."[81]

Rice said that she was practicing about an hour a day at the time,[82] but in Smitherman's memory it was more like four or five. Either way, Smitherman recalls that Rice's mother kept her on a schedule and that she had little time for recreation. "She would get up, read, play the piano, eat a little something, go back to playing the piano, read a little more," Smitherman recalled.[83]

The Rices were considered overprotective of Condoleezza, even in a neighborhood where children were given strict instructions on what homes they could go to and when. "She really didn't get out much," George Hunter III, Vanessa's brother, recalled. "Mrs. Rice and Reverend Rice kind of kept her close. There were very few people Mrs. Rice would let her associate with."[84]

Angelena kept a close watch even when Condoleezza played across the street in the garage of her friend Vanessa Hunter. The two girls liked to set up a chalkboard, put their dolls on chairs, and spend hours in the afternoons playing school. Two other girls in the neighborhood, Margaret Wright Bowen and Debra Hawes Crook, often joined in. "I remember us all being teachers, but my mother said she wanted to be the teacher more," Vanessa Hunter recalled.[85] What Vanessa Hunter's mother remembered most was that Angelena rarely took her eyes off her daughter, and that Condoleezza let her know it.

"I would have the door open, and the garage door open, and she said, 'Mrs. Hunter, if you shut the garage door I'm going to have to go home because my mother can't watch me,' " Carolyn Hunter recalled. "I said, 'Condoleezza, I might have to close that door because flies are coming in." ' Carolyn Hunter also pointed out the inequities to her daughter's young friend: "I said, 'Well, Condoleezza, I can't watch Vanessa in your house.' "[86]

The Rices formed an unusually tight unit with their daughter, and were known in the neighborhood as an inseparable threesome. But outsiders did not see the real extent of the bond. Condoleezza was an assertive child who always knew what she wanted, and within the family she was often treated as an equal to her parents. As part of her training, she was given wide latitude in making decisions. "They worked a democratic form of house," McPhatter recalled. "They got together and they discussed what was going to take place, what was going to be for dinner, what they were going to wear and what they were going to do. She ended up making all of the decisions, but her mother directed it that way."[87]

The device that Angelena and John Rice used to instill such responsibility in their daughter was to make her "president" of the family. "Because we had to organize ourselves," Rice said years later. "So that, for instance, let's say that we were going to go to Denver the next day, we had to have a family meeting and determine what time we were going to get up and what time do we have to be on the road. And somebody had to organize the meeting, so I was the president of the family."[88] Rice, who appeared to be speaking without irony, was asked if "president of the family" was some sort of child-rearing strategy of her mother's to teach her leadership. Rice laughed off the question. "I won it fair and square, my mother and I voted for me," she said.[89]

President or not, Rice was an unusually decisive child. "She never pondered over things," McPhatter said, recalling that as early as the age of four, Condoleezza would rattle off exactly what she wanted for dinner when her mother asked. "She'd just come off the top like that," McPhatter said. "Ann would cook exactly what Condoleezza said. And John would eat exactly what Condoleezza said. And he would enjoy it! It didn't bother me. If I didn't want it, I didn't eat it. I would go home."[90]

The "president" made decisions during family travels, too. "They went a lot of places in the car, and she was always the person in charge of the food, when we eat," recalled Clara Rice, Rice's stepmother, who heard the stories from John Rice. "If she was sleepy, and they wanted something out of the lunch thing, she'd say, 'The store is closed, I'm sleepy. When I wake up, we can eat something.' "[91]

By the time she was nine, Condoleezza had progressed so far in her music that she was providing accompaniment for her mother at church, where daughter played piano and mother played organ. "I can still see her, walking, tiptoeing, across the front of the church, going from the piano to the organ, perhaps to say something to her mother, or getting a piece of sheet music," recalled Smitherman, a member of Westminster. "She had long, pretty hair. And her mother always kept it in the Shirley Temple–type curls. Braids on special occasions, if she had a special recital on Easter or Christmas."[92] On some Sundays, Condoleezza traveled to other churches to play at recitals, always under Angelena's close guidance. "It would reinforce her confidence," said Connie Ray, Rice's aunt. "Condoleezza's mother believed in her being exposed to different situations as much as possible."[93]

But the Rices sometimes drew the line at popular culture. For a grade school variety show, Condoleezza was planning to dress up with friends as the Supremes until her parents told her that impersonating the most successful black musical group of the 1960s would somehow be undignified. The Rices decided that their daughter should perform a solo tap dance instead, and went so far as to hire a tap dance teacher and select her costume. "I had this peculiar outfit, and my father stood there by the stage with his arms crossed to make sure nobody laughed," Rice said. "That's the way my parents were. I was always supposed to do something different and special and slightly more refined."[94]

The Rices made sure that their daughter was schooled in French as well. When she was eight, they sought out Danetta Thornton Owens, one of John Rice's fellow teachers at Ullman, who had a master's degree in modern foreign languages from the University of Indiana, a rare academic credential for a black teacher in the city's public schools at the time. Owens taught Rice for an hour each Saturday, and said she was struck not only by her intelligence but by John Rice's full-time focus on the betterment of Condoleezza Rice. "It wasn't by happenstance, it was by design," Owens said.[95]

There were also typing classes, ballet and tap lessons through her father's church youth group, and, from the time she was five, instruction in etiquette. Rice's mother had helped start Tots and Teens, an alternative in Birmingham to the black social group Jack and Jill. Every Saturday afternoon, Rice arrived with the other girls in frilly dresses and learned manners offered by Tots and Teens at her father's church. "They would sit you at a table and say, 'Use this fork first, make sure that your napkin is in your lap, don't eat until everybody is served,' " Rice recalled. "It was just kind of another thing to learn."[96]

Despite the nonstop lessons, Rice was not the only child to be pushed so hard. Rice stood out in Titusville for her talents on the piano and for her poise, but perfectionism and drive were hardly unique qualities in the striving community. The Rices were intense, but many other ambitious parents insisted that their children take ballet, music, and language classes. "Condi was not, at that time, perceived to be the only little kid who was so disciplined," recalled Odessa Woolfolk, a Titusville resident who taught history at Ullman High School when John Rice was the guidance counselor and was later a founder of the Birmingham Civil Rights Institute. "Back in those days, and even before that era, parents in the black community had aspirations for their kids. And they were told that if you study and get ready your time will come, and if you prepare yourself, even though we lived in a segregated world at that time, in the future things will be better."[97]

Although Rice would bristle at her parents' involvement during high school and college, she never thought to object as a child. In the view of one relative, she subconsciously absorbed the family mission of achievement, although at great emotional cost. "As a five-year-old, you don't even know you're on the mission," said Connie Rice, Rice's second cousin, who had a similar upbringing and is now a civil rights lawyer in Los Angeles. "But you know you're going to get straight As, and you know you're going to the piano recital, and you know you're going to get the standing ovation. What that does is—and you're not even aware of it—it makes you very remote. And as soon as I met Condi I recognized that effect."[98]

Rice, who got to know her second cousin only as an adult, rejected what she considered Connie Rice's psychobabble. "I kind of thought achievement was a good thing," she said when asked about her cousin's remarks. "And the fact that my parents wanted me to know how to do a lot of things was a good thing. I'm really glad that they did, because now I can play the piano and play with Yo-Yo Ma, and I can understand a French conversation with President [Jacques] Chirac."[99] In short, she said, "I can do all these things that enrich my life now. So why should I resent that, as if somehow it was armor? My parents' point of view was that you're going to be better and nobody will be able to question who you are, and that will make you strong. Gee, I just liked taking the lessons, I didn't have a whole kind of psychological experience about it."[100]

Many of Rice's broader lessons came through her father's church youth group, a collection of some thirty-five high school students who John Rice insisted be exposed to the wider world—the arts, history, religion, sports. Rice took the group on field trips to concerts, museums, and college campuses, and usually brought his young daughter along as a mascot. In the afternoons and evenings he opened up the church for chess lessons, ballroom dancing, Ping-Pong, and other pursuits. Once a month he even had a dentist come in, with his own dental chair, for checkups. Since there were so few places for blacks to go in Birmingham, the church provided a social and civic life.

"It was Monday night, ballet and tap, Tuesday night, chemistry and algebra tutoring, Wednesday night, the dentist came, Thursday night you had choir practice," Rice said.[101]

By all accounts, Rice's father had created one of the most vibrant church youth groups in town. Counseling was clearly his calling, not pastoring or preaching or thundering from the pulpit. "He was like a Presbyterian preacher, the kind of preach-under-control type, not a typical black Baptist preacher jumping-around-wiping-sweat-off type," recalled George Hunter III.[102]

Rice recruited his youth group members from Ullman High, from friends of friends, and from word of mouth. A student did not have to be a member of the church to belong. "The reverend, he was what you'd call live—he was jovial, happy, and loved," said George Hunter III, a member of the group. "He wasn't like an average adult with a youngster. He was a really nice person—always trying to help me."[103]

The biggest draw was the Friday night parties in the Fellowship Hall, where the kids played the Temptations, Ike and Tina Turner, and Jerry Lee Lewis. "The reverend used that as a recruiting tool," said George Hunter III.[104] Outside of church, Rice even took the group on field trips to two synagogues in town, Temple Emanuel and Temple Beth-El, for a rare intermingling of races. "We would go in and the rabbi would explain the customs and what they did," Eva Carter recalled. "It was just a different world."[105]

Many youth group members say to this day that John Rice changed their lives. "Besides my parents, he had the most profound impact on my life of anyone I can remember," said Carter. As a child, she said, "I remember almost being a little jealous of Condoleezza." Carter's parents had not gone to college, but John Rice encouraged her. "You have this person telling you, you can achieve anything, you can do whatever you want to do, if only you get an education, and we believed it," Carter said. Her mother didn't know what credit hours were, but John Rice advised her to go to his alma mater, Johnson C. Smith University. "Reverend Rice always said, 'Now, you're my future,' " Carter said.[106]

John Rice's reach extended to the poor black families who lived in the projects behind Westminster. "He would literally go to the government projects at the back of the church, and knock on people's doors and say 'you know your daughter's really smart, and she ought to be going to school and I'm going to get her a scholarship,' or, you know, 'your son's really smart,' even though this kid would probably have ended up working in the steel mills," Condoleezza Rice recalled. "My dad was determined that this kid was going to go to college, and that was the way he was his entire life."[107]

The outreach upset some of the class-conscious church members, particularly the older men. "My father told me once that these kids were out behind the church at one of his picnics or something, throwing dice, you know, playing dice," Rice recalled. "And one of his members said to him, 'See, Reverend, they're not ready to be with us.' It just rankled him."[108] Another time, Rice said, a church member tried to take home a Christmas basket of fruit and canned goods that was meant as a donation for a poor family. "And my father said, 'You can afford this, why would you do that?' " Rice said.[109]

Money was as much a dividing line as education among Birmingham's blacks, where economic status was displayed not only in houses and cars but fashion. The women of Titusville dressed when they went out—to church, school meetings, grocery store errands—and not just because it was the era when that was expected. The clothes advertised their status over working-class blacks, and something more. Years later, Rice was in a Holocaust museum in Israel looking at a photograph of an immaculately dressed Jewish couple in the Warsaw Ghetto when someone asked, "What do you think that's about?" Rice knew exactly. "That's about control," Rice said. "Your outward image is critical to reminding people that you still have control. They're not diminishing your humanity."[110]

Birmingham's department stores were open to blacks with money, up to a point. Angelena took her daughter on frequent shopping trips, but with results that sometimes undermined her resolve that her daughter should never know of her second-class status among whites. In 1961, in one often told story about Rice's childhood, Angelena took the six-year-old Condoleezza dress shopping at Berger-Phillips, one of the fine downtown department stores. But as they headed toward the whites-only dressing room, a saleslady stopped them, took the dress from Condoleezza's hands, and told Angelena her daughter would have to try it on in a storage room instead.[111]

As Rice tells it, her mother drew herself up and confronted the white saleslady. "My daughter will try on this dress in a dressing room, or I'm not spending my money here," Angelena said. Faced with losing a commission, the saleslady wilted, led them to an out-of-the-way dressing room, and furtively guarded the door for fear she would be dismissed from her job.[112]

Around the same time at another department store, a saleslady scolded Rice for touching a hat on display. (In those days, Birmingham's blacks had to put on skullcaps before trying on hats so that no black head would ever come in contact with fabric that might touch a white head.) Angelena, furious, loudly told her daughter to go around and touch every hat in the store. "And I went happily around touching every hat," Rice said.[113] While other children might have been embarrassed by such an outspoken mother, Rice said her reaction—at least the reaction she claimed in retrospect, as an adult—was one of pride. "Because she was always on my side," Rice said.[114]

In yet another episode, Rice was waiting to see a department store Santa Claus, a white man, when her father noticed that Santa put the white children in his lap but kept the black children standing at a distance. "And my father said to my mother, 'If he does that to Condoleezza, I'm going to pull all that stuff off his face and you're going to have to come get me out of jail for Christmas, but I'm not going to let him treat my daughter that way,' " Rice said.[115] In her telling of the story, when her turn came with Santa "it was plop, right in the lap," an outcome she attributed to the look her father gave Santa when her turn came up.[116]

By 1962, the situation in Birmingham's downtown department stores had become so offensive to blacks that Fred Shuttlesworth organized a shopping boycott during the crucial Easter season.[117] Rice's parents observed the boycott, but got around its inconveniences when they asked Genoa, Condoleezza's aunt—who by then lived in Virginia—to send them their daughter's new Girl Scout uniform from Norfolk.[118] The good life they had created for Condoleezza continued on.

CHAPTER 2

The Year of Terror

Birmingham, 1963

The year 1963 in Birmingham shattered Condoleezza Rice's comfortable cocoon. Up until then, her age and her parents' determination to shelter her had shut out much of the city's savagery. As a child, Rice never knew about an unspeakable crime that spread horror through Titusville, the Ku Klux Klan's castration in September 1957 of a young black man, Edward "Judge" Aaron, to warn that the same thing would happen to Fred Shuttlesworth if he attempted to integrate the city's schools.[1] As a child, she did not know that Bull Connor, Birmingham's brutal commissioner of public safety, had allowed the Klan to go into the city's bus station on Mother's Day 1961 and beat up the Freedom Riders, the black and white students trying to integrate buses in the Deep South.[2] She did not know then that her city was called Bombingham, or the Johannesburg of America, or that Arthur Shores's daughter had been presented at a black debutante party but was so afraid of the city's violence—the Shoreses' home would be blown up twice—that she slept with her father's Colt .45 under her pillow.[3]

The year was the dividing line in Rice's childhood, a demarcation between relative innocence and an awareness of race that would feed an anger she carried into adulthood. Decades later, Rice looked back and called it the "crucible" year, the same word that Martin Luther

King used in his eulogy to the four girls killed in the bombing of the Sixteenth Street Baptist Church. Rice's set story of her life—that her upbringing nurtured and empowered her despite the terror in Birmingham's streets—has always left out the element of rage.

Rice was eight when the year began on a sour note, at least for the civil rights leaders who had placed their hopes in President John F. Kennedy. On January 1, one century to the day after Abraham Lincoln's Emancipation Proclamation became law, Kennedy sidestepped what Martin Luther King had been quietly pushing on him for more than a year—issuing a second Emancipation Proclamation to end segregation by executive order.[4] Two weeks later, when George Wallace stood in the portico of the state capitol and declared "Segregation forever!" at his inauguration as Alabama's new governor, King had already begun planning what would be a perilous, epochal campaign of life and young death in Birmingham, by then the most racially explosive city in the United States. In 1960, Harrison Salisbury of *The New York Times* had outraged the city's white hierarchy with a searing but accurate front-page description of Bombingham: "Every channel of communication, every medium of mutual interest, every reasoned approach, every inch of middle ground has been fragmented by the emotional dynamite of racism, reinforced by the whip, the razor, the gun, the bomb, the torch, the club, the knife, the mob, the police and many branches of the state's apparatus."[5] The article included one of the more notorious boasts of Bull Connor: "Damn the law, we don't give a damn about the law," Connor said in 1958. "Down here we make our own law."[6]

That winter, as Rice blazed through fourth grade at Brunetta C. Hill, King planned his assault on Birmingham. In a meeting in Savannah he told his closest associates that "some of the people sitting here today will not come back alive from this campaign."[7] But King felt he had no choice: He had become a celebrity preacher for his role in organizing the Montgomery bus boycott of 1955 and 1956, and was frustrated that he had not been able to spread its success to other cities.[8] In 1961 he lost a power play to gain control of what he saw as an ideal base for his movement, the five-million-member National Baptist Convention, and by 1962 he was branded a failure for not ending segregation in an ambitious campaign in Albany, Georgia.

For his own survival, King would now have to stage a showdown in Birmingham, as Shuttlesworth had been pleading for him to do for years. "If you can break the back of segregation in Birmingham, Alabama, then you can break the back of segregation all over the nation," Shuttlesworth told King that winter.[9] Decades later, Shuttlesworth summed up the essential equation: "He needed Birmingham as much as Birmingham needed him."[10]

John Rice and Birmingham's black middle class did not have the same sentiment. King's pending arrival in the city that spring set off alarms in Titusville, where the view was that confrontation would make things worse. There had been some signs of improvement: The beating of the Freedom Riders had been so shocking—the photographs ran all over the world—that Birmingham's moderate whites, worried about their ability to attract business to the city, had engineered Connor's ouster through a referendum that changed Birmingham from a commission to a mayor–city council form of government. The change eliminated Connor's job and forced him to run for mayor. He lost in a run-off on April 2, as moderates had anticipated. Connor refused to recognize the election results (a court would eventually decide against him), but his defeat spread hope that the city's ugliest days were behind it—and made the black middle class question King's timing.[11]

But King arrived on the night of the election, and a few days later met with the pillar of the black bourgeoisie, A. G. Gaston, a businessman much admired in the Rice household. Gaston, who owned the motel where King would stay during the siege, saw King as an outsider and considered an alliance with him a potential risk in his relationships with white creditors, but he was also worried that if he opposed King he might end up on the wrong side.[12] Gaston and a group of black leaders heard King out—his immediate goals were the desegregation of lunch counters, drinking fountains, and bathrooms in Birmingham department stores—but the response was that they were making progress and could handle things themselves.[13]

One of those at the meeting was James Montgomery, the doctor to Gaston and Shuttlesworth, a friend of King from their days at Morehouse College, and the Titusville resident who knew the Rices. After about half an hour he spoke up, outraged. "What the hell are you all talking about?" Montgomery recalled that he told the group. "What's all this progress we're making? Everything is segregated, all the lunch counters got signs on them, all the hotels you can't walk in the doors as a human being."[14] In an interview decades later, Montgomery said the group was of the view that "the time is not ripe yet for some of these things, so put them on the back burner." Montgomery paused. "And they'd been putting them on the back burner since slavery," he said.[15]

John Rice was not among the pastors at the meeting, but his feelings about King were consistent with the cold reception of the black bourgeoisie. Years later, John Rice's widow, Clara Rice, the woman Rice married after Angelena died, said she was surprised to learn from Rice that "he didn't like Martin Luther King," although she didn't know "if it was the movement he wasn't quite with, or if it was Martin himself."[16] Condoleezza Rice presented a more politically palatable view of her father. "He was supportive of King, and he tried to support Shuttlesworth and those people," she said, drawing a distinction between Shuttlesworth and his supporters and her own family. But, she said, "I think he was ambivalent about some of the tactics."[17]

Rice said she once asked her father why he hadn't marched in the streets with King, and his answer was that he was afraid he would not be able to hold to King's principle of nonviolent resistance. "He said, 'If somebody strikes me, I'm going to fight back, and then I would have ended up dead, and you would have been left without a father,' " Rice said. "I'm not sure he fully accepted the concept of nonviolence."[18]

Whatever Rice may have told his young daughter, he told Shuttlesworth something else. "He told me plainly that he was just afraid his church would be bombed," Shuttlesworth said. "His church was a very nice building, and he was concerned that it might not get restructured if it was bombed."[19] In Shuttlesworth's recollection, Rice was worried that the black Presbyterian church, which had nowhere near the membership and money of the Baptists, would simply not have the funds to rebuild. But Shuttlesworth said that he perceived Rice as sympathetic to the movement, and that Rice was "thankful to God that somebody was coming to Birmingham who didn't fear Bull Connor."[20]

Shuttlesworth saw Rice every week or so, an odd pairing given the bad feelings about Shuttlesworth among the city's black middle class. Their meetings seem to have been as much an accident of geography as of anything else, although Rice appeared, at least in Shuttlesworth's telling, interested in Shuttlesworth's ideas. Their conversations occurred because Westminster Presbyterian was near the homes of Shuttlesworth's mother and one of his key followers, and so Shuttlesworth stopped by to see Rice when he was in the neighborhood. "He was just a man not forward in his nature," Shuttlesworth said. "He was not expressionistic, let us say. He was a simple Presbyterian preacher." But, said Shuttlesworth, "he loved me. He just loved to talk to me."[21]

The protests got off to a slow start. On April 3, some five dozen blacks sat in at lunch counters at the downtown department stores, but the waitresses, rehearsed ahead of time to avoid confrontation, turned off the lights, and said the stores were closed.[22] Newberry's was the lone establishment to challenge the sit-ins, and by the end of the day, only twenty people had been hauled off to jail—a whimper of a beginning for King.[23] Few blacks were willing to protest, and the campaign went so rapidly nowhere that by Good Friday, April 12, King got himself arrested—for marching against an injunction—in the hope that his own jail time would bring much-needed attention to the campaign.[24] During nearly nine days in solitary, he lashed out at a group of white ministers who had called his campaign "unwise and untimely"[25] with his "Letter from Birmingham Jail," a now famous jewel of the civil rights era that laid out the moral justification for the movement. But in April 1963 the letter was largely ignored, and by the time King was out of jail, late in the month, the Birmingham campaign was near failure.[26]

Desperate, King listened to the urgings of one of his more radical and brilliant lieutenants, James Bevel, that he permit children to join the marches.[27] Bevel had been conducting daily workshops in nonviolence to enthralled Birmingham high school and grade school students, most of them Baptists, and he argued that they were old enough to join a movement that embodied Christian teachings.[28] King did not buy all of Bevel's argument, but he also realized that without children the Birmingham campaign was finished, and he eventually acquiesced.[29]

John Rice was aghast at the news. "Oh, he wasn't ambivalent about that," Rice recalled of her father. "He really, really did not favor the children's march. He said, 'I would not send my child.' "[30] John Rice, like other members of Birmingham's black middle class, thought King had gone too far, and that the marches were nothing less than exploitation. "The question was, are you using these children?" said Freeman Hrabowski, the president of the University of Maryland, Baltimore County, who was a protégé of John Rice and one of the few black students from Titusville to participate in the marches and go to jail. "And that's a legitimate question, it is. There was no right and wrong answer."[31]

Either way, King's Birmingham campaign turned Condoleezza Rice's life upside down. Rice's parents, fearing trouble, frequently kept her home from school—Angelena would count thirty-one days that her daughter missed from March through the end of 1963—and sent her to her grandmother's house instead.[32] King's organizers were blanketing the county's black high schools with leaflets urging students to march, regardless of whether they had permission from teachers or parents.[33] No such leaflets were distributed at the Hill school, but Rice's parents were taking no chances. They were terrified, as everyone was in Titusville, by the night riders—whites who raced through black neighborhoods brandishing shotguns out of car windows and shouting racist slogans. "The period between March or April of '63 and September of '63 was just very violent," Rice recalled. "That was when Arthur Shores's house was bombed a couple times, that's when night riders used to come through communities, that's when, because of the way the marches were being handled they were pulling kids out of school. I didn't go to school—a lot. It was just a very tense time."[34]

The first children's march began on May 2, only two miles from Rice's home, at the most fashionable black church in town, the venerable Sixteenth Street Baptist. (The church was chosen not for the sentiments of its middle-class members but for its location near City Hall, the downtown merchants, and Kelly Ingram Park, a central gathering place.) That morning, nearly eight hundred students missed roll call, even as R. C. Johnson, Alma Powell's father and the principal of the all-black Parker High School, locked the school's front gates. It was all in vain—his students simply scampered over them.[35] That afternoon, fifty teenagers emerged from Sixteenth Street Baptist, singing "We Shall Overcome" like a ragtime march.[36] A waiting phalanx of police warned them of a court order against demonstrations, arrested them, and then hauled them into paddy wagons.[37] More demonstrators emerged from the church, some as young as six. By the end of the day, nearly one thousand children had marched and some six hundred were in jail.[38] King and his followers were elated.

The marches resumed with greater intensity on May 3, a day that would be seared in the memory of Condoleezza Rice and the history of the civil rights movement itself. Buoyed by the spectacle and excitement of the day before, another thousand children turned out to march. But with the jails full, Bull Connor's troops were under orders not to make more arrests and instead to stop the marchers from getting into the downtown business district. To do that, firemen turned hoses on a group of sixty students, who were drenched and quickly retreated. But when ten students stood their ground, the firemen advanced and, at close range, pummeled them with water from special monitor guns that forced the flow from two hoses through a single nozzle mounted on a tripod.[39] The guns, capable of knocking bricks loose from mortar or stripping bark from trees at a distance of one hundred feet, rolled little black girls down the street like tumbleweed.[40]

Carolyn McKinstry, a tenth grader at Parker High School who would befriend Condoleezza Rice as an adult, got hit so hard with the water that it ripped off a section of hair from the side of her head.[41] "I remember thinking to myself when I was hit with the hose—nobody told me anything about water," McKinstry recalled years later.[42] Like many of the others, McKinstry, a member of Sixteenth Street Baptist, had joined the march as a thrill, after she heard King speak outside the church and saw a big poster at school that proclaimed, "It's Time!"[43]

To drive the students back further, Connor's forces then loosed growling German shepherds on the crowd. Outside the Jockey Boy restaurant, one white dog handler grabbed a fifteen-year-old black boy, Walter Gadsden, as the dog, teeth bared, charged the boy's torso.[44] An AP photographer standing nearby captured the image that came to symbolize the racial horror of Birmingham, and by the following morning the picture was all over the world. At the White House, President Kennedy said the photograph made him "sick."[45]

The photograph sickened John Rice, too, not least because it proved to him the costs of King's decision to use children and the limitations, as he saw them, of nonviolent resistance. "You know, water hoses and police dogs and nobody fought back," Condoleezza Rice said years later. "I think that was hard for him. I think he understood the logic of it, and it was very powerful, but personally, I think, he was not somebody who could do that."[46]

John Rice, like the rest of Birmingham, nonetheless understood the history unfolding before him. In the days after the photograph appeared, Condoleezza Rice said that her father took her to the county fairgrounds, where most of the arrested students were being held, either in the 4-H Club Building[47] or in outdoor pens.[48] Her father put her up on his shoulders, she said, her legs dangling down on his chest, so she could see through the milling crowd of frantic parents what was happening:[49] "He would raise me up to see, going among the kids, saying, you know, are you okay, is there anything we can do for you, and so forth."[50]

Most of the children were from the projects and working-class homes, but two of Rice's middle-class students, Freeman Hrabowski and George Hunter, had marched and were in jail. Rice did not see them that day, but both recall that he did not discourage them from demonstrating,[51] even though Hrabowski knew that Rice was opposed. Most teachers at the time were as well: Bull Connor had ordered any demonstrating student over the age of sixteen expelled from school[52] and parents had been told by employers that they would lose their jobs if their children took part.[53] But Hrabowski, then an awkward and precocious twelve-year-old high school student, still plunged in, and spent five terrifying days in jail watching "bad things" happen—to this day he will not discuss what he saw—and trying to comfort a group of even younger boys who cried for their mothers.[54] He was stirred to hear King preach outside the jail about "what you do this day will have an impact on generations yet unborn," and he insisted, years later, that "Reverend Rice always believed it, even when he and other teachers had their doubts about strategy."[55]

As an adult, Condoleezza Rice would bristle when anyone suggested that her father and the black middle class had kept a safe distance from King and the cataclysmic events of Birmingham that year. "Well, sure," she said, acknowledging the criticism, but pointing out that black teachers had also falsified attendance records that spring when the school board tried to find out who had marched to keep students from graduating.[56] "So they did their part, but they had different views of what their own roles were," Rice said. "And they still educated more kids and put more kids in a position to be able to take advantage of the civil rights movement than anybody else."[57]

John Rice did get involved at close range in his own neighborhood. A shrapnel bomb went off that spring near the Titusville Public Library, just a block from Westminster, shattering the library's windows and damaging homes nearby.[58] Around the same time, a gas bomb was hurled through the Rices' neighbor's window, forcing Rice and her parents to evacuate for a day. "The odor was so strong it stifled the whole community," John Rice recalled.[59] Knowing they had no protection from Bull Connor's police force, the men of Titusville organized nightly patrols of their own.

Once a week, John Rice took out his shotgun and joined his shift of two other men at a checkpoint, the entrance to his street. For the next three hours, guns in their laps, the men patrolled the neighborhood by car. By dawn they were home, ready for a day at work. John Cantelow, Condoleezza Rice's band teacher at the Hill school, was a block captain in a system that included more than one hundred men.[60] Despite the numbers, Rice's strongest memory of the time is of never feeling safe.

"I blocked out for a long time that it was—" She paused, looking for the right word. "Traumatic's the wrong word, because I obviously wasn't ultimately traumatized by it—but how really frightening it was. Because my parents were very good at protecting me. But it was pretty frightening, and I think as an adult I look back, and sometimes I look at terrorist incidents and kind of remember what that was like, not to feel safe in your home, you know, to have your father out with a shotgun."[61]

Rice has memories from the same period of Connor, who by this time she was following closely in the news. "I was fascinated by him, because he was kind of the personification of evil," she said. "You know, who is this man and why is he doing these things? And he would get on television and say the most awful things. He had that pronunciation of Negro that was particularly appalling: the Nigras. And I would watch him, and I was always taught not to hate, but I think I hated him."[62]

Birmingham streets remained a battleground into the second week of May, when Kennedy sent in Burke Marshall, the assistant attorney general, to try to mediate an end to the violence. But thousands of demonstrators blanketed downtown before a truce was finally announced on May 10, when Birmingham merchants agreed to desegregate their department stores and King emerged triumphant.[63] The siege of Birmingham would take its place in history.

By June 11, attention shifted to Tuscaloosa, where Governor George Wallace made his stand in the schoolhouse door to try to stop the integration of the University of Alabama. That same evening at the White House, Kennedy introduced his civil rights bill in a speech to the nation. Rice and her parents watched on television from home. "I didn't have a sophisticated understanding of what it meant, I just thought and my parents thought this was going to be a good thing," she said. "I had such a crush on John F. Kennedy, you know, anything John Kennedy did was fine."[64]

Later that summer, Rice and her parents went on a family trip to Washington, where Rice posed for a picture outside the White House gates. The grainy black and white photograph, now a classic, shows a pretty child dressed in the very best that Angelena could buy—a sleeveless, light-colored summer dress, a necklace and charm bracelet, a big bow in a braid of hair, Mary Jane shoes. Behind the eight-year-old Condoleezza Rice is the North Portico entrance of the White House that would become so familiar to her decades later, but what is most striking about the photograph is the extreme self-possession evident on her young face. As the family lore always had it—and as virtually every newspaper and magazine profile of Rice now mentions—the young Condoleezza vowed to her father on the spot, "I'll work in that house someday." It was an extraordinary statement, if true, for a child living under the segregated terror of Birmingham.

Years later, Rice said she had no memory of the line and that it was her father who had told the story over the years. "Either he remembered it or it was made up in his head, but I can't vouch for the story myself," she said.[65] She first heard it from him when she went to work in the administration of George H. W. Bush. "He said, 'You've fulfilled your promise—you said one day you'd work in that White House.' I said, 'I did?' And then he told this to every person who wrote an article about me from then on. All I remember is that it was miserably hot, and that my mother let me take off my socks. If you'll notice, I'm not wearing any socks in my little Mary Janes."[66]

That August of 1963, King delivered his "I Have a Dream" speech from the Lincoln Memorial, before the largest demonstration in American history at the time. He had a message that resounded in Birmingham: "I have a dream that one day, down in Alabama, with its vicious racists, with its governor having his lips dripping with the words of interposition and nullification; one day right there in Alabama, little black boys and black girls will be able to join hands with little white boys and white girls as sisters and brothers."[67] Rice watched the speech on television with her parents, and as an adult recalled that "you couldn't not see there were major things going on around you and that big change was coming."[68]

Less than two weeks later, on September 4, Birmingham's public schools were at last desegregated. It had been nine years since the Supreme Court struck down school segregation in *Brown v. Board of Education*, but the court had not said how its mandate should be implemented, and Alabama, like other Southern states, slow-walked and legislated its way around the landmark ruling. The delays came to an end in July when the Fifth Circuit Court of Appeals, in response to a lawsuit filed by one of Shuttlesworth's followers,[69] put the Birmingham schools under federal court order to desegregate. The decision, which opened the door for the first five black students at three different public schools, predictably set off another round of violence.[70] Arthur Shores's home in Smithfield was blown up at the end of August and again on September 4, when whites also shot and killed a black man, mistakenly believing that he was Shuttlesworth.[71] The opening of the three schools was reset for Monday, September 9. The Hill school was not affected, but like all of Birmingham, the students and faculty were on edge for the rest of the week.

Sunday, September 15, was unusually cool and overcast.[72] At Sixteenth Street Baptist Church, Carolyn McKinstry, who had been blasted by Bull Connor's fire hoses only four months earlier, stopped in to say hello to five friends primping in the downstairs bathroom in preparation for the 11 A.M. service—Denise McNair, Cynthia Wesley, Carole Robertson, and Addie Mae and Sarah Collins, who all ranged in age from eleven to fourteen. McKinstry went upstairs, but on her way stopped to answer the phone in a small office, part of her volunteer duties at the church. The caller said "three minutes," then hung up. Thinking nothing of it—Sixteenth Street Baptist was getting a lot of such calls in those days—McKinstry walked toward the sanctuary and was suddenly rocked by what felt like an earthquake. As the windows crashed in, she heard someone yell "Hit the floor," and then everything got dark.[73] The next thing McKinstry heard was the sound of feet rushing for the doors. She stumbled her way through the church's back entrance.[74]

At the time of the explosion, 10:22 A.M., Condoleezza Rice was sitting in a front pew of Westminster Presbyterian. Later, she recalled feeling a strange sensation. "I remember feeling it, not so much hearing it," she said. "And everybody did. And Mrs. Florence Rice, who was my father's cousin by marriage, we were just getting ready to start church, and she came in and she said, 'Oh my God, oh my God, they've blown up Sixteenth Street Baptist Church.' "[75]

John Rice, without any details of the blast, started speaking from the pulpit as scheduled at 11 A.M. "We went through the service because nobody really knew what had happened, we didn't have cell phones in those days or breaking news or anything," Rice recalled. "And I don't remember much except, you know, being scared."[76]

Parnell Jones, the principal of the Hill school, was at home in Titusville that Sunday morning and he heard the blast, too. "I looked out and saw smoke and said, 'Lord, what happened?' " Jones recalled. "Then the phone started ringing."[77]

Rev. Abraham Woods, one of King's lead organizers in Birmingham, had jumped in his car when he heard the noise, even though it wasn't unusual in those days to hear a bomb go off in Birmingham. "So I went on down there," he recalled decades later. "I stood there and I'm telling you, the kind of feeling that I had at that time, to hear the screaming . . . you were overwhelmed with grief. And I did have some thoughts: 'If I had a massive weapon I would shoot down every white person I saw. This is the last straw.' "[78]

The scene at the church was bedlam. Outside, on the northeast side of the building, a seven-by-seven-foot hole had been blown in what had been the wall of the women's lounge. Rescue workers had already begun to dig through the wreckage, and after layers of bricks were removed, someone said, "I feel something soft."[79] There were four bodies, stacked horizontally, like firewood: Denise, Cynthia, Carole, and Addie.[80] As the bodies were brought out of the debris, the gathering crowd sobbed and prayed.[81] Sarah Collins, Addie's sister, was found moaning and with her face spurting blood, but still alive.[82]

Condoleezza Rice doesn't remember exactly when she heard that her friend Denise had been killed, but she thinks it was sometime that Sunday afternoon. "It was horrible," she said. "It was the first time I knew anybody who died. And I just remember really being sad and being kind of angry, like why did that happen to Denise? I don't remember having the kind of bigger picture in mind. That all comes later as you reflect on things."[83]

Denise was a full three years older than Condoleezza, a chasm at that age, and it is a stretch to call the two close friends. But Denise and Condoleezza had been playmates in the kindergarten that John Rice started at Westminster Presbyterian.[84] Denise's father, Chris McNair, still has a photograph he took of John Rice handing a smiling Denise, dressed in a white graduation gown, her kindergarten diploma. The two girls sang together in kindergarten musicals and played with dolls at the home of Denise's grandmother, who lived across the street from the church. Maxine McNair, Denise's mother, recalled the Condoleezza Rice who played with her daughter as "a quiet, obedient little child."[85]

Revulsion at the church bombing soon spread swiftly beyond Birmingham. "Dear God, why?" King silently asked himself when word of the blast reached him as he was about to step into the pulpit at Ebenezer Baptist in Atlanta.[86] As he prepared to return to Birmingham, King wired George Wallace that "the blood of our little children is on your hands" and sent a telegram to President Kennedy warning of "the worst racial holocaust this nation has ever seen."[87] In Washington, Kennedy sent Burke Marshall back to another Birmingham riot scene, this time one so dangerous that the local police and FBI refused to risk taking Marshall to meet with King at a supporter's home on Dynamite Hill. Marshall got there only after an intrepid team of local blacks, wearing homemade Civil Defense uniforms, threw him facedown in the back of a car and rushed him up to Dynamite Hill, where hired bodyguards were protecting the homes.[88] Many of Birmingham's middle-class blacks were seething against King as the real cause of the bombing,[89] but King was unrepentant. "What murdered these four girls?" he said to reporters. "The apathy and the complacency of many Negroes who will sit down on their stools and do nothing and not engage in creative protest to get rid of this evil."[90]

King's words seemed aimed squarely at Birmingham's black middle class, but if Rice ever heard them she does not recall them.[91] She does remember how deep and hard the bombing hit her family and friends. The girls were products of the middle class, "sweet princesses" as King would call them in his eulogy, who had done nothing more than turn up for church on a Sunday morning. They had not marched in the streets, they had not gone to Jim Bevel's workshops, they had not jumped the fence at Parker High School. They had merely been there in their pretty dresses to sing in the choir or to help lead the congregation on Youth Day. Like Condoleezza Rice, Denise McNair was a budding star, and her family and the others had layers of ties in the community. Carole Robertson's teacher was Willie Mae Jones, the wife of Condoleezza Rice's band teacher at the Hill school. Cynthia Wesley's father had taught history to Odessa Woolfolk in high school, and now Woolfolk taught at Ullman High School, where John Rice was the guidance counselor, and where Cynthia was in the tenth grade when she died. Denise McNair's mother taught at the Center Street School, where Condoleezza Rice's friends from Honeysuckle Circle were enrolled. Denise's father was a wedding photographer in the community, and for a time he had been the neighborhood milkman, too.

"Before we felt protected by our families, by the men in the neighborhood," recalled Marion Sterling, a childhood friend of Rice whose family owned the funeral home where Denise McNair was taken and had the side of her face reconstructed for her funeral. "We had Boy Scouts and Cub Scouts and good high school sports. We had a world that provided the haircuts, movie theaters, fraternities. Then that bomb went off, and even though there were other acts of violence occurring, it was horrifying. That's when I learned that as a child, I could be killed, too. It was so close to you."[92]

The funeral was Wednesday, September 18, three weeks to the day after King's "I Have a Dream" speech, at Sixth Avenue Baptist Church. Police estimated that more than four thousand people overwhelmed the sanctuary,[93] including so many pastors of both races that it became the largest interracial gathering of clergy in Birmingham's history.[94] The Rices, dressed in their Sunday best, took Condoleezza to pay respects to her schoolmate. It was the first funeral she had ever attended, and she spent it with the overflowing masses outside the church's door. "We didn't actually make it into the church," Rice said. "It was so crowded that we just stood outside and watched the people go in, and watched the coffin go by, little coffins."[95]

Rice recalled that she held her mother's hand through the service, and that her father kept his arm around her. But most of all she was stunned by the size of the coffins. "I just remember they were small," she said. "That's what struck me, they were small. I remember vaguely they were pastel of some kind. You know, white or pink, not coffin color."[96]

Inside, King preached over the three open caskets of Denise, Addie, and Cynthia. (Carole Robertson's parents had held a private service for their daughter the day before, despite King's personal entreaties to them to join in a mass funeral. "For an hour he pleaded with them to permit their daughter to be eulogized jointly with the others," Taylor Branch wrote in *Parting the Waters*. "In doing so, he proved to the point of callousness that he was anything but squeamish about confronting the human costs of his leadership.")[97]

King's eulogy at the mass funeral offered no apologies. He hammered the federal government, Southern Dixiecrats, Northern Republicans, and "every Negro who has passively accepted the evil system of segregation and who has stood on the sidelines in a mighty struggle for justice."[98] He tried to comfort the families, acknowledging that life could be hard as "crucible steel," but that "no greater tribute can be paid to you as parents, and no greater epitaph can come to them as children, than where they died and what they were doing when they died."[99] They fell "between the sacred walls of the church of God," he preached, and their deaths were not in vain. He held out the hope that "this tragic event may cause the white South to come to terms with its conscience."[100]

Rice did not hear the sermon outside the church, but four decades later she would echo King's words when she returned to the site of the bombing as a favored daughter of Birmingham and the new American secretary of state, an office unimaginable for a young black girl in 1963. The bombing of the church, she said in a speech in Kelly Ingram Park, "was meant, just a few weeks after Martin Luther King had said, 'I have a dream,' to tell us that no, we didn't have a dream and that that dream was going to be denied." The four girls were denied the chance to grow up, she said, but "in their death they represent for us the very tragedy to triumph that we're celebrating because we were not denied. Birmingham was not denied, and because Birmingham was not denied, America finally came to terms with its birth defect. It finally came to terms with the contradictions that when the founding fathers said, 'We the people,' they didn't mean many of us."[101]

By this point Rice had taken on a forceful tone. "Whenever I think of Addie and Denise and Carole and Cynthia," she said, "I think, too, of what occurred there and what they represent, which is that when America experienced its own homegrown terrorism, it was meant to shatter our spirit."[102]

It was one of the first times in public that Rice had incorporated her childhood into the Bush administration's fight against terrorism. There were people that day in Birmingham, black and white, who, however proud of her accomplishments, were offended by what they saw as the political opportunism of a woman who was claiming a city she had left four decades before. "Her narrative has been carefully crafted to show what she wants to show," said Robert G. Corley, a white professor at the University of Alabama at Birmingham and a city historian who is a friend of Carolyn McKinstry. "The reality for her is that she grew up in Birmingham when it was segregated, but she did not experience segregation in the way that some of her contemporaries and peers did. There's a difference, too, for the people who stayed here. Carolyn lived through that bombing and she really experienced it. Every time she talks about it, it's about her own kind of healing, in a way. Condi's relationship to the event was much more distant. Her thinking about it has been more sort of intellectual."[103]

James Montgomery, the black doctor to Birmingham's civil rights leaders, had a similar reaction. "She was very well received, and I'm happy about that," he said. "But now most black people understand that Condoleezza Rice's politics and our politics are not the same. I'm not sure she ever had the real black experience, I'm not sure of that at all. You leave a place at eleven, you don't have much of the experience."[104]

Carolyn McKinstry said that in recent years Rice has had a lot of questions about the bombing. "She'll ask me about how I felt about what happened," McKinstry said. "I was really afraid for a long time. I think I suffered from some depression during that time, and I didn't know what it was then. But we also talk about how we see it today." Looking back, she said, "I think Condi's life was a little more sheltered than mine," since Rice was an only child and McKinstry was one of six. "All of us were sheltered to some extent," she said, "but I don't think she experienced some of the things we did."[105]

Two months after the church bombing, while Birmingham was still in shock, John F. Kennedy was assassinated in Dallas. Like everyone else, Rice remembers where she was, geography class at the Hill school. Her teacher announced that the president had been shot, and then the students filed out for recess. "And we came back, and I heard her at the door, talking to another teacher, and she said, 'My God, the president's dead, and there's a Southerner in the White House, what's going to happen to us now?' " Rice remembered.[106] Kennedy's death was "another blow," Rice recalled, but the new fear in Birmingham was that Lyndon Johnson would not advance civil rights. "After the bombing of the church, there was a sense that the nation was starting to rally, and then that happened," Rice said. "And people wondered if there would now be a stalling out, because he was a Southerner."[107]

History quickly proved Birmingham's fears unfounded. In less than a year, on July 2, 1964, Rice and her parents watched on their living room television as Johnson signed the Civil Rights Act. With King in the second row in the East Room of the White House, Johnson declared that "those who are equal before God shall now also be equal in the polling booths, in the classrooms, in the factories, and in the hotels, restaurants, movie theaters, and other places that provide service to the public."[108]

Only days later, John and Angelena Rice took their nine-year-old daughter to test the new law in the formerly whites-only restaurant in the Tutwiler Hotel, the most elegant dining room in town. "I remember walking in and the people kind of looking at us like, 'Oh,' " Rice said. "I remember people looking up and thinking this is strange but maybe remembering that it's now okay. And we were actually seated and we ate. I remember that I ate spaghetti."[109] She said she felt "proud," and dismissed the suggestion that she must have felt awkward. By that point, Rice said she had dined out in integrated settings on summer trips up North—"it wasn't as though I had never been in a restaurant," she said—but it was the first restaurant she had been to in Birmingham other than one at A. G. Gaston's motel. "A. G. Gaston's was the only restaurant that was both black and that my mother considered clean enough," Rice said.[110]

More than four decades later, Birmingham blacks who lived through the events of 1963 still get tears in their eyes and fury in their voices when they recall the church bombing. The city had healed up to a point, but among African-Americans there was enormous anger beneath the surface. In an interview, Rice acknowledged feeling the same anger—"of course," she said—but in the next breath distanced herself from it, and said her anger was "not so much for myself, my life is perfectly wonderful, really." She concluded that "my anger is more for my grandparents."[111]

Rice's disavowal of anger—anger is a form of vulnerability, after all—was undermined by her own behavior in what she perceived as racist encounters as an adult. One of the more revealing episodes, a mirror of the Birmingham shopping confrontations of her mother that is relevant here, occurred at a jewelry counter in Palo Alto, when Rice was at Stanford. Rice asked to see the better earrings, the white salesclerk pulled out the costume jewelry, Rice snapped that she wanted the good jewelry, ugly words were exchanged, and then Rice unloaded on the woman. "Let's get one thing straight," she told the clerk, as recalled by her friend Chip Blacker, who was there. "You're behind the counter because you have to work for $6 an hour. I'm on this side asking to see the good jewelry because I make considerably more. And I'm asking to see the good jewelry." At that point a manager appeared, apologized, and showed Rice the good jewelry.[112]

Rice later said that "I can feel racism at a hundred paces," and firmly added, "I know the difference. I know. I know when somebody's reacting to me because of color."[113] She said she had "antennae" for it, but in the same conversation said the antennae could sometimes be wrong. She told a story about how her Aunt Theresa had warned her to be careful of the Ku Klux Klan when Rice was a student at Notre Dame in the 1970s—the Klan rose to prominence in Indiana after World War I—and Rice, who thought her aunt was overreacting, still had her guard up when her car overheated in South Bend one hot summer day. She walked to a service station and was told brusquely by the white mechanic that she'd have to put the car "over here." Rice, thinking that she and her car were being relegated to second-class status, angrily shot back, "Why? Why do I have to bring it over here?" The mechanic, she said, meekly responded, "Well, if you brought it over here and put it in the shade, it might cool down." Mulling over her reaction, Rice said that "I think there is a reflex that you have to be very careful about, and I consistently tell myself, give people the benefit of the doubt—don't assume."[114]

Rice's assessment of the civil rights movement reflected the self-help philosophy of her family but also resentment toward a narrative as it had been shaped by whites. "What I always disliked was the notion that blacks were somehow saved by people who came down from the North to march," Rice said. "You know, black Americans in Birmingham and in Atlanta and places like that were thriving and educating their children and being self-reliant and producing the right values in those families, and in those communities. And when segregation did lift they were more than prepared because of what blacks had done on their own."[115] Segregation was collapsing of its own weight before federal law dismantled it, she told *The Washington Post* in 2001. "Segregation had become not just a real moral problem, but it had become a real pain in the neck for white people," she said.[116]

Birmingham was changing, but Condoleezza Rice would not be there to see it. In 1966, John Rice moved the family to Tuscaloosa and started a new job as dean of students at Stillman College, the school where his father, Granddaddy Rice, had run out of cotton and then trained as a minister on scholarship. Rice had always been more interested in student counseling than tending a congregation, and had sought the position.[117] Condoleezza Rice would insist that her family did not leave Birmingham because of the bloodshed, although John Rice would later tell a family friend in Denver that escaping racism was one reason he eventually left the South.[118]

Birmingham was in any case only fifty miles away, and Rice and her mother made the trip back at least once a week for piano lessons at the music conservatory at Birmingham Southern College, where Rice had enrolled in 1964 as the first black student. The family still shopped for clothes in Birmingham, made visits to Westminster Presbyterian, and saw family and friends. "Our lives were still pretty Birmingham-focused," Rice said.[119] In Tuscaloosa, Rice again skipped an academic year, seventh, and entered Druid High School, an all-black school, as an eleven-year-old eighth grader. The acceleration was the idea of Rice's parents, who viewed Tuscaloosa schools as inferior to those in Birmingham and thought their daughter would spend seventh grade repeating material she already knew.[120]

Rice was freer in Tuscaloosa than she ever had been in Honeysuckle Circle. She was older, of course, but at Stillman there was not the fear of violence that had marked so much of her childhood. "It was nice for me, because I could romp around the campus as an eleven-year-old, without much supervision," Rice said. The family went to basketball games and football games and heard Robert F. Kennedy and the NBC anchor Chet Huntley speak at the University of Alabama, the institution that dominated Tuscaloosa. "It was a really nice life," Rice said.[121]

The Rices spent the summers of 1967 and 1968 in Denver, as they had in 1960, 1961, and 1964, when they were still living in Birmingham. John Rice was slowly working on a master's degree in student personnel administration, and two schools that offered programs were the University of Denver and New York University. New York was too expensive, as the family discovered when John Rice studied there during other summers. So they settled on Denver, where Angelena attended summer classes and Condoleezza learned to ice-skate. The lessons had been Condoleezza Rice's idea—she was captivated by Carol Heiss, the American figure skater who won the gold medal at the 1960 Olympics in Squaw Valley, California, and Tenley Albright, the U.S. figure skater who won the 1956 Olympic gold medal and went on to Harvard Medical School and a career as a surgeon. "I had watched skating on TV and I saw these girls skating and I said, you know, 'Could I do that?' " Rice said. "And so that was my summer activity while my parents went to their school." In short, Rice, said, her skating school "was high-priced child care."[122]

In the fall of 1968, John Rice finally got the kind of job he had been pursuing for years: assistant director of admissions at the University of Denver, with an emphasis on recruiting minority students to the largely white institution.[123] The family packed up again.

CHAPTER 3

Josef Korbel and the Power of Stalin

Denver, 1969–1974

The move west pulled Condoleezza Rice out of the confines and comforts of her segregated black environment and into a foreign world, the nearly all-white suburbs of Denver. African-Americans made up less than 10 percent of Denver's population in 1970.[1] There were virtually no blacks in the faculty housing where the Rices first lived, or in the South Denver neighborhood near the university where the Rices eventually bought a modest split-level at 3161 South Waxberry Way.

John Rice selected an equally white educational institution for his daughter: St. Mary's Academy, a private Roman Catholic girls school in the affluent suburb of Englewood, about ten minutes from the university and fifteen minutes from the Rice home. It was a very long way from the Hill school. Founded by the Sisters of Loretto in 1864, St. Mary's was one of the oldest educational institutions in Colorado, academically rigorous, and a favorite for daughters of University of Denver faculty members and upscale Irish Catholics.[2] Its twenty-four-acre campus, anchored by a white-columned, red-brick Georgian-style mansion that housed the school's administrative offices, sat on University Boulevard, just down the road from large tracts of open land that would later be developed into some of Denver's most expensive gated communities. Virtually all of St. Mary's graduates went on to college, although not necessarily to high-powered careers. "It was expected that they would get married and have children, and would get jobs, maybe as teachers or nurses," said Therese M. Saracino, one of Rice's teachers.[3] Still, the school had been affected by the feminist movement and by the expectations of the Sisters of Loretto—in 1969, nuns still made up about half the faculty—who were strong proponents of women's education. The message of the school, Saracino recalled, was "You prepare yourself—don't expect some man to take care of you for the rest of your life."[4]

Rice started in January 1969, in the middle of her sophomore year, when she had just turned fourteen. She was one of four black students in her St. Mary's class of eighty-seven,[5] and by all accounts—Rice's and St. Mary's—the school was welcoming. Still, Rice was more acutely aware of her skin color than she had ever been in Birmingham. "Race was everything in Birmingham—so in a sense it was nothing," Rice said in a 2002 interview. "In Denver race suddenly became more of a factor because I was actually interacting with people different from me."[6]

Rice has never spoken publicly of any more anxious feelings about the change, and in subsequent interviews she backed off from even her modest admission that she felt different at St. Mary's. "The amazing thing is that I don't remember having any sense of really strangeness about it," Rice recalled. She said that she was comfortable in Denver because she had ice-skated there in the summers, and that her overwhelming feeling about the move was one of excitement since she would be able to skate year-round. "That was the great benefit from my point of view," Rice said. "And I don't particularly even remember thinking, 'Oh, this school is all white.' "[7]

Years later, Rice said that her father chose St. Mary's because he thought the Denver public schools of the late 1960s had a "trendy" curriculum, with too much emphasis on creative spelling and not enough on basics. "What he liked was Catholic schools," Rice said. "Very rigorous, very traditional, lots of languages, Latin, lots of mathematics."[8] But a factor in John Rice's choice had to be the racial turmoil in Denver's public schools at the time. In 1969, the city was at the beginning of a bitter, quarter-century struggle over forced busing that was roiling both black and white communities. Had her parents sent her to public school, Rice said there was a chance, irrespective of her skin color, that she would have been bused en masse with the white students from her nearly all-white neighborhood high school more than ten miles away to Manual, a troubled, nearly all-black and Hispanic high school. "It did happen to kids from my neighborhood," Rice said.[9] (Court-ordered busing began in Denver after a Supreme Court ruling in 1974, when Rice was in graduate school, but as early as 1968 there was a possibility that the Denver public schools would make a limited and voluntary system mandatory. Still, in 2007 a spokeswoman for the Denver Public Schools could find no record of students from Rice's neighborhood being bused to Manual.)[10] But to John Rice, even the prospect that his own daughter would make the journey across town to a minority school in the name of achieving racial balance was a ludicrous and appalling consequence of busing.

Rice quickly established herself at St. Mary's as a bright, hard-working student, unusually poised for her age. "You know those people who were born thirty-five?" said Joy Gerity, who taught Rice American literature in her junior year and AP English her senior year. "She was always sort of ahead of herself. She was a very mature kid."[11] Rice stood out in class, Gerity recalled: "She could talk about ideas, she could see relationships, she could understand consequences in a different way than other kids her age."[12] Gerity easily imagined that Rice would be successful. "You would think, hmm, she's going to be a great prosecuting attorney," Gerity said. "She had a mind."[13]

But soon after arriving at St. Mary's, Rice ran into what would be the first in a series of race-tinged episodes questioning her intellect. In a story that has become part of the lore of her life, a St. Mary's high school guidance counselor informed Rice, based on her standardized test scores, that she was either—Rice's telling of the incident varies—not college material[14] or "maybe junior college material"[15] despite her grades and musical accomplishments. In the stories, Rice casts herself as hurt and stunned by the assessment but says her supportive parents encouraged her to ignore it and move on.

In an interview in January 2007, Rice told another version of the episode, this time with her role changed from victim to parental consoler. The guidance counselor, Rice said, called her in to go over her scores on the PSAT, the precursor to the SAT test administered by the College Board. (Rice said as an aside in the interview that she didn't know if the PSAT, a widely administered and much discussed test, was still given.) "I didn't do very well," Rice said. "First of all, I'm not a particularly good test-taker. And secondly, I was about two years younger than everybody else."[16] She said she didn't remember her exact score, but she did recall that it predicted a combined result of about 1,000 on her verbal and math SATs—an average score that would have made the Ivy League and other elite colleges a big reach.[17]

The guidance counselor, Rice recalled, said, " 'Now, you may need to consider junior college because, you know, test scores like this would mean you're not college material.' And I thought, 'Yeah, right.' And I went home and I was kind of laughing with my parents about it. I said, 'You won't believe what this lady said,' and my parents, oh, my goodness, they hit the ceiling. They were ready to go up and you know, tell her off and she should never do that to any child again. And I said, 'Look, I don't believe her, all right? So don't worry about it.' "[18]

Whatever Rice's reaction at the time—and it is hard to imagine that a fourteen-year-old black girl, newly arrived in a nearly all-white school, would not have been devastated—the telling aspect of this version is that Condoleezza Rice portrays herself as cooler and more resilient than even her ambitious parents. Perhaps that confidence was part of her jumble of feelings, or perhaps it is how she has chosen to employ the anecdote in the service of her life's story, or both. Rice did say that her parents were right to be upset and that if the guidance counselor had made the remark "to a child who had a less secure family background," then "yes, it might have had damaging effects. It was the wrong thing for a counselor to be saying. But I had to keep my parents from going up to school just about every six weeks." They would get upset about "just about anything," Rice said. "You know, I didn't get to play the full program for the glee club."[19]

Teachers at St. Mary's remember other black parents as difficult, but not the Rices. "There were some parents of blacks who, well, if not exactly militant, were suspicious of whites," Gerity said. "They wanted to make sure their kids were getting what other kids were getting. But the Rices were not confrontational. They just wanted to make sure that she was learning and that she was challenged."[20]

"It's because I wouldn't let my parents go!" Rice said. "I saw no reason for them to go fight my battles at school. As a matter of fact, I would never let them go up to school."[21] The only time she said she did remember her mother marching into a classroom was when she was in fourth or fifth grade at the Hill school and the teacher gave her a C in music. "There was no way to keep my mother from going to the school, especially since I learned later that the music teacher and my mother had had a kind of battle in college between them," Rice said. In short, "I was doing fine at St. Mary's. I was happy, I felt like I was getting a good education. To a certain extent, St. Mary's wasn't the center of my life anyway, skating was more the center of my life."[22]

Rice has often been referred to as a "competitive ice-skater," which was technically accurate, but by her own admission not the truth. "I was terrible," she said. "I couldn't bend my knees. I had a judge say to me once, 'It's amazing you can do a double-jump—you never actually leave the ice.' "[23] Nonetheless, she said, "I loved the discipline of getting up and skating. I loved athletics. I was a tomboy, you know, but skating—this is a generational thing—skating was a sort of an acceptable tomboy thing for a girl to do because she wore pretty dresses and skated to music and yet you could go out and be, you know, an athlete."[24]

She insisted it didn't bother her that she had so little talent. "In some ways it's probably one of the most important experiences in my life because I was good at piano," Rice said. "And to do something that I was really not very good at, and go out and fall and have a terrible time and have to get up the next day—I probably learned more from being really bad at something and very dedicated to it."[25]

Around the same time, Rice had a far more serious setback: Her mother was diagnosed with breast cancer. It was the spring of 1970, when Rice was fifteen, and old enough for Angelena to tell her everything. "We were all shocked," said McPhatter. Angelena had a mastectomy and was told by the doctors that they had rid her of the cancer and that she would be fine.[26] Condoleezza put up a brave front, reassured family and friends, and on the surface appeared to deal with

Angelena's illness from a "50,000-foot-level" of emotional distance.[27] But decades later she said she feared her mother's death in those years "every waking day."[28]

By the fall of 1970, at the beginning of Rice's senior year, she had completed all the courses she needed to graduate. Rice was still fifteen, but her parents argued that she should leave St. Mary's—which would save them part of the $1,000 annual tuition—and get an early start at the University of Denver, where Rice planned to enroll as a piano major in the Lamont School of Music. Piano had continued to be central to her life. Rice had already won a young artists' competition and performed Mozart's Piano Concerto in D Minor with the Denver Symphony Orchestra, and her parents had taken out a loan to buy her a $13,000 used Chickering Grand.[29] But for the first time in her life, Rice said no to her parents and said that she wanted to graduate from high school in the spring, like the rest of her class. The three reached a compromise: Rice would attend her last year at St. Mary's while she started college part-time. The university covered half the tuition as a perquisite of her father's administrative position, and the other half came from a scholarship.[30]

The schedule was brutal. Rice was up at 4:30 A.M., arrived at the ice rink by five, and skated until seven. She changed clothes at the rink and headed to the University of Denver for three classes, at 8, 9, and 10 A.M. At lunchtime she went to St. Mary's to practice piano for an hour and then took classes there all afternoon. After school Rice went home for more piano practice and homework, and sometimes she would go back to the rink in the evenings.[31] Asked if she was happy in this period, Rice said "very."[32]

But in her first months at Denver, Rice experienced a racial incident. In her often told version of the story, a professor in a lecture class was speaking in a positive way about William Shockley, the Stanford physicist who was then promoting a theory that blacks were genetically less intelligent than whites. Rice, in a class of 250 mostly white students, was outraged. "I raised my hand and said, 'You really should not be presenting this as fact because there's plenty of evidence to the contrary,' " Rice told *Essence* magazine in 2001, in a recounting that has appeared in many other magazines and newspapers. " 'Let me explain to you: I speak French, I play Bach, I'm better in your culture than you are.' "[33] (The statement may have been a bit of a boast; in 2006, Rice said that while she could understand a French conversation with President Jacques Chirac of France, "I can't speak it, because I was never very good at French.")[34]

The anecdote has always been used to illustrate Rice's self-assurance in the face of racism before hundreds of white students, and in an interview in January 2007, she started by telling it much the same way—although she said, when asked, that there were other black students in the class. (That recollection triggered a brief segue into a present-day defense of herself as a black Republican. "They didn't say anything, which I found appalling," Rice said. "You know, sometimes this notion that if you're conservative you have no concept of race is just bizarre. I've probably spoken about these issues more than my liberal friends. And on this one, I wasn't just going to sit there.")[35]

But the real difference in Rice's telling of the anecdote was her account of the reaction of the professor, Robert Eckelberry. He was taken aback, she said, but the next time he held the class he repeated his views. "And I took him on again," Rice said.[36] At that point Rice said she went to the dean to complain, and shortly thereafter was called in to see the professor in his office. He drew a line on the chalkboard and told her, she said, " 'Now, here's most black people. Here's most white people. Now, you're up here someplace, obviously.' " As she recounted the story, Rice raised her hand above her head to indicate that the professor had drawn the line that represented her as higher than the ones for most blacks and most whites. "He said that," she said, "you know, 'You're different.' He turned out to be one of my biggest supporters."[37]

Rice said she assumed that the dean had admonished the professor, but that in her view, his chalkboard assessment of her abilities was genuine. She said the professor later worked hard to get her an internship in local government that she couldn't accept because of her piano schedule. "I don't think he was trying to make amends," she said. "I think he genuinely decided that anybody who would do that in class had to have some value. And he really—he was very interesting."[38]

The theme of the standard version of the anecdote has always been Rice's superiority over her white tormentor—"I'm better in your culture than you are"—and her expanded version builds on that, to display superiority over most whites in general. But it also, if not quite turning the original anecdote on its head, significantly changes its meaning. As Rice tells it, she is less of a victim and much more the victor, as if by sheer force of her excellence she has won a convert—not to the belief in the intelligence of blacks, but to herself.

Eckelberry was a political science professor at Denver for sixteen years, a period when he was also a Republican member of the Colorado state legislature, and in 2007, at the age of sixty-nine, was practicing law in Littleton, Colorado. In an interview in August 2007, he said he did not know who Shockley was and had never mentioned Shockley in a lecture at DU, and he called Rice's story "a complete fabrication." Eckelberry did say that he had given a lecture at the university called "The Nature of Man" on whether people were products of nature or nurture, and that in that lecture he "might have" talked about the differences in intelligence scoring between the races. "I think it's pretty well known that Asians score the highest," he said. "These are facts—is that racist?" Eckelberry said he did not remember any encounter with Rice in his office, or drawing a line on a chalkboard to represent the level of her intelligence. But he did remember her. "She would come up after class, and the impression I had of her was that she was very articulate," he said. "Got an A in the class, very pleasant. I would say her writing skills were not that great, but she was a very bright young lady."[39]

Around this same time, Rice's father was trying to bring some race awareness to Denver's campus on his own. In June 1969, in addition to his work in admissions, John Rice took on a new job and title, assistant dean of the college of arts and sciences, and by the 1970 winter academic quarter had introduced a seminar called "The Black Experience in America." The seminar was designed to offer "a real knowledge of the black man and his problems to the university community,"[40] according to one of its press releases, and for the most part featured politically moderate African-American speakers in tune with John Rice. But Rice, perhaps to attract attention or to expose students to a wider spectrum of views, or both, also invited more-radical speakers. Among them were two U.S. Olympic track medalists, Lee

Evans and John Carlos—Carlos raised his fist in a black power salute at the 1968 Mexico City Olympics—and Louis Farrakhan, at that time a top leader of the Nation of Islam who was not yet known as an anti-Semite.[41]

Condoleezza Rice's tangle with Eckelberry was a rough spot in the otherwise pleasant if too busy life of a music student who was enjoying a new college social life and paying little attention to the outside world. "I was not frankly all that current-events-oriented," she recalled.[42] Rice pledged the Alpha Chi Omega sorority—she was the only black member until her senior year—and in the spring was presented at a black debutante ball sponsored by the Owl Club, a venerable African-American men's service organization. The girls were selected based on grades and achievement, but their white ball gowns and full-length white gloves reflected the proud social traditions of Denver's black elite. The ball fell on the same night as Denver's graduation, where Rice's father was delivering the baccalaureate sermon. "So he had to go in his robe and tuxedo pants and then rush to present me at the Owl Club," Rice said.[43] That same spring, Rice went to the St. Mary's prom on the arm of a Denver hockey player,[44] the start of a fascination with athletes that would continue into adulthood.

Rice spent her sophomore year preparing for piano performances at the Lamont School of Music, where she was among the best students. She also continued her ice-skating and worked briefly for the school's daily newspaper, *The Clarion*, a job she detested. Rice wrote a few articles, including one about the preservation of statues at Denver's stadium, was promoted to news editor, discovered she wasn't good at writing on deadline, battled with the chief editor, and left. "I didn't have enough time to do it," she said. "And I can't actually remember whether he fired me or I quit, but some combination of those things, because I really hated it."[45]

If anything suffered, it was her academic work. "The truth is that I was a terrible procrastinator, so a lot of times I wasn't all that well prepared," Rice recalled. "I don't ever remember thinking that I was an exceptional student. I did think I was a good pianist."[46]

But that summer, Rice faced the first real crisis of her seventeen years: She attended a prestigious summer music camp in Aspen, encountered eleven- and twelve-year-olds who could play on sight what it had taken her a year to learn, and came to the realization that she was not a prodigy. The students were from all over the country, including Juilliard in New York. "I was among the best students at the Lamont School of Music," Rice said. "I was not among the best students at Aspen."[47]

Years later, Rice assessed her seventeen-year-old abilities. "I didn't have a couple of essential ingredients," she said. "One is I'm not really particularly talented. I mean, I'm sort of technically okay, but I never felt that I was able to go to that next level. You listen to certain people and you think, 'My God, that's a gift, that person just has a gift.' " She defined gifted as "you know it when you see it. A great piano teacher once told me that a good pianist can get maybe thirty shades of color on the piano. A very good pianist can get fifty or sixty shades on the piano. For a great pianist, it's limitless. They can do things with that instrument that shouldn't be possible with just strings, wood, and ivory. And you hear it in the great pianists. I knew fairly early that it wasn't there."[48]

Rice has talked frequently about this period in her life, and usually says that she suddenly saw a future teaching thirteen-year-olds to "murder Beethoven" or of playing at piano bars and Nordstrom rather than at Carnegie Hall.[49] Her comments are always lighthearted and reflect no sense of the personal catastrophe that serious piano students who aren't good enough for concert careers typically face at this point in their lives. But her sense of failure must have been profound: Piano had been at the center of Rice's world since she was three years old. The $13,000 grand was still in the living room, and she had plans to attend a prestigious music program in Germany the following winter. Most of all, her future life as a concert pianist had been her parents' biggest dream.

"Look, it *was* a huge moment of crisis," Rice said, when pressed about her feelings at the time. "But in my own way, I didn't exactly express it as a huge moment of crisis. I just knew I had to get out of music."[50] When she came home from Aspen and told her parents of her decision to quit piano and change her major—even though she had no idea what her new major would be—there seems to have been a battle, although Rice refers to it as a "very vivid" conversation.[51] Her parents told her, she said, that she would end up as a waitress at

Howard Johnson's, and she responded, "Well, I'd rather be a waitress at Howard Johnson's than teach piano." Rice told her parents that it was "her life" and they responded that it was "their money."[52] In the end the three agreed that if she wanted to give up piano, she could not take another four years to finish college, and that she had to graduate in the spring of 1974—less than two years away—as planned.[53]

Adrift and confused, the normally focused Rice started her junior year in search of a new major. First she tried English literature, in part because her Aunt Theresa, her father's sister, had a Ph.D. in the subject from the University of Wisconsin. But Rice found it too "squishy"[54] and "hated it."[55]

Next she tried political science—"because I had always kind of an interest in politics"[56]—but the first course she took was on state and local government. An early project was to interview the water manager of the city of Denver. "He was sitting in this little hole-in-the-wall office, and he told me enthusiastically about all the things he was doing to manage the water of Denver, and I thought, 'I don't like this, I can't believe people do this,' " Rice recalled.[57]

Finally, in the spring of 1973 Rice wandered into a course called "Introduction to International Politics," taught by Josef Korbel, a sixty-three-year-old Czech refugee who had founded Denver's Graduate School of International Studies and was a university elder statesman. In one of the great coincidences and complications of modern American diplomatic history, Korbel also happened to be the father of Madeleine Albright, who would become the only other woman secretary of state. (Albright at the time was married and living in Washington, and she and Rice would not meet until after Korbel's death.)[58]

For Rice, like Albright, Korbel would be one of the great influences of her life. Until she met him, Rice had shown almost no interest in foreign policy—she once told an interviewer that until then she had been "completely oblivious, really, to international politics."[59] But when Rice heard Korbel speak to her class on Stalin, she "fell in love"—the phrase she has used in virtually every interview she has given about this moment in her life.[60] "I mean, there was no earthly reason that a young woman from Birmingham, Alabama, a young black woman from Birmingham, Alabama, was going to become interested in the Soviet Union and Soviet politics," Rice said. "So it shows the tremendous impact that a faculty member can have on a student."[61]

Rice's parents were glad that she had found a major but were nonetheless dumbfounded. "Condi is the kind of person who is very sure of herself and makes excellent decisions," her father said in an interview in 2000, less than a year before he died. "But political science? Here's the time for fainting. Blacks didn't do political science."[62]

The lecture that so transfixed Rice was about the ruthless maneuvering and consolidation of power that allowed Stalin to propel himself from general secretary of the Communist Party to effective dictator of the Soviet Union. "It's the lecture that every Soviet specialist gives about the policy swings in which Joseph Stalin engaged in the 1920s, first swinging right and isolating the left, then swinging left and isolating the right, and then swinging back right, and essentially now he had no competition whatsoever," Rice told Nicholas Lemann in *The New Yorker*. In other interviews, she talked about her fascination with the Byzantine nature of Soviet politics "and by power: how it operates, how it's used."[63] Terry Karl, a Stanford political science professor who later taught with Rice, often heard the same thing. "Like some political scientists of the time, she was impressed with the efficiency and effectiveness of how the Communist parties exercised power," Karl said.[64]

Rice's account of this turning point has always had a theatrical, Steven Spielberg–like quality, as if she had been struck by lightning and would then march with uninterrupted fervor toward international studies and the White House. The reality is that while Korbel's class clearly sparked in Rice a fascination with the Soviet Union, it also came in the nick of time—only a year before she was to graduate—and was of enough interest to her that she finally settled on a major: political science. Over the next few years, Rice would spend periods flailing around and thinking about law or business. It was not then a foregone conclusion that she would build a career around the study of the Soviet Union.

What is true is that Rice had never met anyone like Korbel in her life. He was an exotic European intellectual, witty, sophisticated, and courtly, with a pipe, a gray shock of hair, and a formality of dress that extended, at least in his early days in Denver, to fly-fishing in a coat and tie.[65] For Rice, he opened a window to another world, one of twentieth-century history and grand ideas, all spun out in riveting, first-person accounts in class. "He had these eyes that just kind of twinkled, you know, just danced," Rice recalled. "He was the best storyteller in the world, and boy, did he have stories."[66]

Born Jewish in Czechoslovakia in 1909, Korbel studied at the Sorbonne, received a law degree from Charles University in Prague, began a diplomatic career with the Czech Ministry of Foreign Affairs in 1934, and married Andula Spiegelova, the daughter of assimilated Jews,[67] the following year. After the German occupation of Czechoslovakia in 1939, he and his family, including two-year-old "Madlenka," fled to London, where Korbel served as the head of the Czech government-in-exile's broadcasting department and as an aide to Edvard Beneš, the exiled Czech president, and Jan Masaryk, the exiled Czech foreign minister.[68] Two years later, in a small church in the British countryside, Korbel and his family were baptized as Catholics[69]—a decision taken to protect them from the Holocaust that was kept secret until 1997, when *The Washington Post* published an article about Madeleine Albright's Jewish roots.[70]

After the war, Korbel returned to Prague, where he was named the first Czechoslovak ambassador to Yugoslavia, an important post that gave him access to Marshal Tito, the Yugoslav Communist leader.[71] The Korbels' Belgrade posting ended with the takeover of the Czech government by the Communists in February 1948—although Korbel served the new Communist regime for the rest of the year as a member of a United Nations commission mediating the dispute over Kashmir between the newly independent nations of India and Pakistan.[72] Many of Korbel's wartime colleagues were bitter that he kept ties to the Communist government as long as he did,[73] but Madeleine Albright has always believed that her father accepted the U.N. post in large part to get the family to freedom.[74]

Either way, the family arrived in America in late 1948 and by early 1949 the Czech government had dismissed Korbel from the U.N. post for anti-Communist views. Granted political asylum by the administration of Harry Truman in the spring, Korbel then got a much needed job offer as a professor at the University of Denver. The position had been arranged by Philip Mosely, a founder of the Russian Institute at Columbia University and a member of the Rockefeller Foundation, who made the call to Denver. Mosely, who often acted as a godfather to Eastern European and Russian émigrés to the United States, had been an adviser to Secretary of State Cordell Hull[75] and was long thought to have ties to the Office of Strategic Services, the forerunner of the CIA.[76] Although it was common practice after the war for the CIA to help refugees from Communist countries resettle in the United States in return for information about the Communist regimes back home, the CIA has neither confirmed nor denied that it assisted Korbel.[77] But many of Korbel's friends say they believe he received help from the agency.[78]

As a student, Rice was unaware of Korbel's past beyond the stories he told that so transfixed her. "I remember going to his house for the first time, and that was probably in my senior year, and he had this beautiful painting on the wall, this beautiful oil painting," she once recalled. "And he said, 'Oh, that was given to me by Tito.' And I thought, 'That was given to you by Tito?' "[79]

In 2007, Rice would say that Korbel's greatest influence on her was his "black-and-white view of the world" that held that "the Soviet Union was bad, the United States was a force for good."[80] It is also true that Korbel looked at the world through the prism of the 1938 Munich accord and the Western appeasement of Hitler that led to the Nazi takeover of Czechoslovakia—a disaster that burned in him the belief that America, as the moral authority of the world, had a duty to stand up to aggression.[81] Korbel's later writings also suggest how much he, like so many others, felt deceived by Stalin's promises to stand up for Czechoslovak independence and not to interfere internally.[82] "The Soviet Union and what it had done to Eastern Europe was for him a moral outrage," Rice said.[83]

But Korbel is nonetheless seen by his former colleagues on the faculty in Denver as a more complicated political figure than the one Rice describes. "He had been a Social Democrat," said Alan Gilbert, a professor at Denver's Graduate School of International Studies who taught courses with Korbel.[84] In London in the 1940s, Korbel had maintained good relations with the Communist members of the Czech government-in-exile[85] and appeared to believe that the Communists and democrats could work together one day in Czechoslovakia.[86] "All his friends were Communists, and he was actually rather critical of them from the left," Gilbert said.[87]

Decades later, both Rice and Albright cited Korbel's pro-America, pro-democracy views as powerful influences on their own. "He talked about how special America was in history—not an empire, not a great power that wanted to conquer territory, but a great power that was basically an idea," Rice said in 2006.[88] Albright said that her father taught her "the importance of America's moral authority" and that "you can't let terrible things happen to people in other countries."[89] But in the winter of 2007, Albright also expressed strong mixed feelings about Rice's embrace of her father—pride about what she called Rice's generosity toward him and anger that Rice and the Bush administration had, in her view, twisted Korbel's legacy. "I think what people do is take the basis of their learning and extrapolate it in a different way," Albright said, adding that she was "very unhappy about what has happened to the term 'democracy' under this administration, where it has now been militarized."[90] She also said that her father would have been upset about the Iraq War because it had "ruined America's reputation in the world" and because there had been no "forward thinking" in its planning.[91]

Asked about Albright's remarks, Rice retorted, "Oh, give me a break," insisted there had been adequate planning for Iraq, and then curtly brought the matter to a close. "Let's not try to put thoughts and words into dead people's mouths," she said.[92]

Three decades earlier in Denver, Rice had gone into Korbel's office after the Stalin lecture and told him she thought she wanted to study the Soviet Union. "But I had no idea what one did with a major that would study the Soviet Union," she said. "I just knew that whatever it was, the job market had to be better than concert piano."[93]

That it undeniably was. In the spring of 1973, the United States was nearly three decades into a superpower rivalry with the Soviet Union that had created a huge demand within the government for experts who knew Russian and could help decipher the inner workings of the Kremlin. The result was a "golden age" of government and foundation funding for Russian studies at universities across the country,[94] with jobs at the State Department, the Pentagon, the CIA, or in academia virtually guaranteed upon graduation.[95] Columbia and Harvard were the first schools to have Russian studies programs, and they remained the two big powerhouses, but they spawned other programs in the West and Midwest, including the one at Denver. By the time Rice took Korbel's class, he had built Denver's School of International Studies into a good regional center. "He had parlayed this very small program into something that was really quite respectable," said Catherine Kelleher, a professor at Denver in the 1970s who would become one of Rice's dissertation advisers and a deputy assistant secretary of defense in the Clinton administration.[96]

For Rice, Soviet studies held the allure of understanding America's main adversary—not only its evil but its power—at the beginning of an electrifying period of détente. Richard Nixon had been the first American president to visit the Soviet Union in a trip to Moscow the previous spring, when he and Leonid Brezhnev had signed SALT I, the first Strategic Arms Limitation Treaty aimed at reducing both countries' nuclear arsenals. In June 1973, not long after Rice wandered into Korbel's class, Brezhnev traveled to the United States and generated huge headlines during a week of talks with Nixon in Washington and California. On that same trip, Brezhnev became the first Russian leader to address Americans on national television.[97] Although Watergate transfixed the nation that summer—the Senate Watergate Committee hearings began in May—and the Yom Kippur War exploded in September, for a young woman suddenly awakened to the mystique of the Soviet Union, the pictures of Nixon, Brezhnev, and Henry Kissinger, the superstar secretary of state, offered a tantalizing glimpse into the inner workings of global diplomacy and the secret power of elites.

With only a year to go at Denver, Rice began making up for lost time. "I ended up with one hundred units of music and forty-five in political science," she said. "So it was a very quick major."[98] She started Russian language classes and read on her own—Dostoevsky, Solzhenitsyn, and Hans Morgenthau's *Politics Among Nations*, the classic text on political realism that argues that nations act in their own self-interest and are primarily motivated by power and national security, not human rights or ideals. Morgenthau's book remains a bible for international relations students, and Rice would speak about its influence on her for years—until, that is, the presidency of George W. Bush, when she moved so abruptly to embrace the idealism of her boss (spreading liberty around the world was "the calling of our time," the president declared in his second inaugural address)[99] that her former colleagues were stunned. Rice, well aware that some of these ex-colleagues said she had changed her stripes for career advancement, would heatedly argue in the second term that her critics were oversimplifying.

Rice had just one other course with Korbel before she graduated with a bachelor's degree in political science that spring. By then she had decided to pursue a master's degree in Soviet studies—but at Notre Dame, not at Denver under Korbel. Rice's father knew the president of Notre Dame, Father Theodore Hesburgh, through Denver's chancellor, Maurice B. Mitchell. Hesburgh and Mitchell, both white, were serving together on the United States Commission for Civil Rights, and John Rice, by then an assistant vice chancellor at Denver, had advised Mitchell as well as Hesburgh on the panel's work.[100] The Rices took their daughter to visit Notre Dame and Hesburgh in the spring of 1972, and she had been impressed. "I just loved Notre Dame," Rice said. "I thought it was beautiful and it would be fun to go there. I almost wanted to transfer, but they had just started taking women and so I decided, well, maybe I'd think about graduate school there."[101]

Notre Dame appealed on two other counts: It was a Catholic school, which was important to John Rice, and it had a Soviet studies program not unlike the one at Denver. Phil Mosely, the Columbia professor who had sent Korbel to Colorado, had in fact urged Hesburgh to start the Notre Dame program as part of his campaign to spread Russian studies across the country.[102] Mosely had even dispatched to South Bend another Eastern European émigré, Stephen D. Kertesz, a Hungarian diplomat who fled his country when the Communists took over in 1947.[103] Much like Korbel, Kertesz helped create Notre Dame's International Studies Department in the late 1940s and built it up into a regional center.[104] Although Korbel tried to talk Rice into staying on at Denver for her master's degree, she was determined to go to Notre Dame and, at the age of nineteen, live away from home for the first time.[105]

Before leaving, Rice enrolled that summer in a Barbizon modeling school at a Denver shopping center. Years later she described it as a lark and as something her mother wholeheartedly endorsed. "She thought I was kind of a tomboy and maybe it would make me a little more elegant," Rice said.[106] The course turned out to be worth it: "I learned how to walk more gracefully, they taught you how to do your makeup." In conclusion, Rice said, "actually, I learned a lot."[107]

CHAPTER 4

Football and the Strategy of War

Notre Dame and Denver, 1975–1980

Rice spent some of her first year away from home partying at South Bend's new discos. Freed from the rigors of her parents' household, the minister's daughter began behaving like a normal college student: She stayed out until the small hours of the morning with a new group of friends. "I did have a good time," Rice said. "I'm not an automaton."[1] "Rock the Boat" was at the top of the pop charts that summer of 1974, and "Shining Star," the hit by Earth, Wind and Fire, one of Rice's favorite bands of the era, was released early the next year. Rice loved to dance and liked to pile into cars with friends and head north. "They'd drive into Chicago, they'd party and then they'd come back," said Rice's friend Deborah Cheatham Carson. "It was like an all-night thing."[2] The young girl who had vowed to her Birmingham neighbors that she would marry a football player began dating some members of Notre Dame's team, but they were casual forerunners to the serious relationship that Rice would soon have with a player for the Denver Broncos.[3]

On campus, Rice studied for her master's degree under George A. Brinkley, a Soviet scholar who was chairman of the school's Government and International Studies Department and Notre Dame's leading faculty member in the field. Brinkley had first heard about Rice when he got a call from the office of Hesburgh, the Notre Dame president and John Rice's friend. The president's office had never before contacted him to alert him to a new student, and Brinkley understood that Hesburgh expected him to give this young black woman special attention. "He believed she would definitely be the best student we ever had," Brinkley recalled.[4] When he met Rice, he, too, was struck by her knowledge, poise, and confidence. In fact, he said, "she felt so well prepared that there would be little benefit for her in participating in seminars with other students or listening to lectures by professors."[5] Rice asked if she could work individually with faculty members writing papers on Soviet government, history, and economics in preparation for a doctorate, and the department said yes.

But in Brinkley's view the arrangement never worked. Rice's papers were well written and substantial, he said, but "they lacked depth and attention to different interpretations and points of view."[6] Rice declined to discuss her work with Brinkley or redo it, and as a result, he said, "her evident skills and potential were not developed into more mature scholarship."[7] By August 1975, Rice got her master's degree in government and international studies, but it was what Notre Dame called a "terminal" master's degree, meaning it would not lead to a Ph.D. program. Brinkley placed the blame on Notre Dame as well as on Rice and concluded that "I believe that we were both disappointed."[8]

Rice returned to Denver and was once again at loose ends. Soviet studies did not seem like a promising career. "I was not looking really to continue my academic training at that point," Rice said. "But it was not a great time to get a job, particularly if the language you spoke was Russian, not Spanish."[9] That fall of 1975 she taught piano, filled in for her father's secretary, and got a job as an executive assistant to a vice president of Honeywell—hardly a position worthy of her education—and then lost it in a reorganization before she even turned up for work.[10] Bored and still vaguely interested in government, she applied to law school as a default position, was accepted at Denver, and having no better idea, decided to go. But once again Josef Korbel interceded, and told her she should become a professor instead.[11] "When I think back on that moment," Rice later recalled, "I don't know if it was a subliminal message, but I had such respect and admiration for him that I took the idea seriously for the first time."[12]

So Rice turned back to the Soviet Union and decided to pursue a Ph.D. in international studies. Her first requirement was to do what she had not done at Notre Dame: write a qualifying master's thesis, since Korbel required one of those students who were on his "Korbel Plan," a year of independent work before formal entry into the doctoral program. Rice's chosen topic, which she titled "Music and Politics in the Soviet Union," connected her two worlds in an analysis of the works of Prokofiev and Shostakovich during the Stalin era.

Working with Alan Gilbert, a new Denver professor who had just received a Ph.D. in political science from Harvard, Rice argued that living under a totalitarian regime forced the two composers to accommodate the politics of their time but did not prevent them from turning out some of the most powerful and important works of the twentieth century.[13] The view is more widely accepted now, but Rice's argument was a relatively progressive one for the mid-1970s—when Shostakovich and, to a lesser extent, Prokofiev were more often qualified as great "Soviet" composers whose conservative tendencies were seen as forced upon them. Now they are more celebrated as simply great composers who found ways to defy their circumstances. "They did enough to stay on the right side of the authorities, and they tried to buy room to write what they wanted to write," Rice said.[14] Gilbert recalled the thesis as "not a fantastic piece" in terms of its scholarship, although he remembered it as "a very interesting thing to read."[15]

Rice took Gilbert's courses in political theory and comparative Communism—eight in all, by his count—some of which he co-taught with Korbel. She did not display then any conservative views, Gilbert recalled. "She wrote papers on Marxist analyses of racism and explanations of the rise of Nazism and the resistance to it in World War II that were basically leftist papers," Gilbert said. "They weren't ideological papers, they were smart papers which happened to think racism was bad and that a lot of white people get hurt by racism as well as black people, stuff like that. She was sympathetic to the Soviet Union during World War II, which I think any sane person would have been."[16]

The following fall of 1976, when Rice formally began Korbel's Ph.D. program, she also voted in her first presidential election, as a registered Democrat, for Jimmy Carter. The reason, or at least the reason she gave in 2006 after service in three Republican administrations, was that she was attracted to Carter as a fellow Southerner. "I had this narrative about reconciliation of North and South; he was going to be the first Southern president," Rice said.[17] Whatever the depth of her feelings at the time, as Bush's secretary of state she dismissed her vote for Carter as the unsophisticated decision of a woman who had spent most of her life as an aspiring, apolitical concert pianist—a stance that ignored the fact that she had spent the two years before the 1976 election immersed in political science and the history of the Soviet Union. "I was a music major until 1974, '73," Rice said. "So I was not the most attuned or sensitive person. I didn't spend hours thinking about what party I would join."[18]

Rice was one of about two dozen students who were master's and Ph.D. candidates in international studies at Denver that fall, and one of a small handful who had Korbel as an adviser. Rice was a frequent guest at Korbel's home for parties and dinners, although he included many other students and faculty members. Korbel wanted his school to be "a little European village," recalled Arthur Gilbert, a professor of international relations at Denver, and treated everyone like extended family.[19] But Rice seemed to have stronger emotional ties to Korbel than the others. "He was very fond of her, that was clear," said Wayne Glass, a lecturer at the University of Southern California who was one of Korbel's other doctoral students. "There was an emotional bond between the two of them that I didn't have. I was not his grandson." For Rice, Korbel was the "ultimate grandfather."[20]

Despite Rice's closeness to Korbel, she was not known at the school for academic brilliance. "Joe had many good students, but the others did not become secretary of state," said Arthur Gilbert. "She was a good, solid Ph.D. student like many others, but nobody said someday she's going to be a superstar."[21] Classmates recalled that although Rice seemed to be adopting anti-Soviet views from Korbel, she was unformed on most other issues and cautious about expressing opinions in class. "I don't think she had her own political database," said Glass, who would go on to work for a Democratic United States senator, Jeff Bingaman of New Mexico. "She would not really offer much to say, but she'd listen to what was being said, and if she was called on to speak, it would be in some summary fashion. She wasn't out there, and she was careful to take the temperature of the room before speaking. It was just that her nature was such that she wasn't the one to throw out ideas for everyone else to grapple with."[22]

Rice did stand out for her skin color in the predominantly white school, and for an elegant, stylish presence that was unusual for a graduate student. "She always was perfectly groomed," said Arthur Gilbert. "She knew a great deal about nice-looking clothes. She would come sashaying in, and this would lead to a very mixed response from the students—that she was social climbing." Rice, he said, "tended to like to associate with faculty members and staff members and people who were in effect in positions of importance, rather than the students themselves."[23]

But Rice was inseparable from her best friend at the school, Cristann Gibson, another of Korbel's Ph.D. candidates and a woman who was the mirror opposite of Rice: white, overweight, acerbic, and from a rich, old-line Denver family. Gibson had written a horror novel under a pen name and had been the lead singer and electric piano player in her high school rock band. "I wouldn't call her counterculture—she was kind of conventionally rebellious," said Jonathan Adelman, a Denver professor who knew Rice and Gibson well. "I can only speculate that for Condi, who grew up in a much more straitlaced, black bourgeois environment, Cris Gibson must have been a breath of fresh air."[24]

In Gibson's view, she and Rice had far more in common than they did not. "There were more similarities than differences, but we looked like Mutt and Jeff," Gibson said. "Her upbringing was very upper-middle-class—intelligence, manners, behavior. We were close to our parents, nonapologetically. I don't think we ever really thought black or white." Both Gibson and Rice still lived at home, but they studied together and ate out together—the chain restaurant Chili's was a favorite—almost every night. "It was burgers and fries, and margaritas, to be honest," Gibson said.[25]

At the same time, much of Rice's social life was focused on a group of about a dozen black football players for the Denver Broncos who brought the attractive young Ph.D. student and sports fanatic into their circle. Rice had met the players through her father, who by then was an assistant vice chancellor and still eager to get African-

Americans, especially the athletes he admired, involved at DU. Haven Moses, a Bronco wide receiver, recalls that he first encountered Rice when Rice invited him and a few other players to a university banquet. "I remember sitting up at the head table," Moses said. "It was some kind of honor night. And then he continued to invite us to certain things. He just wanted to in his way expose us, and I guess we didn't realize it at the time what he was doing, but he had a plan as well. I think he was in his way his own civil rights movement."[26]

Soon Moses and his wife, Joyce, were invited to the Rices' for regular dinners, and over time the friendship grew so close that John Rice talked not only about the racial cauldron he had left behind in Birmingham but about his professional disappointments with the university. "I learned about their past, their struggles, and what he was wanting to do," Moses said. "He was very frustrated, because I think he hit a difficult time at DU as well. He knew that there was more there for him to do, but he wasn't maybe being given that opportunity. So in a sense, maybe he was running into some of the things that he left the South for."[27]

Moses was hinting at John Rice's last troubled years at DU, when Rice was demoted after the chancellor and benefactor who had brought him to the university, Maurice Mitchell, moved on. John Rice did not have tenure, and he battled over a pay cut and other issues with the new chancellor, Ross Pritchard.[28] By 1982, Rice was dismissed, but he reached a settlement with the university the same year that satisfied him and also his daughter,[29] who was nonetheless still angry about Pritchard decades later. "My father challenged him early on because he was a complete and total disaster, and I was actually kind of glad my father got out of there," Rice said in 2007.[30] But the big man from the small pond of Birmingham was fifty-eight, and finding new work was not easy. "I've often thought he was sort of afraid to go on the job market," his daughter later said. John Rice did help set up a nonprofit organization for school dropouts, but otherwise, Condoleezza Rice said, it was "a lot of odds and ends."[31]

For Moses, John Rice's troubles underscored why he was working so hard to ready his daughter for a white world. "He knew that by preparing her with all these tools that she wouldn't have to deal with that stuff," he said. "Those things would open the door for her. Who's going to say, 'You can't, because—'? 'Wait a minute here, I can. I've got this Ph.D., I've got this, I've got this.' So he knew that her résumé, how important it was, and that was going to be her salvation."[32]

Moses and the other players had never met a black woman like Rice, who knew football as if she played it. "She blew a lot of guys' minds, because when she started talking football, she knew formations, strategies," Moses said. After the games, "Oh, she'd give her two cents. 'That was a dumb-ass call! What was the coach thinking about? I could see it up in the stands!' She knew how the ball snapped, how team defenses would move around. So she'd say, 'Why did he call that? He's leaving you wide open. You were lined up this deep in the back, you had this guy beat up all day long!' She knew." The players knew how accomplished Rice was, he said, "but when she was around us, she was one of the boys."[33]

Years later, Rice would repeat a favorite formulation that the strategy of football was like war. "It's all about taking territory," she said. "That's really what it is. And to take territory and continuing to take territory, you eventually end up with the conquest, which is the touchdown."[34] In short, she said, "it's very strategic in the way that warfare once was. I mean, warfare is less like that now."[35]

As a twenty-year-old, Rice's manner was always more flattering to the players than intimidating, Moses said, and men who might have been put off by a female know-it-all lapped it up instead. "She had that charm about her that she could cover any subject and make you feel like you're the one who has all the answers," Moses recalled, echoing what many colleagues would later say was her appeal to George Bush. But the players also knew what effect they had on Rice. "For her to be around those guys, I mean, she lit up," Moses said.[36]

By this time, Rice had become seriously involved with one of the players, Rick Upchurch, a star kick returner. The two had been introduced by a mutual friend, a football player, who had been drafted from Notre Dame to play for the Broncos. They started dating soon after Rice's return from Notre Dame, in the fall of 1975, during Upchurch's first season in Denver. At twenty-three, Upchurch was nearly three years older than Rice, and his upbringing had been as harsh as hers was privileged. Upchurch had been essentially left on his own in junior high school after his grandfather died—"he lived out of a car for a while at a very young age," Moses said[37]—and football had been his ticket up and out. Rice fell for him hard.

"Rick wasn't big, but he was fast and a good athlete," Moses said. "I think Condi was fascinated by his athleticism."[38] Years later, Upchurch would say that he and Rice had been engaged,[39] while Rice would say curtly that it was something less formal than that. "Did a twenty-one-year-old girl probably think she was going to get married at some point?" she said. "Yes." To Upchurch? "At one point I thought probably, yeah." Still, she said, "I did not go out and buy a dress or anything like that." Her father, she said, "really, really liked Rick."[40]

The relationship lasted about a year, but by the fall of 1976, Rice and Upchurch split. "Rick was the sweetest man, he truly was," Gibson said. "He had this smile that was like sunshine—he would light up a room. Everybody was pushing really hard, because they were so good together, but it just wasn't even."[41]

Despite the split, Rice remained part of the Broncos family through her friendship with Moses and his wife, Joyce. At home games she sat with the players' wives and girlfriends, and went to dinner with the team afterward at the Colorado Mine Company, a favorite Broncos hangout of the time. As the team became more successful—the Broncos would go to their first Super Bowl in 1978—the players became bigger celebrities, and Rice was often at the table when the autograph seekers came by. On holidays and weekends, she and her parents went to the Moses home for parties, where there would be Southern food, cards, and music. Rice and Joyce Moses, who was eight years older than Rice and the mother of two children, became close friends. "We shopped together, she'd tell me about books to read," Joyce Moses recalled. "It was wonderful for me. As bright as she was, she didn't lord it over you."[42] In January 1978, Joyce Moses felt comfortable enough with Rice to call her at the last minute and ask if she could baby-sit the Moseses' six-year-old son while she and her husband went to a hastily arranged party before they left for the Super Bowl in New Orleans the next day. Rice came over with her books and her study partner, Cris Gibson.[43]

By this time, Rice was at another cul-de-sac in her academic career. She had passed her first set of Ph.D. exams in Soviet and Eastern

European history, including a grueling all-day oral session in the early spring of 1977. But Korbel, who had led the committee's questioning, had not seemed well. "He looked a little yellow," recalled Gibson, who took her orals around the same time. "We were kind of loath to mention it, honestly."[44] By May, Rice and Gibson were stunned to learn that Korbel was seriously ill with pancreatic cancer, and that he had checked himself out of the hospital to preside over their exams. In what was suddenly an emergency, Korbel asked Rice to step in and teach one of his undergraduate courses, Introduction to International Relations. By July he was dead.

By then Rice was in Washington on a State Department summer internship in the educational and cultural affairs bureau, where she helped arrange American-sponsored arts programs in Latin America and Africa. Korbel's death was devastating to her, and she thought about flying back to Denver—Gibson would be ushering at Korbel's funeral in the university's Phipps Tennis Pavilion—but in the end Rice thought it was too close to the end of the internship and decided she shouldn't. "I actually felt a bit guilty about it afterward," she said.[45] As a condolence gift, Rice sent the Korbel family a planter in the shape of a piano filled with philodendrons, which piqued Madeleine Albright's curiosity enough for her to ask her mother who it was from. Albright's mother said the planter had come from Condoleezza Rice, her father's favorite student—the first that Albright had heard of her.[46]

Rice and Gibson spent the next academic year mourning the loss and floundering. Rice seemed particularly hard hit, and years later described the loss of her mentor as if he had been an exceptionally close family member or soul mate. "Your relationship with your thesis adviser is the closest possible relationship you will ever have with any other human being except perhaps your parents or spouse," Rice said. "And suddenly that person is gone. And I really didn't even know what I was going to do."[47] Korbel, she said, "had been so important in helping build an image of myself, of somebody who was likely to be a good academic and all of those things. I really did feel pretty lost. So Cris and I just kind of did much of nothing that year. We sort of hung out."[48]

Rice's plan had been to turn her master's thesis on Shostakovich and Prokofiev into a Ph.D. dissertation on cultural politics in the Soviet Union, but without Korbel's guidance she struggled. She was also studying for her second set of exams and serving on a committee, along with Gibson and Glass, to find Korbel's replacement.

Help arrived in early 1979. Jonathan Adelman, a young Ph.D. in political science from Columbia University, was the choice of the committee to replace Korbel, and he assumed the role of Rice's adviser. By that time Denver had also hired Catherine Kelleher, a specialist in American strategic studies from the Massachusetts Institute of Technology who came by way of the University of Michigan. Kelleher, who would become a deputy assistant secretary of defense in the Clinton administration, joined the small committee overseeing the dissertations of Korbel's former students, and soon became an important adviser to Rice.

Kelleher found Rice's planned dissertation on cultural politics "still kind of in a shambles" and along with Adelman urged her to do something else.[49] As Kelleher understood it, Korbel had steered Rice away from a dissertation on security policy—warfare, armies, nuclear weapons—because he felt the field was tough for a woman. Kelleher, an expert in security policy, knew that Korbel was right, but saw no need to limit a new generation. Adelman held up his own dissertation, on relations between the Chinese government and its military, as an example. Rice settled on a new topic: relations between the Czech government and its military and the role of the Soviet Union. Her starting point was 1948, the year the Communists took over in Prague and Korbel began his tortured course to the United States.[50]

Rice liked the topic because it was concrete and to an extent quantifiable, as opposed to a dissertation that would involve studying relationships between Soviet leaders. "I did not want to spend my life as a Kremlinologist trying to find out what Brezhnev had said to Kosygin in the men's room," Rice said. "I just didn't know how you did that kind of research. But militaries had things to study, and they had to have exercises and they had to write, and I liked military history and military affairs."[51] There was already a lot of academic work on the Soviet military, but Rice saw a niche in the Czech army and thought there might be more available material because of the brief period of liberalization during the 1968 Prague Spring. She knew she would have to learn to read Czech, but it was close to Russian and she thought it was manageable. Not least, Czechoslovakia would be a connection to Korbel, who had died only eighteen months earlier.

Although Rice needed academic guidance, both Kelleher and Adelman were struck by her self-confidence. "Condi Rice was, even back then, not a person to be trifled with," Adelman said. "I mean, at twenty-four, my joke about her is, she came fully formed out of the womb."[52] Adelman would never forget his first one-on-one meeting with Rice, in early 1979, when the two had their first conversation about her dissertation. Adelman asked her what she wanted to do with her life.[53]

"She sat up straight in the chair, she kind of drew herself up, as her mother must have taught her, stared straight at you, and she said, 'I'm going to become a U.S. congressman—and maybe a U.S. senator,' " Adelman recalled. "Then she proceeded to elaborate a plan on how she was going to do it!"[54] Adelman said that Rice had decided that Pat Schroeder, the Democrat who then represented Denver in Colorado's 1st Congressional District, would not be in the seat much longer (in fact Schroeder went on to serve another seventeen years in the House) and that she thought she had a chance. Rice told Adelman that as a black woman she had appeal and that she was learning Spanish so she could reach out to Latino voters. She also said that even as a Republican she thought she could win, although in Adelman's memory "she didn't make a big deal out of what party she was going to run on."[55]

In 1980, Rice volunteered for Senator Gary Hart, the Colorado Democrat who was running for reelection, although her work for him was minimal. "I think she just came to a couple of meetings and offered ideas," Hart recalled.[56] That November, Rice voted for Ronald Reagan over Jimmy Carter in the presidential election, although she remained a registered Democrat.[57] She had turned away from Carter, she has long said, because he expressed shock that the Soviet Union invaded Afghanistan, a remark the Republicans used against him in the campaign and that she, schooled by Korbel, considered the height of naïveté. "I thought, 'What in the world is he doing?' " Rice said. "The kind of draining away of American power was really troubling to me."[58] By 1982, Rice had registered as a Republican, although in 1984 she advised Hart, who was then running for president. By 1987, she had moved far enough to the right to turn down Madeleine Albright when Albright asked Rice to join her in working on the campaign of Michael Dukakis, who would be the 1988 Democratic presidential nominee. "Madeleine, I don't know how to tell you this, but I'm a Republican," Rice said. Albright was astonished. "Condi, how could that be?" she asked. "We had the same father."[59]

Rice has in part explained her politics by citing her real father, John Rice, who registered as a Republican in Alabama in 1952 and remained a member of the party until his death. But the story is not that simple. Rice had first tried to register as a member of the Democratic Party, which controlled the country registrars in Alabama at the time. He was effectively denied suffrage when he was subjected to a poll test he couldn't possibly pass, as happened with many other blacks. In Rice's case, a white clerk asked him to say how many jelly beans were in a jar. Dejected, Rice learned of another county clerk who would register blacks in secret as long as they registered Republican, a party that barely existed in Alabama. "The Republicans were looking to register anyone they could," Condoleezza Rice said.[60] Rice characterized her mother as politically independent and "not that interested," and proudly told a story of how she had accompanied Angelena as a five-year-old into a voting booth in 1960 and guided her to pick the candidate marked with an elephant, Richard Nixon, over the one with a donkey, John F. Kennedy. "I said, 'Mommy, you're supposed to pull the elephant,' because my dad was a Republican," Rice said. "So, she did. Completely, you know, talked my mother out of voting for the Democrat."[61]

Years later, Adelman would say that Rice never gave up her ambitions to run for office. "I think the biggest thing people miss about her is how political she is," he said in 2006. "They have this notion she's a would-be academic. I mean, here she is, not even doing a dissertation, and she already wants to run for political office, and not just Congress. And when she looked at you, you sort of thought maybe she could." She never said, Adelman recalled, "I want to be an academic" or "I want to be in the policy world."[62]

At Denver, Rice started in on her dissertation in 1979 with renewed focus. Kelleher was impressed with her drive—"she's not out to slit somebody's throat, she just knows what she's after"—and her ability to set goals and limit distractions. "Anything else coming in, other opportunities, might be interesting, but they weren't going to deter her from what she understood to be her first priority," she said."[63] Rice was interested, though, in NBC Sports, which began courting her to be a commentator for the 1980 Summer Olympics in Moscow, which the United States ultimately boycotted because of the Soviet invasion of Afghanistan. Rice's entrée was the local NBC anchor, a friend of her father. In the wake of the Afghan crisis, Rice's Russian language skills and interest in sports—as well as her race and gender—made her a natural choice. Rice went so far as to fly to New York for an interview, but nothing came of it.[64] Kelleher, for one, was glad. "I told her, 'You have to finish your dissertation, then you can go off and be famous,' " she said.[65]

Rice took Kelleher's advice, but through Adelman got a part-time job in 1980 at Science Applications International Corporation, or SAIC, the giant military contractor, which had offices in Denver. As contractors, Adelman and Rice advised the Defense Department on the inner workings of the Soviet military. It was an urgent policy issue after the Afghan invasion, and would only intensify with Reagan's Cold War rhetoric during the 1980 presidential election. "The core was trying to understand how the Soviet military looked at the world and how they would fight nuclear wars," Adelman said.[66] Rice's principal task, which was related to her dissertation topic, was to read Russian military literature and write reports on what the leaders were doing and thinking.[67]

Rice found military intelligence alluring. "It was an exciting world," Adelman said, recalling sessions where scholars and analysts would watch computer-simulated images of imagined thermonuclear exchanges between the United States and the Soviet Union. "You would work on analyses of Soviet military intervention, what they were doing in Afghanistan. It was intellectual. It was challenging."[68]

Rice was a rarity in that world, not only as a black but as a woman. The military intelligence conferences at the time were nearly 100 percent male, peopled with ex-CIA officers and former commanders who would talk about their bombing runs over Hanoi and take off two hours a day to exercise. "It was macho," Adelman said. Rice's entrée was through her part-time job and her dissertation. "She could go to conferences and talk about the Eastern European military," Adelman said. "How would they fight in a war? She knew civil-military relations. That was considered an important topic. She could talk about political succession struggles, all of which are applicable in that particular world."[69]

In the end, Rice's time at SAIC may have been as influential in her metamorphosis from piano student to right-leaning Soviet specialist as Korbel ever was. Adelman, for one, thinks so. "I just can't draw the link otherwise," he said. "Everybody wants to always say what we did here was the most important. I don't think so." Denver's Graduate School of International Studies, he said, was "a typical, very liberal institution. She didn't glom on to much of that."[70]

By the fall of 1980, Rice was in any case planning her next move. Through Kelleher she learned of a Ford Foundation postdoctoral fellowship that would allow her to finish her dissertation at MIT, Harvard, or Stanford, among a handful of other institutions. Rice was awarded the fellowship, and wrote to both Harvard and Stanford to ask if they would take her. Harvard never responded, but Chip Blacker, the assistant director of what was then Stanford's Center for International Security and Arms Control, took notice of the handwritten letter on pale blue stationery with "Condoleezza Rice" embossed in gold across the top. Postgraduate students didn't usually send letters on elegant personal stationery and they didn't usually apply to Stanford from regional schools like Denver. Blacker, curious, called a friend on the fellowship selection committee, Larry Caldwell, who had been Blacker's mentor at Occidental College. Caldwell gave Rice such an enthusiastic endorsement that Blacker called Rice out to Stanford to meet with his colleagues at the arms control center, then readily offered Rice a spot.[71] By January 1981, Rice was headed to Palo Alto. She would be the first African-American and in the first group of women to be a fellow at Stanford's arms control center, a formerly all-male, all-white bastion of the nation's elite.

CHAPTER 5

She Tells Me Everything I Know About the Soviet Union

Palo Alto and the White House, 1981–1991

Rice had never seen a campus as seductive as Stanford. She loved the grand, sun-drenched main entrance lined with the nearly century-old Canary Island palms. She loved the university's cloistered Main Quadrangle of California Mission–style buildings with red-tiled roofs, so reminiscent of Romanesque churches in France and Spain. She loved the Rodin sculptures in the gardens and the views from the surrounding hills of San Francisco Bay. The campus had been created by Frederick Law Olmsted, the designer of the English pastoral landscape of Central Park, but here Olmsted's courtyards of avocado, citrus, and bougainvillea evoked the Mediterranean. Over the next two decades, Rice would re-create herself yet again in this exotic new home. "I just thought it was fantastically beautiful," she said.[1]

Rice was one of four arms control fellows, all women and all selected by Blacker, and in the male-dominated setting the group quickly dubbed itself "The Fellow-ettes." Like the others, Rice had a modest stipend for the academic year. She worked out of a small office at Galvez House, the shabby (for Stanford) building, now razed, that housed the arms control center. She spent her days working on her dissertation, making research trips to the library, and attending academic seminars that caught her interest. Ronald Reagan had been inaugurated in January and the massive American military buildup was one of the urgent issues of the day. For all its scruffiness, Galvez House felt like an important satellite in the national security debate. It was sociable, too. William Perry, a big-fish Stanford graduate, had just returned from Washington as an undersecretary of defense in the Carter administration. Perry, who would become co-director of the center and then defense secretary in the Clinton administration, liked to invite everyone from Galvez House over to his big place in the Los Altos hills for barbecues.[2]

Rice shared a house on campus with one of the Fellow-ettes, Gloria Duffy, who had known Chip Blacker at Occidental and would later become an assistant secretary of defense in the Clinton administration. Rice rented an upright piano, and both she and Duffy fixed dinners and invited over Blacker and the other Fellow-ettes. Duffy recalled that Rice, the only African-American of the group, did not seem to identify herself strongly as black. Rice was also not noticeably political, even though she had voted for Reagan as a Democrat the previous fall. She was bright, but appeared no more academically gifted than anyone else. "Everyone there was a high achiever," Duffy said. "I can't say that I saw back then that she would be secretary of state."[3]

But in those first months at Stanford, Rice did something that echoed both the lessons of self-improvement her parents had so pressed upon her in Birmingham and her attachment in Denver to Korbel. She sought out another older, eminent professor, Sidney Drell, the Stanford theoretical physicist and arms control expert, and asked if he would teach her the technology of nuclear weapons. Drell, who was also a highly connected adviser to the government on national security, readily said yes. "She was one of the boys at the arms control center," Drell recalled.[4] A few days a week, Rice met with Drell at the Stanford Linear Accelerator Center, his office, or his home and eagerly absorbed his instructions. "I had had physics in high school, but what I remembered of it was minimal," Rice said. "So he taught me, really, the physics of nuclear weapons."[5] Decades later, when Rice was secretary of state and confronting Iran over its nuclear program, she said that Drell's teachings had "come in handy as I've had to deal with Iranian enrichment processes."[6]

Rice plowed ahead without apparent angst on her dissertation on the Czech military, and in March gave a lecture about it, as was expected of a postdoctoral fellow. Rice presented the nub of her argument: After the Communists took over in Prague in 1948, the Czech military ended up serving two masters, the Soviet Union and the Czech Communist Party. Thus the Soviet Union was an "internal actor" disturbing the critical relationship between Czechoslovakia's civilian and military leaders. The end result, Rice concluded, was widespread disillusionment with the military and a demoralized Czech army.[7] Rice was unusually nervous—it was her first big talk at Stanford—but she had spent so many years before audiences in concert halls and ice rinks that her performance was smooth and she impressed the faculty. Within weeks Stanford asked if she would be interested in joining the political science faculty in a non-tenure-track position.[8]

The university's affirmative action officer at the time, Cecilia Burciaga, recalled how a faculty member had asked her about hiring Rice. "He came to us and said, 'Look, she'll probably never be a full professor here, she came from an unknown university, but we should give her a nice golden handshake,' " recalled Burciaga, who would surface years later in one of the most acrimonious battles that Rice had at Stanford. "He thought she would have a future at a historically black college. He was surprised she had given a good talk."[9]

Rice was cool to Stanford's overture—she had job offers from SAIC, Occidental College, and RAND, where she had worked a previous summer—but before she could make up her mind, Stanford came back and asked if it would help if the position were changed to tenure track. "And I said, 'Okay, what's going on here?' " Rice recalled.[10] Soon enough, she knew exactly what had happened. Stanford, which normally conducted labor-intensive national searches for faculty over months and years, had moved with lightning speed to hire a promising twenty-six-year-old black woman under an affirmative action program that allowed the university to circumvent the normal process.[11] Rice's interest in going elsewhere had convinced Stanford that it had to do something quickly to keep her.

Still, Rice insisted years later that she soul-searched before accepting an offer that others her age could only dream of. "I really wasn't sure about entering an academic track," she said.[12] She had grown up on college campuses, but she had been put off by the experience of her aunt, Theresa Love, the Victorian scholar at the University of Wisconsin. "I remember going to visit her when I was about probably seven or eight, and she was reading *A Tale of Two Cities*, and I said, 'Oh, Aunt Theresa, have you read that book before?' " Rice recalled. "And she said, 'I've read this book twenty-five times.' And I thought, 'You've got to be kidding. There must be something better in life.' And that was sort of my vision of what academics did. They stayed cloistered, and I couldn't get that out of my mind. But when I really thought about it, I thought you're not going to turn down the chance to teach at Stanford."[13]

The chairman of the Political Science Department, Heinz Eulau, made clear to Rice that she would have to prove herself, and that tenure was far from guaranteed—the standard warning delivered to any new faculty member. Eulau died in 2004, so there is no way to know his version of exactly what he said to Rice, but Rice's recounting of the conversation had Eulau giving voice to her own view that there should be no affirmative action at the time of tenure. "Heinz said, 'Now there's one thing you have to understand,' " Rice said. "He said, 'Very few people get tenure here. And you came in on a special arrangement.' I remember he said, 'You came in on a special arrangement.' And he said, 'But you have to understand, when you come up for tenure, there are no special arrangements. And we don't care what color you are, or what gender you are, there are no special arrangements.' And he said, 'You have three years and then you're reviewed. And after three years, if you're not making it, then you have to leave the university. After six years, you come up for tenure.' And I was so kind of naive in some ways, and I said, 'Oh, yeah, three years, that sounds like about the right length of time, because then I can decide if you like me and I can decide if I like you.' "[14] Only later would Rice realize her presumptuousness in telling a world-class institution like Stanford that it would have to measure up to her. "I just shudder that that's what I said to the department chair, on our first meeting," she said.[15]

Rice did not feel stigmatized as an affirmative action hire, or so she said decades later. "I knew I was as good as anybody they were hiring, so I wasn't worried about that, and they were very clear that if I wasn't good enough at tenure I wasn't going to make it," she said. "I thought that sounded perfectly fair. I was a big champion of exactly that kind of affirmative action when I became provost. Cast your net widely—at an assistant professor level, you're taking a risk anyway. Some people come in with the very best credentials, high-fliers, and don't make it, and some people come in and you don't see that credential, and it's a bet, and they do make it."[16] Years later, after she became provost, Rice's views would be furiously criticized by women and minority faculty members and would in part trigger the investigation at Stanford by the United States Department of Labor.[17]

Rice finished her dissertation in the spring of 1981 and was awarded her Ph.D. in international studies that August in a ceremony at the University of Denver. Still only twenty-six, she returned to Palo Alto, settled into an office in the Main Quad, and spent the fall planning her courses in the preparation period Stanford provided for new professors. "You come from graduate school, you know nothing about being a professor," she said. "It's as if you brought somebody out of medical school and never made them be an intern. And you're about to walk in front of classes of some of the smartest kids in the world, right?"[18]

She debuted as a Stanford assistant professor of political science in the 1982 winter quarter, when she taught three undergraduate courses: Comparative Civil-Military Relations, the Soviet Union in the Third World, and, with Eulau, the Politics of Elites, a course that studied how people in different societies were channeled and chosen for political positions.[19] Her students remember her as meticulously prepared but tentative at first. "She changed over time," said Rose McDermott, a professor at the University of California at Santa Barbara who took Rice's classes as an undergraduate at Stanford in the 1980s. "Early on, she would get nervous."[20]

Rice was more confident when she moved away from the podium and engaged her classes in simulations of international crises, a favorite teaching technique. "All you ever had to do was introduce a lost nuclear weapon," Rice said, recalling how she created catastrophes for the students to handle.[21] Students would be assigned roles as the American president or the Soviet national security adviser and asked to act out their responses. "You had to resolve the crisis, you had to work with your teammates, and you had to research the background not only of your character but of your country," McDermott recalled. "It was phenomenal."[22] One year Rice and Blacker co-taught a simulation of a U.S.-Soviet summit meeting on arms control that required students to negotiate a treaty by the end of the course. Rice was the adviser for the American side and Blacker for the Soviet side, and the students became so wrapped up in their roles that by the end they were in tense all-night negotiations. "I used to have to say, 'Okay, everybody take a break and go to bed tonight,' " Rice recalled.[23]

Rice was looser and funnier in the simulations than she was in her lectures, and the courses made her a popular professor. "It was plain that she was an emerging phenomenon as a teacher," said Donald Kennedy, who was president of Stanford at the time. "She got students very excited about foreign affairs."[24] Kori Schake, currently a West Point professor who worked for Rice on the National Security Council staff in the first term of George W. Bush, took Rice's course in the Politics of Elites as an undergraduate in 1984 and recalled her as "a magnetic field unto herself" who impressed the women students as an unusually pulled-together combination of brains, youth, and style. Rice was heavier in her early days at Stanford than she later was in Washington, but she still dressed better than the average woman professor. "She was what all of us wanted to be," Schake said.[25] In an echo of her father's guidance counseling, Rice also spent large blocks of time in those early days giving her students academic and career advice, and soon the lines for her office appointments were snaking down the hallway and running two and three hours long.[26] In 1984 she won a Walter J. Gores Award, Stanford's highest honor for teaching.

One student who was always in the lines out Rice's door was Jendayi Frazer, a black woman who had grown up as an Army brat in the United States and Germany. Rice gave Frazer guidance on her academic papers, pushed her to pursue advanced degrees, and later rescued her when Frazer was struggling financially in the first year of a Stanford Ph.D. program. To make ends meet, Frazer had been working two jobs, including a midnight to 8 A.M. graveyard shift as a security guard. Overwhelmed, she went to Rice for help. "I pretty much told her I was exhausted," Frazer recalled. "I'd come to class and have been up all night."[27] Rice went to the administration and got Frazer a scholarship to keep her in school. Later, when Rice left Stanford for two years during the George H. W. Bush administration, she set up a fund so Frazer could call her with questions about her dissertation.[28] When Frazer finally finished her dissertation but didn't have the few thousand dollars she needed for filing it with the university, Rice took out her checkbook and lent her the money.[29] (In 2001, Rice brought Frazer with her to the National Security Council staff and then got her appointed as the United States ambassador to South Africa. In 2005, Frazer became assistant secretary of state for African affairs.)

At around the same time in the early 1980s that Rice met Frazer, she also met Gene Washington, a Stanford football star who graduated from the university in 1969 and went on to play for the San Francisco 49ers. Washington was in the NFL for a decade, but by the time Rice met him he was a football commentator for NBC and the host of a sports program on the CBS television affiliate in San Francisco. Washington was African-American, from Tuscaloosa, and just the kind of handsome campus football celebrity Rice found irresistible. Washington, who had been married and divorced, asked the young Professor Rice to play tennis and then took her to dinner, and the two dated for the better part of a year. Rice's friends found Washington charming, although roguish. After the relationship ended, Washington married and divorced again, then took a job as an assistant athletic director at Stanford at around the time that Rice became provost. The two dated again and continued to see each other sporadically after Washington moved to New York City as a National Football League executive in 1994. When Rice moved to Washington as national security adviser in 2001, she and Washington began to see each other more often. Over twenty-five years, he would be a kind of constant in her life who met both her needs and her schedule, but he was more significant to her than a convenient escort. "There's a lot more to our relationship than may appear on the surface," Washington said in 2007. "There are issues of friends, family, Alabama, sports, a whole lot of connecting points, if you will."[30]

In 1984, Rice's interests at Stanford were soon extending beyond Gene Washington and her life on campus. That winter she became a foreign policy adviser to Gary Hart, who was chasing after former vice president Walter Mondale for the Democratic nomination. Hart had been the upset winner in the New Hampshire primary and his rag-tag operation had suddenly exploded into a tsunami of fund-raising and overlapping committees. Rice knew Hart from her days volunteering for his 1980 Senate reelection campaign in Denver, but this time she was recruited by Blacker, a Democrat and a onetime Hart staff member, to play a more substantial role offering ideas and memos on the Soviet Union. "She knew what she was talking about," Hart recalled. "This was not a graduate student fumbling with what to say."[31] Hart remembered Rice as of the realist school of foreign policy—she believed that the U.S. relationship with the Soviet Union should be both cautious and engaged. "She was mainstream," Hart said.[32]

Rice was also giving speeches, serving on university committees, and moving far enough beyond the realm of an ordinary professor that her superiors warned her about losing focus. "More than once I had to say there's some level of concern that you're spreading yourself too thin and taking on too many assignments, and you ought to focus on your core task of getting tenure," said David M. Kennedy, a Stanford history professor who in 2000 would win a Pulitzer Prize for his book *Freedom from Fear*, a history of the Depression, the New Deal, and World War II. "And she would reply, thanks, but I can manage my own life." Kennedy, who was then an associate dean in charge of the Political Science Department and so gave annual performance reviews to tenure-track professors like Rice, said he was struck by Rice's composure in the face of his admonition. Other young professors might have been rattled, Kennedy said.[33]

Rice took a big step toward tenure in 1984 when her dissertation was published as a book by Princeton, one of the top university presses. (Stanford, like most universities, required book publication as a prerequisite for granting the benefits of lifelong job security.) Rice dedicated the book to her parents "for their love and support" and to Korbel "in memory of his love for Czechoslovakia."[34] She concluded, as she had in her dissertation, that the Soviet Union was a wedge between the Czech Communist Party and Czech armed forces.[35] Years later, she joked that she was a "dinosaur" as she recalled that the book was about two countries that no longer existed.[36]

The reviews of Rice's book were mixed. The most negative was in *The American Historical Review*, the leading journal in the field, which criticized Rice for relying too heavily on secondary sources and Soviet propaganda, and referred to her as a man. The review, by Joseph Kalvoda, a Czech-born professor of history and political science at Saint Joseph College in West Hartford, Connecticut, would be resurrected years later in magazines and newspapers when the Bush administration came under fire for the false case it made about the threat from Iraq. "Rice's selection of sources raises questions, since he frequently does not sift facts from propaganda or misinformation," Kalvoda wrote in the 1985 review. "He passes judgments and expresses opinions without adequate knowledge of the facts."[37] Kalvoda, who died in 1999, also criticized Rice for not knowing that a "former military scientist" was in fact a Communist agent, a mistake another reviewer shrugged off as a minor lapse.[38]

That reviewer, Christopher Jones, a professor at the University of Washington and an expert on the Warsaw Pact, praised Rice's book in the journal *Soviet Studies* for its "sheer mass" of research and the "forceful logic" of its opening and closing chapters, and predicted that it would become the standard work in the field, however small the field was.[39] Dale R. Herspring, a Russia scholar who was then an adjunct professor at Georgetown University, took a similar position to Jones in the *American Political Science Review*, calling Rice's book "first rate" and "a must for anyone interested in civil-military relations in communist systems."[40]

Rice gave the book to her mother for Christmas, a timing she later remembered as "really important" because by Easter, Rice's father told her that Angelena did not seem well. "And then around the Fourth of July my father called and said, 'You know, I'm really worried about your mother, she seems to be falling a lot and she can't remember things,' " Rice said. "And so she went to the doctor and she had a brain tumor."[41] The breast cancer of fifteen years earlier had spread. Rice flew to Denver for three weeks, went back to Stanford to teach a summer weekend course for alumni, and had plans to return to Denver on August 15, a Sunday. "So I was all packed and I was going to Denver the next day and I got a call Sunday morning, two o'clock in the morning or something like that, my father's saying,

'Your mother's not breathing,' " and " 'I just wanted you to know we're on our way to the hospital,' " Rice said. "And he called one hour later and said she'd died."[42] The death was shattering to Rice. It did not seem possible that Angelena, her strong, tough mother—the woman who had stood up for her in Birmingham's department stores, who had taught her piano on those hot summer days, who had made her into so much of what she was—was gone. So, too, was the family threesome. As Rice recalled the moment twenty-two years later, her eyes welled up with tears.[43]

At Stanford that night, Rice called up Blacker and asked if he would come over. Blacker immediately did, and learned then that his friend had religious beliefs she rarely displayed in the secular world of Stanford. "She was pretty broken up," Blacker said. "I stayed there overnight, and at seven I drove her to the airport. She was totally composed. I asked her how she could be. She said, 'It's because I honestly believe I will see my mother in heaven.' "[44]

The next month Rice took in a friend, Randy Bean, a documentary television producer who was struggling to make it as a freelancer, couldn't pay the rent, and needed a place to stay. "I was a mess," said Bean, a white Episcopalian minister's daughter from Montclair, New Jersey, who had met Rice in 1982 when Bean was at Stanford on a Knight Fellowship for journalists.[45] As was the case with Cristann Gibson in Denver, Rice appeared to have little in common with Bean, who was a liberal Democrat and as emotional and down on her luck as Rice was controlled and on her way up. But both were football fans and close to their minister-fathers, and they soon became friends. For four months, Bean slept on a mattress in the den of Rice's faculty apartment, and in the evenings the two ate take-out and watched television together. "She defined what loyalty was when I went through a really difficult moment," Bean said. Later, Rice and Chip Blacker would help Bean buy a small house near Stanford as partial investors in a valuable piece of Palo Alto real estate.[46]

Rice spent much of those four months telling Bean favorite stories about her mother, but Bean could not help but notice how self-possessed Rice appeared so soon after the death. "I actually worried about her, but I didn't want to draw it out of her if she wasn't ready to talk about it," Bean said. A few years later, when Bean was struggling emotionally because of deaths in her own family, she leaned on Rice again. Although Bean saw Rice as uncomprehending about her troubles—"she didn't understand how anybody's life could be so destroyed by emotion"—she was grateful that Rice supported her without question. "She was completely there," Bean said.[47] Many years after that, Rice surprised Bean when she told her how vulnerable she had felt after her mother's death. "She said, 'You'll never know how important it was that you were here the four months after my mother died,' " Bean said.[48]

By late October, a little more than two months after Angelena's death, John Rice moved from Denver to Palo Alto to be close to his daughter. "He was as distraught a human being as I've ever seen," Bean recalled.[49] Angelena's death had turned daughter into parent, and now Condoleezza Rice would be the source of her father's stability. Rice had encouraged the move, and in the recollection of Don Kennedy, Stanford's president at the time, she turned to the university for help in getting John Rice settled. "I think I made a couple of calls," Kennedy said. "I was glad of that because it clearly meant a lot to Condi. And Condi was a rapidly developing asset here. You want to make assets like that happy because otherwise Harvard comes looking."[50] With help from his daughter, John Rice rented a small apartment in Palo Alto and began volunteering at Stanford's tutoring center for athletes. "It was just great for him to be out there," Rice said.[51] She introduced her father to a married couple his age, and within a year John Rice had "three wonderful lady friends," at least in the words of his adoring, protective daughter, who portrayed her father as far happier than he had appeared to Bean at the time. "I remember that he said, 'Do you think I'm dating?' " Rice recalled. "And I said, 'Yeah, I think you are.' And he said, 'Is that all right with you?' And I said, 'Sure, I think it's great.' "[52]

By then Rice had started a year-long fellowship at the Hoover Institution to work on what became *The Gorbachev Era*, a collection of essays she edited with Alexander Dallin, an eminent Stanford historian of the Soviet Union. The following academic year, starting in the fall of 1986, Rice was in Washington on a Council on Foreign Relations international affairs fellowship in Ronald Reagan's Pentagon. Rice effectively parachuted into the inner workings of the Defense

Department at a time when arms negotiations with the Soviet Union were dominating American foreign policy. She later called it "one of the best experiences of my life."[53]

Rice worked in a windowless basement room as an assistant to the director of the Joint Chiefs of Staff—Michael Hayden, who would become director of the CIA in George W. Bush's second term, was a colleague—and helped out on a project that assessed the strategic implications of eliminating all U.S. ballistic missiles, as Reagan proposed to do that October at the U.S.-Soviet summit with Mikhail Gorbachev in Reykjavik.[54] The summit ended in failure and disappointment, but the dramatic talks with what seemed to be new Russian leadership under Gorbachev riveted Rice and foreign policy makers around the world.

It was in this tumultuous period that Rice reached out to a charismatic African-American general, Colin Powell, who was then Reagan's deputy national security adviser. "I called him up, actually, and said, 'I'd like to meet you,' " she said.[55] Rice's entrée was Powell's wife, Alma, who had grown up in Birmingham. "And so he had me come over to the NSC and he sort of kept a check on me, you know, would call from time to time," Rice said.[56]

Later that fall of 1986, Rice went back to Palo Alto for surgery to remove uterine fibroids, a nuisance more than a crisis. But for John Rice, the stress of having his only child in the hospital so soon after Angelena's death was evidently overwhelming. The day that Condoleezza Rice was released to go home, John Rice had a heart attack, which put him into Stanford Hospital hours after his daughter had left. "It upset him so because I guess he thought he was going to lose her like his wife," said Clara Rice, Rice's stepmother.[57] As was evident to anyone, John Rice had become enormously dependent on his only child. He talked to her up to five times a day, morning and night, in between classes and on weekends. If he couldn't reach her by phone, he would get upset and sometimes get into his car and drive around trying to find her.[58]

John Rice recovered from the heart attack, but it weakened him, and his big personality seemed to shrink. He really had not been the same since the loss of the job at Denver and particularly since Angelena's death. In Clara's telling, Rice was so unhappy that he had started drinking.[59] His small apartment in Palo Alto was chaos, with stuffing sprouting out of the sofa, and he drove a car so decrepit that under the dash was a mass of wires that entangled passengers' feet.[60] "He told me he actually came to California to just die," Clara said.[61]

The father Rice had worshipped as a child was slipping away, and when Rice went back to Washington to resume her Pentagon fellowship she found herself worrying about him as much as he had worried about her. But that winter, there was at least some good news for her from Palo Alto: She had been granted tenure at Stanford. "I got a call saying it had been voted unanimously out of the department," Rice later said. "And I thought, 'Oh, that's great.' And I remember saying to a young faculty member, 'It's really nice not to be around when you're being voted for tenure, because when you're being voted for tenure and everybody's whispering behind your back, you can't see somebody eye to eye in the hallway.' "[62]

Rice's tenure was a major achievement that would also become a flash point a decade later in her battles with Stanford's women faculty over affirmative action. In the view of friends like Blacker, Rice had a strong tenure case: a book published by a prestigious university press, a collection of essays edited with Dallin, and an article in the academic journal *World Politics* that argued that military decision-making in the Soviet Union operated on what organizational theorists called a "loosely coupled" system—in other words, the Soviet political leadership set the broad outlines of defense policy while the professional military class implemented it.[63] Rice was also considered a stellar teacher and a good mentor to students.

But in the view of faculty members who later became hostile to Rice as provost, her scholarly credentials were thin enough to put her case into question, particularly at an institution like Stanford, where tenure was granted to only half the faculty. Rice had published, but not extensively, and her work was not known for any originality or brilliance. Although the committees that oversaw tenure decisions deliberated in secret, as was the practice, the view among many faculty members looking back was that Rice's good but not weighty academic record was overshadowed by the committee's desire to keep such a promising young black woman at Stanford—in short, a clear case of affirmative action.[64]

Rice always insisted that although Stanford hired her because of her race and gender, affirmative action played no part in the decision to grant her tenure, and that she approved. "I think that when you start having an on-off switch—'Well, you get a little bit of help because you're a minority, you get a little bit of help because you're a woman'—why?" Rice said. "You've had six years to prove yourself. Take a bet when somebody's coming into the university. You know, cast your net widely." In other words, she said, affirmative action at the time of hiring gave people the chance to make it, but by the time of tenure it implied that minorities needed more help. "And that's what you should resent if you're a minority," she said. "What you shouldn't resent is broadening the field."[65]

With tenure, Rice arrived back at Stanford from Washington in the fall of 1987 with a new title, associate professor of political science. The promotion brought her more money, prestige, and confidence, but there was another change in her as well. Rice's colleagues saw that her experience at the Pentagon had instilled in her what would be an enduring awe and fascination with the American military. "It turned Condi from being a Soviet–Eastern Europe specialist to someone who was interested in U.S. power," said Scott Sagan, a Stanford professor who had the Pentagon fellowship the year before Rice and who is now co-director of the university's renamed arms control center, the Center for International Security and Cooperation.[66] Blacker recalled that Rice was also starry-eyed from attending a state dinner at the White House that year with a major contributor to the Republican Party, a black businessman from Fresno. "I remember her coming back just extolling the virtues of Ronald Reagan," Blacker said. "And I told myself, she's lost."[67]

Rice settled in at Stanford, happy to be closer to her father but fretful about his health. John Rice was still drinking like a lost soul,[68] although he managed to get out as a volunteer in some of the local schools. The work turned out to be fortuitous the following year when John Rice turned up as a volunteer in the Menlo Oaks Middle School, where Clara Rice was the principal. As it happened, Clara already knew Condi Rice because Rice, in a coincidence, had briefly played the piano for the choir at Clara's church. (As Clara told the story, Condi Rice was in a supermarket checkout line in Palo Alto when a black man struck up a conversation with her. When the man learned that Rice played the piano, he asked if she would temporarily fill in for the regular pianist, who was ill.) Clara was eighteen years younger than John Rice, but she had grown up in Birmingham and the two immediately became friends. "We talked and then started visiting," Clara said.[69]

Sometimes Clara would go over to John's place to find the stereo cranked up full blast. He told her stories about the old days in Birmingham and his daughter, who doted on him but now had a life of her own. "He just turned the music up loud so he wouldn't think," Clara said. "Because I remember when I started going by there, you just couldn't hear. And I think it was a sense of loneliness, and he thought maybe Condi didn't want to be bothered with him, and he just didn't have anyone. So I was kind of like his savior, so to speak."[70]

Soon John Rice was calling Clara every day. "We were beginning to be like soul mates, and I just didn't believe I would marry him, because he was eighteen years older, and he was sickly, and I had in my mind if I would marry again what I wanted, and it wasn't him," Clara recalled. "But I just kept drawing closer and closer to him, because he was such a good person, and so easy to talk to and be with."[71]

One day late that fall Condoleezza Rice got a call from the office of the new president-elect. Would she be interested in a job in Washington? She would, although she worried about leaving her father behind. John Rice, however, had figured out how to fill the void that would be left by his cherished daughter. "So when she got called by Bush," Clara Rice said, "he wanted to move in with me."[72]

It was actually two calls that came for Rice in November 1988, shortly after George H. W. Bush, vice president for two terms under Reagan, defeated Michael Dukakis to become the forty-first president. Dennis Ross, a Soviet scholar and Middle East expert who knew Rice from his days running a joint Stanford-Berkeley program on Soviet international behavior, asked if she would work for him on the State Department's influential policy planning staff, where he was in line to be director. While Rice was thinking about it, she got a call from Brent Scowcroft, who had been Gerald Ford's national security adviser and was now taking the same position in the new Bush administration. Scowcroft offered Rice a job as his Soviet expert on the National Security Council staff, and Rice, after mulling it over, accepted.[73]

It was not a hard decision. The national security adviser was the chief adviser to the president on foreign and defense policy, one of the most powerful figures in the government, in charge of coordinating the often warring views of the State Department, the Pentagon, the Treasury Department, and other agencies. The national security adviser worked in the West Wing, only steps from the Oval Office, and although Rice would be next door in what was then called the Old Executive Office Building, she would still be working for the White House and in close proximity to the president.

Scowcroft was something of a Soviet expert himself, so he could afford to bring along a talented protégé and still have his own knowledge and experience to draw from. He had known and nurtured Rice since 1985, when he first met her at a Stanford dinner with arms control experts. "Arms control, especially during the Cold War, was a pretty esoteric subject, throw weights, all this kind of stuff," Scowcroft recalled. "So here are all these heavyweights in the field, and we're having this discussion. In the room was this young woman who looked like an undergrad rather than a lecturer, and she participated. She was respectful but assertive and stood her ground. And it really impressed me. I thought, I ought to introduce her into the national security community and get her more widely known." In short, he said, "I sort of launched her."[74] Scowcroft invited Rice the following summer to Colorado to meet with the Aspen Strategy Group, an elite collection of foreign policy experts, and over the years kept in touch.

Rice arrived in Washington at what turned out to be the beginning of an extraordinary period of change and opportunity in the history of modern American diplomacy. From the end of World War II, the managers of the Cold War on the American side had grappled with the terrifying balance of power and the threat of nuclear annihilation posed by the forces of the Soviet Union and the United States. But Rice was in the capital for two years, 1989 and 1990, when what was once thought impossible occurred: the end of the Cold War, the beginning of the dissolution of the Soviet Union, and the reunification of Germany. Rice, who eventually had the title of senior director of Soviet and Eastern European affairs on the seventy-member National Security Council staff, was in a midlevel position and was carrying out the policies of Bush, Scowcroft, and Secretary of State James A. Baker III rather than making any of her own. But she spoke the solid, competent Russian of an American academic, and her superiors turned to her for assessments of Mikhail Gorbachev, his rival, Boris Yeltsin, and how the Soviet Union might react to U.S. tactics. "Her contribution was to help understand how Gorbachev and the Soviets think of things," said Robert Blackwill, a Harvard academic and career foreign service officer who was Rice's immediate supervisor on the National Security Council staff.[75]

Rice frequently found herself in the Oval Office or the Roosevelt Room with Scowcroft and other senior advisers briefing the president of the United States. "Brent would say, 'Well, Mr. President, today we're going to talk about the Gorbachev-Yeltsin problem, you know, how do we handle both of them?' " recalled R. Nicholas Burns, Rice's deputy at the time. "And he would turn to Condi, and Condi would brief."[76] By the end, Rice had forged a personal bond with George H. W. Bush that went beyond the usual relationship of a president to a staff member, and that would later help pave her way into the administration of the son. The senior Bush, Burns said, "was captivated by her."[77]

In the same period, Rice developed close working relationships with a team of men at the White House and State Department—Burns, Blackwill, Philip Zelikow, Robert Zoellick, Robert Gates—whom she later described as pragmatic internationalists, suspicious of both the multilateralism of Carter and the unilateralism of Reagan.[78] Gates was Scowcroft's deputy and a Soviet specialist, Zelikow was a career diplomat and lawyer who handled European policy on the NSC, and Zoellick was the State Department official in charge of German policy. During the forty-third presidency, Rice would hire all of them to work for her except for Gates, and she would later help steer him to the Pentagon as a replacement for Donald Rumsfeld.[79]

At the start of the new Bush administration in January 1989, Rice moved into a spacious third-floor office in the Old Executive Office

Building with a balcony view of the West Wing. She turned her attention to Gorbachev, the foreign official who would dominate her working life. The Soviet leader had been in power since 1985 and had begun reaching out to the West and pushing perestroika, a domestic renewal, of the rotting Soviet system. In a 1988 speech to the United Nations, Gorbachev had even encouraged some independence in the Soviet satellite countries. But the Bush administration was still suspicious of Gorbachev's motives and thought Reagan had been a little starry-eyed when he embraced the Soviet leader in the second term.[80] Scowcroft, for one, was unsure of Gorbachev's prospects and that the changes in the Soviet Union would last.[81]

One of Rice's first tasks was to organize a session for the new president on what he should think of Gorbachev, which was held on an icy Sunday in February at the Bush summer home in Kennebunkport, Maine. Rice sat with the president, Scowcroft, and a half-dozen Soviet specialists she had invited, including Adam Ulam from Harvard and Marshall Goldman of Wellesley and the Harvard Russian Research Center, in Bush's master bedroom, one of the few parts of the house the family kept heated in the winter. With the icy waters of the Atlantic visible through the fogged-up windows, the academics reached the consensus that Gorbachev was committed to drastic reform but that the changes could produce a backlash—a coup d'etat by party hard-liners, the army, or the KGB. Only three weeks into her job, in an intimate setting with the president and men far senior to her, Rice readily spoke up and said she thought the "Achilles' heel" of Gorbachev's program might turn out to be the potential for rebellion in Eastern Europe, and that the independence he was encouraging there could sweep the satellite countries out of his control.[82]

Rice's assertiveness that day set a pattern of willingness, at least then, to speak up and assert her views to those who outranked her. "The White House has a caste system, assistants talk to assistants, that type of thing, but she wasn't afraid to reach beyond her caste," recalled Andrew Card, who was the White House deputy chief of staff for most of George H. W. Bush's administration. Card saw Rice's ability to work with strong personalities like Blackwill, who had a temper and a tendency to speak forcefully and sometimes condescendingly—a "lousy bedside manner," in the words of Card. "Condi was someone who didn't seem particularly fazed by how gruff anybody was," Card said.[83]

Another of Rice's early tasks at the White House was to scrounge up money for economic benefits for Poland, where the Communist government was in talks with the trade union Solidarity that would lead to free elections and ultimately the end of forty years of Communist rule. "She beat the bushes and came up with funds that people were not using for certain programs," Scowcroft recalled. "It was paltry, $150 million or something. I was hoping for a billion. But she did that, and she really helped think through how we went about this, how we encouraged reform in Eastern Europe without bringing about a Soviet reaction. It wasn't revolution, but it was careful diplomacy."[84]

That April, Rice also helped draft a speech the president delivered to a Polish-American community in Hamtramck, Michigan, which linked a modest American aid program for the Polish government to political change in Poland and Eastern Europe.[85] In the careful language of the forty-first presidency, Bush said the stirrings toward open political expression in the Soviet bloc were viewed by the United States "with prudence, realism and patience."[86]

While Rice's attention was focused on matters of state, events in her family competed for attention. In July, Rice paid a visit to Palo Alto to preside over a reception at the Stanford Faculty Club in celebration of the wedding of her father and Clara. Without telling anyone, including Rice, the two had been quietly married in Las Vegas in March. The newlyweds let Rice in on the news in April when they visited Washington, and Rice later professed no hurt that her father had kept his wedding a secret from her. "She was a church lady," Rice said of Clara. "They wanted to live together. She was not about to live with him without getting married. So they got married early. No, it didn't bother me. It was fine."[87] Whatever else she may have felt, Rice's overwhelming emotion at the time was relief that her father would have someone to care for him. She sent out a card with wording along the lines that "Condoleezza Rice would like to announce" the wedding of John and Clara, a construction that put her in an active role and sent the message to friends and family back in Birmingham that she approved of her father's remarriage.[88]

Rice's duties plunged her more and more into the fast-changing situation in the Soviet Union and that fall she had an encounter that became one of the most often told stories about her steeliness in the face of confrontation. On September 12, the White House invited Yeltsin, the former Moscow party chief who was then the leader of the parliamentary opposition to Gorbachev, to a meeting in the West Wing with Scowcroft. In what was to be an encounter reflecting the delicacy of the diplomacy at the time, the president was to drop by unannounced and shake Yeltsin's hand, thereby avoiding the potent symbolism of an Oval Office meeting while Gorbachev was in power. But when Yeltsin's limousine pulled up to meet Rice at the West Wing basement entrance, used by foreign officials and members of Congress in part to avoid the press, Yeltsin thought it was the service entrance and threw a fit. When he learned that his appointment was with Scowcroft and not the president, he threw another fit and refused to get out of the car. Rice stood her ground and told Yeltsin in Russian that if he didn't want to see Scowcroft he might as well return to his hotel. Then she grabbed his elbow and, in the words of Gates, "essentially propelled" Yeltsin up the stairs to Scowcroft's office.[89] "He struck me as mercurial and difficult," Rice later said.[90]

Yeltsin did meet briefly with Bush, but the sensitivities reflected the ongoing debate in the administration over how much to support Gorbachev over Yeltsin, who was considered a democrat and favored by hawks like Dick Cheney, then the defense secretary. But Scowcroft, and Rice, took what they considered the more realist view and supported Gorbachev, the Soviet leader who they saw as in the position to negotiate an arms deal and offer steps to ease tensions with the West. "I never thought he was a democrat, but he was an intellectual," Scowcroft said. "And he was careful and cautious. After all, he was running the country."[91]

But events soon engulfed both Gorbachev and Washington. In November, after months of protests and only hours after East Germany lifted travel restrictions to the West, tens of thousands of Germans took history into their own hands and clambered across the Berlin Wall. The spontaneous act spread euphoria on November 10 and 11 through Washington, Berlin, Bonn, Paris, and London, but the first reaction from Gorbachev, in the words of Rice at the time, was one of "barely disguised panic."[92] On November 10, Rice and Gates received a message from Gorbachev for Bush, hand-delivered by a Soviet emissary, which they found both insecure and threatening.[93] In the letter Gorbachev complained of the "political extremism" he saw in West Germany and warned of the potential for destabilization in Central Europe "on a larger scale." Rice and Gates phoned Scowcroft at home and suggested that he alert the Germans.[94]

Over the next year, Rice was a junior but important player in the delicate dance that transformed the German protests and the crumbling of the Communist regime into the unification of East and West Germany—all without a military response from Moscow and despite the fears of the major powers in Europe who, forty-four years after Hitler, did not want a strong new German state in their midst. No one had expected the Russian satellites to implode as fast as they did, and for the United States the challenge was to manage the process by building consensus among the European powers but asserting American leadership toward the goal of a unified Germany.

The first test of American diplomacy came in December 1989 during a summit of Bush and Gorbachev in a winter gale on the Mediterranean island of Malta, where the two met on the Soviet cruise liner *Maxim Gorky*. To prepare for what became known as the "seasick summit," and in the face of conflicting signals from Moscow, Rice drafted the National Security Council staff's best estimate for the president of where Gorbachev stood on reunification. Her assessment was that the Soviets had lost control of the rebellion in Eastern Europe and were opposed to German reunification, which they thought "would rip the heart out of the Soviet security system." Their "worst nightmare," Rice wrote, was of a reunified Germany allied with NATO that would lead to disintegration of the Warsaw Pact and move the Soviet line of defense back to the Ukrainian border.[95] To avoid alarming Gorbachev, Bush did not push hard or fast for reunification at the summit, and Gorbachev did not at first appear gravely concerned about Germany.[96] He was, however, surprised by Rice, and used her to make a blunt point expressing doubt that the Americans understood his own predicament. At the start of the first meeting on the *Gorky*, Bush introduced Rice to Gorbachev as the woman "who tells me everything I know about the Soviet Union," and Gorbachev responded in Russian, in what Rice took to be a snide tone, with "Well, I hope she knows a lot."[97]

By January 1990, when constant demonstrations on the streets in East Germany were making it clear that the country was disintegrating and reunification was moving faster than policymaking in Washington, the view of the Bush administration shifted. Blackwill asked Rice to make an assessment for Scowcroft of what Gorbachev might do if the United States stepped up the pace for a new democratic, unified, and West-leaning Germany. Rice wrote that the Soviet leader would be alarmed, but that he was in a difficult position and so in her view the United States should go ahead and hit the accelerator. "I believe (and this is a hunch and I guess if we did this that I would spend a lot of time in church praying that I was right) that the Soviets would not even threaten the Germans," she wrote.[98]

The next month Rice accompanied Baker and Gates to Moscow and got a look firsthand at how the country she had studied for sixteen years, since that first day in Korbel's class, was coming apart. Baker was in Moscow to meet with Gorbachev in early talks about how reunification might proceed, and Rice met separately with an adviser to Gorbachev, Vadim Zagladin, whose candor offered a glimpse into the chaos at the Kremlin. Zagladin came to the meeting in a frenzy an hour late and told her, she recalled, "I'm sorry, but every day we come in to see what disaster's befallen us."[99]

The next month, Rice was in Europe and mired in an elaborate forum for the two Germanys and the four World War II victors to negotiate reunification. Known as the Two-plus-Four negotiations, the talks had been the idea of the State Department to let the Europeans and Soviet Union participate in the decision process, but the goal was also to use the talks to insure that America got its way. Nonetheless, the administration saw the negotiations as highly risky because the allies might not stay in line, or worse, Moscow could use its seat on the forum as a platform against the United States. A long memo for the president, drafted principally by Rice, warned that "we should be under no illusions about the dangers that these talks pose," and added that it was "critical that we get the administration's position formulated and then coordinated with the Allies so that we do not mismanage what will arguably be the most important set of talks for the West in the postwar period."[100]

Rice was part of the three-member U.S. delegation sent by Secretary of State Baker to the first Two-plus-Four meeting for midlevel officials in Bonn on March 14, and she reported mixed results to the White House. "The Soviets were not prepared to be very directive or clear about what they want," Rice wrote. "They held their fire today and seemed somewhat unprepared. That's the good news." The bad news, in her view, was signs of weakening Western solidarity—the British wanted a peace treaty with Germany, for example, and the French were resisting coordinated Western attempts to gang up on the Soviets with a German fait accompli.[101]

In March, the White House announced that Bush and Gorbachev would meet for a five-day summit in Washington and Camp David in late May and early June. By April, when Eduard Shevardnadze, the Soviet foreign minister, was in the capital for pre-summit talks with Baker, another crisis was on the table. This time it was Lithuania, which had declared its independence from the Soviet Union on March 11. Gorbachev had responded by sending tanks into the streets of the capital, Vilnius, and the administration warned Shevardnadze against a violent crackdown. But Bush, seeing too much uncertainty in Soviet relations and too much at stake over Germany, chose not to impose sanctions or bluster in public against Moscow. Explaining the president's caution, Rice later told a reporter that Bush was "afraid to light a match in a gas-filled room."[102]

In May, Rice accompanied Baker and Dennis Ross, the State Department's director of policy planning, for more pre-summit talks in Moscow, where Baker found Gorbachev under enormous pressure on Germany and felt the issue was "overloading his circuits."[103] Baker made no headway on what had emerged as the main sticking point between the two countries: The United States wanted a unified Germany to be a member of NATO but the Soviet Union, fearful of the powerful military alliance that would be arrayed on its western border, was reverting to its hardened view of its own security needs. At one point Shevardnadze abruptly canceled a critical negotiating session and a frustrated Baker asked Rice and Ross what they thought was going on. To find out, the two headed to the foreign ministry meeting house and barged in to find a large group of Soviet officials immobilized in a strategy session and in no position to negotiate with the American secretary of state.[104] "We said, you know, 'the secretary's waiting,' " Rice recalled. The Soviets told her, " 'We're not ready, we're not ready.' People were pretty panicked, actually."[105] Zagladin, the Gorbachev adviser, summed up the view in Moscow perfectly when he told Rice on the same trip that "there used to be two Germanys—one was ours and one was yours. Now there will be one and you want it to be yours."[106]

On May 31 in Washington, in an atmosphere of high drama and uncertainty, Gorbachev arrived for a ceremony on the White House South Lawn, and in a meeting later that day astonished the Americans and even his own aides when he said that a unified Germany could choose for itself whether to become a member of NATO—in effect, a capitulation to the U.S. position, because both sides knew that Germany would readily join the Atlantic Alliance.[107] Administration officials, scarcely able to believe what was happening, did not dare announce the apparent agreement until they had it in writing, but at a White House state dinner that evening Gorbachev said in his toast that he expected "major results" from the summit, and Shevardnadze, when asked by reporters if Gorbachev was referring to a unified Germany in NATO, said yes.[108] Rice, who was a guest at the Thursday night state dinner and would be up all of Friday night helping to draft a presidential statement that would include wording on NATO acceptable to both sides, nervously tried to lower expectations. "I wouldn't try to tot it up until after Saturday," she told reporters at the White House.[109]

The air of mayhem in the summit was reflected even in the side agreements. As the deadline approached, Gorbachev and Bush agreed to a trade deal moments before they were to appear in a grand East Room ceremony to sign a series of summit accords, but even that trade agreement was so unexpected that no one at the White House even had a copy of the documents for signature. Someone had to scurry the few blocks to the Commerce Department to fetch them while Rice stood in the Red Room, with Bush and Gorbachev impatiently looking over her shoulder, frantically adding some handwritten comments about the trade deal into the president's prepared remarks. "He said, 'No, you don't have to do that,' and I said, 'Yes—yes, I do,' " Rice said, referring to the president. "Because I wanted the words to be exact."[110]

Later that night, Rice helped draft a statement for Bush to deliver at the joint press conference that would close the summit on Sunday morning. The idea was for Bush to say that while he and the allies believed that a united Germany should be in NATO and Gorbachev did not, they were in "full agreement" that it was a matter for the Germans to decide.[111] Rice passed the draft to the Soviet ambassador, Alexander Bessmertnykh, to show to Gorbachev, then headed to Camp David for the continuation of the summit on Saturday. She attended a dinner there that evening, then waited tensely through the night with Blackwill for the Soviet reaction to the NATO statement. Early Sunday morning Bessmertnykh finally passed the word to Blackwill that Gorbachev had no objection to the president's planned remarks.[112]

The summit was done, hailed as a historic turning point. But for Rice there was an upsetting personal denouement. After the events in Washington, she flew with a group of administration officials accompanying Gorbachev on a cross-country trip that included a stop at Stanford, where Rice helped lead Gorbachev on a tour of the campus and had a seat on stage when he delivered an address at the university.[113] It was a splashy homecoming for Rice, overshadowed only by what appeared to be a racial incident at the end of the visit. Rice was the only black member of the presidential delegation waiting to say goodbye to Gorbachev and his wife, Raisa, at the San Francisco International Airport when a California-based Secret Service agent ordered her to leave the tarmac and stay behind the security barricades. Rice, who was wearing a White House identification pin, objected and said she was a member of the official delegation, but the agent ignored her, placed both hands on her shoulders, shoved hard, and shouted, "I told you to get back there!" As Rice demanded to know the man's identity, White House officials pulled the agent aside, and Rice regained her composure to say goodbye to the Gorbachevs in

Russian.[114] Marlin Fitzwater, George H. W. Bush's press secretary, later said the president was "very upset about it."[115]

On August 2, 1990, Iraq invaded Kuwait and the attention of the Bush administration, and the world, abruptly and dramatically shifted to the Persian Gulf. Rice continued to work on German reunification, but the next month, when she was in Moscow for the signing of the treaty that would pave the way for the two Germanys to finally reunite, the mood was anticlimactic.[116] The treaty, which concluded seven months of the Two-plus-Four negotiations, required the four World War II victors to give up their occupation rights over Berlin and German territory, which had been established at the Potsdam Conference of July and August 1945.[117] "The new Germany is here," Baker said in his remarks at the ceremony, held on September 12. "Let our legacy be that after 45 years, we finally got the political arithmetic right. Two plus four adds up to one Germany in a Europe whole and free."[118] The momentous words somehow did not find their setting at the ceremony, which was held in the lobby of the Communist Party's Oktyabrskaya Hotel rather than in the palaces of the Kremlin and included only one head of state, Gorbachev, who was overwhelmed at the time by the growing Soviet economic crisis and challenges to his leadership. Rice could not help but notice how Gorbachev stood behind the others, hidden among the midlevel officials and not far from the hotel waiters preparing to pour champagne.[119]

Years later, one of Rice's favorite themes was to point out that German reunification was made possible by forty years of allied cooperation and a trust in the structures—NATO, the transatlantic alliance—that were put in place by farsighted diplomats at the end of World War II. But she also said that American power backed by careful diplomacy ensured that the Russians did not feel so crushed in defeat that they responded with war.

"We were in a very good structural environment," Rice said. "The Soviet Union was coming apart. And it had to be managed carefully, and what I think President George H. W. Bush did so well was to manage that in a way that the Soviets actually believed there were no losers. Or they were at least able to pretend that there were no losers. Because people always say, you know, 'They had no options.' Of course they had options. They had three and a half million men in Europe, they had 30,000 nuclear warheads. What was to say they were just going to go quietly into the night? And I think that's the value of diplomacy—letting the other guy have the face-saving way out."[120]

By January 1991, when American bombs were raining down on Baghdad for the start of the Gulf War, Rice had already made plans to go back to Stanford. It was a difficult choice. Although she had no central role in the war, she had helped manage a critical U.S. relationship with a Gorbachev adviser, Yevgeny Primakov, whom Gorbachev had tasked with trying to delay the use of force against Saddam Hussein.[121] Rice knew that her job would get more interesting, and she was right—Yeltsin would be inaugurated in July as the first freely elected president of the Russian Republic. On December 25, Gorbachev would resign and bring to an end the seventy-four-year-old Soviet Union.

But Rice also knew that she had to get back to California if she wanted to continue in an academic career. Stanford, like other universities, generally gave its faculty members only two years away before they risked losing tenure. After her time at the center of the action as the world turned upside down, Rice was also exhausted from her long hours, seven days a week. Burns, her deputy, remembered that she told him, "I want to have some time to myself, I want to have a personal life, I want to work out, I want to have friends."[122]

But there was an odd and in its way prophetic final episode as she left the arena but first flirted with another round of a different sort. Around the same time, Rice turned down an overture to fill the United States Senate seat in California left vacant by Pete Wilson, the Republican who was elected governor in 1990. Wilson, who had four years left in his Senate term, could appoint his successor, and he called Rice in Washington and asked if she was interested.[123] Under California law, Rice would have had to face election in 1992 for the balance of Wilson's term, meaning that she would have had to start campaigning the moment she took office, very possibly against long odds. Rice told Wilson she was flattered but not interested. Years later, Wilson said he didn't know if he actually would have chosen

Rice had she said yes—there were two or three others he was considering—but he came away feeling that her mind was clearly made up. "She really did not have the fire in the belly, and I had made the point that it was pretty much a requirement," Wilson said.[124]

Rice, who would have had the support of the president if she had run in California, equivocated more than Wilson knew. "There were a couple of weeks when she really thought about this, you know, and 'what do I do?' " Nicholas Burns said. But it seemed too daunting. "I remember her telling me, 'I have to raise twenty million dollars to run for the Senate, and I'll have to spend every single moment campaigning,' " Burns said.[125] In the end, Wilson chose a moderate Republican real estate entrepreneur, John Seymour, who was easily defeated the following year by the former mayor of San Francisco, Dianne Feinstein—as Rice very well might have been herself.

To Clara Rice, her stepdaughter's decision was in character. "I've always worried if she comes tumbling down, I'm really going to have to be there to help catch her, because it's going to be hard," Clara Rice said. "I just can't see her taking failure. And I think that's why she has never run for any office. It's always where she's appointed. Because I think she knows she stands the risk of losing. And just the thought of losing, I don't think that would go too well with her."[126]

CHAPTER 6

I Don't Do Committees

Stanford, 1991–2000

Rice returned to Stanford in the spring of 1991 noticeably changed, at least to her old Democratic friends, who found her more confident, more ambitious, and more openly conservative. Terry Karl, the Stanford political science professor who had become good friends with Rice in the late 1980s, was startled that fall when Rice took the side of Clarence Thomas, the conservative African-American jurist Bush had nominated for the Supreme Court, against Anita Hill, a black law professor who said Thomas had sexually harassed her when she was his assistant. Karl knew how much Rice had helped young black women scholars like Jendayi Frazer, and her defense of Thomas did not seem in character. "Condi said, 'I can't believe they're doing this to him,' " Karl recalled. "And I said, 'What are you talking about?' And she said, 'Well, you can't believe her.' " Karl was also surprised to hear Rice tell her that welfare recipients were taking advantage of the government and that they needed to pull themselves up on their own. "I remember saying, 'Condi, there are a lot of people who are ill, who can't get out of poverty because of their circumstances, who can't function and who can't move forward,' " Karl said. "But that argument didn't sway her. Afterward I said to a colleague, 'That woman has a hard streak in her.' "[1]

Although Rice's service in a Republican administration made her suspect to the many Democrats on Stanford's faculty, George H. W. Bush was so popular after the swift victory in the Gulf War that Rice enjoyed plenty of reflected glory. She quickly made clear she would be no ordinary professor. Using her high profile from her White House experience as a springboard, Rice set about launching herself into powerful political, corporate, and foreign policy circles in California and Washington, and effusively promoting George H. W. Bush along the way.

"He has a deep knowledge of international affairs," Rice told an audience at a Stanford symposium on the Soviet Union in May 1991. "More often than not, when something was written for him, he'd improve it, and you'd sit there thinking to yourself, 'I wish I'd thought of saying that.' "[2] A few years later, Rice would work with Zelikow on an exhaustive and widely praised book on Bush I's careful diplomacy, *Germany Unified and Europe Transformed: A Study in Statecraft.*

One of the most important things Rice did was befriend George Shultz, who had settled into a comfortable life as a Republican elder statesman from a top perch at the Hoover Institution, the conservative think tank on Stanford's campus. Rice joined Hoover as a senior fellow in 1991, an appointment that was in addition to her position on the Stanford faculty. She quickly became part of an informal lunch group with Shultz and Sidney Drell, the arms control expert who had taught Rice the physics of nuclear weapons when she first came to Stanford.

"I was impressed with her, and so Sid and I said, 'Let's add her to our luncheon club,' " Shultz recalled.[3] (A fourth member was Lucy Shapiro, a professor of developmental biology at Stanford Medical School.) Every three or four weeks, the group got together for conversations that ranged from physics to biology to economics to politics. "Condi was very much a part of that," Shultz said. "It was the kind of discussion that was really stimulating, and you couldn't predict what was going to come up."[4]

Soon Rice asked Shultz to help her move into a bigger forum. "She came in to see me one day, and she said, 'I feel as if I ought to learn more about management and how it operates, because that's such a big part of how the United States operates,' " Shultz recalled. As Rice knew, Shultz was on the board of Chevron, which had its corporate headquarters in San Francisco. "So I said to Condi, 'How about a big, bad oil company?' " Shultz recalled. "And she said, 'Well, I think oil companies are very interesting companies because they have a global viewpoint.' " Shultz introduced Rice to Kenneth Derr, Chevron's chairman and chief executive, who took Rice to lunch and, Shultz said, "inside of fifteen minutes concluded that she would make a terrific board member."[5] However charming Rice was that day, her contacts and expertise in the former Soviet Union clearly appealed to Chevron. Rice went on the Chevron board in May 1991, only a year before the company signed an agreement with the new nation of Kazakhstan, a former Soviet republic, to invest $10 billion over forty years to develop the country's Tengiz field, one of the largest deposits of oil in the world.[6] Chevron owned half the field, and over the decade that Rice would serve on the board, she worked closely on the deal that culminated in the opening in March 2001 of a nine-hundred-mile pipeline from Kazakhstan to a Russian port on the Black Sea.[7] Rice knew the Kazakh president, Nursultan Nazarbayev, and she traveled to Kazakhstan for Chevron in 1992. In 1993, Chevron named a supertanker after her, the 129,000-ton SS *Condoleezza Rice*. But in the face of criticism about the Bush administration's ties to big oil—including a suit against Chevron charging human rights abuses in Nigeria—the company quietly renamed the tanker the *Altair Voyager* in the spring of 2001.[8] Rice resigned from the board on January 15, 2001, less than a week before she became national security adviser.[9]

In 1991 Rice also joined the board of Transamerica, the insurance giant based in San Francisco, and the following year became a member of the board of the Hewlett-Packard Corporation in Palo Alto. Rice was with Hewlett-Packard only a year, but she remained with Transamerica until 1999 and picked up other board memberships along the way. In 1994 she joined J. P. Morgan's International Council, a paid advisory position, and in 1999 she became a board member of the Charles Schwab Corporation.[10] In the early 1990s, Rice was making an estimated $35,000 in annual board fees from each company, meaning that by her second year back at Stanford, when she served simultaneously on three boards, she likely received around $100,000 to supplement a faculty salary of about $125,000.[11] By the time Rice became national security adviser, she reported annual

Chevron board fees of $60,000 and holdings of more than $250,000 in Chevron stock.[12]

In those early months back at Stanford, Rice also served on a redistricting commission that Governor Pete Wilson appointed to redraw the state's political boundaries, joined the Aspen Strategy Group of foreign policy specialists, and became a member of the Lincoln Club, a Republican group led by Tom Ford, a major Silicon Valley developer whose wife, Susan, became one of Rice's good friends.[13]

The most crucial professional move Rice made in this period was to join the search committee for Stanford's new president. Rice was one of about ten people on the panel, which included faculty, trustees, and students. In keeping with what had now become a pattern, Rice was the committee member who made the biggest impression on Gerhard Casper, the University of Chicago provost and the committee's ultimate choice. As Casper told the story, Rice came with the Stanford group to interview him for the job at his Chicago apartment in early 1992, and she stood out for her answers to his questions about Stanford's budget troubles and other problems of the time. "Condi, who does not beat about the bush, just was extremely straightforward in her answers, to questions going from the finances of Stanford to the political climate at the university," Casper said. "She simply never pretended that things were any different from what they were."[14]

Casper, a German-born intellectual with a law degree from Yale, became Stanford's new president in September 1992. It was one of the few times the university had not selected one of its own as president, but there had been little choice. Stanford was staggering under the weight of a financial scandal and huge budget deficits and the trustees wanted an outsider to clean things up. Specifically, the university faced claims that it had overcharged the federal government by more than $200 million for the indirect costs of government research, and that it had misappropriated the excess money for luxuries like a yacht. (Indirect costs, negotiated between universities and the government, are hard-to-quantify expenses like electricity and water associated with federal grants. Before a whistle-blower set the exposure of the scandal in motion, Stanford had an indirect cost rate of 76 percent, meaning that if Stanford had, say, a $1 million contract to do research work for NASA, the university charged the space agency an additional 76 percent, or $760,000, for indirect costs. As a result of the scandal, in 1991, Stanford's indirect cost rate was reduced to 55.5 percent, which was a major reason it was facing a budget crisis. In 1994 Stanford negotiated a settlement to pay $1.2 million to the government and the government acknowledged that Stanford had done nothing wrong.)[15]

One of Casper's first duties was to find a number two. He dutifully appointed a search committee for provost, a Stanford tradition he viewed as cumbersome and excessively consensual. "Here there was a search committee for everything," Casper said.[16] So when the search committee came up with a list of recommendations, none of them Rice, Casper, according to Chip Blacker and other faculty members, ignored them and picked the young black woman who had so impressed him in Chicago.[17] Casper's version differs: In his telling, he was the chairman of the search committee, he controlled it, and Rice's name did appear on the list of recommendations, although Casper would not say how it got there. He did acknowledge that "as far as I know, nobody outside the search committee, and outside my mind, was thinking about Condi as provost."[18]

On campus that was the understatement of the year. At thirty-eight, Rice was not only the first black, the first woman, and the youngest person to be named Stanford provost, she also had never been a dean or a department head, the normal route for advancement, and was still only an associate professor. (In May, after Casper made his decision, the university quickly made Rice a full professor, a move that drew criticism from other women faculty members who said that Rice had not published enough for such a promotion.)[19] Casper knew his choice would be controversial—among others, he reached out for advice to Shultz, who urged him to make the appointment.[20] Casper later said that "there was no one explanation" for his decision,[21] although the view among many faculty members was that Casper knew that Rice would have the toughness to make budget cuts across the board, including in minority programs, and as a minority herself could give him some political cover.

"I have generally not believed in career patterns," Casper later said. "If somebody strikes me as very good, then why not try her? And Condi after all, when she had been at the National Security Council, had to deal with people who had great egos." Her youth and gender were important in the decision, he said, and "the fact that she was black also wasn't totally irrelevant."[22]

Rice took office in September 1993 at an especially bleak time. As provost, she was the chief academic officer in charge of 1,400 faculty members serving fourteen thousand students as well as the chief budget officer who had to bring costs at the sprawling university under control. Stanford, which was also reeling from the costs of damage sustained by a 1989 earthquake, needed to slash $25 million from what was then its $1.2 billion annual budget.[23] There already had been several rounds of cuts totaling $40 million, and little fat was left. Rice immediately started laying off staff, cutting services, eliminating programs, and letting people know that things would be different under a new regime. "I don't do committees," she infamously said in one of her first Faculty Senate meetings, and she meant it.[24]

Rice quickly dispensed with the existing provost's budget committee of some thirty people and instead formed a small group of about six or eight that met in her office every Monday at 8 A.M. "There wasn't a lot of messing around," recalled Timothy Warner, who attended as the vice provost in charge of the university's budget. Rice called this new streamlined committee the "ungroup" and relied on them for some advice, but, Warner recalled, "Condi and I would sit down and make the decisions."[25] Although Rice had no experience with billion-dollar budgets, she learned quickly and did not always take even Warner's advice.[26] "Condi pushed it very hard, and that was a good thing to do," Casper said. "We were incredibly parsimonious."[27] In two years, Rice had cut the needed $25 million out of the budget and announced that the university was running a small surplus.[28]

Although Rice was now the darling of the board of trustees, she had started to antagonize the faculty for a confrontational style as well as the substance of her cuts. Rice's budget battles spread into other fights over Stanford's curriculum and into standoffs with women, blacks, and Chicanos over affirmative action. Stories circulated on campus about how Rice would lose her temper and publicly berate faculty members who opposed her. "I don't think Condi ever looked for fights, but I don't think she ever couched what she said to avoid fights," said Paul Brest, one of Rice's friends who was the dean of Stanford's law school at the time. "She also played an important role for Gerhard, who hated criticism. She was his lightning rod."[29] Other friends said that Rice lashed out because of frequent condescension from older faculty members. "There were deans who came in and treated her dismissively and felt she could be rolled, and she overreacted to that—'Okay tough guy, I'm going to tell you who's boss,' " said Randy Bean.[30]

The end result was bewilderment on a campus that thought of itself as a community, and not, as Rice saw it, a corporation that needed shaping up. Increasingly under fire, she seemed to have forgotten the lessons she had learned during German reunification about consultative diplomacy. "People will accept all kinds of decisions if they think their voices have been heard," Brest said. "I don't think Condi valued, in that context, hearing diverse points of view, or hearing points of view that disagreed with or challenged her own point of view. So she would come to decisions, whether correct or not substantively, without the kind of consultation that got people to buy in."[31]

But Rice was in a hurry. "Stanford had a very consensual style of decision-making, and I wasn't going to be able to make those changes consensually, and I knew it," Rice said years later. When asked why, she responded, "Because you don't get it done." Her only regret, she said, was that she had sometimes been too harsh. "I learned that, sometimes, my tendency to be very sharp, particularly with people who were in a subordinate position, was not a good thing, because it tended to make people fearful," she said. "And so I learned to do that better."[32] In the view of much of Stanford's faculty, Rice's high-handed style foreshadowed the unilateralism of the Bush administration's first term.

Her relationship with Casper foreshadowed in many ways her bond with George W. Bush. Casper gave Rice a free hand and enormous power, and the two talked and dropped into each other's offices throughout the day. But Rice, in Casper's telling, never challenged him or overstepped her authority. "Condi always knew that the buck stopped in my office, and that the important decisions had to be made by me," Casper said. "And, of course, she was extremely loyal. She will never stab anybody in the back, including her enemies. She will diminish her enemies, cut them down, do whatever. But she will not stab them in the back."[33]

Rice's first big confrontation with minorities came only six months into her job, in March 1994, when in the name of budget cuts she laid off Cecilia Burciaga, Stanford's highest-ranking Chicano administrator. Burciaga was an associate dean in student affairs, and she and her husband and son lived at Casa Zapata, a Stanford dormitory for Chicanos and others interested in multiculturalism. More to the point for Rice, Burciaga had been the affirmative action officer who handled the administrative details of her hiring as a tenure-track professor in 1981, and the two had been friendly. But on the first day of Stanford's spring break, Rice called in Burciaga and told her that although the university thought well of her, the financial situation was so dire that she would have to go. "She just very cavalierly says, 'Not about you, good performance, this is just money,' " Burciaga recalled. "As I was walking out, I heard her say to her secretary, she took a breath and said, 'Who's next?' "[34]

Burciaga's firing triggered protests and a three-day hunger strike by four students in Stanford's Main Quad, just steps from Rice's office. Burciaga had been publicly critical of Stanford's record on improving diversity, and she, for one, thought her dismissal was retaliatory.[35] Burciaga was also popular among students, and her plight got generous coverage in the *San Jose Mercury News*. "What Was Stanford Thinking?" was the headline over a column by Joe Rodriguez, an editorial writer.[36] But Rice was determined to prove her toughness and to make the point that no one was exempt from budget cuts. In private, she was dismissive of the hunger strikers. Several days into the protest, a friend asked Rice how she was holding up. "She said, 'What do you mean?' " the friend recalled. "And I said, 'It's been a really rough week.' She said, 'Well, I haven't missed any meals.' "[37]

The strike ended when Casper and Rice gave in to some of the students' demands—they agreed to consider adding a department of Chicano studies to the university, for example[38]—but the bad feelings on both sides persisted. "I try to be warm," Rice told the *San Jose Mercury News* after the strike. "We're having to do some tough things. You can't pretend there's a fantasy world out there and no one is going to lose a job."[39] Burciaga and her family were given until August 1 to move out of the Stanford dorm, and the following year, Burciaga's husband died of cancer. Burciaga blamed Rice for the stress that she said led to her husband's death.[40]

At around the same time, Rice came under fire from African-American students about Stanford's commitment to them in particular and to diversity in general. Black Student Union members demanded that Rice come and speak to them, and she did, at a protest gathering in a university auditorium. Chip Blacker, who was there, recalled that while Rice was on stage, a white student spoke up and challenged the new provost's commitment to civil rights. "And Condi's face just got super-hard, and her eyes—I don't know if you've ever seen them, but they can be like lasers—and she said, 'I don't need a lecture from anyone on race. I've been black all my life.' "[41]

Rice's rise in a largely white world seemed to have created a new sensitivity in her to suggestions that she wasn't sufficiently black, but success had also given her the platform and self-confidence to aggressively push back. Luis Fraga, an associate professor of political science, recalled how Rice once reprimanded him after they disagreed in a committee meeting about how to award affirmative action fellowships to Stanford Ph.D. candidates. As Fraga recalled it, he thought it was important to consider whether a candidate's dissertation topic related to affirmative action—a study of American politics and race would be more desirable than one on European integration, for example—and Rice did not. Words were exchanged, and after the meeting, Rice asked Fraga to stay for a moment. "She told me, as I recall, 'You cannot tell me that I am not black,' " Fraga said. He was surprised by Rice's interpretation of his remarks, and responded that he was trying to make a point about a university policy and not an assessment of her.[42]

Early in 1995, Rice charged into another controversy, this one over her move to shut down Stanford's Food Research Institute, a seventy-four-year-old center focused on agricultural and economic policy in the developing world. The institute was one of three economic departments at Stanford, and in the view of Rice and John Shoven, the dean who oversaw the institute, the center was redundant and not up to the university's academic standards. In the view of the institute's supporters, Rice wanted to show more muscle with the board of trustees and was opposed on ideological grounds to the institute's advocacy of stimulating growth in the Third World. Scott Pearson, the last director of the institute, fought back, but found he could drum up little support among a fearful faculty. People told him, he said, "I don't want to bring down her wrath on my department."[43] There was as much bitterness about Rice's high-handed style. "One of the problems Condi had going from assistant professor to provost was that she had never run a department," said Walter Falcon, the codirector of Stanford's Center for Environmental Sciences and Policy and a former director of the Food Research Institute. "There's a lot of walking in the hall, there's a lot of cajoling, you can't ram things through."[44]

Rice also tangled with the faculty over the undergraduate curriculum, and again, the rancor was as much about her methods as substance. The acrimony, which predated Rice, focused on what Great Books should be required reading for freshmen. For fifty years, from the 1930s into the 1980s, Stanford first-year students had read the usual dead white males in a mandatory course that was called Western Civilization and then Western Culture. But in 1989 the name was changed to Cultures, Ideas and Values, or CIV in the campus shorthand, and included the slave narrative *Equiano's Travels* and authors like Mary Wollstonecraft along with Locke, Hobbes, and Rousseau.[45] The new course was an opening shot in the culture wars, and buried Stanford under an avalanche of bad publicity that portrayed the university as abandoning the Western canon for political correctness. When the course was first proposed, Stanford students on a march with Jesse Jackson had chanted "Hey, hey, ho, ho, Western culture's got to go." William Bennett, then the secretary of education, had responded by turning up in Palo Alto to deplore Stanford's "unfortunate capitulation to a campaign of pressure politics and intimidation."[46]

By the time Rice was provost, most faculty members said the problem with the course was not its perceived political correctness but its sweeping, superficial approach to literature. Rice ordered a review, and yet again was criticized for her tactics in trying to force change that most everyone agreed was necessary. Rice said the members of a course review committee were not "puppets to whom I surreptitiously passed ideas,"[47] but one professor, Carolyn Lougee Chappell, resigned from teaching CIV to protest what she saw as Rice's domination of the process. Later she challenged one of Rice's statements about the course at a faculty meeting. "She said, 'Don't put words in my mouth, Carolyn!' " Chappell recalled. "She exploded at me."[48]

Marsh McCall, a classics professor who was then the dean of Stanford's adult education program, found himself on the wrong side of Rice when he criticized Casper in the public forum of a Faculty Senate meeting for what McCall thought was a frivolous university advertising campaign. The next day Rice summoned McCall, an elected member of the Senate and a self-described rabble-rouser, and told him that he had hurt Casper's feelings and that he should write him a note of apology, which McCall agreed to do. But then Rice said that since McCall was a Stanford dean, never mind his role as an elected member of the Senate, his criticism amounted to an act of disloyalty against the administration. "She said, 'It really raises the question whether you can be a member of this team, if you're going to fly off the handle in public,' " McCall said.[49] In McCall's view, Rice was trying to shut down dissent, which he saw as "just 180 degrees opposite to my vision of what goes on at a great university."[50]

Rice's most bitter confrontation was with women faculty members over discrimination, even though the women had at first welcomed Rice as one of their own. "I did have high hopes," said Cecilia Ridgeway, a sociology professor.[51] But those hopes faded as Rice made public statements about her opposition to affirmative action at the time of tenure and as at least a half dozen women were denied promotions or appointments on her watch.[52] By March 1998, when Rice upheld a decision to deny tenure to a history professor, Karen Sawislak, the anger boiled over. A group of about a half dozen women humanities professors got together, compiled statistics, and wrote a report that showed there had been a slight drop-off in the tenure rate of women at Stanford.[53]

Ridgeway took on the task of presenting the report in a Faculty Senate meeting, a responsibility that included a run-through with a steering committee the week before. To Ridgeway's surprise, Rice turned up at the run-through and sharply challenged the report's methodology. "For half an hour, she was berating me," Ridgeway said. "I was flabbergasted." To Ridgeway, Rice's performance "was power politics, and the kind you never see in academe. I also thought, she has a temper, and she's going to have to learn how to manage that, or it would give her trouble."[54]

By the time of the meeting, Rice had prepared her own report on women at Stanford, complete with overhead slides, which not only questioned the women's statistics but denied that a problem existed. The result was that at the Faculty Senate meeting in the university's law school auditorium on May 14, 1998, two wildly divergent reports were presented on the status of women at Stanford. Each side analyzed the issue in a different way and angry fireworks broke out. But the indisputable starting point, at least according to the American Association of University Professors, was that in 1998 women accounted for 14.4 percent of tenured professors at Stanford, a figure that ranked the university twenty-fourth out of twenty-six public and private institutions surveyed, including Princeton, Columbia, and the University of California at Berkeley. (Stanford had good company as it scraped the bottom. Harvard, where 14.3 percent of tenured faculty were women, ranked twenty-fifth, and Yale ranked twenty-third, with 15.3 percent. The Massachusetts Institute of Technology was last, with 10.4 percent.)[55]

Ridgeway went first and said her data showed that the percentage of tenure-track women professors at Stanford had declined in recent years and that there was "some slight indication that the slope of tenure rates for women is declining."[56] She also reported that the percentage of women faculty was well below the available pool of women scholars in each of Stanford's schools.[57] Overall, Ridgeway described an increasing sense of unease about the university's commitment to gender equity and diversity.[58]

Rice, up next, disputed Ridgeway. "Given that I'm the provost and I'm the chief academic officer, so I'm the one more responsible for this area, I'd like it to be very clear that I simply do not believe that there has been a turning back," she said.[59] Rice presented statistics that she said showed increases in the percentages of women faculty, both tenured and not, and stated that women and men were granted tenure at Stanford at the same rate.[60] "I want to say this as clearly as I can because a lot of the extrapolation from a few high-profile cases out there, I think, has sunk the morale of a lot of our junior faculty needlessly," Rice said.[61] She repeated her own position that she "strongly supported" affirmative action at the time of hiring but "completely opposed" it at the time of tenure.[62]

A group of about twenty-five women faculty members in the back of the auditorium were outraged. Barbara Babcock, the first woman professor in Stanford's law school, spoke up and said the group in the back wouldn't be there if they didn't feel "a sense of despair and crisis" about the treatment of women at Stanford.[63] Then she told Rice that "if you don't want to call it a crisis, don't call it a crisis, just treat it as a problem that requires immediate, expert attention now."[64] But the most heated and significant exchange occurred between Rice and Susan Okin, a political science professor, who referred to a document signed by a former dean of the school of humanities and sciences, Norm Wessells. Okin, who has since died, said the document indicated that a form of affirmative action was applied at the time of tenure decisions from at least 1983 to 1993.[65] "I would like to know when exactly that policy changed, who changed it, and whom they consulted about the change, and also why it was changed, especially during a period when Stanford is supposedly trying to increase the diversity of the university," Okin said.[66] Rice's response would come back to haunt her. "The Wessells paper is a statement of the policies and procedures in the Wessells administration," she said. "I'm the chief academic officer now, and I am telling you that, in principle, I do not believe in, and in fact will not apply, affirmative action criteria at the time of tenure."[67]

Later, Rice invited some of the women to dinner at Lake House, the provost's official home where she entertained. (Rice lived in smaller faculty housing.) The women thought there would be reconciliation, but in their telling, Rice reprimanded them instead. "She was calling us on the carpet," Babcock recalled. "The message was you're a bunch of whiners and you're old and time has passed you by and this is not going to help the cause of women."[68] A business school professor, Joanne Martin, was so upset that her voice broke as she spoke to Rice, but Rice, in the recollection of Babcock, remained "cool and untouched" throughout the evening.[69]

Six months after the Faculty Senate meeting, the United States Department of Labor began an investigation into whether Stanford had engaged in gender discrimination and violated federal affirmative action laws in its hiring and promotion of women faculty.[70] The probe had in part been triggered by Rice's comments on affirmative action in the Faculty Senate. Her words "contain the suggestion that she doesn't believe in affirmative action programs and the university doesn't have one," Gary Buff, the Labor Department attorney who forwarded the case for investigation, told the *San Jose Mercury News*. "If that's the case, that's a potential violation."[71]

The Labor Department inquiry grew out of a complaint brought by a half dozen women researchers at Stanford who compiled statistics, Rice's statements, and case studies into a four-hundred-page report that they then forwarded to investigators. Karen Sawislak, the history professor who was denied tenure, was one of the case studies, as was Colleen Crangle, a former research scientist at Stanford's medical school who won a gender discrimination case against the university and then settled on appeal.[72] As Crangle saw it, Rice had been the beneficiary of affirmative action at the time of tenure, even though she denied it, but now her view was "putting up the drawbridge after I've had my opportunity."[73]

A letter signed by Pete McCloskey, Jr., a former Republican congressman who represented Palo Alto, accompanied the complaint and pointed out that Rice "has consistently and publicly stated her opposition to 'goals and timetables' " on affirmative action, even though goals and timetables were required by federal law.[74] The investigation proceeded, and at this writing, in 2007, it remains ongoing, in part because the original complaint has been enlarged to include racial discrimination and now twenty-eight individual cases. But a number of the original faculty members have settled with the university and withdrawn.[75]

The interpretation of the statistics remains in dispute. Stanford's position in 2007, in a carefully worded formulation, was that during Rice's years as provost, from 1993 to 1999, the proportion of women coming up for tenure who received tenure was higher than the proportion during the previous twelve years, and that the proportion was the same as for men.[76] But in 2002, Stanford's Web site displayed charts and figures showing that from roughly 1994 to 1999, the tenure rate for women faculty at Stanford declined to 40 percent, from 56 percent during the previous six years. Those statistics are no longer available on Stanford's Web site.[77]

Eight years later as secretary of state, Rice still stuck to her objections about the women's methodology by arguing that the women had effectively compared apples to oranges. In other words, Rice said, the women asserted that the percentage of women Ph.D. students in biology at Stanford was *X* but the percentage of women biology professors was less than *X*, and therefore women biology professors were underrepresented on the faculty. But to be accurate, Rice argued, the women should have compared the number of biology professors to the pool the professors came from themselves—the pool of women biology students when the professors were in graduate school. That pool, she said, would have reflected the fewer women in the field at the time and, not incidentally, produced better numbers for Stanford. "When people like me came along, the pool of women was smaller than it is now," Rice said. "Now the pool's larger. So if you want to know what should the percentage be, you don't look at what the pool looks like today, you look at what the pool looked like when I was a graduate student."[78]

The puzzle was why Rice resorted to elaborate academic arguments and took such a hard line against the women when she might have defused the situation by simply acknowledging a problem. If she had been willing to appoint some of the women to a committee or a review process, however distasteful for her, she might have been able to invest them in some sort of change. That, at least, was what Rice said she learned from her front-row seat in George H. W. Bush's negotiations with the Soviet Union. But in this case Rice herself had become the issue, and she seemed to see the women as Barbara Babcock said she did—privileged complainers who had faced less discrimination than she had. Most of the women were white, most were in the first warhorse generation of feminists, and most saw raising objections about their professional treatment as a duty and a cause, not a cry of victimhood. But to Rice, who was raised to never dwell on the unfairness in society, the complaints amounted to a broadcast of weakness. Rice wanted to deal from a position of strength, which was a lesson she imparted to one of her students, Kiron Skinner, who became a professor at Carnegie Mellon University. Once when someone had treated Skinner badly, Rice told her that "people may oppose you, but when they realize you can hurt them, they'll join your side."[79]

In part to counter the stress of her job, Rice turned back to the piano after a few years as provost. In the process she revealed a part of her personality that was rarely on display in public. In the fall of 1995, she sought out George Barth, a Stanford music professor, for lessons. Rice had played piano for Clara Rice's church choir, but it had been a brief experience years before. "She showed up and told me that she felt matters came to a head when a friend of hers asked her to play hymns and she could hardly do that," Barth said. "I thought to myself, this is a busy person with a lot of responsibility, it's going to be something superficial."[80] But Rice had recently joined a chamber music group at the invitation of Paul Brest, Stanford's law school dean, and they were preparing to play the Brahms F Minor Quintet in a performance to celebrate a new endowed professorship. Rice told Barth she wanted to learn it.

"I thought, 'Holy cow, the Brahms F Minor, that's a mighty difficult piece,' " Barth recalled. "So I said, 'Okay, we'll go to work.' And man did she work."[81] Barth helped Rice with voicing—deciding whether to bring out the soprano or tenor in a piece, for example—and also with fingering, or planning what fingers to use for which keys in a particular piece of music. "There is standard fingering, but some of the greatest pianists use nonstandard, and the fingering shapes the music in certain ways," Barth said. "She was coming back to me after a long time. I noticed certain rhythmic things that suggested stiffness, so some of the natural curves of the music would not come through as they might."[82]

After a little more than two years, Rice and Barth played Brahms's two-piano version of "Variations on a Theme by Haydn" in a performance for the university. In preparation the two had practiced for ten hours a week, an insignificant amount of time for a professional but an "unheard of" commitment, in Barth's words, for a provost. "I could see sometimes the stresses that she felt," Barth said. "We had some interesting conversations about going out on stage and performing. And she said, 'What do you do if things are falling apart, and there's a memory lapse?' " His answer was only to do her best. "I think she was kind of shocked by the riskiness of it," Barth said.[83]

By this time Rice and her chamber group were spending a week each summer with the Muir String Quartet at music camp, in Park City or Snowbird, Utah, or in Bozeman, Montana. The idea was to learn from the pros, and Rice and the three other chamber players spent eight intense hours a day in practice. Brest, the violist, found Rice to be a different personality when she played with the group.

"Condi was just tremendously open, very collegial," Brest said. "She was completely open to being coached and being corrected." It was not a situation of a personality change as extreme as *Dr. Jekyll and Mr. Hyde*, Brest said, because in his experience "Condi is unfailingly polite even when it's clear she's annoyed."[84] But it was striking. "You can see one characteristic when she is in authority, like provost, and another when she is a colleague playing chamber music," he said.[85]

Mike Reynolds, the cellist in the Muir Quartet, found something else in Rice when he worked with her in the summers. "Condi tends to be conservative by nature, but musically she's incredibly liberal," Reynolds said. "She's very creatively open. She takes big chances musically, which is one of the reasons I like playing with her. In a Brahms quintet you'll have your hands on one end of the keyboard, and suddenly you have to go to the other end. It's just huge, huge reaches and leaps. And some pianists take that little extra millisecond of time to make sure they hit every note, but she just goes for it because the music demands it. Therefore, she doesn't hit every note perfectly, but it allows the desperation of the music to come out, which is what the music wants to have happen."[86]

Not surprisingly, Rice agreed with that assessment, but saw in it one of the reasons she gave up piano back in Denver. "I tend to think that music is a place where passion comes out," she said. "And that's been an evolution for me in my music. I was much more focused on technical perfection when I was younger and doing this as a potential career, to the point that I think I was probably not very musical."[87] When she returned to the piano as provost, Rice found the Brahms pieces she played at seventeen to be entirely different at thirty-nine. There was "creativity and passion and understanding of the depth of the music," Rice said. "And I have a feeling that when I played as a college student, as a musician, somebody really doing this as a career, that I played the notes, not the music."[88]

Rice's other passion at Stanford was football, and as provost she devoted large amounts of time to the school team, not least because Casper had no interest. Rice went to every home game the moment she arrived at Stanford, and in 1988 asked for and won a spot on a search committee that selected Dennis Green, an African-American, as the new coach.[89] Green would go on to coach the Minnesota Vikings, and in 1994, Rice was directly involved in luring Tyrone Willingham, another African-American and then an assistant Vikings coach, to be head coach at Stanford.

Rice was always proud of her record on minority recruitment in football, particularly on a campus where her commitment to civil rights had been questioned. Years later, she told ESPN that many college athletic directors did not do enough to seek out black coaches. "I know a little bit about recruiting college coaches and you can very easily fall into that," Rice said. "You know, you call five people and they tell you their top two or three candidates and you look up and none of them are African-American. And so you have to push beyond the kind of normal channels."[90] In 1999, Willingham coached Stanford to its first Rose Bowl appearance in twenty-eight years, a game that Rice watched from the press box with Ted Leland, then Stanford's athletic director. With two minutes to go, when Stanford recovered a fumble and sealed the victory, Leland recalled that Rice jumped up and shouted, "There is a God!"[91]

Rice's other interest as provost was a program she started with her friend Susan Ford for poor Hispanic and black students in East Palo Alto. The two, with John Rice's involvement, created the Center for a New Generation, an after-school enrichment program and summer session that targeted the brightest middle school students. Rice and Ford were criticized for helping the smartest instead of the neediest, but Rice's perspective, straight out of Titusville, was that ambitious students would benefit the most from the kind of community support she had as a child. The program started in 1992 with one hundred students and a first-year budget of about $150,000, was expanded into grade school, and later merged with the Boys and Girls Club. Most of the money for the center came from Susan Ford and fund-raising, but Rice directed some of her board fees to the program.[92]

By the end of 1998, Rice had been provost for more than five tumultuous years, a longer tenure than most, and in December she announced she would be stepping down. She said she planned to take a leave of absence to work in "the private sector," and would eventually return to teaching political science at Stanford.[93] But as insiders in Republican circles knew, George W. Bush had already decided to make Rice the foreign policy adviser for his 2000 presidential campaign. By the time Rice officially resigned six months later, she readily said that she would be "doing some work obviously for Governor Bush."[94]

Rice's departure was greeted with relief by much of the faculty but with accolades from supporters who admired her backbone and what they saw as the discipline she and Casper imposed on the university. "Stanford was brought under control," George Shultz said. "Its costs were gotten under control, its budget got balanced, and the sort of looseness that had come to this university, like many others, was gotten out of the system."[95] Stephen Krasner, a former chairman of the Political Science Department and the director of the State Department's Policy Planning Staff under Rice, viewed her tenure with Casper as vital to Stanford's survival. "I think it saved the place," he said.[96]

Rice remained unapologetic to the end. "I knew that if I could force through—and I had Gerhard's total backing—if I could force through the difficult decisions in the first couple of years, then Stanford could really take off, and we could do all those faculty hires that people had wanted to do, and we could have a campus again that people were proud of, and we could do all the special programs that people wanted to do, and we could have massive numbers of new graduate fellowships," Rice said. "But we had to do the hard stuff first. And if I'd soft-pedaled the hard stuff, we weren't going to be able to do the good things later. And I think people appreciated it in the end."[97]

But Rice also said, even after four years as national security adviser and two as secretary of state, that the provost position was the toughest job she ever had. "I think in its own way it was," she said.[98] At a farewell gathering at Stanford, Chip Blacker remembered that Rice told the crowd that "if I had to do it all over again, I might not have come on quite as strong."[99] With Blacker in private, she was blunt. "Maybe I was too much of a hard-ass," he recalled that she said.[100]

—

Condoleezza Rice first met George W. Bush in a White House receiving line during his father's presidency, and saw him next in 1995, shortly after he was sworn in as Texas governor. Rice had been in Houston for a Chevron board meeting, and had stopped in Austin at the invitation of George H. W. Bush. It was not a promising get-together. Rice chatted with the younger Bush about sports and family, but then felt like a potted plant when she and the former president sat through a lunch the younger Bush had with the Texas House speaker and lieutenant governor.[101]

The first meaningful meeting between the two occurred in April 1998, when Governor Bush was thinking of running for president and happened to be in San Francisco for a Republican fund-raising dinner. The next day, at Shultz's invitation, Bush came to Stanford and sat down in Shultz's living room with a half dozen Hoover scholars. Among them were Martin Anderson, a former adviser to Ronald Reagan, and also two economics professors, John Cogan and John Taylor. As usual, Rice, the provost and national security aide in Bush I, was the only woman and black in the room.

The gathering was a get-to-know-you session and an early tryout for both sides. Shultz, who had felt excluded by the senior George Bush after his service in the Reagan administration, was taking the measure of the son. The son, in turn, was taking the measure of the Republican elders as potential advisers for a future presidential campaign. Nothing was said out loud about politics or any nascent Bush campaign, and the discussions focused on economics and touched on the International Monetary Fund. But one of the things Shultz most remembered from that day was that Rice and the younger Bush connected. "Particularly when foreign policy things came up, Condi had a lot to say," Shultz said. "And you can tell when people click. And he was interesting, I thought, because he pitched into the discussion. He seemed to like the give-and-take."[102]

Things went so well that Bush invited Rice, Shultz, and Anderson down to the governor's mansion in Austin for a follow-up session in July. Dick Cheney, the Bush I defense secretary and at that time the chief executive of Halliburton, was there, too, as was Paul Wolfowitz, then the dean of the Johns Hopkins School of Advanced International Studies. This time Bush was direct, and told the group that he was thinking of running for president and wanted their help.[103]

The next month, the elder Bush invited Rice back to Kennebunkport. The younger Bush was there, too, for what seems to have been an arranged meeting with Rice by the father for the son. It may have worked better than the elder Bush ever expected. Over two long days, Rice and the younger Bush fished, worked out, and discussed sports and the state of the world. While Rice ran on a treadmill at the Kennebunkport compound, the younger Bush used the rowing and cycling machines. "What about relations with Russia, what about relations with China?" Rice quoted Bush as saying.[104] "We were working out next to each other and we continued to talk about these issues while huffing and puffing on whatever machine we were on," Rice later said.[105] Bush struck her as "curious and probing," with an expertise in foreign policy that "was like that of an attentive person—I mean somebody who read the newspapers, watched television, would have known basics."[106]

The younger Bush, who had just stepped down as managing partner of the Texas Rangers, had never met anyone like Rice. She could talk baseball, football, and foreign policy all at the same time, but she did not sound like an intellectual and she never made him feel inadequate or ignorant. On the contrary, Rice made Bush feel sharper, particularly when she complimented him on his questions. Bush did not know many black people well, and it made him feel good about himself that he got along so easily with Rice. It was hard not to see that she was also attractive, athletic, and competitive, and, like him, underestimated for much of her adult life.

For Rice, Bush was a refreshing change from the academia of Stanford. She liked his directness, his humor, and of course his power as the expected front-runner in the Republican Party. Although he had traveled very little, he was curious about the world, particularly about the leaders she knew, and he had good instincts about what drove them politically. She admired the first President Bush, but she was charmed by this potential President Bush. She could see that he needed her far more than his father had, and that made her feel important and vital. It was either then or shortly afterward that Bush made the decision to put Rice in charge of foreign policy for his presidential campaign.[107]

"I like to be around her," Bush said in the spring of 2000. "She's fun to be with. I like lighthearted people, not people who take themselves so seriously that they are hard to be around." Besides, he said, "She's really smart!"[108]

That fall, Wolfowitz joined with Rice as a second foreign policy adviser, and in January 1999, while Rice was still provost, the two assembled what would be the Bush campaign foreign policy team. The group included Robert Blackwill and Robert Zoellick from the first Bush administration, and also four former Pentagon officials from past Republican administrations: Richard Armitage, Richard Perle, Steve Hadley, and Dov Zakheim. The group met first in Austin with Cheney and Shultz, and then over a weekend in Rice's home at Stanford.[109] This was the group that named itself the Vulcans, after the statue in Rice's hometown, and over the next two years Rice would work with Wolfowitz and the others in preparing foreign policy position papers and educating the candidate.[110]

Rice, who was the closest of the Vulcans to Bush, had a job on her hands. She winced in November 1999 when Bush failed a pop quiz by a television reporter who asked him if he could name the top person in power in Taiwan, India, Pakistan, and the Russian republic of Chechnya. Bush managed to come up with Lee Teng-hui in Taiwan, although he referred to him simply as "Lee," but he struggled painfully to name the military leader of Pakistan.[111] "General, I can name the general," Bush replied, but he failed to produce the name Pervez Musharraf.[112] Similarly, Bush could not name the prime minister of India at the time, Atal Behari Vajpayee, or the Chechen leader, Aslan Maskhadov.[113]

The next day, Bush spoke to Rice on the phone and asked, "So who's the prime minister of Italy? Do *you* know?" Rice, ever the understanding tutor, told him that he should be thinking about his "vision" for the world and not spending time trying to remember every fact and figure about foreign policy. "Somebody will always be able to catch you on that game, you know, what's the capital of this," she told him.[114] The following year, that seemed to happen when a writer for *Glamour* magazine asked Bush about the Taliban, the oppressive Afghan regime. From either a failure of hearing or recall, Bush could only shake his head in silence. When the writer gave him a hint—"repression of women in Afghanistan"—Bush replied, "Oh. I thought you said some band. The Taliban in Afghanistan! Absolutely. Repressive."[115]

By then, Rice had written the most comprehensive outline of what foreign policy was to be like in a George W. Bush administration—a 6,600-word article, "Promoting the National Interest," in the journal *Foreign Affairs*. The article, much discussed among the foreign policy intelligentsia, was unusually critical of the Clinton administration for deploying American forces in conflicts like Haiti, and questioned the moral impulse to spread American democracy when what really mattered, Rice wrote, were the relationships between the great powers. "The belief that the United States is exercising power legitimately only when it is doing so on behalf of someone or something else was deeply rooted in Wilsonian thought, and there are strong echoes of it in the Clinton administration," Rice wrote. "To be sure, there is nothing wrong with doing something that benefits all humanity, but that is, in a sense, a second-order effect."[116] Rice also made clear that there was no need for an invasion to overthrow Saddam Hussein because regimes like Iraq and North Korea were "living on borrowed time, so there need be no sense of panic about them. Rather, the first line of defense should be a clear and classical statement of deterrence—if they do acquire WMD, their weapons will be unusable because any attempt to use them will bring national obliteration."[117]

In less than two years, the article would be a relic of another era, remembered more as a political pamphlet than a serious analysis of foreign policy. By the time Rice was secretary of state, it was an embarrassing reminder that she had derided some of the very policies she ended up embracing. Bush, in any case, said in a news conference in 2005 that he had never read it, a statement that was hard to believe about a document that had served as the central explanation of his foreign policy in the 2000 campaign. But Bush insisted it was so. "I don't know what you think the world is like, but a lot of people don't just sit around reading *Foreign Affairs*," Bush said, chortling, in an interview a few days after the news conference. "I know this is shocking to you. I know what Condi thinks. I spent a lot of time with her in those days."[118]

On December 12, 2000, the Supreme Court ruled 5–4 that

Florida's electoral votes should go to Bush, and Rice's student became the new president. It was clear that she would be national security adviser, and five days later, on Sunday, December 17, at the governor's mansion in Austin, Texas, Bush announced his decision. Rice, who spoke only briefly at the announcement, said that she would promote the president-elect's vision of "humility with strength" around the world.[119]

Back in Palo Alto, Rice's father was seriously ill. He had been bedridden for ten months, after a serious arrhythmic episode in February 2000, which had coincidentally occurred when he was home without Clara in the middle of an interview with *George* magazine about his daughter's success. (The reporter, Ann Reilly Dowd, called 911, then Rice at her Stanford office. Rice rushed over. "Daddy, it's Condoleezza," Rice told her father in a strong, clear voice as paramedics surrounded him while he lay unconscious on a stretcher. "We're going to the hospital. We're going to take good care of you.")[120]

On that Sunday, December 17, Clara Rice sat her husband up in bed to watch his daughter on television with Bush. "We're not sure if he really understood that she was going to work for him," recalled Clara, who said that her husband, for whatever reason, was not a fan of the president-elect. "He had the strangest look on his face, he wasn't smiling, he didn't look happy when he was looking at her, so I don't know if he really knew what was going on, or knew and didn't like it, you know. I don't know today what that look was all about."[121]

A week later, on Christmas Eve, John Rice was dead. Rice had been tormented about whether she should leave for Washington with her beloved father so sick, and in the end he made the decision for her. She was at his bedside when he died. "Say hello to Mom," she said as he slipped away.[122]

Nine days later, Rice left for Washington, leaving her father and Stanford—her family for nearly two decades—behind. "She literally in the blink of an eye lost him and her entire support system out here," said Randy Bean.[123] In Washington, Rice had a new title, a new office, a new place in the world—and something more. "I think she moved her familial needs from Palo Alto to the Bush family," Bean said. In becoming national security adviser, "I think it really, really filled a bigger need than a job."[124]

CHAPTER 7

Bin Laden Determined to Strike in US

The West Wing, 2001

George Walker Bush was sworn in as the nation's forty-third president on January 20, 2001, and in a fourteen-minute inaugural address sought to project unity and humility after one of the most divisive elections in the country's history. "We will show purpose without arrogance," the new president promised in a cold Washington drizzle, echoing his campaign pledge that America would be a modest actor on the world stage.[1] Rice, the foreign policy coach who had helped Bush reach this pinnacle, sat on the West Front of the U.S. Capitol only a few rows back from the lectern, sandwiched between Margaret Spellings, a Texas transplant who would be sworn in the next day as the president's domestic policy adviser, and Alberto Gonzales, another Texan who would be the new White House counsel.

For Rice it was a bittersweet moment after the chaos of the transition and a period of grief. Only three weeks earlier she had buried her father in Palo Alto, where he now lay in Alta Mesa Cemetery near Angelena, whose remains Rice had exhumed from Denver almost a decade before. Rice was keenly aware that she was experiencing one of the most important events of her life without the two most important people in her life, but she was comforted by her belief that somehow her parents knew. "I feel a connection so strongly with my parents all the time, I don't feel that connection has broken," she later said. "I don't know that they're sitting in heaven saying, 'Oh, goodness, I wonder why she said that'—I hope not. But there's a kind of spiritual connection that makes you sense that you haven't lost them, and they haven't lost you."[2]

Rice had wept with emotion on her way to the inaugural service that morning from St. John's Episcopal Church in Lafayette Square to Capitol Hill, but she composed herself in time to offer the talking points of the new administration to the press. "He's going to be the president for everybody," Rice told NBC's Maria Shriver in an interview on the inaugural platform shortly before Bush took the oath of office. Feeling magnanimous, Rice added unusually glowing words about the administration she had treated so dismissively during the campaign. "I want to say that the Clinton foreign policy team has been terrific," Rice said, singling out Josef Korbel's daughter, the departing secretary of state, Madeleine Albright, as well as Clinton's national security adviser, Sandy Berger, and the defense secretary, William Cohen. Rice termed all of them "fantastic."[3]

That evening, Rice celebrated with the extended family that had come to town. Genoa McPhatter, or Aunt Gee, as Rice called her, was there, as were Aunt Connie and Uncle Alto, Rice's cousin Lativia, her stepmother, Clara, and her friend Susan Ford. Rice had a date for the inaugural balls, Rollin B. Chippey II, a Harvard- and Yale-educated African-American lawyer from the San Francisco office of Morgan, Lewis & Bockius. Chippey had been introduced to Rice by a mutual friend and she had been seeing him in California, but it was not a long-term relationship. Still, Chippey got star treatment. After he and Rice went in a group with Rice's family to one of the inaugural balls, the two were invited into the presidential limousine to travel from party to party with the Bushes for the rest of the evening. "Rollin had the best night of his life," Susan Ford recalled.[4]

The next day, Rice showed her family her big new office in the northwest corner of the West Wing, one of the most coveted pieces of real estate in Washington. It was being redecorated—Rice would later hang a 1930s painting of a black church revival meeting in the sitting area and display football helmets from the Cleveland Browns and San Francisco 49ers in the shelves—but everyone could see the view out the windows of Pennsylvania Avenue and Lafayette Park and how close it was to the Oval Office. "It was just like fairyland," Connie Ray recalled. "We just had to pinch ourselves."[5]

Rice, who had worked her entire life to get to this point, shared her family's sense of wonder. She did not know that only months into the future she would be sucked into a vortex of terrorism, or that some of the 9/11 hijackers were at that moment at a training camp in Afghanistan, where they had learned how to storm cockpit doors and butcher a camel in preparation for using knives on passengers.[6] The festive atmosphere in Rice's corner of the White House reflected the early expectation that foreign policy would not be a problematic preoccupation of the new administration. Bush's initial foreign policy goals—getting tough on what he saw as the military threat of China and scrapping the Antiballistic Missile Treaty, the arms accord that Richard Nixon had signed with the Soviet Union nearly thirty years earlier—did not seem likely to provoke any serious crises. Overall, the focus of the new administration was to be on domestic policy, principally education reform and the tax cuts that Bush had made the centerpiece of his campaign.

As national security adviser, Rice was following in the footsteps of a long roster of powerful men—McGeorge Bundy, Walt Rostow, Henry Kissinger, Brent Scowcroft, Colin Powell, and Sandy Berger, among them—in a relatively new position in American history. The Truman administration established the National Security Council along with the CIA and Defense Department as part of the overhaul of the nation's national security system after World War II. Its purpose was to coordinate foreign and defense policy among several cabinet agencies and provide streamlined national security advice to the president, who served as the NSC's chairman and chief client. In the forty-third presidency, the council consisted of seven standing members: the secretaries of state, defense, and treasury, the vice president, the national security adviser, the chairman of the Joint Chiefs of Staff, and the director of national intelligence. The separate position of national security adviser as it is now known did not come into existence until the Kennedy administration, when Bundy, an intellectual and bureaucratic powerhouse and a close friend of JFK, was allowed by Kennedy to effectively operate as a mini–State Department inside the West Wing. Other presidents and national security advisers interpreted the job differently over the years, but Kissinger was the most powerful of all, and remains probably the most influential foreign policy figure of the entire era in which the United States has been a global leader.[7]

In contrast with Kissinger, Rice saw her job as essentially a staff position with three main responsibilities: translating Bush's instincts into policy, reconciling competing views within the government, and operating as a gatekeeper—although she likened herself to a "transmission belt"—for the president on national security. "I found myself pretty often saying to the president, 'You know, you really ought to sit down with X,' or calling up X and saying, 'You know, I really think you ought to go talk to the president,' " Rice said.[8] By far, Rice considered the most important part of her job as providing advice to the president, although within clear limits set by Bush. Rice could challenge or coax him, but in the end he was boss.

"I don't talk the president into almost anything, all right?" Rice would say two years into her job. "I just want that understood. You can't do that with the president. What you can do with the president is make your arguments."[9] As had been the case with the other important men in her life—Casper, Korbel, Scowcroft, her father—Rice would do what the president wanted. Richard Armitage, the deputy secretary of state in Bush's first term, went so far as to call Rice an "acceleratron"[10] who reinforced Bush rather than putting on the brakes when needed. One of the president's closest friends, Roland Betts, an owner of the Chelsea Piers athletic complex in New York City, who saw Bush and Rice together during weekends at Camp David, had a similar view. "I think to say that 'she worked for him' is probably a pretty good way to put it," he said. "In a policy debate he has the upper hand. She'll always make her point, but once he makes his decision, and it could be based on something she said or somebody else said, she goes along with that. She doesn't take him on."[11]

Rice soon established a pattern to her days. She rose at 4:30 A.M. at her temporary apartment in the Lansburgh Building in downtown Washington—Rice would later move to a permanent apartment in the Watergate—and ran for a half hour or more on her treadmill. She was at the White House by 6 A.M., which gave her an hour before the president was in the Oval Office to read the thick overnight file her staff had assembled on what had happened around the world while America slept. The file contained what were still called cables, a vestige from the days when the U.S. Foreign Service relied on the telex machine, but in reality were printed-out e-mail messages from American embassies about developments over the previous twenty-four hours overseas. The file also included e-mails from Rice's staff and memos that she had requested on specific issues—the state of affairs in the Middle East, for example. Rice usually raced through the major newspapers at home before arriving at the White House, but the file contained what her staff considered important articles from foreign publications. In short, the folder represented the state of the world as the White House cared about it on that particular day.

At 6:45 A.M., to round out the picture from the written record, Rice usually had a ten-minute conference call with Powell and Rumsfeld to get their sense of developments and their plans for the day. (Later, when Rice's relationship with Rumsfeld deteriorated, she was more often on the line with just Powell.) Next a CIA analyst brought her an overnight compilation of the most sensitive intelligence gathered by American spy agencies and went over the highlights with her. The end result was that when Bush arrived in the Oval Office around 7 A.M. and picked up the phone for Rice, which was often his first call of the day, she was ready. "What's going on?" Bush liked to ask.[12] Depending on the news and the president's mood, Bush either listened on the phone or asked Rice to come straight to the Oval Office to tell him more in person.

From the outset, a pattern established itself that was based on the chemistry between Bush and Rice. However grim the information, Rice usually cheered the president up. "He used to look forward to seeing Condi," Card recalled.[13] As Rice soon learned, the calls from the president continued through the morning and afternoon and sometimes well into the evening. She frequently found herself in the Oval Office six and more times a day. Often it was just she and Bush, talking about whatever was on the president's mind. He was her client, and a demanding one.

By 7:30 A.M., assuming the president didn't need her and she didn't have a call overseas, Rice sometimes went to the White House senior staff meeting in the Roosevelt Room, where Card went around the table and asked everybody—Karl Rove, the political adviser, and Ari Fleischer, the White House press secretary, among others—to report on their upcoming plans. The meeting was a recitation of schedules and upcoming presidential events, and often devolved into complaints about what was in the morning papers, grousing about individual reporters and how to push back.

Whether or not the meeting was done, at precisely two minutes to eight Rice and Card left to participate in the most important meeting of the day, the president's CIA briefing. George Tenet, the CIA director, attended with an agency briefer who was assigned directly to the president. As Rice, Card, and the vice president looked on, the analyst presented Bush with a blue three-ring loose-leaf leather notebook with "President's Daily Brief" stamped across the top. (It was the same CIA document that Rice had seen an hour earlier, although now she would go over it in more detail.) Inside the notebook was a series of top secret short reports, no more than ten to twelve pages in all, of what the CIA considered the most important information of the previous twenty-four hours, including potential terrorist threats and reports on the health of foreign leaders.[14]

The analyst would introduce each article, explaining background and context, and then hand it to the president to read.[15] Sometimes there would be additional material, like the "nitty-gritty," as Tenet put it, on how the CIA had obtained the secrets in each item.[16] Bush studied each one carefully and often tossed out questions as he was reading, at which point Rice and the others joined in. The PDB, as it was called by the ten senior officials who saw it each morning, had been around since at least the Ford administration, but it was little known outside the top circles of government. That would change—and turn Rice's life upside down—the following year.

Not everything went harmoniously for Rice in this settling-in period in the White House. To her amazement, a confrontation erupted between her and Vice President Dick Cheney over which of them was to run National Security Council meetings in Bush's absence. Rice would win the argument, but it provided a foreshadowing of battles to come.

The fight began in the very first days, when Rice assumed that by tradition she would run the NSC meetings—usually three a week—

when the president did not attend or was not in town. But she soon learned something she found alarming: Cheney, who expected to play a major role in foreign policy, had pushed Bush to appoint him chair of the sessions rather than her.[17] "She threw a fit," a former administration official recalled.[18]

Rice, in a pattern that would repeat itself over the next four years, went directly to the president to reclaim her territory. She was determined, as she later put it, "to get it fixed," and made the argument to Bush that it "wasn't appropriate" for Cheney to run the meetings since that had not been the role of vice presidents in the past.[19] Rice knew that Cheney saw himself as different from his predecessors, with nearly unprecedented influence over a president who brought almost no foreign policy experience to the White House. As a former defense secretary and White House chief of staff, he had run a team advising Bush on whom to choose as vice president after Bush got the Republican nomination in the summer of 2000. The fact that the candidate chose Cheney himself reflected how brilliantly Cheney would manipulate the process of advising Bush. Had he even partially supplanted Rice as national security adviser, he would be able to change the role from that of honest broker to one of maneuvering the process for his own ends. Ultimately Cheney found other ways to make the process conform to his goals.

Only days into the administration, Rice found herself in the extraordinary position of challenging the powerful new vice president, but she saw it as a move that was critical to her own stature and effectiveness. "Mr. President, this is what national security advisers do," Rice told Bush.[20] Bush, in Rice's telling, readily agreed to her wishes.[21]

The first NSC meeting was on January 30 in its usual spot, the White House Situation Room, the storied crisis center underneath the West Wing. (In reality it was something of a low-tech dungeon, in dire need of a makeover to bring its 1985 communications into the twenty-first century. But that would not happen until late 2006.[22]) The president convened the meeting and made an initial announcement, as Rice knew he would. "Condi Rice is my national security adviser," Bush said, in the recollection of several participants. "She will run these meetings in my absence."[23] Bush then told the group—including Cheney, Rumsfeld, Powell, Tenet, Treasury Secretary Paul

O'Neill, and General Hugh Shelton, the chairman of the Joint Chiefs—that he would be seeing all of them regularly, but he expected them to debate policy in these meetings, and that Rice as national security adviser would report the results of all their discussions back to him. It was the first but hardly the last time that Bush would support Rice in power struggles between the major players of his administration.

Bush moved on to the stated topic for the meeting, "Mideast Policy," but the discussion of the shattered peace process between Israel and the Palestinians was brief. Clinton had tried desperately in his final days to reach a settlement between Ehud Barak, the Israeli prime minister, and the Palestinian leader, Yasser Arafat, but the talks ended in failure when Arafat rejected a final offer that outlined the contours of a Palestinian state, including 90 percent of the territory he was demanding. The second Intifada, a Palestinian uprising against Israel that had begun in late 2000, continued to rage, and the Israeli government had fallen. The hard-line Ariel Sharon, who took a tougher stance against Arafat than did Barak, was thought likely to become the next prime minister.

No one saw much hope for progress in brokering a negotiated settlement, particularly Bush, who announced to the meeting that he was reluctant to get involved and that Clinton had overreached and made the situation worse by his failure. Powell disagreed and said that as bad as tensions were, a hands-off approach for the United States, which had unique influence in the region, was untenable. Cheney and Rumsfeld backed the president and said he should not waste his political capital in the dispute. Rice, who would much later invest her own political capital into the Middle East in 2006 as secretary of state, did not speak up at the meeting. Brand-new in her job, determined to be an "honest broker" between competing views, she did not see it as her role. But later she said she agreed with Bush, Cheney, and Rumsfeld. "I thought that in light of the breakdown of Camp David and the launching of the second Intifada, and Sharon coming to power, there was absolutely no prospect of a Middle East peace process that was going to lead to anything," she said. "I just didn't see it."[24]

The discussion then shifted to Iraq, the most important subject of the meeting. As two men in the room that day knew firsthand, the president's father had made the decision to leave Saddam Hussein in Baghdad after the U.S. military expelled Iraq from Kuwait, its mission in the 1991 Persian Gulf War. The first Bush administration—including Powell, then the chairman of the Joint Chiefs, and Cheney, the defense secretary who in 1991 was more often than not allied with Powell[25]—believed that if the United States went beyond its original mission and marched into Baghdad to oust Saddam, it would lose the support of the international coalition that backed the war and, worse, become bogged down in an open-ended occupation. The White House at that time assumed or at least hoped that Saddam was so weakened by the war that he would fall on his own.

Instead, the United States spent the next decade trying to contain Saddam through United Nations economic sanctions and the creation of "no-fly zones." The zones, patrolled by American and British warplanes, banned the Iraqi air force from the skies in the north to protect a vulnerable ethnic minority, the Kurds, and in the south to protect another minority terrorized by Saddam, the Shiites. From time to time, usually in response to Iraqi provocations, the planes bombed Iraqi military and intelligence facilities in a kind of low-grade war that Americans largely ignored. The U.N. had also sent in weapons inspectors to make sure that Iraq did not build up another arsenal after the Gulf War, but in 1998 Saddam kicked them out. The Clinton administration, heeding the loud voices of influential hawks, especially in the Republican-controlled Congress, responded by adopting an official policy of "regime change" that sought to topple Saddam through pressure, chiefly sanctions that banned Iraqi oil exports except those used in exchange for imported food and "humanitarian" goods.

Clinton launched air strikes against Saddam's weapons facilities in December 1998 that were surprisingly effective, although the extent of the damage to the regime was not known at the time.[26] But by the start of the Bush II administration, the new president had concluded that the patrols of the no-fly zones were putting American pilots at too much risk and that Saddam was circumventing the curb on oil exports. Bush considered the sanctions so full of holes that he referred to them as "Swiss cheese" in an interview with *The New York Times* at his ranch in early January 2001.[27] Clearly Saddam was still getting enough money to prop up his regime.

"We have a regime change policy that isn't really regime change," Rice told the group.[28] Powell spoke up and said he thought the sanctions could be strengthened by focusing more on controls of weapons and less on restrictions of food. Rumsfeld, who had been part of the conservative coalition arguing in the 1990s that Saddam should be dealt with aggressively, said he didn't see why the administration was bothering with sanctions in the first place.[29] He was of the view, buttressed by evidence, that Saddam was able to sell enough oil to maintain his armed forces as a potent military threat in the region. Tenet then pulled out several surveillance photographs showing command and antiaircraft formations on the edge of Baghdad and structures he identified as possible chemical weapons factories. Everyone got up to look at the clusters of buildings in the desert, but it was hard for the untrained eye to reach any firm conclusions about their purpose. On-the-ground American intelligence inside Iraq was poor to nonexistent, Tenet acknowledged.[30]

As the meeting drew to a close, Bush gave out assignments: Powell should draw up guidelines for more effective sanctions, Tenet should report back on improving intelligence in the country, O'Neill would investigate how to financially squeeze the regime, and Rumsfeld should examine military options, including "how it might look" to use U.S. ground forces in Iraq's north and south.[31] The atmosphere had suddenly changed, although participants took away different messages from the session. To O'Neill, the former Alcoa chief executive who was new to the issue, Iraq loomed as a more urgent priority than he had ever imagined and the meeting set the tone for what was to come.[32] In Rice's mind—and Powell's—the assignments represented a shift to a tougher approach that did not then set a high priority on military action. "We had spent an inordinate amount of time—and this I really want to be understood—from the time we came in until after 9/11 trying to figure out something else on Iraq," Rice later said. "I went to more meetings about strengthening sanctions than I did about anything else."[33]

Rice chaired the follow-up session, on February 5, which was held with only the national security principals and without the president and therefore called a principals meeting. A decision had already been made by the White House to give money to Iraqi exile opposition groups for anti-Saddam activity inside the country, and now the participants reported back on their Iraq assignments of the week before.[34] Powell told the group about plans for what had been dubbed "smart sanctions," while Rumsfeld outlined a new set of "response options" for U.S. and British pilots patrolling the skies over Iraq. Pilots would have latitude to bomb radar, antiaircraft, and command-and-control centers beyond the no-fly zone lines. The idea was to make the pilots less vulnerable while tightening the noose on Saddam, and the president readily gave his approval.

By then, Rice was already under pressure on another front from a man who would become a serious threat to her own credibility, Richard Clarke, the National Security Council's counterterrorism chief. Clarke, a holdover from the Clinton administration, worked in the Eisenhower Executive Office Building in the ornate French Baroque edifice across an alley to the west of the White House. He happened to occupy the former office of Oliver North, the Reagan-era official who secretly sold weapons to Iran to support the Nicaraguan contras. No one had ever accused Clarke of waging his own foreign policy, but like North he was an odd keeper of secrets, passionate, deathly pale, and, by his own account, obsessive about terrorism. Rice later described him as someone who "broke china."[35] Clarke ran the administration's Counterterrorism Security Group, or CSG, and he was desperate for the new national security adviser to pay more attention to what he considered an imminent danger, Al Qaeda, the worldwide alliance of terrorist groups founded by Osama bin Laden.

Five days into the administration, Clarke sent Rice a memo urgently asking her to convene a meeting of the National Security Council principals—Cheney, Rumsfeld, Powell, herself, and the others—to review policy on Al Qaeda. "Al Qida is not some narrow, little terrorist issue that needs to be included in broader regional policy," Clarke wrote, using a less common spelling of the group. Clarke added that the principals needed to decide whether Al Qaeda was "a first order threat" or a " 'chicken little' over-reaching," although he made clear his own view that the United States "would make a major error if we underestimated the challenges Al Qida poses."[36]

Attached to the memo was a thirteen-page document that Clarke had developed in December 2000 as the Clinton administration came to an end. Entitled "Strategy for Eliminating the Threat from the Jihadist Networks of al Qida: Status and Prospects," the paper warned that Al Qaeda had a network of terrorist groups in the United States and forty other countries and was "actively seeking to develop and acquire weapons of mass destruction."[37] Still, Clarke estimated that the United States could "roll back" Al Qaeda as a serious threat to the United States in three to five years if enough resources were committed. To that end, he suggested ways to step up the fight: destroying terrorist camps in Afghanistan where Al Qaeda trained as well as giving "massive support" to the Northern Alliance, the Afghan fighters who opposed the repressive Taliban government that ruled Afghanistan and gave Al Qaeda safe haven. Clarke also proposed using the Predator—an armed, unmanned aircraft—against terrorists in Afghanistan that coming spring. Domestically, he proposed expanding the antiterrorism task forces that operated in major U.S. cities and accelerating the FBI's translations of wiretapped conversations of terrorist suspects in the United States.[38]

Faced with recycled material from the Clinton White House, Rice was determined to develop what she considered a comprehensive new plan against terrorism that bore the thinking of the Bush administration, and so she did not respond directly to Clarke's memo or strategy paper.[39] She would later insist, before the entirety of Clarke's paper was made public in 2005, that "no Al Qaeda plan was turned over to the new administration" and that Clarke had simply "suggested several ideas."[40] Subsequently Rice would say that while Clarke was insightful about Al Qaeda, his memo focused on overseas threats that had little bearing on the terrorist attacks. "Does anybody really think that arming the Northern Alliance would have prevented September 11?" she said in 2007.[41]

From the perspective of the post-9/11 world, Rice's dismissal of Clarke's warnings in the early months of 2001 looked defensive, wrongheaded, and semantic. Her approach seemed that of a cautious academic who had not been in government in a decade and thought she had the luxury of time. But Rice was also taking her cues from the president, who belittled the idea of catching terrorists one by one and who agreed with Rice that a counterterrorism policy had to be developed slowly so that diplomatic, financial, and military planning could mesh.[42] Rice recalled that the president told her that spring that he was "tired of swatting at flies,"[43] a reference to what the new administration considered Clinton's piecemeal approach to combating terrorism.

"We decided to take a different track," Rice later said.[44] She saw that the most urgent priority was to come up with a counterterrorism strategy that incorporated broader U.S. policy toward countries in the region, particularly Pakistan, which was actively supporting the Taliban at the time. "The problem was you didn't have an approach against Al Qaeda because you didn't have an approach against Afghanistan, and you didn't have an approach against Afghanistan because you didn't have an approach against Pakistan," Rice later told the 9/11 Commission. "And until we could get that right, we didn't have a policy."[45]

In Clarke's view, Rice was moving slowly because she failed to connect the dangers brewing on the other side of the world with the threats on American soil. "I think basically she didn't want to be bothered with homeland security or terrorism," he said. "She was hired to do grand strategy and worry about China and Russia."[46] When Clarke first briefed Rice during the 2000 presidential transition, he recalled that she did not understand the fundamentals about terrorism. "She had heard about bin Laden, but she thought of bin Laden as a guy with a few camp followers," Clarke said. "When I said 'Al Qaeda,' she said, 'Stop, what's that?' When I said it was an organization of tens of thousands of followers and millions of dollars in scores of countries, she said she didn't know that. And moreover, why should she? She was a Soviet Union specialist."[47]

Whatever counterterrorism strategy the administration was going to adopt, Clarke would not be as central to it as he wanted. Although Rice had decided at the start of the administration to keep him and his entire staff—"I wanted somebody who would continue the Clinton policies until we could get new policies in place," she later said[48]—she downgraded Clarke's position. Clarke's title would still be national counterterrorism coordinator, Rice determined, but he would not be the de facto "principal" he had been in the previous White House, and therefore would not be at meetings with Cheney, Rumsfeld, Powell, herself, and the others.[49]

Rice, who was engaged in a streamlining of the NSC staff from what she saw as the messy and unfocused Clinton years, concentrated on the fact that Clarke's staff was an "interagency" committee that crossed the boundaries from foreign policy into domestic threats and had people assigned to it from other parts of the government. Rice told Clarke that his staff did not belong under the NSC structure, and like other heads of interagency committees he should report through the deputies.[50] In short, Clarke would now attend the second-tier meetings with the deputy national security adviser (Hadley), the deputy defense secretary (Wolfowitz), the deputy secretary of state (Armitage), and others. If Clarke wanted any input into the new counterterrorism strategy that Rice was methodically developing on a global scale, then he would first have to reach consensus on a plan with the deputies and recommend that proposal to the principals. The principals would review the proposal at their own pace before handing it off to the president for final consideration. Clarke found the process dangerously slow, but he consented and set to work.

Rice was in any case occupied in the first months of the administration with the president's first foreign trip, a brief foray to Mexico, where Bush met with the new president, Vicente Fox, at Fox's ranch in the state of Guanajuato. As a candidate, Bush had declared that relations with Latin America would be a major priority. The White House had built the Mexico visit around the theme of immigration reform, but the trip demonstrated right away how much Iraq would demand attention. On February 16, the day that Bush had a joint news conference with Fox that was to be the public centerpiece of the visit, the Pentagon launched air strikes against military communications targets—radar systems and command-and-control facilities—deep inside Iraq, including on the outskirts of Baghdad. American military commanders had requested the strikes as part of the new "response options"—the ones that the president had just approved—to bomb Iraqi antiaircraft sites beyond the no-fly zones.[51] Although Rice and the president had been briefed about the plans for the strikes, they did not know how extensive the bombing would be. "What they didn't tell us was that this particular one was going to come very close to Baghdad and likely set off the Baghdad air-warning system," she later recalled.[52]

In the middle of Bush's talks with Fox, Ari Fleischer slipped into the room and motioned Rice away from the table.

"Why are we bombing Baghdad?" Fleischer whispered to her.[53]

"What?" Rice asked the press secretary incredulously. "Why are we doing what?"

"The news reporters are telling me that there are wire stories that we're bombing Baghdad," Fleischer responded, as Rice recalled it.

Rice excused herself, found a television set, discovered that the United States was indeed bombing Baghdad, and quickly retrieved Powell and Karen Hughes, Bush's top communications adviser, from the meeting. "One by one we're all leaving the table," Rice recalled. "The president's thinking, 'What's going on?' "[54]

As Bush remained virtually alone in the room with the Mexicans, Rice conferred with the others about what to do. Fearful that the White House would appear incoherent or incompetent, Rice returned to the conference room and asked if there could be a short break. Rice, Powell, and Hughes then briefed Bush on the bombing and told him he should express no surprise to reporters at the upcoming news conference. Instead, they suggested he refer to the strikes as "routine"—which Bush did, three times.[55] "It was really a problem because, you know, we go to Mexico to show our interest in Mexico and this important relationship, and the press conference is all about, 'Why are you bombing Baghdad?' " Rice recalled.[56] To her relief, the news accounts described the strikes as a well-planned action on the part of the new administration. "I learned to ask a lot more questions after that briefing," Rice later said.[57]

The next month, Rice established her role as the president's enforcer in two separate episodes. On March 7, she got a call at home at 5 A.M. from the president, who was angry about a story in that day's *Washington Post*: "Bush to Pick Up Clinton Talks on N. Korean Missiles." Bush read the major newspapers in bed every morning, even though he liked to say that he did not, but he often just skimmed the headlines and always avoided the editorials and opinion articles that criticized him.[58] On this morning the *Post* headline caught his eye and the accompanying article was just the kind to get under his skin.

Bush learned that Powell, his superstar secretary of state, had said at a news conference the day before that "some promising elements were left on the table"[59] by the Clinton administration as it frantically tried to negotiate a deal in its final days to try to persuade North Korea to abandon its nuclear ambitions. The negotiations had grown out of a 1994 accord with the Communist dictatorship, called the "Agreed Framework," that promised American aid and eventual diplomatic recognition of North Korea if it froze and ultimately dismantled its nuclear weapons program. "We do plan to engage with North Korea to pick up where President Clinton and his administration left off," the newspaper quoted Powell as saying.[60]

Rice did not think that what Powell had said was so damaging to the administration's objectives, but she knew how touchy the president was to a suggestion that he might be taking the lead from the Clinton White House. Although Bush and Clinton had gotten along well when they met on the morning of the inaugural, Bush was contemptuous of Clinton's behavior with Monica Lewinsky and what he considered the undisciplined nature of a White House with no adult supervision. The White House was still reviewing what its approach on North Korea would be, and now here was Powell getting out in front of the president and embracing Clinton. Complicating matters was Bush's impending meeting at the White House that morning with the South Korean president, Kim Dae Jung, who Bush knew would ask him to follow Clinton's lead and continue the U.S. support of South Korea's "sunshine policy" of economic and social incentives to lure the North toward national reconciliation.

Rice picked up the phone to call Powell. "We have a problem," she informed him.[61]

Powell, who had been friends with Rice since he was Reagan's deputy national security adviser and she was a young professor on a fellowship in Washington, was at first taken aback that a woman he had helped along now seemed to be reprimanding him. On the other hand, he knew that Rice was making the call on behalf of Bush. "She said the president was deeply upset, and that made her deeply upset,"

Powell recalled. "It was really the president's upset-ness that she was conveying."[62]

Powell did not see it as a huge conflict and was agreeable to defusing it. "He said, 'Let me fix it,' " Rice said. "And I said, 'Yeah, I think that's really a good idea.' "[63]

Only hours later, Powell dutifully back-pedaled. He slipped out of the talks between Bush and Kim in the Oval Office and, surprising a group of reporters waiting in the West Wing hallway, volunteered his assessment of the still-in-progress meeting. "The President forcefully made the point that we are undertaking a full review of our relationship with North Korea, coming up with policies that build on the past, coming up with policies unique to the administration, the other things we want to see put on the table," Powell said. "And in due course, when our review is finished, we'll determine at what pace and when we will engage with the North Koreans." For good measure, Powell added that although "there was some suggestion that imminent negotiations are about to begin, that is not the case."[64] Minutes later, Bush ended the meeting with Kim and, in comments to the waiting reporters, made it official: The new administration was putting aside Clinton's negotiations for a deal with North Korea and talks would not resume anytime soon. "When you make an agreement with a country that is secretive, how are you aware as to whether or not they are keeping the terms of the agreement?" Bush said.[65]

There was no easy answer to Bush's question. North Korea posed a difficult dilemma for him, just as it had for his predecessor. The regime of Kim Jong Il had an unsavory record of deception, authoritarian repression of dissent, and near-total isolation. Clinton had gambled with his 1994 agreement, which pulled the United States back from the brink of an attack. But the agreement was a mixture of promises by the United States to get North Korea to change its behavior and hopes that it wouldn't cheat. The Bush team and Republicans in general were never happy with it. In pulling Powell back, the White House wanted to signal a change, but the only course it had to offer was more tough talk, a refusal to bargain, and renewed economic, political, and military pressure on the North. That approach stirred anxieties in South Korea and China, which worried that it would lead to war. It would take years for Bush—and Rice—to alter the approach on North Korea and even longer for the new approach to bear fruit. Although Powell publicly laughed off the incident weeks later when he told reporters that "sometimes you get a little too far forward in your skis,"[66] privately he saw the president's decision as a missed opportunity that cost the administration critical time. He also learned that Rice, whatever her personal views, was not a reliable ally.

Less than a week later, Rice was once again sorting out trouble with Powell and exposing her vulnerability to being outmaneuvered by Cheney. This time it was the Kyoto Protocol, the 1997 international agreement that bound industrialized nations to cuts in emissions of carbon dioxide and other heat-trapping greenhouse gases that most scientists blamed for global warming. The Europeans and Japan were big supporters of Kyoto, but Bush, Republicans in Congress, and the American energy industry opposed the agreement, named for the Japanese city where it was negotiated, as potentially harmful to the U.S. economy and unfair because developing countries like China and India had balked at agreeing to its obligations. Still, Bush had pledged during the presidential campaign to try to regulate emissions of carbon dioxide from American power plants, and the new administrator of the Environmental Protection Agency, Christine Todd Whitman, had only days before described the president's campaign pledge as if it were already policy.[67] In the meantime, the White House had appointed a task force, led by Cheney, to come up with a new energy policy.

On the morning of March 13, Rice called Powell. "We're going to have to do something on Kyoto," she abruptly told him.[68]

"Right now? Why?" Powell asked.

Rice said that Senator Chuck Hagel of Nebraska and three other Republicans, who opposed not only Kyoto but Bush's pledge on emissions, had sent the White House a letter asking for a "clarification" of his policy—a pressure tactic that was part of the loud opposition from conservatives and the energy industry to Bush's campaign promise. In response, and unknown to Rice, the vice president's office had drafted a letter for Bush to sign that cited rising energy prices and said Bush no longer believed that the U.S. government should impose cuts in emissions on American power plants.[69] It was a reversal of the president's campaign pledge and would set off a wildfire at home and overseas. "I knew that for Colin and Christie, this was going to be really a problem," Rice recalled. For Powell, the letter's omission of any diplomatic language, like promising to move forward together in some way on emissions, was destined to infuriate the Europeans. Worse, no one in Europe knew the letter was coming.

Years later, Rice would sidestep blaming the vice president, but she did point a finger at his office. "They handled it basically as a kind of legislative affair, as a domestic issue," she said. "I really don't think people knew the foreign policy implications."[70] Nobody, she added, was thinking about "the fact that we've just gotten into office, basically, and that this is the first administration pronouncement on this, and therefore there has to be this groundwork laid."[71] But it was an international agreement that was being repudiated, and the fact that she was not part of the process was an ominous breakdown of internal communications and a sign that she was not entirely on top of issues with foreign policy implications.

The Kyoto fiasco unfolded in almost comic fashion. Cheney was about to hand-carry the explosive letter up to Capitol Hill, and in Rice's recollection, she told Powell to get over to the White House as quickly as possible to try to intercede.[72] In Powell's recollection, he told Rice he was coming over and asked her to slow the letter down.[73] Either way, it was too late by the time Powell reached the White House. He found the president, Rice, and a few others in the Oval Office, where a stunned Whitman had just been informed by Bush that he was reneging on his emissions pledge and effectively undercutting her at the EPA.[74] Cheney, meanwhile, had just left for the Hill with the letter in his pocket.

"He was gone," Rice said of the vice president, when asked why she had not tried to stop him herself, given her feelings. "I didn't know, I didn't see it. It's not like I was looking at the vice president. The vice president was gone."[75]

Powell was astounded. "They all got together . . . and said to hell with everybody else and they just signed it with no reference to our allies, no reference to 'Let's work with them and find a way forward on carbon emissions' or whatever," he later recalled. "Cheney was anxious to get it up there, so he just walked it up."[76] The letter, and the administration's confirmation at the end of March that it opposed

Kyoto, enraged Europe and effectively paralyzed environmental advocates around the world in negotiating a replacement agreement for the next six years. (In May 2007, Bush finally reversed course and called on other nations to join the United States in agreeing to a global goal of reducing greenhouse gases. But even that shift was distrusted in Europe as a ruse.)

For Rice, the episode was emblematic of Cheney's power, but in this case she did not see herself as losing out to him. Rather, she knew that the president was completely in line with the vice president's views and so she did not consider it her role to object. Powell could not believe how much Rice had allowed the vice president to outflank her, but the real problem was that Rice was presiding over a process that made people like Powell feel they did not get a chance to have their say.

What struck other people about Rice in this period was her immovable tone. One administration official was stunned in the early days of the administration during a meeting in the Roosevelt Room when Rice informed Sergei Ivanov, the visiting Russian national security adviser, that the United States would be withdrawing from the ABM Treaty—a nonnegotiable position that the administration had not yet taken in public. "She laid it on the line—'we're not going to do it, we're abandoning it, you're going to have to deal with it, next subject,' " the official recalled. "It wasn't exactly a dialogue."[77]

Similarly, when Rice's old friend from the University of Denver, Wayne Glass, stopped in to see her in those early days, he was taken aback by her absolute assuredness that withdrawing from the Antiballistic Missile Treaty that had helped curb a U.S.-Soviet arms race for three decades was the right thing to do. What Bush wanted to build in the absence of the treaty was a scaled-back version of Reagan's space-based, spectacularly ambitious "Star Wars" system. Reagan's Cold War–era system had been aimed at defending against a massive nuclear holocaust by the Soviet Union. The new missile defense system sought by Bush was planned to intercept an attack now considered more likely—a relatively smaller, less sophisticated one from a rogue state. Few experts thought it would work, and many worried that it would lead to a new generation of arms built to defeat it. "She said, 'I don't get it,' " Glass recalled. "How come you guys think the

ABM Treaty is so good?' My sense was she pretty much bought the party line. There was no honest exchange between the two of us that showed me she saw shades of gray."[78]

The administration finally had its first real foreign policy crisis in the spring, a standoff with China over a downed American spy plane that in retrospect was a footnote to the catastrophic events of the next six years. "It was a huge crisis at the time," Rice later recalled.[79] On April 1, a U.S. Navy EP-3 reconnaissance plane flying off the Chinese coast collided with a Chinese F-8 fighter jet, and the pilot and plane plummeted into the South China Sea. The American plane, though damaged, landed on the Chinese island of Hainan, where the Chinese detained the twenty-four-member American crew for eleven days. Powell successfully took charge of the negotiations and secured the return of the crew. It was a victory for the secretary of state and the outcome pleased Rice. It also gave Powell a sense that his diplomatic skills were valued despite the rebuffs he got on other issues.

By then Rice had bought an apartment in the Watergate that overlooked the Potomac River and was just minutes from the White House. She had renovations done and then moved in at the end of March, thanks largely to her Aunt Gee and Chip Blacker's partner, Louis Olave, who had packed up Rice's house in Palo Alto and unpacked her in Washington. Rice, who was working six or seven days a week and was never much of a nester, was relieved to have someone take care of it all. "I would come home every day, more boxes would be unpacked," Rice said. "Finally all the boxes were unpacked. I remember Gee saying, 'But you're not going to be able to find anything.' I said, 'I don't care, just put it away.' "[80]

Rice spent many, if not most, of her weekends with the Bushes at Camp David. She and the president were busy with the national security briefing and other work on Saturday mornings, but in the afternoons they worked out in the gym together or watched football games on television. Other times Rice and Laura Bush went on long walks together or worked jigsaw puzzles. Sometimes Rice would bowl in the Camp David bowling alley with Andy Card and his wife, Kathleen. Like the other guests, Rice ate her meals with the first couple at a big table in a communal dining room, but always had a cabin to herself on the grounds. "I sit with my reading and my cup of coffee, and especially if it's winter, I make a fire," Rice once said. "It's really not tough duty."[81]

On the weekends that Rice was in town, she attended services at National Presbyterian, a largely white establishment church in northwest Washington, and went on Sunday afternoon shopping trips to Saks Fifth Avenue in the Washington suburb of Chevy Chase. She had no security protection in those pre-9/11 days, so she drove herself in the Mercedes she had bought while she was Stanford provost. Sometimes on Saturday evenings she would go to concerts at the Kennedy Center, just next door to the Watergate, with her friend Mary Bush, a Republican business executive who had been a member of John Rice's church youth group in Birmingham.

On Good Friday that first year, Rice went to the Kennedy Center to hear the Brahms Requiem with Steve Hadley and his wife, Ann. Later she would look back on the evening as one of the last moments of normalcy for a very long time. "I remember it was a lovely April evening, and I remember walking back and thinking, Oh, this is going to be great. You know, I live next door to the Kennedy Center, I'm going to be walking over to the Kennedy Center to things, and it was so peaceful and it felt so good," she said.[82]

On May 1, Rice's sense that things were right with the world continued when a tragic part of her past was resolved. In Birmingham, a state court jury of eight whites and four blacks convicted a former member of the Ku Klux Klan, Thomas Blanton, for the 1963 bombing of the Sixteenth Street Baptist Church that had killed Rice's friend Denise McNair and the three other girls. After the verdict was announced, Denise's parents, Chris and Maxine, exchanged hugs in the courtroom with Doug Jones, the United States attorney who prosecuted the case. Alpha Robertson, the only other surviving parent of one of the victims, said that she knew that her daughter Carole would have been pleased. "I'm very happy that justice came down today, and, you know, that's enough, isn't it?" said Robertson, who had watched the day's proceedings from a wheelchair in the front row. "You know, I didn't know if it would come in my lifetime."[83]

Blanton, who was sentenced to four terms of life in prison, one for each of the girls who died, was the second of four original bombing suspects to be convicted. The other, Robert Chambliss, had been convicted in 1977, but a third suspect died without being charged and a fourth was ruled mentally incompetent. Blanton and the others had not been prosecuted in the 1960s in Birmingham in part because of concerns that they could never have been convicted in that era by a Birmingham jury.[84] Rice was in her office when she heard the verdict.

"They finally caught the bastard," Rice remembered thinking.[85] She had followed the trial from a distance, and thought about Denise and how the McNairs must be feeling. The following year the McNairs saw her at the White House. "They came to my office and they sat, and I remember joking around with Mr. McNair, who'd been the photographer in Birmingham, and I said, 'You took pictures of my birthday parties,' and he said, 'I bet I could still find some of those pictures if I looked back,' " Rice said. "And then we started talking about Denise, and he said, 'You know, she would have been fifty now.' And I just remember thinking how terribly sad that was."[86]

For the rest of May, the administration was consumed by domestic and political concerns. Cheney's energy plan was released on the sixteenth and Senator James Jeffords of Vermont announced he was leaving the Republican Party on the twenty-fourth, which threw control of the Senate to the Democrats and plunged the White House into its first political crisis. Rice spent her time preparing herself and the president for two major foreign trips: Europe in the first half of June and the annual summit of the world's major industrialized democracies, the Group of Eight, in Italy in July. But as Rice worried about the ABM Treaty, Russia, and China, Richard Clarke was once again sounding alarms.

That spring he e-mailed Rice, as he later wrote, that Al Qaeda was "trying to kill Americans, to have hundreds of dead in the streets of America."[87] The CIA and other American intelligence agencies were noticing a dramatic surge in the reporting of terrorist threats, although most were about planned attacks overseas.[88] At this point, Rice did seem to get the message. The development of the administration's counterterrorism strategy was moving sluggishly along—the first meeting to review it had not been held until March 1[89]—and now Rice decided that the time had come to give it a push. On May 29, in a meeting about terrorism with Tenet and others, she asked Clarke and his staff to draw up a draft of what was called, in White House parlance, a national security presidential directive to combat Al Qaeda.[90] Clarke produced a draft by June 7 that outlined an ambitious, multiyear plan of covert action, diplomacy, law enforcement, financial squeezing, and, if necessary, military action.[91] Rice was pleased. In her view, this was the comprehensive new counterterrorism strategy she had wanted since the start of the administration. In Clarke's view, it was essentially the same strategy paper he had given Rice in January.[92]

By this time, Clarke had had enough of the Bush administration's slowness on his issues. He asked Rice to reassign him to a position overseeing cyber security outside the NSC. "Maybe I'm becoming like Captain Ahab with bin Laden as the White Whale," Clarke recalled that he told Rice at the time. "Maybe you need someone less obsessive about it."[93] He planned to move to his new job on October 1. Rice later said that if Clarke was frustrated, he never expressed it to her.[94] In the meantime, the draft of the presidential directive on counterterrorism began to lumber through the relevant agencies—the CIA, the State Department, the Defense Department, the Treasury—so that officials could sign off on it before it went in final form to the president for his signature.

Late the next month, after Rice returned with Bush from Europe, Clarke was once again bombarding her with alarms. On June 25, he told Rice that six separate intelligence reports showed that Al Qaeda was warning of a pending attack, and on June 28 he wrote her that one Al Qaeda intelligence report warned that something "very, very, very, very" big was about to happen.[95] Most of the warnings pointed to attacks overseas, but by the Fourth of July holiday threats were pouring into American intelligence agencies at such a disturbing rate—Tenet would later tell the 9/11 Commission that "the system was blinking red"[96]—that on July 5, Rice grew unusually concerned. She called Card and with him directed Clarke to assemble the top officials from the country's domestic agencies.[97] As a result, officials from the FBI, the Coast Guard, the Secret Service, Customs, the Federal Aviation Administration, and the Immigration and Naturalization Service met in the White House Situation Room, although Rice and Card did not attend.[98] "I'm the one who initiated that meeting and said maybe you better gather up the domestic agencies and just run it past them," Rice said with some defensiveness years later.[99]

But what actually happened was the most colossal failure of intelligence and planning since Pearl Harbor—a series of events and missteps that would forever help define the Bush administration and Rice's tenure at the White House. Clarke recalled that he told the meeting that Al Qaeda was planning a major strike on U.S. interests, and although he said that the CIA thought it would probably be in Israel or Saudi Arabia, he himself held out the possibility of a domestic attack. "Just because there is no evidence that says it will be here, does not mean it will be overseas," Clarke recalled that he told the group. "They may try to hit us at home."[100]

Despite the dire warnings, there was confusion about how the agencies were expected to respond and little happened. Some officials who attended the meeting said they were told not to disseminate the information, which they interpreted to mean that they could brief their superiors but not send out advisories to the field.[101] The FAA did have authority to issue security directives and sent out several over the course of the summer, but most simply urged the airlines to "exercise prudence," and none increased security at checkpoints or on board aircraft.[102]

As for Rice, her response to the meeting was weak at best. Under later public grilling from the members of the 9/11 Commission, she described her follow-up as having constant conversations with Clarke—"I talked to Dick Clarke about this all the time"—and noted that Clarke worked with the chief counterterrorism official for the FBI.[103] But she pointed to no other specific action that she took after the meeting. When one of the commission members, Timothy Roemer, asked her if it wasn't the responsibility of the national security adviser to make sure that the FBI responded adequately to terrorist threats, Rice retorted that "the responsibility for the FBI to do what it was asked was the FBI's responsibility."[104]

Rice's statement was accurate, since the FBI was a domestic agency that did not fall under the authority of the national security adviser—a reflection of what was then wrong with a system that had built a wall between the nation's domestic security agencies and foreign intelligence services. But in retrospect, Rice's response was an overly narrow reading of her function and it seemed obvious that she could have done more. She was, of course, not the only top official to fail in anticipating a terrorist threat at home, but she presided over one of the crucial nodes of communication that suffered a breakdown.

Later, Andy Card would recall Clarke as "a pants-on-fire kind of guy" and Rice as a levelheaded administrator who "did not succumb to emotional outbursts" of people like the counterterrorism chief. "When someone came in and said, 'The sky is falling, the sky is falling,' she did see them as a little bit Chicken Little," Card said. Asked specifically if he was referring to Clarke's warnings to Rice, Card replied, "Or anybody that would come in. She'd say, 'Calm down and let's take a look at it. Let's take a look at it.' I don't remember us being particularly jacked up over the terrorist threats."[105]

But the warnings continued to build at such a rate that the CIA's counterterrorism team, led by Cofer Black, felt compelled to consolidate the threats into a single, strategic assessment for Tenet. On July 10, Black presented his findings to the CIA director, who had been losing sleep over the terrorist warnings and now was shocked by what he heard.[106] Al Qaeda was going to attack American interests, possibly within the United States itself. "The briefing he gave me literally made my hair stand on end," Tenet recalled.[107] He picked up the phone and told Rice he needed to see her immediately, and Rice instantly made the time. Tenet, Black, and an undercover CIA official, identified by Tenet as "Rich B.," made the fifteen-minute drive from CIA headquarters in Langley, Virginia, to the White House. What happened over the next hour would become the focus of a bitter dispute between Rice and Tenet and would be central in the debate over whether she responded adequately to the terrorist threats in that summer of 2001.

Clarke and Hadley were in Rice's office when the group from the CIA arrived, and as Tenet recalled it, Rich B. passed out briefing packages and opened with a line designed to get everyone's attention: "There will be a significant terrorist attack in the coming weeks or months!" He told Rice and the others it was impossible to pinpoint a day, but that the signs were unmistakable. As evidence, he had a chart in the briefing papers that displayed seven specific pieces of intelligence collected over the previous twenty-four hours, all predicting an imminent attack. The attack will be "spectacular" and aimed at inflicting mass casualties against U.S. facilities and interests, Rich B. told the group. He argued that the United States had to go on the offensive and take the battle to Afghanistan.

At the end of the briefing, Rice turned to Clarke and, as Tenet recalled it, asked, "Dick, do you agree? Is this true?" Clarke, as Tenet told it, put his elbows on his knees as his head fell into his hands and gave an exasperated yes.

Rice then looked at Black and, in Tenet's recollection, asked, "What can we do?"

Black responded, in Tenet's recollection, "This country needs to go on a war footing *now.*"

"Then what can we do to get on the offensive now?" Rice asked, as Tenet recalled it.

Either Tenet or Black then told Rice—Tenet later wrote that he couldn't recall who it was—that the CIA wanted broad new powers from the president, including the authority to kill Osama bin Laden, which was prohibited under an executive order that banned assassinations by the U.S. government. Tenet had raised the issue with Hadley four months earlier, but the CIA director had been told to wait as the new administration sorted out its policies toward Pakistan.[108] Now Tenet was making the case more urgently to Rice, who assured him, Tenet wrote, that something would be done.

As Rice later told it, the information Tenet presented to her on July 10 was not as specific to that meeting as he recalled. "This is in the context of very high threat warnings almost every day," she said. "And we would talk about them in the Oval and we'd come back and talk about what to do with them."[109] In her recollection, Tenet was calling her attention to intelligence reports that she had already seen, and that described potential attacks overseas—something similar to the Al Qaeda bombing of the USS *Cole* in October 2000 or the 1998 bombing of U.S. embassies in Kenya and Tanzania. "Everyone would say you can't rule out an attack on the homeland," Rice said, but "there was nothing that pointed to an attack on the homeland."[110] Rice was more concerned at that point about a terrorist attack at the upcoming summit in Genoa, where Italy closed the airspace over the city and mounted antiaircraft batteries at the airport because of threats.[111] "It wasn't as if this was a single important meeting," she said. "This was a meeting in a context of a constant stream of high-threat reporting."[112]

Tenet, Black, and Rich B. left the meeting, depending on the account, in one of two frames of mind about Rice. In his 2007 memoir, *At the Center of the Storm*, Tenet described himself as encouraged by Rice's assurances, which "were just the outcome I had expected and hoped for" although "the tragedy is that all this could have been taking place four months earlier."[113] Tenet described Black and Rich B. as similarly encouraged as they congratulated each other for getting the "full attention" of the administration.[114] Tenet was even more positive about Rice in his public testimony to the 9/11 Commission. "I was talking to the national security adviser and the president and vice president every day," Tenet said in his nationally televised hearing on March 24, 2004. "I certainly didn't get a sense that anybody was not paying attention to what I was doing and what I was briefing and what my concerns were and what we were trying to do."[115] But in Bob Woodward's 2006 *State of Denial*, Tenet and Black are described as leaving the meeting feeling frustrated and brushed off by Rice, despite the dire nature of their warnings; Black is quoted as saying that "the only thing we didn't do was pull the trigger to the gun we were holding to her head."[116]

Whatever Tenet's state of mind, Rice's response to the meeting was to direct her deputy, Hadley, to try to hurry along the deployment of the Predator, which Hadley did the next day.[117] Weeks later, Hadley and the other deputies from the Joint Chiefs, the CIA, and the State and Defense Departments met and concluded that it was legal for the CIA to kill bin Laden with the Predator because, they determined, the strike would be an act of self-defense that would get around the ban on assassinations.[118] Even so, the Predator was not yet ready for combat, and the deputies left the harder issues—who would authorize the strikes, who would pull the trigger—to be decided by Rice and the other principals. The slow pace of government ground along.

By mid-July, Rice was again focused elsewhere, this time on the upcoming Group of Eight summit meeting in Genoa. Rice laid the groundwork for the trip in a July 13 speech at the National Press Club that offered the first public overview of Bush's foreign policy, including the determination to break with several of the international security arrangements that had guided American policymakers since the Cold War. More significant, the speech signaled that Rice, more than Powell, was becoming the face of that policy. In an implicit argument for why the United States should abandon the ABM Treaty and pursue a national missile defense system, Rice immodestly referred to herself as one of the former "high priestesses of arms control" who had "eagerly anticipated those breathtaking moments of summitry where the centerpiece was always the signing of the latest arms control treaty" and then "the toast, the handshake and, with Brezhnev, the bear hug."[119]

But Rice now cast herself as a high priestess of a changed world in which the United States needed to protect itself against weapons of mass destruction in the hands of rogue states. "We cannot cling to the old order, like medieval scholars clinging to a Ptolemaic system even after the Copernican revolution," she said. "We must recognize that the strategic world we grew up in has been turned upside down."[120] If there was an irony in her statements, it was that she saw the need to anticipate new threats after the Cold War, but her response—a new missile system—was not the kind that would be needed in the face of terrorists with chemical and biological weapons, or even box cutters.

The next week, it was Rice, not Powell, who was at Bush's side at the Group of Eight summit in Genoa. Although Powell attended a session for the Group of Eight foreign ministers in Rome several days before the summit, he did not stay for the main event, as was sometimes the practice of secretaries of state. But it was seen as unusual that Powell did not make an appearance at Bush's first G8.[121] Afterward, Rice headed to Moscow to meet with the president, Vladimir Putin, about the ABM Treaty, a subject that would become a source of rising tension between the United States and Russia for the next six years. The United States did not have plans at that point to deploy missiles in Poland and the Czech Republic, which would set off angry threats from Putin in 2007, and the meeting focused largely on the

U.S. plans to withdraw from the treaty. "She was very clear with Putin," recalled Daniel Fried, the NSC's senior director for European and Eurasian Affairs who handled Russia. "He needed to know that we were really going to do this, but we were going to give him lots of warning."[122]

Back home, Washington's foreign policy establishment took notice that it was Rice, not Powell, who was dealing directly with the president of Russia; Ivo Daalder, a fellow at the Brookings Institution who was writing a history of national security advisers, observed in *The New York Times* that no national security adviser since Kissinger had gone on a routine diplomatic mission to Moscow.[123] Rice's Russian was rusty, but she was confident enough to correct her English-to-Russian translator when he left out portions of what she was saying.[124]

Rice was back from Moscow in late July. For the first time in months, she was relieved to hear relatively good news from Clarke: the spike in intelligence about a coming Al Qaeda attack had diminished, although Clarke warned that another report suggested that an attack had simply been postponed for a few months and would still happen.[125] Clarke said that the government should remain on alert, but within days Bush left to spend the month of August at his Texas ranch, Congress went on recess, and Washington descended into its usual late summer torpor. Rice, who was due at the ranch later in the month, tried to catch up on work at the suddenly peaceful White House. In retrospect, it was the lull before the day of fire. Tenet thought of it as an eerie quiet. Much later he learned that bin Laden was waiting to attack until the president and Congress returned to Washington, after Labor Day. "He knew our habits and customs well," Tenet wrote.[126]

August 6, 2001—a day that would come to haunt both Rice and Bush—was steamy in Washington and hotter still in Crawford, Texas, where the president went for a four-mile run before the temperature began to climb above 100 degrees.[127] Afterward, Bush sat down in the new house on his 1,600-acre ranch for his daily intelligence briefing, delivered as usual by a CIA analyst but this time without Tenet, who did not typically make the trips to Crawford. On this morning, the familiar leather notebook stamped with "President's Daily Brief" contained a separate one-and-a-quarter-page report with a provocative title: "Bin Laden Determined to Strike in US."

Rice had seen the PDB that morning at the White House, and remembered that she talked to the president about it by phone, although later she could not recall if she and the president specifically discussed the separate bin Laden report.[128] Rice did know that the CIA had prepared the report in response to questions from the president that spring and summer. Bush had asked several times during his intelligence briefings whether any threats pointed to an attack inside the United States. The answer, at least as outlined in this new report, was not reassuring, but as Rice read through it, the information struck her as "historical" in nature and based on old reporting.[129] To her, the only thing unusually alarming about the report was its heading—"an explosive title on a nonexplosive piece," as she later described it.[130]

Rice was right in that much of the report reviewed bin Laden's previous plots and activities as far back as 1993, but it did in fact contain information about current threats—a revelation that would be as explosive as the title when the White House, under pressure from Congress and the 9/11 Commission, finally declassified the report and made it public in 2004. The report said, for example, that Al Qaeda had for years maintained an active presence in the United States, was suspected of recent surveillance of federal buildings in New York, and might be preparing for domestic hijackings.[131] The report also said that in May 2001—only three months before—the American embassy in Abu Dhabi had received a call claiming "that a group of bin Laden supporters was in the US planning attacks with explosives."[132] Finally, the document reported that "the FBI is conducting 70 full field investigations throughout the U.S. that it considers Bin Ladin–related."[133]

Rice knew that the CIA and FBI were checking out the information about the current threats, but the investigations had turned up nothing so far. At some point after she and the president saw the August 6 report, the FBI interviewed two Yemeni nationals involved in apparent surveillance of Federal Plaza, but the incident was determined to be "tourism related."[134] Rice saw nothing "actionable" in the report[135]—no dates, no specific places of where bin Laden might strike—an assessment that was echoed by the president. "There was not a time and place of an attack," Bush later said, describing his reaction to the report. "It said Osama bin Laden had designs on America. Well, I knew that."[136]

What Bush and Rice did not know in that late summer of 2001 was that somewhere in the CIA was the information that two known Al Qaeda terrorists had come into the United States, and that somewhere in the FBI was information about strange happenings at U.S. flight schools.[137] Specifically, Bush, Rice—and for that matter, most of the government—did not then know that the CIA had failed to put two of the 9/11 hijackers and known Al Qaeda terrorists, Khalid al-Mihdhar and Nawaf al-Hazmi, on a watch list after the agency learned they were in the United States.[138] They did not know that FBI headquarters in New York had ignored a July 2001 memo from an FBI agent in Phoenix advising that bin Laden might be sending students to civil aviation schools in the United States.[139] Finally, they did not know that FBI headquarters had failed to see the significance of an Islamic extremist, Zacarias Moussaoui, later sentenced to life in prison for conspiring in the 9/11 attacks, who was paying cash for flight lessons on 747s in Minnesota that August.[140]

The deceptively sleepy summer drew to close, and by September 4, the first day that Bush was back in Washington after more than a month at his ranch, Rice and the other principals finally met to finalize the counterterrorism strategy on Al Qaeda that Clarke had urgently called for in January. That morning, Clarke sent Rice an impassioned personal note: "*Decision makers should imagine themselves on a future day when the CSG* [Counterterrorism Security Group] *has not succeeded in stopping al Qida attacks and hundreds of Americans lay dead in several countries, including the U.S.*," Clarke wrote. "What would those decision makers wish that they had done earlier? That future day could happen at any time."[141]

Rice later insisted that she did not think of Clarke's note as another dire warning but as encouragement to move aggressively ahead. "What he was doing was, I think, trying to buck me up so that when I went into this principals meeting, I was sufficiently on guard against the kind of bureaucratic inertia that he had fought all of his life," Rice said.[142] In any case, the group reviewed the planned counterterrorism strategy, the national security presidential directive, which was essentially the proposal that Clarke had sent to Rice in June. The plan, a multiyear program to pressure and hopefully topple the Taliban in Afghanistan, was approved with little discussion.[143] By September 10, it was on Rice's desk awaiting the president's signature.[144]

That evening, Rice had dinner in Washington at the home of the British ambassador, Christopher Meyer, who invited David Manning, then the chief foreign policy adviser to the British prime minister, Tony Blair. It was just the three of them, and Manning, who happened to be in town, recalled it as a pleasant, easy time. The three discussed the expansion of NATO and the ABM Treaty—"ancient history," as Manning later put it.[145]

Rice did not even remember the dinner. The interlude on the eve of the horrible events of the next day, she said years later, "was many, many lifetimes ago."[146]

CHAPTER 8

After the Day of Terror

Washington, Fall 2001

The first Camp David war council was held four days after the day of terror, on September 15, a Saturday. The day before, Bush had traveled to what became known as Ground Zero and in an indelible moment of his presidency grabbed the bullhorn in the smoking ruins of the Twin Towers. Rice had skipped the New York trip to go early to Camp David to prepare for the meeting, which began shortly after 9 A.M. in the conference room of Laurel Lodge, the main building of the mountain retreat. Everyone was there—Bush, Cheney, Rumsfeld, Powell, Tenet, O'Neill, Attorney General John Ashcroft, the military brass, and a few deputies, including Paul Wolfowitz, Rumsfeld's number two, whom Rice knew from her days with the Vulcans in the 2000 campaign.

The group knew that the question was not whether but how and when to strike back, and the meeting started out as Tenet's show. The CIA director distributed a briefing packet titled "Going to War" with a picture of bin Laden on the front cover inside a red circle with a slash superimposed over his face, and then outlined what the United States had in store for it in the treacherous mountains of Afghanistan,[1] where the Russians in the twentieth century and the British in the nineteenth had suffered humiliating defeats at the hands of a savage and tenacious enemy. One of Rice's most vivid memories from the meeting was the moment that someone unfurled a map of the country and the group gathered around. "Everybody looks at it and says, 'Oh, God, Afghanistan, isn't that where great powers go to die?' " Rice recalled. "It's just terrible, hostile territory."[2] The neighborhood was rough—the United States had no relations with Iran, the country on Afghanistan's western border, and tense relations with Pakistan, the sometimes U.S. ally to the east and south. "You kind of look around and you think, well, this is going to be—not good," Rice said.[3]

Rice's worries were shared by others and led to new discussion: Should they think about launching military action elsewhere as an insurance policy in case things in Afghanistan went badly?[4] Rice then asked whether they could envision a successful military campaign beyond Afghanistan—an opening that put Iraq on the table.[5] It was hardly a surprise, since that morning the war council participants had been given briefing materials that included a Defense Department paper specifying three priority targets for initial action in a war: Al Qaeda, the Taliban (which was the ruling regime of Afghanistan), and Iraq.[6] Only three days earlier, on the evening of September 12, Bush had told Richard Clarke, at least in Clarke's recollection, to explore possible Iraqi links to 9/11 and to "see if Saddam did this."[7] Clarke was astonished, as he later recalled in his book. Although Bush later said he believed that the details of Clarke's September 12 recollection were incorrect, he acknowledged that he might well have spoken to Clarke at some point, asking him about Iraq.[8]

At Camp David that morning, Wolfowitz seized Rice's opening about possible military campaigns beyond Afghanistan and launched into an argument for striking at Saddam Hussein.[9] Wolfowitz, a hardliner with a mild manner that masked a single-minded determination to confront enemies in the Cold War and now the looming war on terror, had been a leader among conservatives in the 1990s advocating "regime change" in Iraq. He told the gathering at Camp David, according to one account, that there was a 10 to 50 percent chance that Saddam was involved in the September 11 attacks.[10] For her part, Rice later described herself as put off by Wolfowitz's breach of protocol—deputies did not normally speak up so forcefully in principals meetings—rather than by the substance of his remarks. "Don may have said something like, 'The question of Iraq presents itself,

Paul wants to say something,' but Don didn't offer an opinion about Iraq," Rice recalled. "And I think the president was a little taken aback because Paul's not a principal and so I think he just wanted it off the table because it was a distraction."[11]

Bush, who evidently at that point thought an attack on Iraq carried too many risks,[12] took Card aside during a break and told him to tell Wolfowitz to settle down.[13] The chief of staff quickly delivered the message. "I kind of walked over to him, I didn't do it in a nasty way with Wolfowitz, I just said, 'Cool it on the Iraqi talk, let's stay with the challenge we know we have to meet,' " Card recalled.[14] By the end of the morning, Bush said he had heard enough debate about Iraq, and the afternoon was dominated by what to do in Afghanistan.[15] That evening after dinner, perhaps to break the tension and lighten the mood, Ashcroft sat at the piano and led the group in a sing-along of "Ol' Man River," "Nobody Knows the Trouble I've Seen," and "America the Beautiful."[16] The next afternoon, Sunday, September 16, Bush told Rice that the focus would be on Afghanistan, although he wanted to keep plans for Iraq on the table.[17]

Three weeks of planning for a war in Afghanistan culminated on Sunday, October 7, as U.S. and British forces opened a bombing campaign in what the White House described as the first phase of a war against terror. "On my orders, the United States military has begun strikes against al Qaeda terrorist training camps and military installations of the Taliban regime in Afghanistan," Bush said in a televised statement from the White House at 1 P.M., a little more than a half hour after the first explosions were reported in Kabul, the Afghan capital. Once the military operations started, the national security adviser's role became one of channeling information rather than pushing for policy decisions. After the president's speech, Rice went to a late lunch with Bush and the senior staff in the Roosevelt Room. Karen Hughes, Bush's confidante from Texas and now counselor to the president, asked Rice, "What do we do now?"[18] Rice replied, "Now we wait."[19] As Rice told reporters at the time, "Once the operation starts to unfold, it's unfolding, and you are not participating in its unfolding."[20]

But at least at the beginning, the unfolding was uncertain. Over the next days, Rice watched and worried from afar as cruise missiles blew up Al Qaeda training sites and Taliban air defenses around the cities of Kabul, Jalalabad, and Kandahar. The bombing was so extensive and Afghanistan's infrastructure so pitiful that within forty-eight hours Rumsfeld was complaining that he was running out of targets to hit.[21] "We're pounding sand," Bush later told Bob Woodward.[22]

As Rice and the others began to debate the effectiveness of the military operation, more threats of terrorist attacks poured into Washington. The reports were so intense that the FBI issued a national warning and ordered its agents to curtail their investigation of September 11 to pursue leads that might prevent a second, possibly imminent, round of attacks.[23] In response, Cheney began sequestering himself in his "secure location."

Soon the country was on edge about biological warfare, too. On October 5, the photo editor of a Florida tabloid newspaper died after apparently inhaling anthrax spores in a letter, and worries spread the following week when an employee at NBC News in New York tested positive for the disease after handling two threatening letters addressed to the network's anchor, Tom Brokaw. On October 15, these fears further intensified when aides to Senator Tom Daschle, the South Dakota Democrat who had become majority leader six months earlier, opened a letter laced with anthrax. The police shut down the Capitol mail delivery system and suspended all public tours as the FBI investigated whether bin Laden or a deranged American was behind the new attacks. The reports of the attack had the effect of heightening a sense of vulnerability and anxiety throughout the country. For many Americans, the fear of being exposed to the deadly anthrax germ overshadowed war in Afghanistan.[24]

Rice was reeling not only from the nonstop crises but a new flood of classified intelligence that was pouring into the White House. Since the first few days after September 11, the president had asked for and received his daily "threat assessment," the extensive, detailed compilation of what United States intelligence services and law enforcement agencies had picked up about potential terrorist activity. The assessment, which eventually ran from five to twenty-five pages but in those early days was inches thick, included a summarizing chart, or what the White House called a matrix, that listed the nature of each threat, the potential target, the method by which the United

States gathered the intelligence, any corroborating information, and who had been notified, as Card put it, "to mitigate the concern."[25]

Rather than easing fears, the daily assessment underscored them. The assessment was now the first thing that Bush saw each morning, usually between 6:45 and 7 when he arrived in the Oval Office. Bush then reviewed the assessment along with the President's Daily Brief in his CIA briefing at eight. As with the PDB, Bush, Cheney, Rice, and Card all discussed the assessment with Tenet and the agency briefer. "The briefer might say, 'I want to call your attention to number three, we take this seriously,' or 'We've had some information from another source that sounds similar, so we're going to see if they marry up,' " Card later explained.[26] The assessment was reviewed a second time at the start of Bush's next briefing, with the FBI director, Robert S. Mueller III. That briefing, which was sometimes also attended by Tenet, was intended to focus on threats inside the United States, but also to force the FBI and the CIA to view the information as a whole—which was exactly what they did not do in the months leading up to September 11.[27]

The upshot was that Bush, and Rice, were now exposed to more detailed, raw intelligence than any other president or national security adviser before them. Much of what they saw was unreliable, and some was included simply because no one dared leave out the slightest potential warning sign of a future attack. "We went from basically no information to floods," Rice recalled. "It just started flooding with everything. So now you were getting un-assessed intelligence. You know, just anything anybody said that might be a threat."[28] The assessment, she said, had a powerful effect on Bush's state of mind and her own. She felt like she was constantly on edge, in a state of paranoia, but rational paranoia, as even old threats—and Iraq would soon be one—took on new meaning. She was worried about her own safety, but also about the terrifying prospect of another 9/11 on her watch. Bush shared her anxieties.

In retrospect, Rice came to believe that these frantic, emotional weeks affected the psyche of Bush and his inner circle in ways that anyone outside could scarcely appreciate. Although Rice said that she spent little time second-guessing her decisions in the months before September 11, the months afterward were filled with dread about repeating what everyone realized had been errors of omission and complacency. The determination of the White House to go to extra lengths, in Rice's view, was essential to understanding the climate of the later decisions to invade Iraq and to test civil liberties severely over the next six years.

"I think that's what people have to understand," she later said. "Your response isn't to go back and beat yourself up about 9/11. It's to try to never let it happen again."[29] That was the reason, she said, that the White House pushed so hard for a secret eavesdropping program that the Justice Department at one point declared illegal and refused to support. "Why wouldn't you want to know that somebody inside was having a conversation with somebody outside about a potential attack on the United States?" Rice said. "If I could have known that on September 9, might we have been able to do something?"[30]

By the end of October, the Afghan war had bogged down and the word "quagmire" began rumbling across Washington's chattering elite. The Pentagon had bombed the Al Qaeda training camps and destroyed the Taliban's air defenses, but Taliban fighters were still dug in the mountains and hollows of Afghanistan against the Northern Alliance, the loose confederation of anti-Taliban warlords and tribes that was supported by Washington. "Like an unwelcome specter from an unhappy past, the ominous word 'quagmire' has begun to haunt conversations among government officials and students of foreign policy, both here and abroad," R. W. Apple wrote on the front page of *The New York Times*. "Could Afghanistan become another Vietnam?"[31]

But the stalemate broke shortly afterward and by early November the United States was obliterating the Taliban front lines. Elite teams of American commandos, who had secretly infiltrated into Afghanistan in mid-October, had begun operating on the ground with the Northern Alliance, some even on horseback, and radioing in air strikes to American pilots with the enemy's exact position.[32] CIA teams and the Army's Special Forces—the Green Berets—were soon directing five-hundred-pound bombs at Taliban defenses around the northern Afghan city of Mazar-e-Sharif.[33] Mazar fell on November 9 and Kabul on November 12, although there were still problems in the Taliban stronghold of Kandahar in the southeast. There was no sign of Osama bin Laden.

Rice was nonetheless relieved as the defeat of the Taliban and possibly Al Qaeda seemed imminent. But her attention was diverted to a new problem, this one again with Cheney as the driving force for a policy that was deliberated and decided without any participation by her. Unbeknownst to Rice, on Saturday, November 10, Cheney had chaired a small White House meeting in which the participants approved a directive on what to do with prisoners of the Afghan war.[34]

The problem they dealt with was a real one. American and allied forces were at that moment seizing a large and motley assortment of enemies in Afghanistan. Many of them were officially affiliated with the Taliban regime but others were simply using the country to wage their jihad, or holy war, against the West. To Cheney and the Defense Department, these warriors were not the sort of enemies contemplated by the Geneva Conventions or other international agreements covering the treatment of prisoners of war. In Cheney's eyes, these new enemies not only needed to be seized and incarcerated, they needed to be interrogated—harshly—to uncover new threats.

The November 10 directive authorized the United States to detain anyone suspected of terrorism, allowed them to be held indefinitely, and stripped them of any access to civilian or military courts. The detainees would be tried instead by closed military tribunals with no promise of a presumption of innocence. By January, the administration would decide that the detainees were "unlawful combatants" who had no rights under the Geneva Conventions, and that they would be imprisoned on the southeastern tip of Cuba at the U.S. Navy facility at Guantánamo Bay—far away from American shores and courts.

On November 13, Cheney brought a four-page text of the directive to his weekly private lunch with the president, who signed it later that day in the Oval Office without even taking time to sit down.[35] Almost no one else saw it, Rice and Powell included. "What the hell just happened?" Powell demanded, a witness said, when CNN announced the order that evening.[36] Rice was incensed. Like the decision on the Kyoto treaty, driven by Cheney months earlier, the decision on what to do about the prisoners of the Afghan war was made without consideration of its impact on foreign policy or how much it would hurt America's standing in the world. It is not clear that if Rice had been more involved the outcome would have been any different, but the directive showed a basic flaw in the administration's decision-making process that Rice was either powerless or unwilling to control. As secretary of state, Rice would successfully push the president to make changes in the policy on detainees, but in the fall of 2001 she was simply sidelined. "That shouldn't have happened," Rice later said of the decision and the process.[37]

The following week, on November 21, Bush told Rice that he had asked Rumsfeld to do more serious planning on Iraq. Although the United States was still making progress in Afghanistan, the war would not be over until the following month, when Kandahar finally fell. In Rice's view, Saddam Hussein remained on the back burner in this period. It would not be until the spring of 2002 that she and the president began talking about Iraq, as she later put it, in a "different way."[38]

While the Afghan war dominated the headlines, Rice was focused at the end of 2001 on preparing for the formal announcement, months in the making, that the United States was abandoning the ABM Treaty. The treaty, a cornerstone of the Cold War, embraced the principle of "mutually assured destruction" that held that the United States and the Soviet Union, with thousands of missiles aimed at each other, would not launch an attack that would bring a disastrous retaliation. By barring the development of antiballistic missiles that could actually block an attack, the treaty preserved the idea of mutually assured destruction that helped prevent nuclear war for nearly three decades.

But Rice, who had been immersed in the issue since her days as a graduate student in Denver, had moved on with the rest of the hawks. When Bush announced his decision in the Rose Garden on December 13, it represented a triumph of conservative thinking that the treaty had outlived its usefulness. In the post–Cold War era, the idea of shooting down incoming missiles became more attractive as worries spread about the nuclear programs of Iran and North Korea. The new fear was that terrorist groups could launch missiles bearing chemical, biological, or nuclear weapons. The fear became more real after September 11, and Bush and Rice seized the opportunity to scrap the ABM Treaty to meet it.

Putin, who had discussed the U.S. withdrawal from the treaty with Rice the previous summer in Moscow, reacted to the president's December 13 announcement only mildly, calling it "erroneous."[39] He may have thought the system was impractical or unlikely to be completed, as did many experts, or he may have been thinking of retaliating with his own defensive actions years later. Rice, in any case, was a believer that the new threats necessitated new ways of thinking about arms control. "Clearly we are not against all arms treaties," she said several months before Bush made his announcement, then ticked off the short list of accords that Bush thought were a good idea, chiefly the Nuclear Nonproliferation Treaty. "But the threats have changed and with them the definition of our interests has to be adjusted."[40] What would not become clear for some years, however, was how much this action—and others, like the expansion of NATO to include countries once in Moscow's orbit—would provoke Russia toward a more belligerent approach to the West. By 2007, Putin was citing the scrapping of the ABM Treaty as a reason for why he wanted to abandon another treaty that limited the size of Russian armed forces facing Europe.

Rice went to her Aunt Gee's in Norfolk that Christmas, happy to be with family and relieved that one of the most harrowing years in her life was almost over. By December 28, she was back at the White House for a videoconference with the president in Crawford. Tommy Franks, the commanding general of the United States Central Command, was at the ranch, while Cheney was on the screen from Jackson Hole and Rumsfeld was on from his Taos, New Mexico, retreat. Powell and Tenet joined Rice from Washington. Franks summarized the situation in Afghanistan—Hamid Karzai had been sworn in on December 22—and then moved on to the new front, Iraq.

Franks presented Bush with the Iraq war planning that the president had requested: a twenty-six-page paper, which had also been sent by classified computer to Cheney, Powell, Rice, and Tenet.[41] It called for 400,000 U.S. military personnel for an invasion and close to six months for the buildup.[42]

As Rice's year drew to an end, another war was beginning.

CHAPTER 9

We Don't Want the Smoking Gun to Be a Mushroom Cloud

The White House, 2002

Rice was fretting about the axis of evil. Iraq was the most obvious threat, but should Iran be in it? It was mid-January 2002, two weeks before the president's State of the Union address, and Rice and Hadley were deep in debate over an early draft. Franks, who had been the top commander in Afghanistan, was proceeding with the early phase of the war plans for Iraq. Bush had told Michael Gerson, his chief speechwriter, that he wanted a warning about Saddam Hussein in the address.[1] Gerson in turn asked David Frum, a conservative writer on the White House speechwriting staff, to come up with some phrasing that would provide a justification for war.[2] Frum, who felt that Bush needed to establish a connection in American minds between 9/11 and the threat of Saddam Hussein—even though there was no evidence linking Iraq to the attacks—saw one obvious similarity. Afghanistan and Iraq were both rogue regimes that had alliances with international terrorist groups. This collective alliance between rogue states and terrorists was probably the single greatest danger to the United States, and to drive the idea home, Frum thought of using a sinister synonym for alliance, axis.[3]

In Frum's mind, "axis" echoed the alliance of the three Axis powers in World War II. He then came up with the idea that this new alliance could be called an "axis of hatred."[4] Gerson, an evangelical

Christian, liked Frum's phrase, but he changed it to something more theological: an axis of evil.[5] Gerson wrote a new draft for the president, and as an example of this axis of evil between rogue states and terrorists, cited a single country, Iraq.[6]

When Rice read the draft, she was pleased with the formulation "axis of evil" but was nervous that it would be too explosive if the president cited only Iraq. "I thought people would read it as, 'We're getting ready to go to war with Iraq,' which we weren't," Rice said, evidently meaning that in her own mind at this stage Franks's war plans were still tentative.[7] To tone it down, Rice and Hadley suggested adding other countries from the administration's list of rogues—North Korea, certainly, and maybe Iran. "We felt Iraq alone was a problem, North Korea clearly fit, and the question was, did Iran fit?" Rice later recalled.[8] At the time, the extent of Iran's nuclear ambitions wasn't fully documented—it would not be until August 2002 that Iranian dissidents would blow the whistle about two nuclear power plants in Arak and Natanz, in central Iran—and the country did have an elected president and a small reformist movement. It was different from North Korea and Iraq in another way, too. Iran had cooperated with the United States in ousting the Taliban in Afghanistan and had an interest in opposing Al Qaeda. On the other hand, Iran provided money, weapons, and training to numerous terrorist groups in the Middle East, especially Hezbollah, which had been a sponsor of attacks on Americans, Israelis, and others. In the end, that did it. "The reason Iran made it was the terrorism link," Rice said.[9]

On January 29, the president brandished the phrase "axis of evil" in the State of the Union address, his first since the terrorist attacks of September 11. North Korea was "arming with missiles and weapons of mass destruction," Iran was "aggressively" pursuing weapons of mass destruction, and Iraq had "plotted to develop anthrax, and nerve gas, and nuclear weapons for over a decade," the president said. Then he made his point: "States like these, and their terrorist allies, constitute an axis of evil, arming to threaten the peace of the world."[10]

It was a verbal nuclear explosion with fallout around the globe. The "axis of evil" countries denounced the United States, and the European allies were apoplectic about what they saw as American war mongering. The president had to go so far as to reassure the South

Koreans on a trip to Seoul the following month that the United States had no intention of attacking North Korea.[11] Rice, who had backed into the phrase without thinking it through, was stunned by the reaction. First, no one had caught the distinction that they had all tried and failed to make—the axis was supposed to be the alliance between rogue states and terrorist groups, not one made up of Iraq, Iran, and North Korea. In fact, it was a distinction in their own minds and was not well explained in the text. Second, both Rice and Gerson had assumed the headline would be the president's call toward the end of the speech for promoting American values—or the "nonnegotiable demands of human dignity" like religious tolerance, free speech, and respect for women—in the Islamic world.[12] But because Americans were focused on the possibility of another war, the "axis of evil" overshadowed everything else. It would be another year before Bush returned to the idea of spreading democracy as a factor in his decision to invade Iraq.

Ten days later, with the furor over the speech still raging around the world, Rice was in Wyoming for a quiet weekend with the president and first lady that underscored how much she had become a member of the family. On February 8, Rice flew with the Bushes on Air Force One to the opening of the Winter Olympics in Salt Lake City, and then went on with them to the vacation home in Jackson Hole of the president's friend Roland Betts. He and his wife, Lois, had been close to the Bushes for decades. Betts had been a Yale classmate of the president and had helped set up Bush as the managing partner of the Texas Rangers in the 1990s. On this weekend, it was just the two couples and Rice. They sat by the fire, gazed out the windows at the Grand Tetons, and walked in the snow along the Snake River. Inside, the group watched the Olympics, played pool, worked a jigsaw puzzle, and used the Bettses' gym.

It was a curious fivesome, although Rice, who slept in the bedroom of one of the Bettses' grown daughters, showed no signs that she felt like the odd woman out.[13] She broke away on Saturday morning for the intelligence briefing—the briefer arrived and conducted it in the Bettses' living room for only Rice and Bush, with no one else allowed—but otherwise blended in. After more than a year of weekends at Camp David, Rice had become close to the first lady, and spent hours with her in conversation and long walks. Rice also had an easy relationship with Betts's wife, Lois, an African-American, although Lois's upbringing as one of fourteen children in a poor family in New Jersey had little in common with Rice's Titusville roots. "She and Condi can yak," Betts said.[14]

The respite was brief. The following month, the White House got sucked into an issue that Rice and the president had thought they could safely ignore, the Arab-Israeli conflict in the Middle East. On March 27, as Arab leaders were meeting in Beirut to discuss a Saudi peace plan that lifted people's hopes because it called for the ultimate recognition of Israel, a Palestinian suicide bomber blew himself up at a large Passover seder in a crowded hotel dining room in Netanya, a popular Israeli beach resort. More than twenty people were killed and more than one hundred others were injured, among them many children. The militant Palestinian group Hamas took responsibility, and Israel's leaders, reacting with fury to an attack on families celebrating one of the most important Jewish holidays of the year, sent Israeli ground troops and tanks to storm Yasser Arafat's headquarters in Ramallah, the unofficial Palestinian capital.[15] Israeli troops simultaneously launched a major military incursion into the Palestinian territories in the West Bank as Ariel Sharon, the Israeli prime minister, said that Israel had tried to extend its hand in peace, "but all we get back in response is terrorism, terrorism and more terrorism."[16]

In Washington, Bush came under mounting pressure to abandon his passive approach and do something. Although he had called for a Palestinian state in a speech to the United Nations in November 2001—the first American president to formally do so—Bush had essentially contracted out the Middle East problem to a series of unempowered envoys who failed to make much progress. Anthony Zinni, a retired Marine general, had been dispatched by the administration into the escalating bloodshed in late November, but he was unable to negotiate a cease-fire. Zinni, a Roman Catholic, was in Israel attending his first seder, on March 27, when he first got news of the Passover bombing. Zinni later wrote that "I knew immediately we had come to the end of our road."[17]

Bush had decided much the same thing himself, and that there was little the United States could do to nudge the parties toward peace or even a suppression of hostilities. But he could also not be seen as indifferent to the downward spiral of events. By April 1, he concluded that he would have to send Powell to the Middle East.[18] The secretary of state did not want to go, and both he and the president knew that the trip would be futile. But Powell had enormous stature in the region, and neither he nor anyone at the White House had a better idea at a time when a full-scale war could break out at any moment. "The president said, 'You've got to go, it's going to be ugly, you're going to get beaten up, but you've got a lot of firewall to burn up,' " Powell recalled, referring to Bush's regard for his reputation.[19]

Three days later, Bush announced in the Rose Garden that he was dispatching his secretary of state to the region as peacemaker and effectively thrusting his administration into the central role in the conflict he had sought to avoid. "The storms of violence cannot go on," the president said. "Enough is enough."[20] Bush told the Palestinians that "blowing yourself up" does not help the cause, and he urged Sharon to stop the military incursions into the West Bank.[21] Powell then headed off for what turned out to be one of the low points of administration diplomacy—and ten of the most miserable days of his life.[22]

The secretary of state was the public face of the administration in the crisis, but Rice had a central role as the conduit and shaper of the president's approach. Once again, she aggravated Powell. As he traveled from fruitless meetings with Sharon in Jerusalem and with Arafat at his battered compound in Ramallah, Rice was constantly on the phone with him asking for updates. She repeatedly admonished him to slow down and to avoid putting too much pressure on the Israelis to compromise their security concerns. As before, Powell felt that Rice was not speaking for herself but representing the views of Bush and Cheney, this time about investing too heavily in the Middle East.

"She was conveying whatever angst existed in the White House that day," Powell recalled. "It was cautionary and wanting to know what I was doing so she could report it to the president."[23] By the end of the trip, with no truce and no prospects in hand, Powell came up with the idea of announcing that the administration was exploring the possibility of a peace conference in the region. "I had to say something, so I cooked up a regional conference, but they didn't even want that," Powell recalled. Exhausted, he dug in with Rice. "I finally told her, late at night, 'You may not like it, but I'm the one who's here and I've got to say something,' " Powell said.[24] Rice backed down, but when Powell returned, he discovered that the president had no interest in any peace conference, which Bush feared would become a forum for bashing Israel. Whatever Rice's views of the matter might have been, this was a time when she went with the overwhelming imperative at the White House to avoid undercutting the beleaguered Israeli leadership. The troubles in the Middle East raged on.

But siding with the hard-liners on Israel earned Rice no credit with them on other matters, especially when it came to Rumsfeld. A little more than a year into the administration, the secretary of defense was doing nothing to hide his lack of regard for the national security adviser, at least when the president wasn't around. Rumsfeld had been defense secretary in the Ford administration a quarter century earlier, and in the view of one of his colleagues he saw Rice as a glorified Russian studies graduate student who was not up to the job.[25] In meetings Rumsfeld would read while Rice spoke, or he would be so dismissive of her comments that he made other senior officials in the room uncomfortable.[26] Card described Rumsfeld as "a little bit old school" and "a little bit sexist" in his dealings with Rice.[27]

Relations between Rice and Rumsfeld would deteriorate steadily over the next four years, but at this early stage Rumsfeld was already agitated that Rice was regularly on the phone to Sergei Ivanov, the Russian defense minister. Rice had known Ivanov for years, and in the first months of the administration he had been her counterpart as Putin's national security adviser. After March 2001, Ivanov became Russian defense minister and therefore Rumsfeld's counterpart, but Rice still continued to use Ivanov as a channel to Putin. To Rumsfeld, Rice's dealings were an unauthorized incursion into his territory by a woman who did not necessarily know what she was doing. "It drove Rumsfeld crazy," recalled one of Rumsfeld's colleagues.[28]

Late in April, Rumsfeld retaliated when he was in Moscow with a group of American officials to meet with both Putin and Ivanov. While Rumsfeld and the Americans waited before the meeting in a room in the Kremlin that the Americans assumed was bugged, Rumsfeld let loose. "Rumsfeld says, 'Did you know that Condi called Sergei Ivanov last week and talked to him about whatever it was?' " one of Rumsfeld's colleagues recalled. "And I said, 'No, I didn't.' And he said, 'Can you believe that shit?' Everybody's looking at the walls, and I think he wanted them to hear."[29]

Rice had a respite in April, when she performed a movement of Brahms's Violin Sonata in D Minor with the celebrated cellist Yo-Yo Ma during an arts award presentation at Constitution Hall. Ma, who first met Rice at Stanford, had suggested the duet, and afterward he pronounced her "a good musician."[30] For Rice, the piano student who gave up pursuing a concert career, the event was one of the highlights of her years in Washington, if not her life. She soon hung a large color photograph of herself with Ma outside her West Wing office that showed their arms raised together in triumph.

The next month, Rice was in the center of a firestorm over the first revelations about the clues to the September 11 attacks that the administration had missed the summer before. Congress had been unwilling to criticize the CIA and FBI in the months after 9/11, particularly as the agencies focused on trying to thwart new attacks. But that began to change on May 8, when Mueller, who had become FBI director a few days before the attacks, told a Senate subcommittee that his agency had not paid enough attention to a memorandum from an agent in Phoenix who had detected a disturbing pattern of Middle Eastern men at American flight training schools.[31] This was the first public disclosure of the memo that had been sent to FBI headquarters in July 2001 and ignored, and the news triggered a prickly reaction from the Democrats on the subcommittee. "The American people are entitled to know why red flags were ignored, and I think the F.B.I. has a lot of explaining to do," Senator John Edwards of North Carolina told Mueller.[32]

All but one paragraph of the memo was classified, but some members of Congress and their staff members were allowed to read it. A week later *The New York Times*, citing government officials, reported for the first time that the memo mentioned bin Laden by name and also suggested that his followers could use the flight schools to train for terror operations.[33] The *Times* article, on May 15, set off a day-long explosion that got even louder that evening when CBS reported for the first time the existence of the August 6, 2001, President's Daily Brief, the one that referred to potential attacks on American soil. That night, in response to the revelations by CBS, the White House finally acknowledged that Bush had been warned by American intelligence agencies in early August 2001 that bin Laden was seeking to hijack aircraft but that the warnings did not anticipate that he would use them as guided missiles for a terror attack.[34]

The news sent the capital into a new uproar that did major harm to Rice's reputation. The next afternoon, as Democrats demanded investigations, Rice was sent out to brief the press and do major damage control. Instead, she made things worse in one of the more clumsy performances of her life. Rice had spent that morning reviewing documents and fielding practice questions from her staff—including from Richard Clarke, who had been called in to help because of his terrorism expertise—but when she went before reporters in the White House briefing room, Rice discussed the PDB only in generalities, and with a detached, academic air. "Now, on August 6, the president received a presidential daily briefing which was not a warning briefing, but an analytic report," Rice said. "It mentioned hijacking, but hijacking in the traditional sense."[35] A short time later, she emphasized her point as if she were speaking to a classroom: "I want to reiterate, it was not a warning. There was no specific time, place or method mentioned."[36]

Steve Holland of Reuters pressed her. "Why shouldn't this be seen as an intelligence failure, that you were unable to predict something happening here?" he asked. Something seemed to snap in Rice, and she departed from her professorial tone. "Steve, I don't think anybody could have predicted that these people would take an airplane and slam it into the World Trade Center, take another one and slam it into the Pentagon, that they would try to use an airplane as a missile, a hijacked airplane as a missile," she responded. Her language was so blunt and vivid that it produced the opposite of its intended effect, feeding speculation that Rice had foreknowledge of the plot, or at least that she knew a great deal more about the August 6 PDB than she was letting on. Her refusal to get into specifics that day particularly angered the families of the September 11 victims, who two years later would wage a successful campaign insisting that Rice testify publicly to the 9/11 Commission.

Later that spring of 2002, Rice's attention was once again on the chaos in the Middle East. She had been part of a spectacular showdown over the administration's policy at Bush's Crawford ranch late in April, when Crown Prince Abdullah came for a visit and told Bush—as well as Cheney, Powell, and Prince Bandar, the Saudi ambassador—that the Palestinians were suffering and that the United States had to get Sharon to ease their desperate condition.[37] Arafat was still under siege and Israeli forces remained entrenched in West Bank cities, but when Bush responded about the difficulties of making progress, Abdullah and his aides, in a ploy they had planned in advance among themselves, stormed out.[38] Powell chased after them and got into a shouting match with Bandar, but eventually the Saudis came back in. The group settled down and the mood shifted as Bush tried to make amends. By the end Abdullah was telling Bush, "I love you like a son."[39]

The happy talk did not obscure the fact that the crown prince had made his point in a blunt fashion. Abdullah's power with the president lay in the history of ties between the Saudi and Bush dynasties and his country's strategic importance in any future U.S. invasion of Iraq. Now Rice and everyone else realized the need for a renewed peace effort that looked bold without putting too much pressure on Israel. In the short term, Bush had to get Sharon to pull back his forces from at least parts of the West Bank. "Call Sharon and tell him my ass is on the line," Bush told Rice at the end of the meeting, in the recollection of a Saudi official.[40] Administration officials later professed no memory that Bush had uttered the words, but they perfectly described the box the president found himself in between the Saudis and Israel.

As the prospect of an Iraq invasion loomed and the White House realized it had to persuade the Arabs and Europeans that the president cared about more than threats to Israel, the administration began to engage in a major rethinking of the Middle East. As Rice later described it, the new approach was largely Bush's idea, although she was its articulator. "The president began to question the fundamentals of what we were doing," Rice said. "Not, were we sending enough people out or did we have a good enough security plan, or were we pushing this party hard enough or that party hard enough, but did we have some fundamental problems here?"[41] More and more, Bush saw Arafat as the main obstacle to peace. Whatever the merits of the view, it was a convenient way for Bush to avoid putting pressure on Sharon. "He had begun thinking that the real problem was that there wasn't a reliable interlocutor," Rice said. "He'd been very impressed by the fact that President Clinton had gotten all the way to the end and Arafat couldn't bite."[42] She was referring to Clinton's attempts to present the contours of a Palestinian state to Arafat in his final weeks in office, only to have the offer rejected by the Palestinians as they returned to violence.

For Rice, this turbulent period in the months before the Iraq War marked an important milestone in the evolution of her thinking, not only on Arab-Israeli politics but on the problem of thoroughly undemocratic regimes in the region. It was the beginning of what she would later call "transformational diplomacy" aimed not just at navigating the obstacles but actually reforming them. At an NSC meeting in this period, Rice recalled, the president "had given this little speech in the Situation Room to the principals. We came in to talk about what to do, and he said, 'Look, the key is that you're just going to have to have somebody who will fight terror on the Palestinian side.' That was not surprising. And he said, 'The Palestinians are capable of that, and won't it be an irony when democracy in the Middle East first grows in the rocky soil of the West Bank?' . . . And he said, 'Israel is a democracy, so if there's a chance for peace, the Israelis are going to seize it, their prime minister will have to seize it because of democratic pressures, but we need an accountable Palestinian leadership.' "[43]

The president's musings gave way to what became the June 24 speech in the Rose Garden, a major departure in U.S. policy. Bush demanded the ouster of Arafat before the United States would support a Palestinian state and he called on the Palestinians to back free elections and economic reforms.[44] Rice, who took the lead in conceptualizing the speech, saw it as the beginning of the notion that one day there could be a democratic Palestine, and possibly a democratic Arab Middle East with Iraq as another outpost of freedom. This rosy view would prove to be one of the most central of the administration's tenets in the region, and also one of the most dubious. Even at the start, the speech set off huge fights between the White House, the State Department, and the Pentagon.

Once again, Rice and Cheney were on opposite sides. The arguments focused not only on specifics, like what timetable to set for Palestinian statehood—"within three years," Bush eventually said[45]—but how explicit to be in calling for Arafat's ouster and even whether to give the speech at all.[46] A little more than a week before Bush was set to deliver it, another argument broke out at a June 15 meeting of the principals. Rice, who was participating by videoconference during a trip to California, started hand-wringing. "I thought we'd come to an agreement on what the elements in the speech were going to be, and it completely fell apart," Rice recalled. "The speech was enough of a departure to make traditionalists in the Department of State nervous and maybe not enough of a departure to make people who wanted to break altogether."[47] Rumsfeld and Cheney were strongly opposed to anything that might require Israel to accept a Palestinian state that could become a source for terrorism on its border. Although the defense secretary eventually signed on, Cheney was still arguing against the speech on the morning of June 24.[48]

"I think he just thought the president shouldn't be giving a speech on the Middle East, which kind of implied that if something happened we might reengage," Rice said.[49] A few days before the speech, Cheney had spoken up in an NSC meeting. "There was just a sense of was the president inserting himself in something that he didn't have an answer for, and that was possibly going to make things worse or certainly not make them better?" Rice said. "And so, was it time for the president of the United States to put his capital into this issue?"[50] For perhaps the first time, Rice expressed an opinion in an NSC meeting, coming down on the risky side of an American president laying out his own vision of a future Middle East political arrangement.

"I think you have to do it, and I think you have to do it now," Rice recalled that she told the president. "Just because there's disorder doesn't mean the president of the United States can't have a view."[51] Bush, as was his practice, said that he would think about it, but Rice knew which way he was headed. Over that weekend, the president inserted a sentence into the draft explicitly calling for Arafat's ouster, then delivered the speech as written on Monday.[52]

The call for Arafat's ouster coincided with the slow unfolding of the administration's plans for Iraq—a series of incremental steps, each one making the next more inevitable. Many of the major developments, from the battle plan to the demand that Saddam disarm to the decision to begin a massive troop buildup in Iraq, were laid out by Rumsfeld, Cheney, and Bush. Yet in each case Rice facilitated them as a logical consequence of what had already been decided. In not challenging the moves toward war, she saw herself as carrying out Bush's wishes. It would not be until the end of 2002 that she would actually recommend war to the president as a course of action, but her advice was almost irrelevant because war had become inescapable. Publicly Rice was one of the most aggressive promoters of confronting Saddam, yet inside the White House she did not so much prod the process as get drawn along in its wake.

There were obvious signs that war was in the offing from the beginning of the year. Back in March, Rice had had dinner in Washington with her British counterpart, David Manning, Blair's foreign policy adviser, who reported two days later in a memo to Blair that "Condi's enthusiasm for regime change is undimmed."[53] Nonetheless, Manning said that Rice told him that Bush still had to find answers to the "big questions," including how to persuade international opinion that military action was justified and "what happens on the morning after?"[54]

The war talk continued into April, when Rice had breakfast with the president, vice president, and Andy Card in the dining room behind the Oval Office and discussed Rumsfeld's latest battle plan "and all the things that would have to go with it."[55] On June 1, Bush delivered a crucial speech that filled out his thinking on the threat of Saddam. He told nearly one thousand graduates at the United States Military Academy at West Point that the Cold War doctrines of containment and deterrence were irrelevant and that sometimes the only strategy for defeating America's new enemies would be to strike them first.[56] The new doctrine was known as preemptive war, and although the president never mentioned Iraq by name, his intent was clear.

By July the chatter about plans for an impending U.S. invasion had begun to filter into Washington's bureaucracy. Richard Haass, the director of policy planning for the State Department, found it difficult to believe what he was hearing, so when he went to see Rice in early July for one of their regularly scheduled meetings, he raised his concerns about a war. Rice immediately cut him off. "Save your breath," she told him, in Haass's recollection. "The president has made up his mind."[57] Haass, taken aback, asked Rice if she was sure and if she had thought about the consequences, but Rice made clear that she wanted no more talk on the subject. "The tone of it was, this is not a productive use of our time," Haass recalled, referring to the pros and cons of an invasion.[58] In retrospect, he said, "I think things were pretty far along, that they had in their own minds pretty well decided to go to war unless something fundamentally changed."[59]

Haass's view was shared by top British officials, who on July 23 met with Blair at 10 Downing Street and heard a stark report about Iraq from Sir Richard Dearlove, the director of the British spy agency MI6. Dearlove had just been to Washington and told the group what he had learned about the administration's plans for an invasion—and what he termed Rice's support. "Military action was now seen as inevitable," Dearlove reported, according to minutes of the meeting taken by Matthew Rycroft, a Downing Street foreign policy aide. "Bush wanted to remove Saddam, through military action, justified by the conjunction of terrorism and WMD. But the intelligence and facts were being fixed around the policy. The NSC had no patience with the UN route, and no enthusiasm for publishing material on the Iraqi regime's record. There was little discussion in Washington of the aftermath after military action."[60]

Rice would always maintain that the final decision to go to war was not made until months later, in early 2003,[61] but that was a semantic and academic distinction that did not reflect the onrushing reality around her. Certainly by the summer of 2002, Rice was heavily involved in elaborate war preparations. On August 5, Franks came to the White House to present his latest plans to the president at a National Security Council meeting, where Rice and the others listened to what was then dubbed the Hybrid Plan. As its name suggested, the Hybrid was a combination of two earlier plans that had been under discussion at the Pentagon since late 2001: the Generated Start, which called for a long buildup and 275,000 troops,[62] and the Running Start, which called for an immediate air war and far fewer troops.[63] Rumsfeld thought the Generated Start was unnecessarily slow, with too many troops, while the military commanders viewed the Running Start as risky.[64] To bridge the difference, the Hybrid called for the president to give a five-day notice to his military commanders to mobilize, eleven days to transport troops and aircraft to the region, sixteen days for an air war, then 125 days for a ground war with tens of thousands of troops.[65] The president—and Rice—liked what they heard because it made the war seem efficient, quick, and low-cost.

But Powell was uneasy about the optimism behind these plans. As the architect during the 1991 Gulf War of the doctrine of overwhelming force, Powell thought the Hybrid Plan called for too few troops and too little planning for postwar Iraq. His larger concern was whether Bush had fully understood the huge implication of the war he seemed about to launch. He asked Rice to arrange a meeting with the president, and that same evening, August 5, over a long dinner in the White House, as Rice listened, the secretary of state presented Bush with what later became well-known warnings.

"You're going to be the proud owner of 25 million people," Powell told the president. "You will own all their hopes, aspirations and problems. You'll own it all."[66] A war with Iraq would tie down most of the U.S. Army, Powell said, and would suck the oxygen out of everything else the United States wanted to do. If Bush was determined to go ahead, Powell concluded, he would urge getting approval of the United Nations Security Council for support and diplomatic cover. He predicted that the Security Council would first seek the return of weapons inspectors, and there was always a chance, Powell said, that Saddam might comply and give up whatever arsenal he had hidden and developed since the 1991 Gulf War. In that case Bush would have to take yes for an answer and give up on war.

Rice held back that evening and let Powell make his case, leaving her own views a matter of inference even for the secretary of state.

"She was interjecting from time to time, but not essentially debating it," Powell later said. "She didn't disagree with anything I said, and her characterization of it was that it was very useful."[67] The next morning, Powell got a call from Rice, who told him she thought that the evening had been "terrific,"[68] and also one from Card's office asking him to come over and brief the chief of staff.[69] Powell assumed that Rice had conveyed her enthusiasm about his points to Card. Still, he had learned the hard way that he could not always count on Rice as an ally and even now he was not sure how strongly she supported his position. "I think she accepted it," he later said. "I can't say she was a champion of it."[70] His uncertainty about her views showed either her determination to keep her cards close or to reserve final judgment until she saw which way Bush was leaning. It was not in either case a reassuring performance and it deepened the distrust between them.

Bush left August 6 for nearly a month at his ranch, and the following week, on August 14, Rice chaired a principals meeting in Washington. The group approved for the president's signature a top secret document, entitled "Iraq: Goals, Objectives and Strategy," which laid out broad goals for a military operation that sought both to win a war and to transform a nation. The document grandly stated that the United States would use "all instruments of national power" to free Iraq, acting alone if necessary, and would help the Iraqis "build a society based on moderation, pluralism and democracy."[71] At the same time, Rice took a major step toward managing the execution of the war and speeding the process further along. She created an interagency group of people from State, the CIA, the Joint Chiefs, and the White House who were charged with coordinating the government's preparations leading up to the invasion, including securing bases in the region and getting overflight permission from other countries.[72] The body was called the Executive Steering Group and to run it Rice chose Franklin Miller, the NSC's senior director of defense, who had been in the Situation Room with her on 9/11.[73]

For the American public, it was a summer of speculation without firm evidence that a war was coming. But the experts in Washington could see what was happening. On August 15, Rice was greeted by an opinion article in *The Wall Street Journal* written by her old boss and mentor, Brent Scowcroft. Entitled "Don't Attack Saddam," the article argued that an invasion of Iraq would divert the United States from the war against terrorism and bog the country down in an expensive, bloody, and long-term occupation.[74] Scowcroft, who remained close to the first President Bush, had sent the former president an advance copy of the article, and after hearing nothing back, knew that the president's father had no objections.[75] Rice knew the article would be seen in Washington foreign policy and political circles as a message from father to son about the consequences of Iraq, and both she and the president were furious. She picked up the phone and called Scowcroft.[76]

The two had sharp words, and Scowcroft ended up apologizing. "I don't want to break with the administration," he told her.[77] If Rice had the slightest hesitation about scolding the man who had plucked her out of Stanford and brought her to the National Security Council staff, she never showed it. Her loyalty was to her current boss, not her old one, no matter how much the old one had done for her. Scowcroft understood that Rice was channeling the president's anger, but the encounter upset him. How had a woman who had seemed to believe in the careful diplomacy of Bush I become such a hawk? Scowcroft confided to friends that he was bewildered by what had happened to Rice. "He told me several times, 'I don't understand how my lady, my baby, my disciple, has changed so much,' " said a senior European diplomat.[78]

The next morning, Sunday, August 16, Bush conducted a National Security Council meeting by videoconference from Texas. Rice was still in Washington and others in the group were spread out on vacation around the country. The purpose of the session was to let Powell make his pitch for going to the U.N. that he had outlined to Bush in front of the whole group.[79] The secretary of state repeated his arguments, and he got support, even from Cheney.[80] The plan was now for the president to use an annual address he was to deliver to the United Nations General Assembly in September to make the case against Saddam Hussein, and to call on the U.N. to confront him or risk irrelevance. Although there was no agreement on what specifically Bush should say, everyone seemed to be with the program. Bush called Gerson in Washington and, with Rice on the line, gave him general instructions for the upcoming speech.[81]

Rice left minutes after the NSC meeting for the president's ranch and arrived there by mid-afternoon. As she had the year before, she divided her August time in Crawford with Hadley and another deputy to make sure that a national security aide was always with Bush. It was a custom that had been followed by Clinton on his summer vacations, too, although his aides got the breezes of Martha's Vineyard rather than the inferno of central Texas. Rice didn't like the heat and she didn't love the dry prairie setting, but she did like the relative quiet and the long walks she took with the president and first lady. Rice was by now so close to them that sometimes she even stayed in a bedroom of the new ranch house that the Bushes had built for themselves. More often she stayed, as she did on this trip, in what was called the Governor's House, the renovated original ranch house a short distance away.

This trip to Crawford was anything but peaceful. On August 26, a frustrated vice president, angry about Scowcroft and all the talk of the U.N., struck out on his own. In a speech to a Veterans of Foreign Wars convention in Nashville, Cheney declared that there was "no doubt" that Saddam had weapons of mass destruction and that "many of us are convinced that Saddam will acquire nuclear weapons fairly soon."[82] A return of U.N. inspectors to Iraq, Cheney asserted, would simply bring "false comfort."[83] Only ten days after everyone appeared to be on board, the vice president was now issuing a virtual declaration of war. The speech created big headlines around the world and inevitably led to the widespread assumption, especially in Europe, that Cheney was reflecting the president's views. Powell, vacationing in the Hamptons, was incensed at what he viewed as a deliberate effort to undercut the U.N. approach. Rice, still in Texas, was not happy, either. She had not seen a copy of the remarks beforehand,[84] and although Cheney had told Bush he intended to give the speech, Bush had said okay without reviewing the details of what Cheney might say.[85]

What followed was another pivotal moment in the growing tension between Cheney and Rice, and an indication that the vice president considered himself above and outside the interagency process that Rice was still struggling to master. Rice took her concerns about the Cheney speech directly to the president. "I said, 'This is a problem because we just agreed that we're going to the U.N. and it's going to make it seem when you go to the U.N. that you've already decided, and that's going to be a problem,' " Rice recalled that she told Bush. "And the president said, 'Well, why don't you call Dick and tell him what you want him to do?' "[86]

Rice called the vice president and told him, she recalled, "You know, Mr. Vice President, this is going to be a problem because it's going to trap the president."[87] She told him that Bush was planning to call for weapons inspections as a way to prevent war and that his speech would cast doubt on the president's true motives. In Rice's telling, it had "not occurred" to the vice president at that point that Bush would specifically ask for a return of weapons inspectors in his U.N. address, and therefore, she said, the vice president did not realize the damage he was doing.[88] That version is theoretically possible, since Gerson was still fleshing out the language in the speech, and there would be fights in the weeks ahead about what, precisely, Bush should ask the U.N. to do. But Cheney had been part of the National Security Council meeting on August 16 when Powell presented the case for going to the U.N., and Rice's description of an in-the-dark vice president seems disingenuous.

In any case, Rice said that the vice president at least agreed to try to undo the damage in another speech he was set to deliver three days later. She quickly wrote an insert for the speech and sent it to Cheney's office. "I basically undid what that speech had done," she later said.[89] On August 29, in remarks to Korean War veterans in San Antonio, Cheney dropped the "false comfort" line and said instead that "inspections are not an end in themselves"—hardly a ringing endorsement of their effectiveness, but not an outright rejection, either.[90]

Rice returned to Washington battered by the storms of August, but the tempest had only begun. Both she and Bush knew that the administration had lost control of the war debate over the summer as the commander in chief had vacationed in Texas. The vacuum had been filled not only by Scowcroft but by other prominent Republicans who saw a rush to war. Bush was now determined to end the disarray and present a united, coherent front. Iraq would be front and center. The White House shifted gears and embarked on an energetic campaign to try to convince the public of the imminent danger of Saddam Hussein.

On September 2, the president had lunch with an unhappy Powell and told him, with Rice at the table, that he was skeptical that weapons inspections would work but that he was committed to going to the U.N. to try.[91] The decision ended a debate between the Defense Department, which argued that the United States already had legal authority to attack Iraq because Saddam had been in "material breach" of ten years of Security Council resolutions, and the State Department, which countered that none of the existing resolutions authorized the use of force.[92] On September 3, Card gathered Rice, Hadley, Scooter Libby, White House communications chief Dan Bartlett, and others in the Situation Room for the first meeting of what would be called the White House Iraq Group, or WHIG, whose purpose was to promote the war. On September 4, Bush announced that he would seek a resolution from Congress supporting military action against Saddam Hussein, which he—and Rice—thought would strengthen the administration's hand at the U.N. On September 6, in an interview in his office, Card went so far as to characterize the push to Iraq as a sales campaign that the White House had waited to launch until the summer doldrums were over. "From a marketing point of view, you don't introduce new products in August," he said.[93]

The campaign got going in a big way that weekend. On Saturday, September 7, Bush met at Camp David with Prime Minister Tony Blair, who insisted that Bush first take a diplomatic track and seek a U.N. resolution demanding weapons inspections, the road the administration was already moving down. But the fact that Blair also supported the president's drive to go after Saddam Hussein was welcomed as just the endorsement the White House needed.[94] On Sunday the administration blanketed the morning television talk shows with Cheney, Powell, Rumsfeld, and Rice, who all talked up the dangers of Saddam Hussein. Cheney took the hardest line, but it was Rice's appearance that was the most memorable, and probably the most infamous of her career as national security adviser. Under questioning on CNN's *Late Edition with Wolf Blitzer*, she dismissed views that the threat from Iraq was overstated, and asserted that there had been recent shipments into Iraq of specially designed aluminum tubes "that are only really suited for nuclear weapons programs." Rice acknowledged that there would always be some uncertainty about how quickly Saddam could acquire nuclear weapons. Nonetheless, she said, "we don't want the smoking gun to be a mushroom cloud."[95]

The line was apocalyptic, and in the eyes of Democrats and some Republicans it amounted to over-the-top fear-mongering. At the least it made Rice into a fearsome saleswoman of the coming war. She had picked up the "mushroom cloud" line from Gerson, who had used it in one of the Iraq strategy meetings the previous week, and had decided it would work well on television.[96] "I liked it," Rice later said. "What it meant was, we've almost always been surprised by nuclear explosions—India, the Soviet Union, China. We almost never get it right. And usually when we know that somebody's got a nuclear weapon, there's already been an underground mushroom cloud. So that's what that meant." Rice said that she didn't regret using the expression, although "I regret that people took it as such a big deal. Maybe the language was just too colorful."[97]

Rice's claim about the aluminum tubes—echoed that morning in a front-page story in *The New York Times*—was in many ways more powerful as a spur toward war. Her expressions of certainty, made so emphatically to Blitzer, ignored disagreements among intelligence experts. Almost a year before, Rice's staff had been told that the government's foremost nuclear experts—officials in the Energy Department—seriously doubted that the tubes were for nuclear weapons and more likely were intended for small artillery rockets.[98] But Rice and the White House embraced the disputed theory that the tubes were for nuclear centrifuges, which had first been championed in April 2001 by a junior analyst at the CIA.[99]

Rice later acknowledged that she was aware of the conflicting views, but an administration official said that Rice had believed the CIA.[100] "Somebody walks up to somebody and says we have some doubts about this, but you've got the CIA, who's responsible for it, saying that's what they are,"[101] the official said.

The administration's rollout of its Iraq plans proceeded to the next step on September 12, as Bush stood in the chamber of the United Nations General Assembly at U.N. headquarters in New York and challenged the heads of state and foreign ministers of nearly two hundred countries arrayed before him to act to disarm Saddam Hussein or risk irrelevance. "All the world now faces a test, and the United Nations a difficult and defining moment," Bush said.[102]

The moment of the speech was actually defined by an omission in Bush's text. There was supposed to be a crucial sentence demanding weapons inspections, but the actual line had been left out of the final prepared text of the speech and Bush, catching the omission, had to improvise.[103] Instead he said vaguely, "We will work with the U.N. Security Council for the necessary resolutions." The White House later insisted that the line had been dropped inadvertently, but the mistake reflected the fact that the drafts kept changing as Powell and Cheney argued up to the last minute about the importance of the inspections and whether they would be an impediment to war.[104]

Eight days later, as Powell began negotiations with the Security Council on an Iraq resolution, the administration released a document that effectively served as its philosophical justification for a preemptive use of force in Iraq. Entitled "The National Security Strategy of the United States of America," the document was required by Congress of each president as a statement of administration policy. This one, supervised by Rice and written by her old friend and colleague Phil Zelikow, codified the central themes of Bush's address at West Point the previous June: Preemption was to be the new foundation of American defense, relegating containment and deterrence to the side as outdated. "As a matter of common sense and self-defense, America will act against such emerging threats before they are fully formed," the document stated in an opening section that was signed by Bush.[105]

Although nations have on occasion gone to war with others to defend themselves against the possibility of an attack, the concept seemed to be taking the United States into uncharted legal territory, possibly in violation of the U.N. charter's ban on unprovoked war. The administration's justification was accompanied by some serious legal exegesis by Zelikow. "For centuries, international law recognized that nations need not suffer an attack before they can lawfully take action to defend themselves against forces that present an imminent danger of attack," the document stated. The problem for the administration was that scholars considered preemption legal in the face of an imminent, often visual threat—an enemy army massing at the border, for example, not simply suspicions about a weapons program. To get around this hurdle, the document asserted that such conditions did not apply when modern terrorists could conceal weapons of mass destruction and use them without warning. "We must adapt the concept of imminent threat to the capabilities and objectives of today's adversaries," the document declared. In conclusion, it said, "to forestall or prevent such hostile acts by our adversaries, the United States will, if necessary, act preemptively."[106] Rice went so far as to call the new concept "anticipatory self-defense,"[107] but to many scholars she was dissembling. Acting without an imminent threat was considered preventive war and was historically regarded as illegitimate, since Japan used that justification in support of its 1941 attack on Pearl Harbor.[108]

The administration intensified its campaign to prepare for war when, late on the evening of October 1, with the ink still wet on its covers, the CIA delivered a frantically assembled assessment of Iraq's weapons capability to the Senate Select Committee on Intelligence.[109] The assessment, called a National Intelligence Estimate, had been requested in early September by senators on the committee who wanted written information to help them decide whether to vote for the war resolution that would soon be before Congress. In response, the CIA crashed out an assessment in nineteen days—rather than the usual six to ten months—that flatly asserted that Iraq had chemical and biological weapons and was reconstituting its nuclear program. Two years later, the Intelligence Committee would issue a scathing report condemning the major findings in the assessment as unsubstantiated by the CIA's own reporting[110] and Tenet himself would term it "flawed analysis."[111] But at the time it served as the backbone of the administration's case against Saddam Hussein.

Bush stepped up the drumbeat on October 7, when he said in a nationally televised address from Cincinnati's Union Terminal that Iraq could attack the United States or its allies "on any given day" and that the Iraqi regime had ties to Al Qaeda.[112] The evidence for those links, it turned out, were largely circumstantial. In 2004, the 9/11 Commission said there had been prewar contacts between Iraq and Al Qaeda but no "collaborate operational relationship," a finding that was backed up subsequently by a declassified Pentagon report in 2007.[113] The president repeated Rice's warning that he did not want the smoking gun to be a "mushroom cloud" and he likened the threat from Iraq to the Russian missiles placed in Cuba that provoked the Cuban Missile Crisis of 1962.[114] His wording escalated the sense of urgency in the White House, where it was clear by now to Card that the United States was going to war.[115] Three days later, the House of Representatives backed Bush on military force against Iraq, 296–133, and the Senate followed at 1:15 A.M. the next day, October 11, in a vote of 77–33.

The next week Rice signed off on one of the most critical and ultimately disastrous decisions the administration made on the march to Baghdad: She agreed with Powell and the president that the Pentagon would have control of postwar Iraq. Although an invasion was still hypothetical, Rumsfeld was already thinking about the occupation that would follow. Studying the precedent of the U.S. occupation of Germany and Japan in the 1940s, he insisted that the Pentagon be in charge in Iraq.[116] The State Department had led the postwar efforts in the Balkans and Afghanistan, but Powell agreed that after a major military invasion like the one planned for Iraq the Defense Department as a practical matter had to serve as the main authority. As Rumsfeld decreed it, there would be a civilian administrator to oversee reconstruction and governance and a U.S. military commander in charge of security and retraining of the Iraqi army, but both would report to him.[117] Now the Defense Department would have the authority for administering and rebuilding an occupied country for the first time since World War II.

Rice later said she did not view it as a difficult decision, and that there was not much debate about it. "It was not at all controversial," she said. "I mean, how else were you going to do it?"[118] In her mind, the Balkans did not apply. "It was a wartime environment, you didn't want several chains of command, and DOD was going to be in the best position to carry it out. It was clearly going to be a different kind of war. You were going to be in a serious war where you're going to defeat the regime."[119] What she failed to anticipate was the Defense Department's lack of experience in civilian administration and, even more important, in brokering political compromises among the feuding Iraqi factions that would be scrambling for power once Saddam was gone. The Defense Department was still thinking that a group of Iraqi exiles who had been pressing for "regime change" since the 1990s could simply be installed by fiat. Arabists at the State Department knew that Iraqis inside Iraq would not accept the exiles, but State was frozen out of the decision—a turn of events for which Rice bore some responsibility.

By this point Powell was pushing the U.N. resolution, now called 1441, through the Security Council. The negotiations were torturous because the whole world seemed skeptical of American motives. The fear in the Security Council was that 1441 would automatically trigger a war, so language had to be devised making it clear that the success of weapons inspections, and a voluntary disarming by Saddam, would avert a conflict. Tony Blair, Bush's biggest ally, needed the language more than anyone to prove to his British audience that he favored war only as a last resort. Powell worked closely in this period with his counterpart in Britain, Jack Straw, the foreign secretary, while Rice was on the phone almost daily with her British counterpart, David Manning, Blair's foreign policy adviser. Despite Manning's concerns about Rice's enthusiasm for regime change, he saw her as an ally who would take British concerns directly to Bush to secure British participation in the looming war. "I had always said to Condi, 'You know, there's no question in our minds that you can do this on your own if you want,' " Manning recalled. " 'The prime minister is not insisting on a joint policy. But if you want us with you, we've got politics, too.' " Rice, he said, "got it."[120]

On the morning of November 8, in a considerable triumph of Powell's diplomacy over seven difficult weeks, the Security Council voted 15–0 to give Iraq one last chance to submit to weapons inspections and disarm or face "serious consequences"—obvious code words for war. The vote was a huge victory for the administration, and within an hour the president was in the Rose Garden. "The resolution approved today presents the Iraqi regime with a test—a final test," Bush declared. "Iraq must now, without delay or negotiations, fully disarm."[121] Ten days later, Hans Blix, the chief U.N. weapons inspector, arrived in Baghdad with Mohamed ElBaradei, the director of the International Atomic Energy Agency.

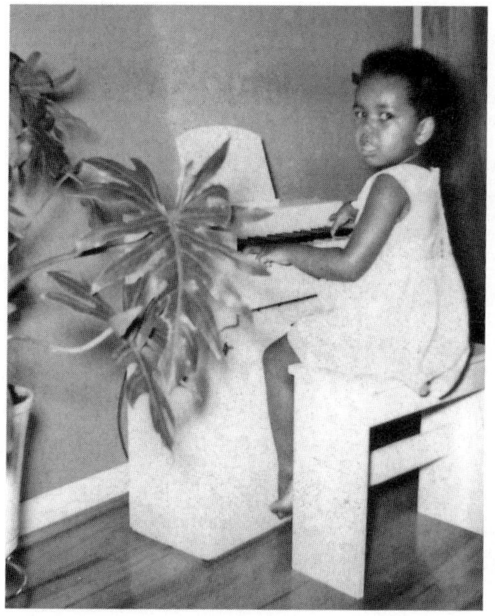

Condoleezza Rice, age three, at a child's piano. (*Courtesy of the Rice family*)

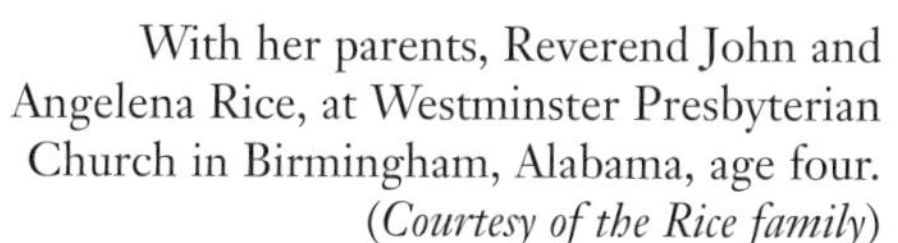

With her parents, Reverend John and Angelena Rice, at Westminster Presbyterian Church in Birmingham, Alabama, age four. (*Courtesy of the Rice family*)

On her Uncle Alto's Jaguar, age five. (*Courtesy of the Rice family*)

Reverend John Rice hands a kindergarten graduation diploma to one of his daughter's playmates, Denise McNair, who was killed with three other girls in the Sixteenth Street Baptist Church bombing in Birmingham in September 1963. (*Courtesy of Chris McNair*)

The second grader at the Brunetta C. Hill School, age seven. (*Courtesy of the Rice family*)

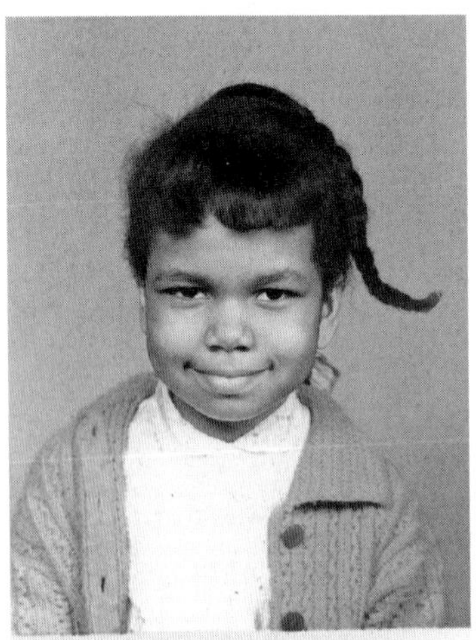

With a department store Santa Claus. (*Courtesy of the Rice family*)

Outside the White House, age eight, in the summer of 1963. "I'll work in that house someday," Rice vowed, according to her father. She herself has no memory of ever saying it. (*Courtesy of the Rice family*)

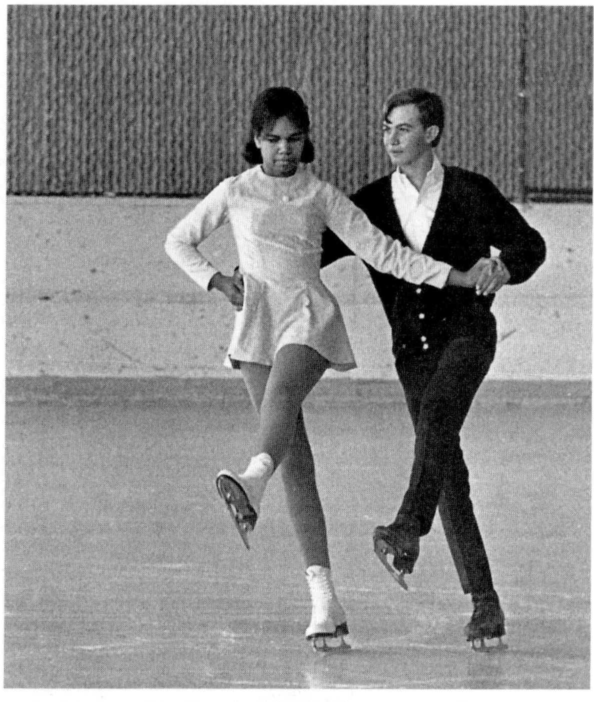

Competitive ice-skating in Denver, age thirteen. "I was terrible," Rice said. (*Courtesy of the Rice family*)

The Owl Club debutantes, Denver, 1971. Rice is in the back row, fourth from the left. (*Denver Public Library, Western History Collection, photo by Burnis McCloud*)

Condoleezza Rice, "Outstanding Senior Woman" at the University of Denver, with her parents, 1974. (*Courtesy of the Rice family*)

Condoleezza Rice, Ph.D., age twenty-six, University of Denver, August 1981. (*Courtesy of the Rice family*)

Professor of political science,
Stanford University, 1983.
(*Ed Souza/Stanford News Service*)

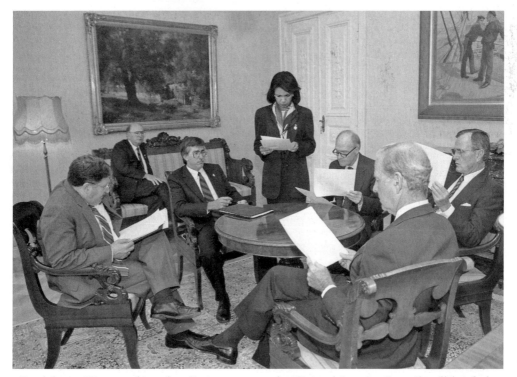

Condoleezza Rice, age thirty-five, Soviet expert on the National Security Council staff, briefs the men during talks in Helsinki between President George H. W. Bush and Soviet president Mikhail Gorbachev, September 1990. Left to right: John Sununu, Marlin Fitzwater, Dennis Ross, Rice, Brent Scowcroft, James A. Baker III, President Bush. (*George Bush Presidential Library*)

The Stanford provost talks to students about the fall of Communism, September 1995.
(Linda A. Cicero/Stanford News Service)

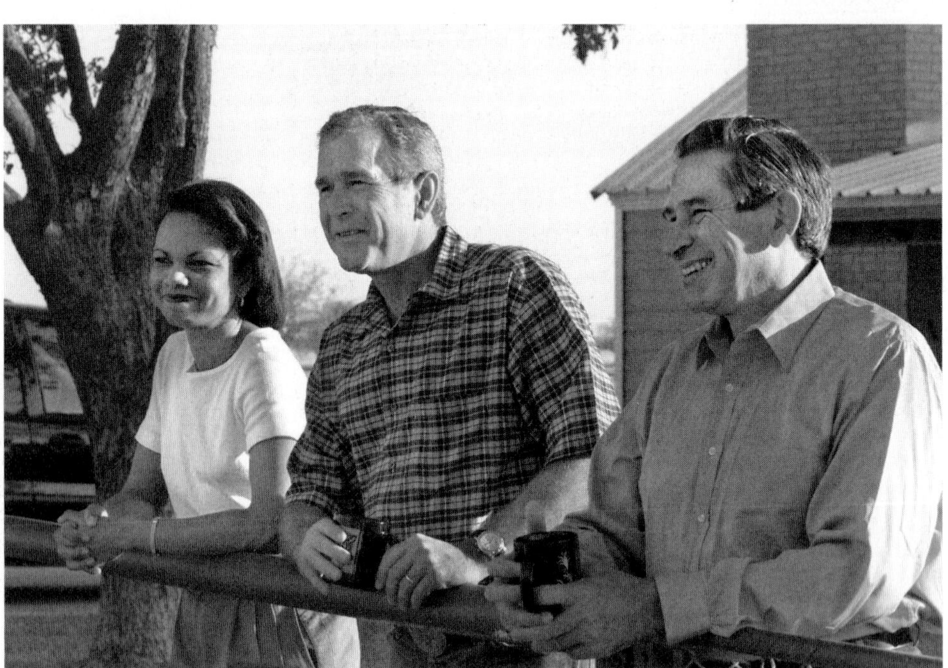

The Vulcans: Texas governor and presidential candidate George W. Bush with his top campaign foreign policy advisers, Rice and Paul Wolfowitz, at his Crawford ranch, September 2000.
(Paul Buck/AFP/Getty Images)

The new national security adviser briefs the president at the ranch, with Andrew H. Card, Jr., the White House chief of staff, February 2001. (© *Ron Sachs/Corbis Sygma*)

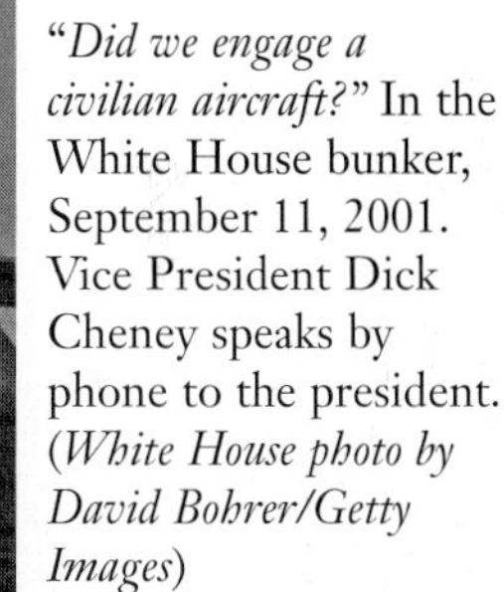

"*Did we engage a civilian aircraft?*" In the White House bunker, September 11, 2001. Vice President Dick Cheney speaks by phone to the president. (*White House photo by David Bohrer/Getty Images*)

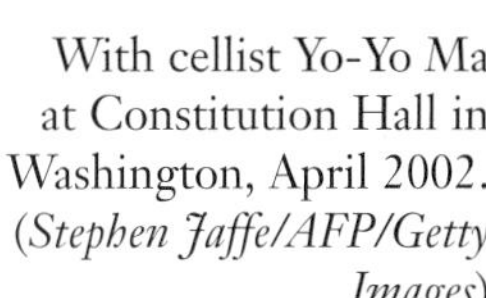

With cellist Yo-Yo Ma at Constitution Hall in Washington, April 2002. (*Stephen Jaffe/AFP/Getty Images*)

Running down the White House driveway to make the motorcade driving President Bush to a three-mile race at Fort McNair in Washington, June 2002. (*Tim Sloan/AFP/Getty Images*)

With (left to right) Secretary of State Colin Powell, Vice President Cheney, communications director Dan Bartlett, and President Bush in the Oval Office, November 2002. (*White House photo by Eric Draper*)

In the Oval Office less than two weeks before the start of the Iraq War, March 6, 2003. (*White House photo by Eric Draper/Redux*)

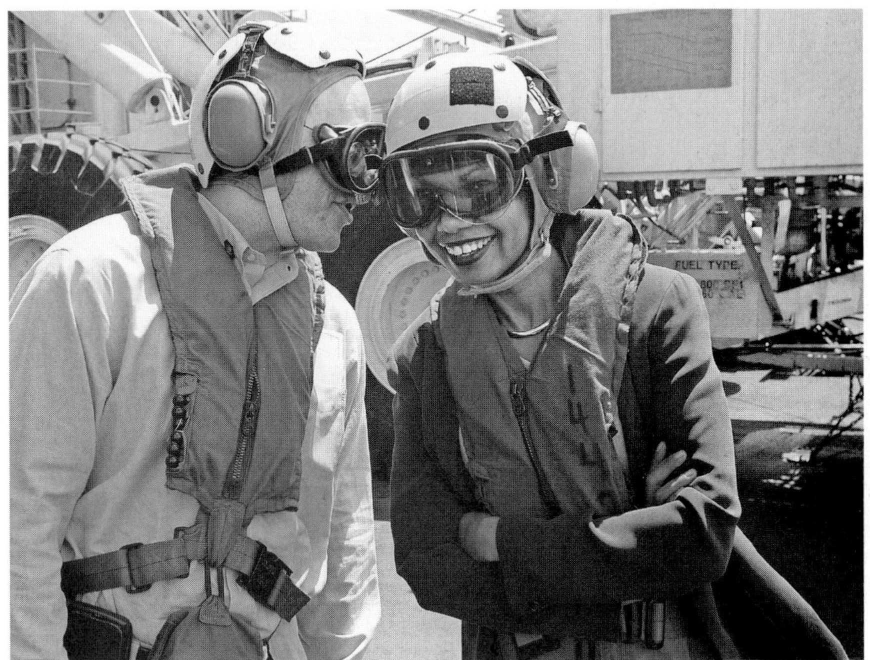

"Mission Accomplished": aboard the U.S.S. *Abraham Lincoln* with Ari Fleischer, the White House press secretary, waiting for Bush to land on May 1, 2003. (*Vincent Laforet*/The New York Times/*Redux*)

A private moment with Laura Bush while the president and Prime Minister Junichiro Koizumi of Japan hold a joint news conference at the ranch, May 2003. (© *Brooks Kraft/Corbis*)

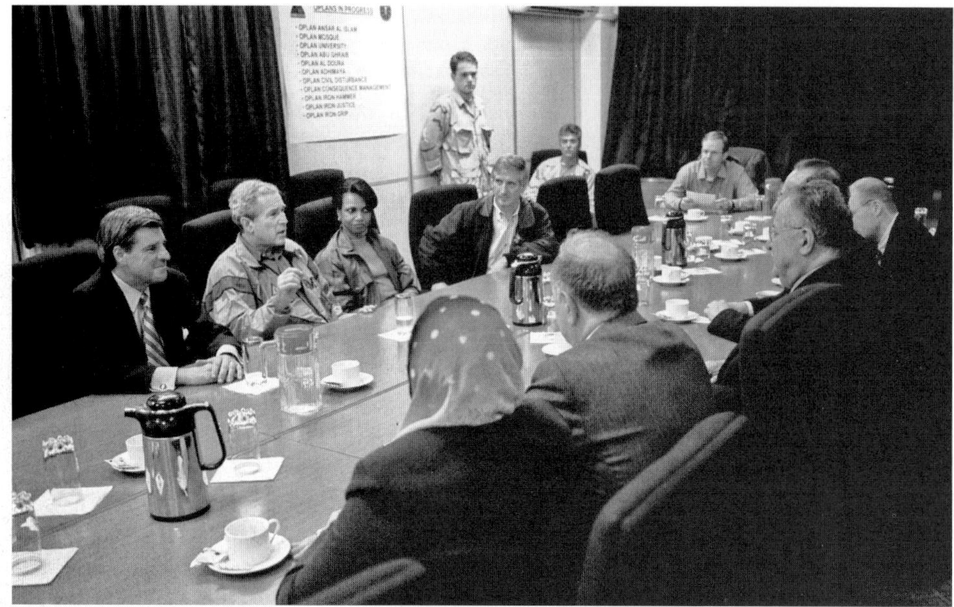

"We looked like a normal couple": with Bush on his secret trip to Baghdad, Thanksgiving 2003. On Bush's right is L. Paul Bremer III, the top American civilian administrator in Iraq. On Rice's left is Card. The Americans are meeting with members of the Iraqi Governing Council. (*White House photo by Tina Hager*)

Testifying to the 9/11 Commission, April 8, 2004.
(*Stephen Crowley*/The New York Times/*Redux*)

“Madame Secretary”: Bush kisses Rice after announcing his nomination of her as his second-term secretary of state, November 16, 2004. (*Doug Mills*/The New York Times/*Redux*)

In the lion’s den: at the Institute of Political Studies in Paris, February 8, 2005. (*Jerome Delay/AP Images*)

"Who wouldn't give her ensemble a double take—all the while hoping not to rub her the wrong way?" writes Robin Givhan of *The Washington Post*. Rice and her boots, Wiesbaden, Germany, February 23, 2005. (*Reuters/Kevin Lamarque*)

At Rashtrapati Bhavan in New Delhi, March 2, 2006. (*Reuters/Jim Young*)

With Defense Secretary Donald Rumsfeld at a hearing on Capitol Hill, March 9, 2006. (*Paul J. Richards/AFP/Getty Images*)

With her chamber music group in her Watergate apartment, March 26, 2006. (*Stephen Crowley*/The New York Times/*Redux*)

With Jack Straw, the British foreign secretary, in England, March 31, 2006. (*Reuters/Matt Dunham*)

A change in policy: On May 31, 2006, in the State Department's Benjamin Franklin Room, Rice offers to talk to Iran, with conditions. (*Doug Mills*/The New York Times/*Redux*)

"Is an Israeli teardrop worth more than a drop of Lebanese blood?" Rice with Prime Minister Fouad Siniora of Lebanon in Rome after announcing that there would be no immediate cease-fire in the Middle East conflict, July 26, 2006. (*Andreas Solaro/WPN*)

Rice with (left to right) the president, Defense Secretary Robert Gates, Vice President Cheney, and General Peter Pace, the chairman of the Joint Chiefs of Staff, after an Iraq meeting at the ranch, December 28, 2006. (*White House photo by David Bohrer*)

With the president's mother and wife at Walker's Point, the Bush family compound in Kennebunkport, Maine, July 1, 2007. (© *Brooks Kraft/Corbis*)

Greeting President Vladimir Putin of Russia in Kennebunkport, during a tense time in U.S.-Russian relations, July 1, 2007. (*Reuters/RIA Novosti/Kremlin* [*USA*])

Gene Washington, director of football operations for the National Football League, Rice's friend for twenty-five years. (*David Drapkin/Getty Images*)

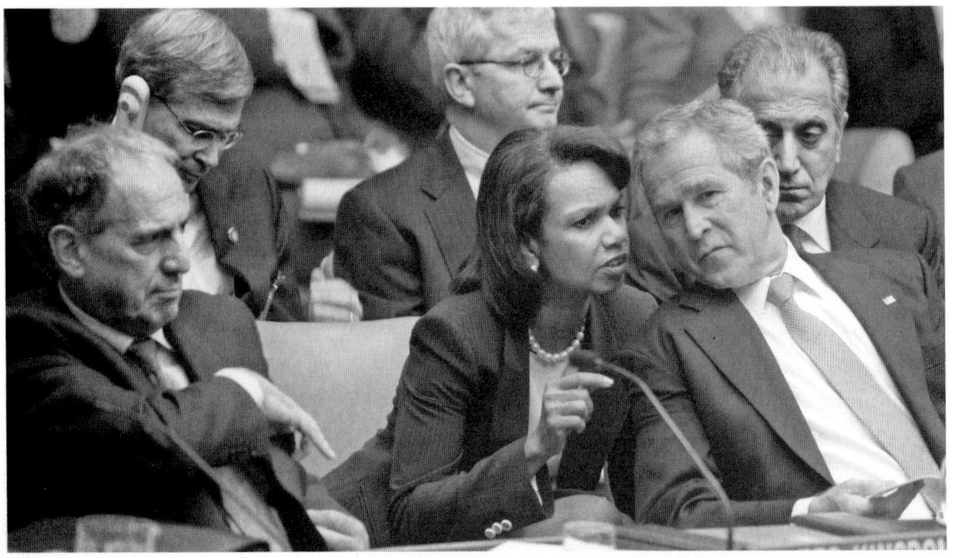

Rice whispers to President Bush in the United Nations Security Council chamber on the same day that President Mahmoud Ahmadinejad of Iran addressed the UN General Assembly, September 25, 2007. (*James Estrin*/The New York Times/*Redux*)

Rice arrives at a press conference in Jerusalem with Israeli Foreign Minister Tzipi Livni on October 17, 2007. (*David Furst/AFP/Getty Images*)

Inspections formally began on November 27 and got off to an inauspicious start. The Bush administration wanted the inspection process to quickly prove the case against Saddam, and the initial hope was that he would flunk the Security Council's first demand—providing a "full, accurate and complete" declaration of all his weapons programs. But what Iraq submitted in early December was an elaborate and confusing inventory of past stockpiles, along with an assertion that it had no weapons to declare.[122] The declaration was dismissed out of hand in Washington. Rice and the others realized if they were going to pursue war, Bush would have to prepare the case for it more publicly with real evidence of what Saddam had and was hiding.

On December 21, Tenet arrived in the Oval Office to present his best case on Iraq's weapons to Bush. Rice was there, as were Cheney and Card. It turned out to be a less than stellar performance. At the end, after all the charts, photos, and transcripts of intercepted conversations, Rice, for one, was underwhelmed. She was not surprised when Bush turned to Tenet and said, "I've been told all this intelligence about having WMD and this is the best we've got?"[123] Tenet responded, in the most memorable phrase he ever uttered, "It's a slam dunk case!"[124]

Bush remained unimpressed. "Needs a lot more work," he told Rice and Card.[125]

With the weapons inspections stalled and the CIA unable to prove its case, Rice was finding the pressure unbearable. Bush was now so frustrated and on edge that he was calling her constantly, asking for updates on Blix. Nothing had been found, Blix wasn't as aggressive as the president had expected, and now the inspectors wanted to take time off for Christmas. The Defense Department had started deploying troops to the region, and the concern at the Pentagon was that an invasion had to start before the desert heat exploded in the late spring, making a war all the more difficult. Bush felt increasingly boxed in by the military and U.N. calendars.

Right before Christmas, while Rice was once again in the Oval Office talking to Bush, he suddenly surprised her. "Do you think we should do this?" he abruptly asked.[126] Rice knew the president meant war. Although they had talked endlessly about Iraq, Bush had never asked her point-blank before for her opinion. Now it was just the two of them alone in the big office. Rice remembered that she was standing near the doors to the Rose Garden, and that she felt the weight of the moment.[127]

"Yes," she told the president. If Saddam didn't respond, she said, the United States would have no choice.

"Everybody knew what consequences meant," she later said. "We would have to carry through."[128]

CHAPTER 10

No Way to Run a Railroad

The White House, 2003

Rice was in Powell's face, chest to chest, demanding answers. "Can't you make it any better?" she asked, in the recollection of Lawrence Wilkerson, one of Powell's top aides.[1] It was late on Sunday, February 2, 2003, and the national security adviser and secretary of state were closeted with Tenet and a frazzled group of other officials from the White House and vice president's staff in the director's conference room at CIA headquarters in Langley, Virginia. In three days, Powell was to take a seat before the United Nations Security Council and present to the world the administration's case against Saddam Hussein. Bush had asked Powell to do it—the secretary of state had far more credibility in the eyes of the world than anyone else in the administration—and Powell had reluctantly agreed, knowing that his reputation would be put to the test. The White House quickly sent Powell a ready-made speech to make the case, but the document bore the distinctive stamp of the vice president's office and Powell found it so full of overheated rhetoric and un-sourced allegations that he turned to Wilkerson to clarify and clean it up.[2]

Wilkerson, appalled by what he read, decamped for a week to the CIA to go over the speech line by line and to make sure there was solid evidence to back every claim. The process turned into a nightmare of arguments over the meaning of intercepted conversations, aluminum tubes, and grainy pictures of supposed Iraqi weapons facilities. Now here was Rice, after Powell and his top aide managed to focus the case on its most persuasive points, demanding to know why Powell couldn't make it any stronger.

"As if *he* were the one manufacturing the intelligence!" Wilkerson said.[3] Powell later said that he was accustomed to Rice's demanding manner and he took no offense that evening, but to Wilkerson, Rice's treatment of Powell was galling. "Here was the first officer of the land, the secretary of state, the honored position in the cabinet and everything, being essentially challenged by this woman who was once his protégée and was a staffer, you know! And it just struck me. I had to go out in the corridor one time because I was afraid I was going to say something."[4]

Rice did not push to include specific assertions in the speech the way members of the vice president's staff did, Wilkerson said, and her input focused more on the theatrics of the presentation. "Hers was more of a constant approach of, 'Was that profound enough? Was that convincing enough? Was that dramatic enough? Was that really all there was? Wasn't there more?' " Wilkerson recalled.[5] But it was obvious to him that Rice was feeling the pressure to ensure that Powell's speech made the most compelling possible case for war.

On February 5, Powell's big day, Rice watched his presentation on television in the dining room off the Oval Office with Bush, Hadley, and Fleischer. There was a sense of watching an unfolding play—Bush was eating cheese and crackers and drinking a Diet Coke—as Powell laid out his case in New York.[6] Despite the concerns that Rice expressed to Powell at the CIA, she felt he had pulled together a persuasive brief, and she watched intently as he displayed satellite photographs on two huge video screens of what he said were chemical and biological facilities. Powell presented recordings of Iraqis referring to "nerve agents," and what sounded like attempts to remove incriminating material before the arrival of U.N. inspectors. At one point scratchy-sounding voices in Arabic that said, "We evacuated everything," "Remove," and "Forbidden ammo," echoed eerily in the chamber.[7] Powell concluded his case with an urgent tone: "Leaving Saddam Hussein in possession of weapons of mass destruction for a few more months or years is not an option, not in a post–September 11th world."[8] The initial reaction to the presentation was positive, and it would take more than a year for the public to learn that one of the most alarming of Powell's claims—that Iraq had a fleet of mobile laboratories to manufacture biological weapons—was based on false information that an Iraqi defector had given to the CIA.[9] For now, Powell had convinced much of the public that Saddam posed a threat. Rice was relieved.

She knew, as did Powell, that the president had already decided to go to war and had laid plans that were all but irreversible. In Rice's mind, Bush had made the final decision shortly after New Year's, when he had told her at the ranch that he thought the weapons inspections weren't working and that Saddam was getting more confident, not less.[10] The weapons were clearly there, Bush was convinced, and the Iraqis were simply hiding them or moving them around. More than 100,000 American troops were massed in the Gulf, and Bush told her he couldn't keep them there forever. In three months, maybe less, it would be too hot to launch an invasion. "Time is not on our side here," Bush told Rice, in one account of the conversation. "Probably going to have to, we're going to have to go to war."[11] Less than two weeks later, on January 13, Bush told Powell the same thing. "I really think I'm going to have to take this guy out," the president said, as Powell remembered the conversation.[12]

Despite the president's decision, the drive to war kept running into impediments. Rice's job was to keep it on track. The most serious obstacle arose when Blair had flown to Washington on January 31 to tell Bush that the British needed a second Security Council resolution citing the failure of Saddam to comply with demands that he disarm and explicitly authorizing military action. Bush, impatient, insisted that the first resolution, 1441, already sanctioned the use of force by stating that Iraq would face "serious consequences" if Saddam failed to give up his weapons. But Blair needed the second resolution to assuage critics of the rush to war at home, and Bush grudgingly agreed to help his ally. It was a fateful decision that led to a torturous new process in the U.N. and ultimately a huge diplomatic setback for the administration.[13]

Rice was in the meantime at odds with Blix, who was carrying out the weapons inspections in Iraq at what she and the president considered a maddeningly slow pace and with Delphic, on-the-one-hand, on-the-other-hand pronouncements about whether Saddam was complying. She was particularly incensed when Blix reported to the Security Council on January 27 that "Iraq appears not to have come to a genuine acceptance—not even today—of the disarmament," but then went on to state that the country was cooperating on the "process" of inspections, if not the "substance."[14] In other words, Iraq was opening the doors to the suspected sites but had not, for example, produced "convincing evidence" that it had destroyed all of its anthrax after the 1991 war.[15]

Rice held a tense meeting with Blix at the White House on February 11, and afterward colleagues said he had felt pressured by her to make his reports more definitive.[16] But Rice's admonitions to Blix seemed only to backfire. Blix's next report to the U.N., on February 14, was almost defiantly ambiguous. Iraq was still cooperating on process but not on substance, Blix said, citing a document indicating that Iraq had one thousand tons of a chemical agent that inspectors could not actually find. "One must not jump to the conclusion that they exist," Blix told the Security Council in an excruciatingly lawyerly formulation. "However, that possibility is also not excluded. If they exist, they should be presented for destruction. If they do not exist, credible evidence to that effect should be presented."[17] Blix, a former foreign minister of Sweden and the onetime director of the International Atomic Energy Agency, was seen at the White House as a ditherer and at the United Nations as a cautious diplomat who did not want to be the cause of the war.[18] One thing was certain: The more Rice made demands on him, the more he dug in.

As if the problems with Blix and Blair were not enough, Rice was having even more trouble with Rumsfeld. As the administration hurtled toward an invasion of Iraq, the defense secretary was doing what he could to keep everyone outside his small circle at the Pentagon—including the national security adviser—in the dark about the crucial details and decisions of the changing war plans.[19] Since August 2002, when the White House had approved Tommy Franks's initial plan for a lean invading force, the military strategy for Iraq had gone through several revisions. By early 2003, Franks's original plan had been overhauled by Lieutenant General David McKiernan, designated as the land commander in the coming war, who added more troops.[20] By mid-February there was a U.S. force of 140,000 in the region, with plans for only 78,000 for the ground attack[21]—not as many as McKiernan and his planners wanted, but the number they were able to squeeze out of Rumsfeld, who was determined to prove his point that wars could be won with a minimal but lethal force.[22] McKiernan's battle plan in the meantime had been renamed by one of his aides as "Cobra II," after Operation Cobra, the code name for General Omar Bradley's advance from Normandy into German front lines to liberate France in World War II.[23]

Rice knew only the broad outlines of the Iraq plan and had struggled to get details out of the Pentagon, where there was considerable discord over how many troops were needed to invade and occupy Iraq. When Rumsfeld came to brief the president and National Security Council on the latest invasion plans, he would distribute slides and handouts just before the meeting and take them back immediately afterward, showing his distrust of the ability of his colleagues to keep secrets.[24] Sometimes Rumsfeld chastised senior staff members for taking notes during meetings, or brought thick packets of information for the president that the others were not allowed to see.[25] Frank Miller, who had worked for seven secretaries of defense over twenty-two years and was now director of the NSC's Executive Steering Group, which coordinated Iraq planning throughout the government, was frequently in a rage over Rumsfeld's high-handedness. "Rumsfeld deliberately withheld as much information from people as was possible, much more so, I think, than was the case in any administration that I ever worked in," he later said.[26] For Rice, it was another instance of Rumsfeld's disdain, but one that she was not equipped yet to challenge.

Instead, Rice adopted a stealth strategy that avoided a major confrontation with the defense secretary a month before the war but got her what she needed. She assigned three people on her staff—Miller, Marine Colonel Tom Greenwood, and Kori Schake, the NSC's director of defense strategy and one of Rice's former students at Stanford—to ferret out war planning information from the Defense Department on their own. Together the three had many decades of ties to the Pentagon and Rice knew they could work the building, either through phone calls, computer access, or personal visits. Sometimes Greenwood would put on his uniform as though he were visiting friends at the Pentagon, find the slides or documents he was looking for, then spirit it all back to Rice.[27]

"We were bringing her vast amounts of information that we had already gone through and synthesized, and if she needed something else, she'd ask us," Miller said.[28] As someone who had mastered the corridors of the Pentagon that were mysterious even to defense policy intellectuals like Rice, Miller had the job of determining what information was important for her to see: "What's going on, what's strange, what's not right, what are some of the four-stars thinking, what is the secretary being told this morning, what's the chairman being told?" Miller said.[29] In his book *State of Denial*, Bob Woodward later wrote that Rumsfeld would not even return Rice's phone calls about war planning or troop deployments in this period,[30] but Rice claims it wasn't so. "I don't know where this comes from," she said.[31] Either way, her relationship with Rumsfeld was a major source of frustration to her and a sign of her inability at a crucial moment to control the process and her unwillingness to involve Bush in clarifying her prerogatives.

Rice later belittled her predicament, saying it was just a matter of the defense secretary's personality. "Don is a bit of a curmudgeon, all right?" she said. "And he can be kind of irascible and short and I'd known Don for years, and that's just Don. It wasn't just Don in the context of my being national security adviser, it's just who Don is. And so I pushed back, and you know, he'd push back and I'd push back."[32] She also insisted she didn't take Rumsfeld's style personally. "I never felt somehow disrespected by Don," she said. "I just felt Don was pushing and shoving the way Don did."[33] But the lack of communication was to have far-reaching consequences as the war foundered in later years.

Rice, who always rejected any suggestion that she was no match for Rumsfeld, cast her problem as natural given the nature of the military bureaucracy. "I used to work at the Pentagon, I know it's a very closed shop," she said. "I know that if you wait for things to come up through OSD"—the Office of the Secretary of Defense—"to NSC, you won't ever see them. And you won't get all the information, because the Pentagon homogenizes stuff before it comes up. This isn't Don's Pentagon, this is any Pentagon."[34] Her comment showed that she was more interested in navigating the system than in changing it to make it work for her. It was a tentative approach demonstrating that after more than two years as national security adviser, Rice was still feeling her way in the job.

In the meantime, no one, Rice included, had focused much attention on postwar Iraq, a shortcoming that would have catastrophic effects in the months ahead. The planning had been the responsibility of the Pentagon since Rumsfeld had taken control of the postwar strategy in October 2002, but there had been little immediate follow-up. In early January, Douglas Feith, an undersecretary of defense for policy and a member of Rumsfeld's inner circle of believers in preemption and military transformation, finally contacted Jay Garner, a retired three-star general who had overseen the relief effort in Kurdistan, in northern Iraq, after the 1991 Persian Gulf War. Feith asked if Garner would run a new civilian postwar planning office and eventually take it to Iraq, and Garner accepted the challenge without knowing what a challenge it would become.[35] Feith told Garner that he probably wouldn't have to be in Iraq for long, perhaps just ninety days, because Feith predicted that by then an Iraqi government would be formed and an American ambassador dispatched to Baghdad.[36]

Feith worked with Frank Miller on the NSC staff because of the early Iraq planning that Miller had done for Rice the summer before, but it was not a happy relationship. Miller found Feith's approach ideological and almost willfully naive. Feith would come to meetings, Miller said, and "launch into some political peroration of the goodness of democracy against the badness or evil of fascism or Saddam. You know, the flavor of the day, completely avoiding the issue at hand, burning up time on the clock."[37] Tommy Franks, no less impatient with Feith's ideological certainty, once referred to him as "the fucking stupidest guy on the face of the earth."[38]

On March 10, only days before the start of the invasion, the president, Rice, and the rest of the national security team finally sat down for an NSC meeting in the Situation Room to review the basic postwar strategy.[39] Miller told the group that Garner's operation, now called the Office of Reconstruction and Humanitarian Assistance, or

ORHA, would move into Baghdad within days of the invasion and take on the monumental tasks of providing humanitarian relief and reestablishing basic services. There would also be a purge of all elite members of Saddam's Baath Party from the government and security forces, totaling only about 1 percent of the party membership. The idea was to be more lenient toward ordinary Baath members, who had not been close to Saddam and who might be needed to run a future government.[40] But after the meeting, in another Pentagon end run around Rice's system, Feith's office drafted an order that made the purge much deeper by banning regular members from holding management positions in every Iraqi ministry, affiliated corporation, or government institution.[41] As was by now typical, the order was not shown to Rice and Powell, and few outside the Pentagon knew about it.[42]

A second U.N. resolution explicitly authorizing war was meanwhile meeting stiff opposition at the U.N., where even the administration's allies were balking at going to war while the results of the inspections remained inconclusive. The European public, convinced that Bush didn't care whether or not Iraq really had weapons, was overwhelmingly opposed to an invasion. The United States needed nine of fifteen votes in the Security Council for passage, but by March it could count only on itself, Britain, Spain, and Bulgaria to vote in favor. France, Germany, and Russia were all opposed. Under Security Council rules, a no vote from any of them would amount to a veto even if the United States could get enough from everyone else. France took the lead in a lobbying campaign against the United States, and its foreign minister, Dominique de Villepin, at one point declared at a fiery news conference that "nothing, nothing" justified war against Iraq.[43]

Bush and Rice saw France's tactics as an irresponsible power play by President Jacques Chirac, but France and Germany saw a war as likely to drag the West into a gigantic clash of civilizations with the Muslim world. In one rueful moment in the Oval Office, Rice told the president that the administration's strategy after the war should be "Punish France, ignore Germany, forgive Russia."[44] Bush laughed, but Rice's words were uttered ironically. They reflected the frustration of the moment but not the future reality in which the United States would need European help to stabilize and reconstruct Iraq.

Rice's comment also underscored that the war was now a foregone conclusion and that the last-minute diplomacy and continuing weapons inspections were becoming irrelevant. Blix had told Powell that he thought he could wrap up inspections and come to a conclusion about Saddam's weapons on April 15.[45] But Powell, who knew that American forces could not sit around in the desert until then and that the window for the invasion was mid- to late March, told him that was too late.[46] On March 12, after Mexico and Chile refused to support the second resolution, Bush told Blair they didn't have the votes and that their effort was doomed.[47] Their fatal mistake, for which Rice bore responsibility along with Powell, was in failing to determine whether they had the votes before going ahead. As a result, the war looked even more like an adventure waged in defiance of world opinion.

On March 16, a last-ditch summit in the Azores for Bush, Blair, and President José Aznar of Spain to meet about making a final stab at diplomacy was nothing more than show. The real thinking and the eerie self-confidence of the administration was reflected more accurately by Cheney, who went on *Meet the Press* the same day to declare that U.S. troops in Iraq "will, in fact, be greeted as liberators."[48] The following morning, March 17, the United States, Britain, and Spain officially withdrew the second resolution. That evening in a primetime speech from the White House, Bush gave Saddam Hussein forty-eight hours to leave Iraq.

On the morning of March 19, Rice took her seat in the Situation Room with the president and the rest of the National Security Council for the long-planned opening of the war in Iraq. There was a theatricality to the scene, as if the participants knew they were actors in a drama that would soon be spun out by the White House spokesmen as their version of history. Tommy Franks and nine of his senior commanders appeared on a secure video link in the room, beamed in from positions in the Persian Gulf. There were now more than 240,000

American forces in the region. Franks, who was at Prince Sultan Air Base in Saudi Arabia, said that each commander would brief the president.[49] One by one they did, and afterward the president asked them all the same thing. "Do you have everything you need?" he said, as Rice recalled it. "Are you ready to go?"[50] The answers were all yes. "The rules of engagement and command and control are in place," Franks said. "The force is ready to go, Mr. President."[51]

Bush then gave the command he had prepared for the occasion: "For the peace of the world and the benefit and freedom of the Iraqi people, I hereby give the order to execute Operation Iraqi Freedom. May God bless the troops."[52] Tears welled up in his eyes.[53] The president then went for a walk alone on the circular jogging track on the South Lawn and Rice returned to her office, tense but relieved that the long months of buildup and uncertainty were over. The war plan now called for forty-eight hours of stealth operations—U.S. commandos were at that moment crossing the border from Jordan into western Iraq—followed by a "shock and awe" bombing campaign on Baghdad and a nearly simultaneous ground invasion from Kuwait.

Rice thought the afternoon would be relatively quiet but she soon got an urgent call. "The president wants you in the Oval right away," she was told.[54] Rice hurried down to find Tenet and top CIA officials showing Bush maps, including a hand-drawn one, of Dora Farms, a complex southeast of Baghdad on the Tigris River that was used by Saddam Hussein's wife. The CIA had intelligence indicating that Saddam and his sons might be there that evening. It was a chance to decapitate the Iraqi government in a single air strike, and the best-case scenario, or fantasy, was that it would somehow end the war before it began.

Rice was skeptical. "I remember thinking that it seemed far-fetched that we could be so fortunate, actually," she said. "And it was all still unfolding."[55] While the group was there, one of the CIA officials was called away from the Oval Office to take a secure telephone call at the desk of the president's scheduler.[56] He was told that a new piece of intelligence had just come in: If Saddam was going to be at Dora Farms that evening, he would be in a bunker.[57] The information escalated the risks. Unmanned Tomahawk cruise missiles, which could be launched from distant ships, would not be enough to destroy a bunker that the intelligence showed was buried under layers of dirt and concrete. The United States would also have to use manned F-117 stealth fighter jets which could carry two-thousand-pound "bunker buster" bombs, a much heavier payload than a cruise missile. The problem was that the F-117 pilots would have to fly into the teeth of Baghdad's antiaircraft defenses and surface-to-air missile sites before the "shock and awe" bombing campaign could suppress them.[58] There was a significant risk that the pilots would be detected and shot down.

The entire war council was now in the Oval Office—Cheney, Rumsfeld, Powell, Card, Tenet, Myers, Hadley, Rice—debating what to do. There were open telephone lines to the commanders in the field, and at one point Myers left to order the coordinates of the Dora Farms site into the guidance systems of the cruise missiles.[59] Bush hung back while the group talked, knowing he would have to make the decision. "It was clear he was uncomfortable, and I was uncomfortable, too," Rice said. "I mean, everything was in place. The war plan was in place. And what I remember was it just seemed like a totally bizarre scene. Because here we are in the Oval Office, this information is literally coming in moment by moment, and people are drawing things on pieces of paper, it must be here, and poor Dick Myers is running down the hallway trying to get the right coordinates to go after this thing, and you know, I thought it was right to take the shot, but there was a kind of sense of this isn't any way to run a railroad."[60]

Myers gave Bush until 7:15 P.M. to make the decision. The timing was for the pilots, who needed to fly from their base in Qatar and reach Baghdad before the sun came up, or else they would be easy pickings in the morning light for Saddam's air defenses.[61] Late in the day in the Oval Office, Bush went around the room and asked the advisers what they would do. All said yes. Bush then did something revealing. He asked everyone but Cheney to leave the room. Alone with the vice president, he asked him what he would do, and Cheney was unequivocal. "I think we ought to go for it," he said, in one account of the conversation.[62] It was another sign of Cheney's power and secrecy and of how much the vice president worked outside the regular circle of presidential advisers. Bush called everyone back in and at 7:12 P.M. gave the order to execute the strike.[63] "Let's go," he said.[64]

Rice was on edge and uneasy about the improvised tactics. "It seemed a little bit not orderly to me," she later said. "If you're going to give it a shot, you didn't have time to plan it by its very nature."[65] The moment undercut her desire to be in control and seemed to encapsulate a deeper problem with her inability to manage the situation. "So people were doing their best, but I'm an orderly person," she said. "And at some level it was my responsibility as national security adviser to make sure it was an orderly process. But there was no way to make this an orderly process!"[66]

Rice called Manning, her counterpart in London, who was at a dinner party. "David, there's a little change in plans," she told him, and then asked him to wake the prime minister. Manning, who remembered Rice's voice as "completely calm," said that Rice quickly laid out the case as "I have this intelligence, I've thought very hard about it, it may or may not be the right thing to do, but if it shortened hostilities and saved lives, the president thought it was the right thing to do."[67]

As the White House waited, two F-117s flew from Al Udeid Air Base in Qatar into the Iraqi air defenses ringing Baghdad and dropped four of the two-thousand-pound bombs on the bunker. At nearly the same time, forty-five Tomahawk cruise missiles fired from ships and submarines in the Red Sea and the northern Persian Gulf hit Iraqi command structures surrounding the bunker.[68] It was around 10 P.M. in Washington, and Myers quickly reported to Hadley that the pilots had successfully dropped their bombs but were not out of hostile territory. At 10:15 P.M., with the fate of the pilots still unknown, the president addressed the nation from the Oval Office, withholding the crucial details of what was happening. "On my orders, coalition forces have begun striking selected targets of military importance to undermine Saddam Hussein's ability to wage war," he said. "These are opening stages of what will be a broad and concerted campaign."[69]

Close to 11 P.M., Myers told Hadley that the pilots were out of hostile airspace and on approach to land. Rice called the president. "The pilots are out of harm's way," she told him.[70] The next day, nearly twenty-four hours ahead of the original plan, the first U.S. ground contingents crossed the Kuwait border into Iraq. The following day, Friday, March 21, missiles and bombs rained down on Baghdad for the start of the "shock and awe" campaign, much of it covered live on CNN. Ari Fleischer told reporters that Bush was far too busy to look at it, but that was hardly the case. In fact the president, and Rice, were avid consumers of the war coverage on the cable networks and spent much of that weekend at Camp David keeping track of the war on television while getting their own reports from the region. Saddam, it turned out, was not hit, and when U.S. forces examined the Dora Farms site after the fall of Baghdad, there was no underground bunker and no evidence that Saddam had even been there on March 19.[71] It was a small intelligence failure that reflected a much larger problem of the faulty intelligence that surrounded the war.

Rice was on edge but cautiously optimistic that the war would go well. She told friends at the time that she was convinced that the postwar phase would be like the successful American occupation of Germany after World War II, and that it would be possible to plant democracy in a shattered Iraq. Some of Rice's friends were stunned that she actually seemed to believe Bush's argument in the final days of the war buildup that a liberated Iraq could spread freedom across the Middle East. They could only surmise that Rice's experience working for the Bush I administration as the Soviet empire dissolved and Eastern Europe turned quickly to the West had distorted her perspective.

But there was something else going on. Rice's embrace of the president's democracy agenda drew on the wellsprings of her own experience in Birmingham, where blacks had been effectively told they weren't "ready" for democracy under segregation. Rice seemed to be reacting viscerally because of the condescension she herself had felt growing up. She had never given much thought to how segregation related to her career in foreign policy, but now the swirl of events after September 11 and her search for answers to why some Arabs in oppressive circumstances resorted to terrorism gave her a powerful connection to the idea that she would later try to develop on her own in her first two years as secretary of state.

The war, meanwhile, moved quickly. Sandstorms and unexpected resistance from Saddam's elite militia, the fedayeen, slowed down the invasion force at points on the long march north, but by April 5 the Army's Third Infantry Division had rolled into the heart of Baghdad.[72] With victory in sight, Bush flew to Northern Ireland to meet with Blair on April 7 about postwar Iraq. Rice, reflecting the self-confidence she and others felt at the moment, had said that only countries that had spilled "blood and treasure" would be involved in carving out a new nation.[73] The United States was at least initially determined to take the central role so that the White House could control the political process leading to a new Iraqi government—one with pliant, pro-American leaders who would cooperate with the military and U.S. economic interests in the region.

A skirmish soon broke out over Blair's insistence that the United Nations be brought in to participate in running postwar Iraq. Powell sided with Blair, but Rice resisted the idea as unnecessary and cumbersome. In this case, at least, she shared the skepticism of Cheney and other hawks about what the U.N. could accomplish, especially after Blix's performance on inspections. But even with her close relationship with Bush, she could go only so far in challenging him before the president made clear he was in charge.

The episode unfolded as Bush met with Blair at Hillsborough Castle south of Belfast, where the two leaders decided that Bush should say at a news conference that the U.N. would have a "vital" role in postwar Iraq, as Blair wanted. But Rice disliked "vital" because she thought it ceded too much control. In the end the president used the word anyway—not once, but nine times.[74] Afterward Rice expressed concern to him that he had gone too far. "I did it, and that's it," Bush shot back, cutting her off.[75] To at least one official observer of the scene, the exchange showed there were limits to how far Rice could push her boss but also the extraordinary familiarity between the two. "They almost had to go off for a minute to sort it out," the official later said. "And then it blew over."[76]

The next day, April 9, an American tank toppled a twenty-foot statue of Saddam Hussein in Baghdad's Firdos Square. It was the iconic image of what seemed like the end of the war, and Rice was unusually emotional after seeing it on television. When her aides Frank

Miller, Tom Greenwood, and Jeff Kojac came into her office that day for an already scheduled war briefing, they found her standing up with Hadley, waiting for them. "They were very happy. They shook our hands," said Kojac, a Marine officer who briefed Rice on military matters. "Condi's sense of appreciation for the men and women in uniform was visceral, and Hadley had this big smile."[77] Rice's eyes seemed to water up, Kojac recalled. In the happy atmosphere, Rice and Hadley called off the briefing. Kojac and Greenwood walked back to their offices in the Eisenhower Executive Office Building, floored at the celebratory talk they had just heard. "They thought the war was over," Kojac said. "It was incredibly unsettling."[78]

It did not take long for reality to reassert itself. A few hours after the statue was toppled, looters arrived at the Ministry of Industry in Baghdad. No troops had been sent to protect it because no one in Washington saw the need. The looters set upon the ten-story building and stole computers, telephones, furniture, and file cabinets.[79] Hard-core scavengers pulled out wiring and metal ducting from the walls, and two days later the building was torched.[80] The scene was repeated all over Baghdad as American troops, without the orders or numbers to intervene, stood by as thieves raided ministries, hospitals, and even the National Museum of Antiquities, which lost artifacts dating back to ancient Mesopotamia. The only government building protected at the time—other than Saddam's Republican Palace, the headquarters of the American occupation—was the Ministry of Oil, belying the claim in Washington that oil was not what the war was about. At the Pentagon, Rumsfeld dismissed the looting at a briefing on April 11 with his now-infamous phrase, "stuff happens,"[81] and publicly the administration took the position that disorder was to be expected.

But in private, Rice was shaken and bewildered. "It was the one time I saw her flabbergasted," recalled Kojac, who was one of those now regularly briefing Rice on the occupation. "She's a very cool personality, but it was plain she was frustrated that things were out of control. She wanted to know why it was happening."[82] If Rice did not understand the reason for the looting, she did understand how lethal it was to the image of the United States. "This is bad, we've got to stop it," she told David Manning, as Manning recalled the conversation.[83] She told him she knew the chaos would cause the United States to lose public sympathy very fast.[84]

Jay Garner, the American who was in charge of ORHA, the Office of Reconstruction and Humanitarian Assistance, and was supposed to run Iraq, was in the meantime marooned at a beachfront villa in Kuwait. The violence in Iraq was so bad that the military refused to let him move into Baghdad, and Garner was reduced to sitting back and helplessly watching the looting on CNN. He and his team from Washington had drawn up a list of sixteen key ministries and sites around the capital that they wanted the military to protect upon the fall of the city.[85] (In a measure of how badly prepared they were, they had consulted a *Lonely Planet* guidebook to help locate the buildings.)[86] But their list never made it to Baghdad.[87] Now Garner's team tried to guess which of the ministries being pillaged on CNN might be the ones they were in line to manage. "It was like,'There goes your ministry! There goes mine!' " recalled Robin Raphel, the interim trade minister, who was also in Kuwait and assumed that soldiers were on the way to save Iraq's infrastructure but then realized with anger that they were not.[88]

In Washington, Rice was already frustrated that Garner could not even begin to do his job. "The first sign that this was going to be a problem was they got stuck in Kuwait," she recalled. "They couldn't even get in."[89] When Garner finally got permission from the military to enter Baghdad on April 21, he found a scene of devastation—totally destroyed ministries and no one to staff them. The Iraqi civil servants the United States had been expecting to help administer postwar Iraq had vanished in the chaos. Since the telephone system no longer worked, Garner and his team ended up walking the streets asking passersby if they knew anyone who worked for the government.[90] This was hardly what the Pentagon had in mind when Garner was hired and told to expect a three-month tour before handing the reins to the Iraqis.

By late April, with Garner barely in Baghdad a week, an exasperated Rice told Rumsfeld that Garner's operation needed to be rethought. Garner, who was wearing open-necked shirts and offering hopeful platitudes, was not projecting anything approaching an image of authority. But the larger problem was that Rice had let Feith and the Pentagon take control of the occupation and the political decisions related to it. Instead of anticipating the problems of occupying an alien territory, she allowed her faith in democratic ideals to minimize the problems that would erupt. She also did not see the need to second-guess the Pentagon on something she thought would take care of itself. "I was not going to sit there and try to figure out who Doug Feith ought to be hiring or ought not to be hiring," she said.[91]

But now she felt she needed to step in. "Don and I were coming out of the Sit Room, and I said to him, 'You know, this isn't working,' and he said, 'I know.' And I said, 'You've got to get somebody else out there in a different structure,' and he said, 'I know, I'm putting together a list for the president now.' "[92]

By May 1, the day that Bush landed in a flight suit on the deck of the aircraft carrier *Abraham Lincoln* and triumphantly declared major combat operations in Iraq at an end, Wolfowitz and Libby had already contacted Garner's replacement.[93] He was L. Paul Bremer, a sixty-two-year-old counterterrorism expert and retired diplomat who had been chief of staff to Secretary of State Henry Kissinger in the 1970s. Bremer was known as a highly organized, nonideological veteran of bureaucratic warfare who could get things done, and Rice thought he was an excellent choice to head what would be renamed the Coalition Provisional Authority, or the CPA, the American-run administration in Iraq. She felt a sense of hope as she, too, landed on the *Abraham Lincoln*, just ahead of the president's jet. Despite all the problems, the war seemed a qualified success. Only 139 Americans had lost their lives, and although no weapons of mass destruction had been found, it seemed only a matter of time before they would turn up.

Rice's early hopes about Bremer were soon dashed. Shortly after he arrived in Baghdad in mid-May, the man who became known as the American viceroy issued two sweeping orders that would come to be seen as the most disastrous decisions of the U.S. occupation. First, Bremer outlawed Saddam's Baath Party and dismissed all of its senior members, some thirty thousand people, from their posts. Then he dissolved the 500,000-strong Iraqi army and intelligence services. Bremer later said that he was simply carrying out the order from

Feith at the Pentagon, and that the goal of "de-Baathification," as it became known, was to rid the Iraqi government of the small group of true believers at the top.[94] As for the Iraqi army, he later said that it had already melted away.[95] Whatever the reasoning at the time, Bremer's decrees created a pool of angry, unemployed men who fed the insurgency and drastically undermined the goal of the United States to create a stable Iraqi society.

Despite the enormity of the two decisions, and the effect they would have on the political dynamics of Iraq, they were surprises to Rice, who did not know about Feith's order or about Bremer's timing in carrying it out. But whatever anger she might have felt, Rice seemed determined years later not to be seen as a victim and insisted that Bremer's decisions were simply a function of a bureaucratic breakdown. She knew the decrees were going to happen, she said, she just didn't know when or how. "Specific decisions as to how de-Baathification was going to be carried out were being put in a series of orders that the CPA was issuing in pretty rapid fashion," she said.[96] The CPA issued orders every day, she said, "and buried in the orders were really, really important things. Unless you were reading every order, you wouldn't see them."[97]

Rice said she also believed in a powerful U.S. administrator in Iraq, at least at this point, and that she trusted Bremer to make the right calls without having to impose a system of second-guessing on top of him. "And I was really on that train at the beginning because it was kind of a mess with ORHA and I was glad that somebody who took strong decisions was out there," she said. "But as it started then to unfold, it started to get into areas where he was starting to make policy decisions without policy guidelines."[98] Within months, Rice would take more direct control over Bremer, but in May 2003 Bremer answered not to Rice but to Rumsfeld, since the Defense Department was in charge of postwar Iraq. "My chain of command was the Pentagon," Bremer later said, though his sense of the mounting problems in Iraq was contradicting the Pentagon's optimism about pulling some troops out early.[99] He envisioned a long U.S. occupation, perhaps two or three years.

By early June, Rice's bigger problem was that no weapons of mass destruction had been found in Iraq. The president was resolute on the surface but jittery in private. The weapons had been the reason for the war and the CIA had insisted they were there. Now Bush was feeling political pressure to find them. Bush decided the administration needed a special weapons hunter, and on June 10, David Kay, a former chief U.N. weapons inspector with extensive experience in Iraq, was sworn in as an adviser to Tenet and as head of the CIA's Iraq Survey Group. The group's task was to focus solely on the search for Saddam's weapons, a job that previously had been assigned to the same forces trying to stabilize the country. Once again, Rice believed that he would be the right man for the job, but a year later Kay would place considerable blame on Rice herself for overselling the existence of the weapons in the run-up to the war.

In July, Rice received an unwelcome visitor: Richard Armitage, Powell's deputy at the State Department. Armitage was a bald, barrel-chested weight-lifter the size of a torpedo who swore with abandon and was devoted to Powell. He had obtained the secretary of state's permission to tell the national security adviser of some mounting frustrations at the State Department and elsewhere about Rice herself, and Armitage let loose. He told Rice that the NSC was "dysfunctional" because it had failed in the principal job of resolving differences among the cabinet members.[100] Angry about the denigration of the State Department and what looked like a growing problem in Iraq—the country was already starting "to smell around the edges a little bit," he recalled—Armitage told Rice that Rumsfeld was effectively conducting his own foreign policy on Iraq and other issues and needed to be reined in.[101] The defense secretary came to NSC meetings and refused to take a position, then dealt with the president in private afterward, Armitage said, preventing others from criticizing or reacting to his plans. Other times Rumsfeld would send underlings to the meetings of the deputies and principals—Armitage called them the deputies committee and the principals committee, or the DC and the PC—who had no authority to act without him. He also complained that when there was interagency disagreement, Rice had not pushed for firm resolutions on decisions.

"We got on the gerbil wheel every morning getting ready for these DCs and PCs and we'd argue our positions and not in a nasty way, but we'd argue them," Armitage recalled. "Then we'd get off the gerbil wheel and wait for an answer. No answer would ever come from the NSC, so we'd get back on the gerbil wheel the next morning."[102] There was no accountability, he told Rice, and no follow-through.[103]

Rice listened to Armitage quietly, thanked him for his input, then told him she did not want to read about his comments in the newspapers.[104] "And I said, 'Everybody in town knows this—everybody,' " Armitage recalled.[105]

Armitage thought Rice's reaction was "very brittle" and that he had clearly made her unhappy,[106] but four years later, Rice downplayed the conversation's impact and dismissed Armitage as incoherent. "I barely remember this conversation," she insisted. "I remember saying something like, 'Well, what is it that you think isn't working?' " People become "incredibly inarticulate," she said, "when you ask them, 'Well, what is it that isn't working? Do you not get to express your views?' Well, no, you get to express your views. 'Do you not get access to the president if you need it?' Well, no, you get access to the president if you need it. 'Well, the deputies committee gets locked up, you know? It can't move.' Well, fine. Take it to the principals for a decision. So, since he couldn't articulate what it was, I sort of put it aside because if you think something is dysfunctional, then you probably ought to have an explanation for what that means."[107]

Powell had told Rice of similar concerns, although he had not been as confrontational.[108] He had in any case come to the conclusion that Rice was only partially to blame. Rumsfeld was a powerful obstacle who knew how to exploit the system, but Powell saw the greater problem as the vice president and his parallel national security operation.[109] Rice, at least in Powell's view, did not consider it her place to challenge Cheney in the full forum of a National Security Council meeting, and Armitage, who did not know of the times that Rice had quietly gone to Bush to complain about the vice president, could only see that she treated Cheney very carefully. "She couldn't take him on very often," Armitage said.[110] Armitage, like Powell, ultimately concluded that the president had the national security system he wanted, and that Rice had decided that she could live with it and be selective in her fights with the defense secretary and vice president.[111]

In the weeks after Armitage's confrontation with Rice, Glenn

Kessler and Peter Slevin of *The Washington Post* wrote an article quoting an unnamed "senior State Department official" who described the NSC process as "dysfunctional."[112] Rice called Powell and angrily accused Armitage of leaking the story. After the call, Armitage told Powell he hadn't done it, and then repeated to Powell what he had said to Rice, that everybody in town knew about her shortcomings.[113]

Both Armitage and Powell had come to the view that Rice was more of an enabler for Bush's combative instincts and not enough of a counterweight. "Whatever your president wants, that's all his business, and fine," Armitage later said. Ideally, he explained, a national security adviser should serve as an "attenuator" of a president's emotions by telling him to lower his rhetoric on some occasions and raising his energy level on others.

Armitage's criticisms, as tough as they were, overlooked areas where Rice and Powell shaped foreign policy rather than reacting to events, most notably in easing a civil war in Liberia and expanding American efforts to combat AIDS in Africa. In July both Rice and Powell had urged Bush to intervene militarily in Liberia over the opposition of the Pentagon, and Bush had eventually approved sending a contingent of two hundred marines.[114]

Rice had also pushed Bush to support a five-year, $15 billion program to fight AIDS in the world's poorest countries, which the president highlighted that summer on a trip to Africa. Rice was on the trip with him, and even though she didn't like the term "African-American," she felt a powerful kinship when she and Bush visited Gorée Island in Senegal, a former slave-trading post from which Africans were shipped across the Atlantic. "You can almost imagine these stolen people suddenly arriving on the shore of this absolutely beautiful place and being put in these horrible cells where large numbers of them would die," she told reporters aboard Air Force One en route from South Africa to Uganda. "And when I think of the Gate of No Return, I still have a lump in my throat from thinking which one of my ancestors might have actually gone through that gate on their way to the United States."[115] Later she said of herself and Powell, "AIDS policy would not have happened without us. Colin was involved, but I was really a driver of that policy."[116] In 2007, the president said that the $15 billion program had paid for the treatment of

1.1 million people in fifteen nations, out of nearly 40 million people worldwide that the U.N. reported were living with HIV.[117]

But Iraq overshadowed everything. While she was on the trip to Africa, Rice became embroiled long-distance in the growing crisis over the failure to find Saddam's weapons of mass destruction and the intelligence that justified the war. A bitter dispute opened between the CIA and White House, pitting Rice against George Tenet in an argument that damaged both of them and was never resolved.

The problem had its roots in a sixteen-word sentence in the president's State of the Union address more than six months earlier, in January 2003. "The British government has learned that Saddam Hussein recently sought significant quantities of uranium from Africa," the president said. The claim was important because processed uranium ore, or "yellowcake," was a key ingredient for nuclear weapons. This claim received only modest attention in Washington until Sunday, July 6, when Joseph Wilson, a former ambassador to Gabon, published an opinion article in *The New York Times* under the headline, "What I Didn't Find in Africa." Wilson wrote that in February 2002 the CIA had sent him to Niger, in West Africa, to check out an intelligence report that Saddam had sought to buy yellowcake there. Wilson reported back that he found nothing. But the claim turned up in an early draft of the president's speech in Cincinnati in October 2002 before the CIA caught it and had the White House remove it as unsubstantiated. Somehow, though, the uranium claim made its way back into the State of the Union address that the president delivered only six weeks before the war.

A new firestorm ignited and the question quickly arose over who put the faulty assertion in the speech. Since Rice was in Africa, Tenet, who was making a speech in Sun Valley, called Hadley at the White House. The two agreed that the CIA and the NSC, which were both responsible for reviewing the president's State of the Union address, would share the blame.[118] But before any statement came out of the White House, Tenet learned that Rice, en route to Entebbe on Air Force One, had briefed reporters and laid the blame squarely on the CIA.

"The CIA cleared the speech in its entirety," Rice said, adding that "I can tell you, if the CIA, the Director of Central Intelligence, had said, take this out of the speech, it would have been gone, without question."[119] The next day in Sun Valley, Tenet, turning the other cheek, accepted partial responsibility in a statement acknowledging that he had never read a draft of the speech ahead of time, although it had been sent to him. "C.I.A. Chief Takes Blame in Assertion on Iraqi Uranium," read the next day's headline in *The New York Times*.[120] Although Hadley took his share of the blame ten days later and even offered his resignation to the president for missing the yellowcake claim—Bush refused to accept it[121]—Rice never took any blame for herself or for the NSC and never wavered from the position she took on Air Force One. As a result, Tenet would always feel that she had undercut him, and their relationship became poisoned. Rice's reputation as someone who could stubbornly refuse to accept blame was solidified in the process. Four years later, she still said of her stance: "I'm not blaming anybody. It was a statement of fact."[122]

Rice got no respite in August, the month that is by tradition quiet in Washington but often erupts in scandals and crises. The biggest blow yet to the occupation in Iraq occurred with an explosion at the United Nations in Baghdad on August 16. The blast killed the brilliant and charismatic senior U.N. representative in Baghdad, Sergio Vieira de Mello, who was there to carry out the "vital" role Bush and Blair had called for earlier in the year. The episode shattered international confidence in the country's ability to recover. Rice, for her part, was still smarting from her encounter with Armitage and realized she needed help. She called in a reinforcement: Bob Blackwill, her old boss on the Bush I NSC staff. She knew Blackwill could be difficult and arrogant, but she also felt he was knowledgeable and effective. The only question was whether he would be willing to work for the young Stanford professor who had once worked for him. Blackwill, who had taught at Harvard and had just returned to the United States after a tour as ambassador to India, said he would.[123]

Blackwill was given the title of coordinator for strategic planning on the NSC staff, with responsibilities for Iraq, Iran, and Afghanistan. But within weeks he was dealing almost exclusively with the problems in Iraq—and within the Bush administration itself as it descended into backbiting over everything that had gone wrong. Blackwill was astonished when he attended National Security Council meetings and saw the animosity between Rumsfeld and Powell, how the president never forced discussions, and how little Rice could do to intervene. An image locked in his mind, which he later imparted to Bob Woodward: Rice sat dutifully at one end of the table, the inexperienced president with his legs nervously jiggling sat at the other, while the three bulls of national security—Cheney, Rumsfeld, and Powell—staked out their ground, hoofs pawing and almost snorting defiantly, daring a challenge that never came.[124]

"It was as if Powell and Rumsfeld, who sat next to each other, were on separate planets," Blackwill later said.[125] When one talked to the president, the other would look straight ahead, as if he wanted no part of what was being said. There was no engagement, no real discussion of military strategy or Iraq. Blackwill suddenly understood how difficult Rice's job had been for two and a half cataclysmic years. "The conventional wisdom is, gosh, she didn't manage this right," Blackwill later said. "Well, I just think that's deeply unfair."[126] Blackwill believed that Kissinger and Scowcroft, both strong national security advisers, would have found the clash of egos and worldviews similarly difficult. "Neither one of them could have easily managed a situation in which the vice president is the former secretary of defense and the winner of a war, the secretary of state is both a former chairman of the Joint Chiefs of Staff and the national security adviser, and the secretary of defense is the former secretary of defense and a former chief of staff of the White House," he said.[127]

Rice took a week off at the end of August to attend the U.S. Open tennis tournament in New York and spend a weekend with her Aunt Gee, Mary Bush, and other friends at the Greenbrier resort in West Virginia. While she was away, Blackwill read everything he could find on Iraq—CIA reports, classified documents, internal memos—and came to the conclusion that Bremer's plan for a lengthy occupation of two to three years was unworkable. It was obvious to him that Iraq was the black hole of the administration, sucking the energy out of everything else, and that administration policy there was so far a failure. When Rice returned, Blackwill was ready with a lengthy memo for her that outlined the difficulties as he saw them: There were not enough troops and there was no discernible military strategy to defeat the insurgency or win it over with aid. In addition, the United States was throwing money away trying to rebuild Iraq's infrastructure and the path to Iraqi sovereignty as envisioned by Bremer was too slow.[128] Most important for Rice, the memo said that the "interagency process"—the coordination of Iraq policy between the NSC and cabinet departments—was broken.[129]

The problems in the memo were not news to Rice, but they reinforced her impressions and a determination to assert herself. Over the summer she had grown increasingly frustrated with Bremer, who continued to operate as an independent viceroy and who was reporting back little of what he was doing to her or the NSC. Bremer answered only to Rumsfeld, which meant that whatever information Bremer did provide to the Pentagon never came to her, or, for that matter, to Powell or Tenet. (Powell and Bremer had their own back channel, but they kept it secret from others.)[130] "People were throwing their hands up saying, 'We don't know what the hell is going on out there,' " Bremer later acknowledged.[131] Since his arrival in Baghdad in May, he had spoken daily to Rumsfeld, Wolfowitz, or Feith, and at first assumed that what he told them was being shared with the rest of the bureaucracy. "Obviously it wasn't," Bremer said.[132]

To Rice, it no longer made sense to let Rumsfeld control postwar Iraq, especially its economic reconstruction and political healing. The defense secretary openly disdained the goal of nation building, the view that Bush had held in the 2000 campaign. Rumsfeld was not going to be the mother hen of Iraq's struggle to create a legislature, a justice system, and a cabinet representing its warring factions. "We have to do something," Rice said to Blackwill, as Blackwill recalled it.[133] It was obvious that the NSC needed to get control of Iraq policy, which was now being implemented by all corners of the U.S. government. There were Treasury Department teams tasked with setting up a new Iraqi currency, Energy Department experts trying to revive the country's oil production, and State Department officials who would soon be helping the Iraqis write a new constitution. The NSC was the one body that could coordinate all the money and manpower pouring into Baghdad.

Blackwill encouraged Rice to go to the president to get greater control, and shortly after Labor Day she did. Rice did not criticize Bremer directly—she knew how much Bush admired him for taking the job and putting his life at risk every day—and instead cast the issue as one of policy coordination. "I explained the problem, how we were starting to get decisions out there that we would know after the fact, that had huge policy implications, and we just couldn't work that way," Rice said. "And the Pentagon was not in a position to exercise the kind of oversight that was needed because even they didn't have the right chain for all the political decisions."[134] Rice told Bush that she didn't want to get in the way of quick decisions that had to be made on the ground in Iraq, but that the White House needed to be directly involved in the larger ones, like the timing of elections, which required a political sensitivity that the Pentagon had proved it did not have.[135]

Bush agreed to set up a new task force, the Iraq Stabilization Group, which was to coordinate Iraq policy from the White House and be run by Rice. Early in October, she sent a memo describing the new group to Rumsfeld, Powell, and Tenet. David Sanger broke the story in *The New York Times* on October 6, and wrote that at the State Department and "in some offices in the White House," the decision to create the group was interpreted as a direct effort "to diminish the authority of the Pentagon and Mr. Rumsfeld" in the next phase of the war.[136] Rumsfeld reacted with a predictable roar. He testily told a group of reporters the next day that he had not been informed by the president of the new group and that Rice had simply told *The New York Times* of her plans. He suggested that the NSC was finally doing what it should have been all along—coordinating the work of the many government agencies dealing with Iraq—and that it was "not quite clear to me why" Rice sent him a memo on the subject.[137] When a German broadcast reporter pressed him on why Rice had sent out her directive, Rumsfeld snapped: "I said I don't know. Isn't that clear? You don't understand English?"[138]

The next day Rice called Rumsfeld and tried to settle him down. "I don't want to take over the management of the war," she told him, as she recalled it.[139] She said her goal was to make sure that the White House was part of the major decisions about Iraq's political process that Bremer was making almost daily in Baghdad. "And I walked him through that, and Don's view was, 'Well, okay, fine, so that means Bremer's going to report to you for those things.' "[140]

Rumsfeld was clearly not as acquiescent as Rice described in her rosy version of their conversation, and he later told Bremer that he was unhappy about Rice's control and that he thought it was a mistake for the national security adviser to get involved in the daily political process in Iraq. "The last time the NSC got into operational issues, we had Iran-contra," Rumsfeld told Bremer, referring to the Reagan-era scandal in which Oliver North of the National Security Council staff got involved in trading arms for hostages in Iran and using the money to fund insurgents in Nicaragua. "But she seems to have jumped into this with both feet."[141] Bremer guessed that Rumsfeld, a gifted Washington infighter, saw Rice's move as a surprisingly successful power play by "the national security adviser whom he's tried to cut out of everything."[142]

As was by now clear not only to Bremer but everyone at the White House, Rice and Rumsfeld were settling into a relationship of mutual loathing. Rumsfeld agreed with Powell and Armitage on almost nothing, but he did share their view that things never got decided in NSC meetings and that Rice was unable to manage the process.[143] For her part, Rice thought Rumsfeld was no longer paying attention to Iraq's political and economic needs and that his only interest was in getting the troops out as fast as possible. She understood his aversion to superintending Iraq's political rebirth, but she felt a responsibility to the Iraqis, who, as a practical matter, were in no shape to create a government on their own. She still believed there could be democracy in Iraq, and more important, so did Bush. It was obvious to her that she would have the president's backing on the Iraq Stabilization Group, and it was that support that made it possible for her to publicly challenge Rumsfeld for the first time—a milestone in her tenure as national security adviser.

The tension between Rice and Rumsfeld at White House meetings now sometimes needed outside help to defuse it. Andy Card, the White House chief of staff, considered Rumsfeld and Rice Type A personalities, and he would sometimes call them after a testy exchange to try to smooth things over. "There were times when they'd choose to shut down and I'd have to try to find the switch and turn them on, reengage," Card recalled.[144] He saw it as part of his job to keep the president's top advisers talking to each other, and Rice and

Rumsfeld tested his diplomatic skills. "I would usually ask, 'Is everything okay?' " Card said. "They were frustrated, they'd seem upset. I would say, 'If you tried to send a signal, everybody saw it. The signal's been sent.' "[145]

Fran Townsend, who was the deputy national security adviser for combating terrorism and a friend of Rice, remembered seeing the national security adviser push back against Rumsfeld at a meeting Rice was conducting that fall.[146] Rumsfeld, as was his habit, had suddenly dropped a Defense Department document on the conference table as Rice was leading a discussion on something else. Normally the principals distributed their position papers ahead of time, giving everyone a chance to read them so that there could be a theoretically useful and efficient debate. But the defense secretary's "table drop," as it was called, meant that the discussion Rice was leading would be disrupted while everyone picked up the new paper and read it. The talk would then inevitably turn to Rumsfeld's document, and the meeting's agenda would be derailed. It was the kind of bureaucratic tactic that had maddened Frank Miller in the run-up to the war the previous year.

Rice had had enough. "No, you're not going to do this here," she curtly told Rumsfeld, in Townsend's recollection. "We can have a conversation about your paper, but this meeting's about this one."[147] Rumsfeld snapped back, Townsend recalled, that he might not have distributed his papers so late if he had gotten Rice's documents for the meeting a little earlier—which was what Rumsfeld almost always said, regardless of when documents from Rice arrived on his desk. He grumpily took back his documents to try again next time.

Now that Rice had her Iraq Stabilization Group, she had a new responsibility: keeping track of Bremer. Every day at 6:20 A.M., shortly after arriving in her office, she had the Situation Room place a call for her to CPA headquarters in the Green Zone of Baghdad. It was 2:20 P.M. there, well into Bremer's always chaotic day, and by then he had a long list of things to check with her. Bremer had been taken by surprise by Rice's move to manage Iraq policy, and in one of their first phone calls he asked her why he was now reporting to her and not the defense secretary.

"She said, 'You know, this is too important for the president, I've just got to watch it for him,' " Bremer recalled. "I don't think she mentioned Rumsfeld, but I kind of understood what her problem was."[148] Bremer had himself had bitter fights with Rumsfeld that summer over troop withdrawals, which Rumsfeld kept calling for. "By the end of September, he and I had had some real toe-to-toe shouting matches about, in my view, his completely unrealistic assessment about how quickly we could get out of there and how quickly the Iraqi soldiers and police would be ready to replace us," Bremer said.[149]

Bremer, who knew he was now on a shorter leash with Rice, said he nonetheless found his conversations useful, not least because of her near-instant access to Bush. "I'd ask for guidance if I needed guidance on things, and that was very helpful because she could get the president right there," Bremer said. "I remember one time she called, she was down in Crawford with the president one weekend, and she and I were going through the list and the president walks in and she just handed him the phone."[150] On that day, Bremer got his instructions directly from Bush.

Through her daily conversations, Rice leaned on Bremer to speed up his plan for turning the governing of Iraq over to the Iraqis, which was fast becoming the consensus of Rumsfeld and Powell, too. Shortly after arriving in Baghdad, Bremer had presided over the selection of a U.S.-appointed interim Iraqi government, a twenty-five-member Governing Council, which was dominated by Iraq's majority Shiites and had no real power. Now Bremer had devised an elaborate seven-step process that called for the Governing Council to write a constitution and for elections to be held before the United States would grant sovereignty to an authentic Iraqi government, probably sometime in 2005.

Bremer's thinking—and the original thinking of Rice and the White House—was that granting sovereignty to an unelected Shiite-dominated group like the Governing Council would only antagonize Iraq's Sunni minority. But as the factions on the Governing Council squabbled over the constitution and the Sunni-led insurgency gained strength, the administration decided to reverse course: An interim constitution would be written and sovereignty would be granted as early as June 2004 to empower the Iraqi leadership to reconcile with the political factions on its own. At the same time, U.S. troops would remain in place. Rice thought the new plan represented the first real progress on Iraq, and she told Bremer so in a cheerful phone call on November 13, the day before the plan was to be announced in Baghdad. Bremer, who had just been through six of the most difficult months of his life, cautioned her not to bet on success. "This is, after all, Iraq," he said.[151]

Two weeks later, Rice got a chance to see for herself when she arrived with the president on a secret Thanksgiving Day trip to Baghdad. Like Bush, Rice was on the ground for only two and a half hours and security was so tight that she and the president never left the secure area around Baghdad International Airport, where Bush shared turkey with American soldiers in a mess hall. For Bush, the trip was a minor coup of presidential theater that had the unintended effect of underscoring how dangerous Iraq had remained since he declared major combat operations over on May 1.

For Rice, the trip showed how unusually close she had become to the president at a time of war weariness. The journey began at the president's Crawford ranch the day before Thanksgiving. While Laura Bush and the rest of the family stayed behind, the president and Rice slipped out in baseball caps and an unmarked van and headed toward an airport in Waco, the nearest town. To be as secretive as possible, Bush was traveling without the usual trappings of motorcades, helicopters, and flashing lights. "It's Wednesday night before Thanksgiving and it's wall-to-wall, bumper-to-bumper traffic," Rice recalled. "We had to sit there in traffic, making our way to the airport."[152] It was an odd moment for the two of them, she added, "trying to look like normal folks."[153]

When the president told his story of the trip, he used the same formulation. "I slipped on a baseball cap, pulled her down, as did Condi," he said. "We looked like a normal couple."[154]

Except that they weren't. What they were was a president and national security adviser forming an extraordinary bond. Months after the trip, Rice was quoted in *New York* magazine as referring to Bush as "My husb—" at a Washington dinner party, as if she was about to refer to the president as her spouse and then caught herself.[155] Rice denied ever saying it. “I’m quite sure I didn’t,” she said. “What a dumb comment it would have been.”[156] Two guests did hear the comment, but most others did not.[157]

The next month, there was finally good news out of Baghdad: Saddam Hussein was captured by U.S. forces in a six-foot hole near his ancestral home of Tikrit. Bremer woke up Rice with the news at 1 A.M. Washington time, Sunday, December 14. “I’ll wake the president,” she said. “He wants to know.”[158]

It was a burst of good news in the face of all their troubles and offered some grounds for hope on Iraq. The next day Rice called her stepmother, Clara, in Palo Alto to share her excitement. “She was just telling me, ‘Oh we got him, we got him!’ ” Clara Rice recalled. “And I remember saying, yeah, maybe so, but it’s bin Laden, Condi, isn’t that who you really want?”[159]

Rice refused to have her mood dampened by her stepmother’s skepticism. “She said, ‘Oh, no,’ ” Clara Rice recalled. “And I think about that all the time now, that’s who you wanted, you know.” Clara Rice dropped the subject, and never brought it up again. “I didn’t want to take away her joy,” she said.[160]

CHAPTER 11

Karl's Aide-de-Camp

The Reelection Campaign, 2004

Rice was praying at her desk, head down, hands clasped, eyes closed.[1] She was alone in her office on the morning of April 8, 2004, and in a few minutes she would leave for Capitol Hill and the most important performance of her life: her public testimony to the 9/11 Commission investigating the terrorist attacks three years earlier on New York and Washington. Nearly three thousand Americans were dead, and in the eyes of the victims' families Rice bore a large measure of the responsibility. She—and the White House—had everything riding on how she would explain her actions in that sleepy summer of 2001. The questioning was expected to be hostile from the Democrats on the commission, and although Rice had seemed her usual composed self to her staff that morning, she was obviously nervous. No one was surprised when she asked for a few moments to collect herself and then closed her door. When one White House official quietly peeked in to see if she was ready to head up to the Capitol, he saw the Reverend John Rice's daughter doing what she sometimes did in moments of crisis, which was asking God for strength in what was about to unfold.[2]

Rice and the White House had struggled through a relentless pounding of bad news since the first of the year. Bush's 2004 reelection campaign, although flush with cash and overseen by one of the toughest political teams in a generation, had been jolted day after day by events out of its control in Iraq. In January, David Kay, the weapons hunter who been sent to Baghdad six months earlier, told James Risen of *The New York Times* that the administration had been almost certainly wrong in its prewar belief that Iraq had large stockpiles of weapons.[3] Saddam Hussein had become so isolated and fantasy-riven in his last two years of rule, Kay said, that he had approved money for weapons programs that were actually corrupt money-raising schemes by Iraqi scientists.[4] Saddam was even sending his deputy prime minister, Tariq Aziz, manuscripts of novels he was writing as the United States prepared to attack him.[5] The announcement was a stunning indictment of the intelligence that justified the war, and the leading candidates for the Democratic presidential nomination—former governor Howard Dean of Vermont, Senators John Kerry of Massachusetts and John Edwards of North Carolina—hit Bush daily with a chorus of criticism about administration lies and incompetence.

The effort to stabilize Iraq's political scene was also going badly. Rice spent much of February on the phone with Bremer, who was in round-the-clock negotiations with the Iraqi Governing Council as it lurched toward a March 1 deadline for writing an interim constitution that would lay out how power was to be shared among the country's many factions. By February 29, with only twenty-four hours to go, Rice kept a virtual open line to Baghdad and tried to help Bremer sort out the competing demands of Iraq's three main ethnic and religious groups, the Shiites, Sunnis, and Kurds. "She was very much engaged in the tactical problems we had the last weekend with the Shia walking out and the Sunnis walking out and the Kurds walking out," Bremer recalled.[6]

One of the major sticking points was the role that Islam would have in the constitution. Rice, the former Stanford political science professor who had been through a similar problem with Afghanistan's new constitution only a few months earlier, was by this time on the phone with Bremer every half hour. She and the president pressed for as much religious tolerance as possible in a country newly dominated by Shiite parties demanding that Islamic religious teachings serve as the basis for the nation's new laws. "Her overriding concern was whether this was a constitution the U.S. could live with," Bremer said.[7] In the end the Governing Council members compromised on Islam as "a source" of legislation rather than as "the primary source," which leading Governing Council members had demanded.[8] The constitution was finally approved on March 1, at 4:20 A.M. Baghdad time.

The announcement of the constitution was a relief for Rice, but the next month she faced two converging public relations catastrophes. The first was the publication of Richard Clarke's book *Against All Enemies*, which painstakingly chronicled her sluggish response to his warnings about Al Qaeda in the summer of 2001. The second was the intensifying pressure on Rice to testify publicly to the 9/11 Commission about her role in one of the biggest intelligence failures in American history.

The commission of five Democrats and five Republicans, created by Congress and signed into law by Bush in late 2002 to conduct a wide-ranging, independent investigation of what went wrong and why in the years and months before September 11, had been holding public hearings of government officials and other witnesses since the spring of 2003. Clarke, who was scheduled to testify to the commission on March 24, had moved up the publication of his book, originally set for the summer of 2004, to coincide with his appearance. On March 21, he went on the CBS program *60 Minutes* to launch a first broadside against the White House. "Frankly, I find it outrageous that the president is running for reelection on the grounds that he's done such great things about terrorism," Clarke said on the program. "He ignored it for months. He ignored it for months, when maybe he could have done something to stop 9/11. Maybe. We'll never know."[9]

The next day, *Against All Enemies* offered the first public disclosure of Clarke's vivid e-mails to Rice, like the one in the spring of 2001 that warned her that Al Qaeda was "trying to kill Americans, to have hundreds of dead in the streets of America."[10] The book concluded that Bush's leadership after September 11 amounted to "unthinking reactions" and "ham-handed responses" that had left the country less secure.[11] Clarke's public testimony was even more dramatic. He opened his remarks in a hushed Senate hearing room with an extraordinary apology to the 9/11 families who were in the audience that day. "Your government failed you," he said. "Those entrusted with protecting you failed you. And I failed you. We tried hard. But that doesn't matter, because we failed. And for that failure, I would ask, once all the facts are out, for your understanding and forgiveness."[12] Clarke then proceeded to make his case that the Bush administration ignored the threat from Al Qaeda before September 11. By now his charges were making headlines around the world and his book was soon to be number one on the *New York Times* best-seller list.

The commission had already been seeking Rice's testimony, and now Clarke had in effect thrown down a gauntlet. After his damning performance, Rice's side of the story was needed to ascertain the facts and to maintain a level of fairness in what had become a partisan furor in an election year. But the White House drew a line with Rice and said no. Although Tenet, Rumsfeld, and Powell had appeared before the commission, Alberto Gonzales, the White House counsel, said that as national security adviser, Rice's appearance would violate executive privilege, the principle that holds that White House staff aides should not be forced to disclose private conversations with presidents. Sitting national security advisers "regularly decline to testify publicly on policy matters," Gonzales told the commission.[13]

But Rice saw that Clarke's testimony was a disaster for her reputation and that of the administration. She went to Gonzales and argued with him. "She used to get so angry," recalled an administration official.[14] Rice was desperate to rebut Clarke's charges, and she was convinced that she could make a credible case and perform well under pressure, as she had all her life. Rice, who referred to the attack inside the White House as "our Pearl Harbor," said she also felt a responsibility to cooperate with what she saw as a good-faith effort to get to its root causes. "This was the means the American people, our Congress, had chosen to review the harshest attack on American territory in our history," Rice later said. "And so I felt kind of morally obliged to testify."[15]

With Gonzales dug in, Rice did what she had done so many times before: She appealed her case to the president.[16] But this time, in her telling, Bush could not be moved. "He was just very, very worried about the executive privilege issue," she said. "And I just kept saying this was an extraordinary circumstance."[17]

Rice and her staff decided to go public in a different way, by taking her case to the airwaves. The Sunday after Clarke was on *60 Minutes*, Rice made her own appearance on the program, on March 28, in an interview with Ed Bradley that her press adviser, Jim Wilkinson, had recommended she do. But the report on the national security adviser that aired that evening showed Rice flustered and on the defensive over Bradley's tough questions on why the threats of Al Qaeda were ignored, why terrorism had been relegated to a "back-burner" issue, and why Bush seemed determined to use the 9/11 attacks as an excuse to go after Saddam Hussein. "Ed, I don't know what a sense of urgency, any greater than the one we had, would have caused us to do differently," Rice told him.[18]

She ended up angry at *60 Minutes* for the way it edited the program, angry at Wilkinson, and angry at herself. "I actually thought the interview went pretty well, because I thought I'd made the case pretty well, and I watched it, and I was horrified," Rice recalled.[19] The appearance also had the unintended but obvious consequence of raising the question of why Rice was stonewalling the 9/11 Commission when she had made herself available to CBS. As Bradley asked her on the air, "The secretary of state, defense, the director of the CIA, have all testified in public under oath before the commission. If you can talk to us and other news programs, why can't you talk to the commission and under oath?"[20]

Rice didn't have a good answer. She invoked the principle of executive privilege but clearly understood the dilemma. As she later recalled, "A lot of friends and family were saying, 'What are you doing? Why are you in this position of not being willing to testify on something that's clearly so central?' "[21] The 9/11 families, who had suspected that Rice had something to hide since her May 2002 briefing about planes slamming into buildings, were now even more convinced that she was covering up. They, too, stepped up the pressure on her to testify.

Rice went back to the president, who seemed to be wavering under the adverse publicity seven months before the election. He told her he thought there might be a way to work out an agreement for her to appear. Finally, on March 30, six days after Clarke's testimony, the

White House bowed to the inevitable and agreed that Rice would testify on the condition that her testimony not set a precedent for other national security advisers. (Bush and Cheney, also under fire, agreed for their part that the 9/11 Commission could interview them jointly in a private meeting at the White House.) Rice's testimony was set for April 8.

For the next week, Rice prepared as if she were facing the biggest oral exam of her life. She reviewed documents, assembled facts, and fielded practice questions from her staff—Wilkinson; her counsel, John Bellinger; her spokesman Sean McCormack; and others. Robert Zoellick, the United States trade representative, whom Rice knew from his days as a close aide to James Baker at the State Department in Bush I, came by to help with the practice sessions and make sure that Rice presented a credible case. "He has a good bullshit detector," Wilkinson said of Zoellick.[22] Rice spent hours in the sessions, but she drew the line at going through a "murder board," a mock hearing with a panel of questioners. It had been Wilkinson's idea to have a pseudo-panel "just ask you tough questions and let you respond under fire," but Rice had had enough. "She looked at us and she pointed her finger and said, 'Jim Wilkinson, John Bellinger, either I can wrap my head around this or I can't. I'm not doing a murder board. I'm an academic, I know I can talk for a living.' "[23]

On the morning of the testimony, Rice headed into Room 216 in the Hart Senate Office Building shortly before 9 A.M., ramrod straight, in a sober beige suit, smiling but on edge. The atmosphere crackled as a giant phalanx of photographers stood arrayed before her. "I had never seen so many cameras in my life," Wilkinson later said. Behind Rice in chairs were family members of the dead. When she walked in, they held up pictures of their loved ones and hissed at her. "I'll never forget it," Wilkinson said.[24]

Rice raised her hand to swear to tell the truth and the room exploded with the sound of camera shutters and flashes that almost drowned out the words of the oath.[25] All the major networks interrupted their programming to provide live coverage—the last time they did so for a black woman testifying under oath in Washington was when Anita Hill spoke out against Clarence Thomas in 1991[26]—

and the room was jammed with people who had lined up for hours to get a seat. Rice had been drawing crowds all her life, but now it seemed as if she were in the dock on the way to her execution.

Rice sat down, all alone at a conference table, and nervously read from an opening statement. She smiled often, as she always did in her performances, but in this case her expression seemed too merry for the seriousness of the subject. Her statement laid out the arguments she had been making for years: The Bush administration was working hard on developing a comprehensive counterterrorism strategy in 2001, and while that was underway she took the "unusual step" of retaining Richard Clarke and his entire Clinton counterterrorism team. The threat reporting in the spring and summer of 2001 was not specific as to time, place and manner of attack. The August 6, 2001, President's Daily Brief did not raise the possibility that terrorists might use airplanes as missiles. There were "structural and legal impediments" that prevented the CIA and FBI from communicating in the summer of 2001, and there was no "silver bullet" that would have prevented the attacks.[27]

The questions from the commissioners then began, but after all the buildup, there were few revelations and only slightly more fireworks as Rice stuck to the careful, academic answers that were her trademark. The only real moment of drama came while she was under intense questioning from Richard Ben-Veniste, a Democrat and veteran Washington lawyer who had led the Watergate prosecutions a generation before. He asked Rice if she recalled the title of the PDB. Like the other commissioners, Ben-Veniste already knew the title, but since the document was classified, he had not been permitted to make it public.

Rice took care of that for him. "I believe the title was 'Bin Laden Determined to Attack Inside the United States,' " she flatly replied, getting the wording only slightly wrong.[28] The room was silent as the ominous title sank in. Rice, trying to regain control, started to explain the content of the PDB when Ben-Veniste cut her off. The two quickly got into an acrimonious exchange.

"I would like to finish my point here," Rice said.[29]

"I didn't know there was a point," Ben-Veniste shot back.[30]

An odd lighthearted moment broke the tension later when another of the commissioners, Bob Kerrey, a former Democratic senator from Nebraska, became confused and repeatedly called Rice "Dr. Clarke" during his questioning. "I don't think I look like Dick Clarke," Rice said with a smile, offering a rare public glimpse of her ability to deploy sarcasm.[31]

But the moment that encapsulated both the strength and the inadequacy of Rice's presentation came from a former Democratic congressman from Indiana, Timothy Roemer, who pointedly summarized her situation. "You're the national security adviser to the president of the United States," he told her. "The buck may stop with the president; the buck certainly goes through you as the principal advisor to the president on those issues. And it really seems to me that there were failures and mistakes, structural problems, all kinds of issues here leading up to September 11 that could have and should have been done better. Doesn't that beg that there should have been more accountability, that there should have been a resignation or two, that there should have been you or the president saying to the rest of the administration somehow, somewhere, that this was not done well enough?"[32]

Rice's response was the best that she could come up with. "Mr. Roemer, by definition we didn't have enough information," she replied. Then she added, repeating some of her earlier comments to the commission: "I think we've all asked ourselves what more could have been done. I will tell you, if we had known that an attack was coming against the United States, an attack was coming against New York and Washington, we would have moved heaven and earth to stop it."[33]

At the end of her day of testimony, punctuated by occasional hissing from the families of the victims, Rice was drained but relieved. As if to show the world that she could not be rattled, she took a deep breath and walked back to the families to shake their hands and say hello. Rice knew the gesture would not win them over, but part of her upbringing was to be gracious and to show an inner cool. Years later, she said she thought the hearing had gone well under the circumstances. "You don't spend a lot of time thinking, 'Oh gosh, this is going to be horrible,' " Rice said. "No, I just did it."[34]

The reaction to her testimony was indeed anticlimactic. She had forcefully defended her conduct and that of the president, and had offered no new information on the administration's handling of the terrorist threat before 9/11. "I thought I was pretty effective," Rice later said. "All I had to do was talk. I'm an academic. They would ask questions, I'd respond. I'd done a lot of homework on who the questioners were and what kinds of questions I'd get from them."[35] In the end, the appearance showed her at her best and worst. She was steely, poised, and analytical, but she also displayed no remorse, regret, or any human sense of being tormented by her role in the events. The public was not allowed to see her sweat or to see her true feelings. She had learned long before how to conceal them.

But the issue was not going away. Two days later, when the administration finally declassified the entire August 6 PDB on the Saturday night before Easter, the most incriminating document of the period became public and a part of the 9/11 lore. On the one hand, the actual document, only a page and a quarter, dispelled the notion of some of the family members that Rice and Bush had received a warning in the summer of 2001 about planes flying into buildings. But it was also obvious that the PDB was not all "historical" information, as Rice kept repeating. The document made clear to the public that Bush was warned in the month before September 11 that the FBI had detected "suspicious activity" that suggested that terrorists might be planning a hijacking in the United States.

The release of the document only fanned a debate that would echo through the entire election season. The president's critics said the PDB should have galvanized him to do something more—like ordering the FBI and the CIA to be more aggressive—while his allies said that it contained no specific information he could have acted upon.[36] For Rice, the document would always cast a shadow over her performance at the White House. Even though the job of the national security adviser did not, strictly speaking, extend to the FBI and the domestic surveillance of terrorists, the document would always leave unresolved the doubts about Rice's methodical and cautious approach to the job.

But as so often happens in Washington, the furor of the moment subsided and the capital moved on. Not even three weeks later, on April 28, Rice was consumed with the explosive broadcast by *60 Min-*

utes II of shocking pictures of the notorious Abu Ghraib prison in Baghdad. Built by Saddam for his political enemies, the prison was now used by the Americans to hold thousands of Iraqis, many of them swept up without any charges against them. American viewers saw what became the iconic images of Abu Ghraib: a hooded man standing on a small box with wires attached to his outstretched arms, and naked, hooded male prisoners stacked on top of one another or cowering in terror from snarling dogs. Whether they were being subjected to interrogation techniques or merely humiliated for the amusement and sadistic pleasure of the Americans didn't seem to matter. The pictures had been taken between October and December 2003 as souvenirs by American guards at the prison, and in many of the photographs the guards themselves appeared with big smiles or thumbs-up signs. *The New Yorker* followed with more photographs and a lengthy article by Seymour Hersh several days later, adding to what was now a worldwide furor and a major crisis for the Bush administration.

The Pentagon had been aware of the problem—and the existence of the pictures—but had kept it all secret. In January 2004, the U.S. military launched an investigation into reports of misconduct at the prison and concluded in an internal report in February that U.S. soldiers "have committed egregious acts and grave breaches of international law."[37] That same month Army Lieutenant General Ricardo Sanchez, the top U.S. commander in Iraq, ordered a criminal investigation, and by March the U.S. military had brought charges against six soldiers in connection with the abuse and suspended eleven others.[38] But Rumsfeld not only did not tell Americans, he did not tell the president, and Bush learned about the photographs only months later, after they were broadcast on *60 Minutes II*. On May 5, the president chastised Rumsfeld in the Oval Office and then authorized White House officials to leak the dressing-down to reporters.[39] The next day, the president apologized for the scandal during a brief appearance in the White House Rose Garden, where he said that he was "sorry for the humiliation suffered by Iraqi prisoners and the humiliation suffered by their families."[40]

Rumsfeld followed with a more extensive apology on May 7 at the start of a marathon day of testimony about Abu Ghraib on Capitol

Hill. "These events occurred on my watch," Rumsfeld said. "As Secretary of Defense, I am accountable for them and I take full responsibility. . . . I feel terrible about what happened to these Iraqi detainees. They're human beings. They were in U.S. custody. Our country had an obligation to treat them right. We didn't and that was wrong. So to those Iraqis who were mistreated by members of the U.S. armed forces, I offer my deepest apology." Later in the same hearing, the defense secretary said, "I would resign in a minute if I thought that I couldn't be effective."[41]

Rumsfeld had in fact offered to resign in this period, as Rice well knew. Her closest friends, who understood how difficult her relationship with Rumsfeld had become, were convinced that Rice now favored his resignation. "He appears to have become a liability for the president and has complicated the mission in Iraq," a person close to Rice told *The New York Times* on May 7.[42] The same person speculated that Rice would not be unhappy to see Rumsfeld go.[43] But there were other considerations in play, including Rice's concerns that heeding the worldwide calls for Rumsfeld's head would only weaken the president and do little to ease the furor. As a result, publicly she backed Rumsfeld. Privately she considered it inappropriate to lobby for his ouster.

"Very few things really knocked me off my legs in this whole time, but that did," Rice later said of Abu Ghraib. "And I just thought, 'We really have no chance to recover from this.' "[44] Rice could see that Rumsfeld was devastated and was not surprised, an administration official said, when he told her on the sidelines of an NSC meeting that he had offered to step down.[45]

Whether Rice's judgment was correct or not, within weeks the scandal had broadened. A report by the International Committee of the Red Cross, first disclosed by *The Wall Street Journal*, found that the abuses were not confined to a handful of rogue guards at Abu Ghraib but appeared to be "part of the standard operating procedures by military intelligence personnel to obtain confessions and extract information."[46] Over the next month, leaks in the major newspapers revealed that the administration had effectively authorized the interrogation techniques at Abu Ghraib in a series of secret memos and legal opinions that condoned torture or other acts of cruelty.

Cheney was the driving force behind the new interrogation rules, and his chief counsel, David Addington, had worked with Gonzales and others in writing a particularly crucial document, a Justice Department memo in August 2002 that provided the White House with a rationale for using torture to extract information from Al Qaeda terrorists in captivity abroad.[47] The radical legal reasoning in the document held that international laws forbidding torture did not apply to the commander in chief because Congress "may no more regulate the President's ability to detain and interrogate enemy combatants than it may regulate his ability to direct troop movements on the battlefield."[48] But Rice and Powell, in what was now a familiar pattern, knew nothing about this document until they read about it two years later, on June 8, 2004, in *The Washington Post*.[49]

For Rice, the secrecy of Cheney's actions was a dangerous breach of process and trust. Together she and Powell confronted Gonzales in his office, where Rice angrily told him there would be no more secret opinions on international and national security law and threatened to go to the president if Gonzales kept them in the dark again.[50] *The Washington Post* later reported that Powell remarked admiringly as he left the meeting that Rice had dressed down Gonzales "in full Nurse Ratched mode," a reference to the head nurse of the mental hospital in the 1975 film *One Flew Over the Cuckoo's Nest*.[51] But neither Rice nor Powell went to the vice president with their complaints, and it would be two more years before Rice took on Cheney or Bush on the subject as a more emboldened secretary of state. Her inaction was an indication that at this stage, she would not be able to get the basic policy changed or revised.

As Iraq's security situation deteriorated and the world united in condemnation of Abu Ghraib, there was one thing Rice could do to move Iraq in a more positive direction. That was to arrange for a successful transfer of power to Iraqis in Baghdad, now scheduled for June 30. As the deadline loomed, Rice began hatching plans with Bremer to move up the date to avoid the expected violence. For once, something went right in Baghdad. On June 28, at 10:26 A.M., in a small, nearly secret ceremony inside the heavily fortified Green Zone, Bremer handed Ayad Allawi, the interim prime minister, a leather-bound note from Bush indicating that the Coalition Provisional Authority was dissolved.[52] Rice, who was with the president at a NATO summit meeting in Ankara, Turkey, heard from one of Bremer's aides when the deed was done. She immediately wrote a note for Bush that captured both history and their personal relationship: "Mr. President, Iraq is sovereign. Letter was passed from Bremer at 10:26 A.M. Iraq time. Condi."[53] Minutes later, Bremer, now out of a job as viceroy, flew by helicopter to Baghdad International Airport, where he boarded an American C-130 military transport and left the country. Bremer was done, but Iraq's problems were anything but. What, for example, would be the significance of Iraq's official sovereignty when American armed forces were still in charge of the country and Rice still had to coax a meaningful political process out of the fractious Iraqis?

The issue of the war's original rationale was also refusing to go away. On July 9, the Senate Intelligence Committee said in a scathing, 511-page document that the CIA and other American intelligence agencies had produced false and misleading information before the Iraq War about Saddam Hussein's weapons programs. The committee laid the blame on what it characterized as a sloppy, dysfunctional intelligence structure led by Tenet,[54] who, anticipating the bad news in this and other coming reports, had abruptly resigned the month before.

Less than two weeks later, the 9/11 Commission let loose with a bigger blast, a sweeping indictment of a breakdown in the federal government—the CIA, the FBI, the Pentagon, the National Security Council, the Federal Aviation Administration, Congress—that left the nation vulnerable to attacks that were a shock but "should not have come as a surprise."[55] The executive summary of the report said that senior officials were repeatedly warned about Osama bin Laden but did not respond aggressively, and that across the government there were "failures of imagination, policy, capabilities and management."[56] The commission called for a massive overhaul of the nation's intelligence-gathering system, specifically a cabinet-level national intelligence director who could oversee all fifteen federal spy agencies. The report held the Clinton administration responsible for the lapses as well as the Bush administration. It did not say if one deserved more blame than the other, or if the attacks themselves could have been prevented.

Rice did not fare especially well in the commission's voluminous, massively researched final report, written as a book and overseen by her friend Zelikow, the 9/11 Commission's executive director. Although some of the 9/11 families had called for Zelikow's resignation from the commission because of his closeness to Rice, or at least were suspicious that he would treat her gently, the final report exhaustively detailed Clarke's warnings to Rice and her slow response. The report did not, however, include any mention of the White House meeting on July 10, 2001, when Tenet and Cofer Black ran over to Rice in a panic about the terrorist threat. (Zelikow later said he and some of the commission staff omitted the meeting from the report because they believed that Tenet had conflated it with another meeting and garbled the facts. Zelikow did not dispute that Tenet had warned Rice in this period about the terrorist threat.)[57]

As the 2004 election approached, it was hard to know which headlines were more damaging to the White House: the ones about the current warfare or the false intelligence that preceded the invasion. The failure to find any weapons popped up again as an issue in August, when David Kay, the weapons hunter who had said in January that the administration was wrong in its prewar beliefs about Saddam's arsenal, testified to Congress that the National Security Council had failed to protect the president from the faulty CIA estimates that led to the war. "The dog that did not bark in the case of Iraq's W.M.D. program, quite frankly, in my view, is the National Security Council," Kay said.[58] Kay, who had resigned as weapons hunter at the time of his statements in January, did not use Rice's name, but the implication was clear in his unusually personal remarks.

"Where was the National Security Council when, apparently, the president expressed his own doubt about the adequacy of the case concerning Iraq's W.M.D. that was made before him?" Kay asked, apparently referring to his concern about Powell's presentation to the U.N. Security Council.[59] Bob Woodward in *State of Denial* reported a year and a half later that Robert Joseph, Rice's deputy for weapons proliferation, called Kay after the testimony and in a subsequent conversation tried to convince him that the intelligence failures were not Rice's fault. Kay told him that Rice had failed in her responsibility to vet the intelligence more carefully, and Kay later told Woodward that

"Rice was probably the worst national security adviser in modern times since the office was created."[60]

Rice was hammered with yet another report on the Iraqi weapons fiasco on October 6. Charles Duelfer, the weapons hunter who had replaced David Kay, concluded that Iraq essentially destroyed its illicit weapons capability in 1991 and that at the time of the American invasion it had no chemical or biological weapons and was not trying to restart its nuclear program.[61] The report, at the height of the presidential campaign, was another devastating blow, but the Bush campaign had by now become used to them and was on its way to turning back a challenge posed by the Democratic combatant, Senator John Kerry of Massachusetts.

To help in the campaign, Rice was well into a series of politically attuned speeches in key battleground states. Breaking with the precedent that the national security adviser remain above politics, Rice traveled to Ohio, Pennsylvania, Michigan, and Florida in the weeks before the election and jumped into the middle of the raging argument between Bush and Kerry over the Iraq War and the administration's response to terrorism. Kerry's blistering attacks on Bush as an incompetent commander in chief who had lied about the war and who had failed to find Osama bin Laden rankled Rice—by clear implication, they were attacks on her, too—and she struck back. Rice never mentioned Kerry by name, but her target was clear in a typical speech in mid-October at the City Club of Cleveland, where Rice said there was "a debate in our country" over the war on terrorism.[62]

"For some, it is a limited engagement whose goal is to go after bin Laden and al Qaeda, assume a defensive posture at home, put it out of our minds and just hope they do not attack us again," Rice said, evoking the theme from the president's campaign that Kerry was soft on terrorism and would put the country at risk of another 9/11. "They see a narrow struggle against a narrow enemy. This is a fundamental misunderstanding about what happened to us on that fateful September day."[63]

Like Bush, Rice was trying to change the subject from her own failures to those of Kerry. By contrast, neither Powell nor Rumsfeld gave speeches during the campaign, but Rice wanted to make the trips and the president's campaign encouraged her. Not surprisingly, the

Kerry operation took her to task. "America would be a lot better off if Dr. Rice spent more time worrying about Osama bin Laden's job security and less time worrying about her own," Mark Kitchens, a Kerry spokesman, told *The Washington Post*.[64] Wilkinson defended Rice, saying it was the job of the national security adviser to discuss foreign policy with American citizens, and that the nonpolitical position did not mean that Rice should be inaccessible. But years later, Wilkinson acknowledged that Rice was willing to enter the fray because of her devotion to Bush and to her own reputation. "It wasn't designed to be political, it was designed to go make our case in very important markets," he said.[65] Either way, Rice figured it couldn't hurt.

Rice spent the last days of the campaign embroiled in still another Iraq-related dispute, this one a story about a missing cache of explosives that could have been stolen from under the nose of the U.S. military. Eight days before the election, CBS and *The New York Times* reported that the Iraqi government had warned the United States and international nuclear inspectors that nearly 380 tons of powerful conventional explosives were missing from one of Iraq's most sensitive former military installations, a complex called Al Qaqaa.[66] The explosives, which could produce bombs strong enough to shatter airplanes or tear apart buildings, had vanished sometime after the American-led invasion in 2003.[67] The concern, as voiced by experts quoted in the article, was that they could be used in major attacks against American or Iraqi forces, or even be used to trigger a nuclear weapon.[68]

Kerry, who was running neck and neck with a president struggling to hang on to the White House, immediately seized on the missing cache as "one of the great blunders of Iraq," and charged that, yet again, Bush's "incredible incompetence" had put American troops at risk.[69] Kerry's supporters joined in, among them Madeleine Albright, who told CNN, "It's an outrageous mistake, and one I'm afraid we will pay for for a long period of time."[70] If Rice saw the irony of the daughter of her mentor, Josef Korbel, joining the criticism, she didn't mention it.

In response, the White House first took the position that the explosives may have been removed by Saddam before the war, but then said that it was a "mystery" when the explosives disappeared and that the president would not comment until more facts were known.[71]

Trying one more time to rebut the charge, on October 29 the Pentagon offered up an Army demolition expert, Major Austin Pearson, whose unit in Iraq had destroyed hundreds of tons of ammunition and explosives in a part of the Al Qaqaa complex. But under repeatedly tough questioning at a news conference, both Pearson and Larry Di Rita, the Pentagon spokesman, admitted they did not know for certain if the material the unit destroyed was the same as that reported missing.[72] It was hardly the counterpunch the campaign was counting on and in fact only seemed to reinforce the sense that the Pentagon didn't know what it was doing.

Rice, appalled as she watched the news conference with the president on Air Force One, immediately called the White House. "Get them off the podium!" she ordered.[73] The White House official who took the call could hear the obvious panic on Air Force One. "They were freaking out," the official recalled. "The president was pissed and everyone was angry."[74] Down on the ground, he said, "we were just dying."[75]

Rice spent the last days before the election traveling in an exhausted frenzy on Air Force One. She did not have to be there—she could have sent Hadley or another deputy to cover the need for a traveling national security official with Bush—but she seemed unable to resist the daily combat of the campaign. At one point, Rice told her aides that she felt like she was hanging on to a branch over a cliff like the cartoon character the Road Runner, and that Wile E. Coyote kept trying to chop off a little more of the branch every day.[76]

The night before the election, Rice stayed at the president's ranch, where she and Karen Hughes shared the guesthouse. The next morning she waited while Bush voted in a light rain at the Volunteer Fire Department in Crawford. Rice was bone-tired from a nineteen-hour, seven-stop, six-state campaign swing the day before, but she was too on edge to sleep. She flew later on Tuesday with Bush to one last stop in Ohio, to thank campaign workers in Columbus, then headed back with the campaign to Washington. As Air Force One landed at Andrews Air Force Base, the first exit polls began to come in. Rice watched in the senior staff cabin as Karl Rove, the president's chief political adviser, talked to campaign headquarters on the phone and scrawled figures on a small envelope.

"I could see the numbers, and it was like, 'Ohio, minus thirty, Florida, minus thirty, Alabama, plus one,' " Rice recalled. "And I thought, we're up one in Alabama? This is lost. This is really bad."[77] Although the president was apparently losing massively in the critical battlegrounds, Rice focused on her home state. She knew that if the president was leading Kerry by only one percentage point in reliably Republican Alabama, the election was over.

At this point, Bush walked into the staff cabin and Rice, suddenly emotional, couldn't look at him. "I thought we had lost the election," she said. "I didn't know what to say."[78] After going through so much with him on the roller coaster of the last four years, she couldn't stand to see Bush so vulnerable, and she didn't want to have to tell him she was sorry. She made the excuse that she had to go to the ladies' room and quickly left the cabin.[79]

On the helicopter ride on Marine One to the White House, Rove told the group that he thought the numbers were strange and not to worry until he had sorted them out. "But everybody was pretty down," Rice recalled.[80] When she got to her office, she logged on to her favorite political Web site, realclearpolitics.com, to try to find out more. "I'd become a realclearpolitics fiend," Rice said.[81] There was nothing comforting for her there, but when she checked out the *Drudge Report* she found a flicker of hope for the White House: An early version of the national poll that showed Kerry ahead of Bush was using a sample of voters that was disproportionately female, meaning it was possibly skewed toward Kerry. "I started thinking, 'Well, maybe this isn't bad,' " Rice recalled.[82] Rove in the meantime was frantically e-mailing Republican supporters to tell them that the exit polls had been wrong in the 2000 election and that they were likely wrong now.[83]

Hoping that Rove was right and with little to do, Rice went home at 5 P.M. to try to get some sleep. But she was still too wired and her apartment was lonely. The prospect of watching the television returns by herself was depressing, and within three hours, she was back at the White House. "What else was I going to do?" Rice later said. "Go home and watch by myself and stay nervous at home?"[84]

By 8 P.M., Rice had parked herself next to Rove in his makeshift war room in the Family Dining Room on the state floor of the White

House. Rove called it his "bat cave."[85] In the neoclassical surroundings, underneath a stylish portrait of Edith Carow Roosevelt, Teddy Roosevelt's second wife, Rove had installed a bank of computers linked to Bush campaign headquarters in Arlington, Virginia, and the offices of the Republican National Committee on Capitol Hill. For the next hours, while Bush entertained some thirty friends and extended family members upstairs, Rice stayed downstairs where the action was, as Rove's improvised assistant. "Karl was trying to work, and so I said, 'Give me something to do,' " Rice recalled.[86] Rove told her she could help him keep track of returns by computer. "He would say, 'Now, go to District 14 in Ohio, and what's the difference between the number we need and the number that's come out,' " Rice said.[87]

At 1:49 A.M., Rove was on his cell phone to the secretary of state's office in Nevada, where a victory for Bush was expected to be announced within a half hour.[88] Assuming there would be no recount in Ohio—Fox, NBC, and MSNBC had just called it for Bush—Nevada would put the president over the top. As Rove talked, Rice was listening in. "Congratulations," she said to him, relieved and a little amazed that the White House had managed to eke out a victory in a year when a host of problems—Iraq, the false intelligence before the war, the missing weapons, the blast from the 9/11 Commission—had threatened to derail any victory. "We sure did try to screw things up."[89]

Rice's involvement demonstrated that for all her training as a foreign policy specialist, she was as drawn to the intricate machinery of politics as those around her. But how could she not be? Her future, no less than Bush's, was on the line. The people who criticized her for stooping to join the campaign did not see her as a woman who had once entertained political ambitions and who thrived on the rough give-and-take of public life. It would not be long before the close advisers who knew her taste for politics would push her toward that world again, hoping that this time she would be a candidate herself.

Rice spent the weekend after the election at Camp David in talks with the president about her future in a second term. For most of the year, Rice had said that she wanted to go back to California and a normal life. She was exhausted and intellectually drained as national security adviser, and she wasn't sure she even wanted to stay in Washington for any job for another four years. Rice had always wanted to be secretary of defense because of her background in military affairs, and now because she had seen in the first term that the Pentagon was where the real power was. But even though Rice and Andrew Card both argued that Bush should make a clean sweep of his cabinet for a second term, Rice knew that Rumsfeld wasn't going anywhere in the middle of a war. She also knew that Powell had told Bush that he wanted to leave as secretary of state, and that the president would almost certainly offer her the job.

On Saturday morning in Bush's office at Laurel Lodge, the conversation unfolded as Rice expected. The president asked her to think about replacing Powell. Bush had never been comfortable with his cabinet superstar, and had told close friends that he thought Powell had not traveled enough and was overly preoccupied with how he was seen in the world. Specifically, Bush felt that Powell had not put his reputation on the line and forcefully campaigned for support of the Iraq War in Europe because Powell did not want to hurt his image there. "It's not about you," one friend of the president quoted Bush as telling Powell on several occasions. "Don't worry about what people think of you."[90]

The job of secretary of state would be different now, Bush told Rice. Diplomacy would be central in a second term. After the rupture with the allies over Iraq, it was imperative that the United States reach out to Europe and make progress toward a peace settlement in the Middle East. Bush did not explicitly say so, and Rice later insisted that she laid down no conditions,[91] but she knew that because of her close relationship with the president she would have far more power and a freer hand in the job than Powell.

Rice told the president she wanted to think about it. She had to decide if she had the drive and energy. She knew she was not always diplomatic or in love with the ceremonies and trappings of dinners, choreographed meetings, and endless niceties in Washington and on the road. "I don't love to travel, frankly," she later said. "I like my things, I like my schedule, I like my routine. It's not that I don't like visiting foreign countries, but I don't particularly like getting there and I don't particularly like the sense of disruption in my life. Some of the happiest years of my life were as provost, when I almost never traveled. I got up every day and I did the provost job. I liked that."[92]

On the other hand, she would be a cabinet officer, the first black woman secretary of state and, finally, on a par with Rumsfeld. She could stand up to him as a theoretical equal. There might even be less second-guessing and secret maneuvering from the vice president's office. At the least, she would no longer have to try to rally the warring war cabinet into some kind of agreement. "You know, no more remote control trying to get secretaries to do things," Rice said. "That was the attractive part of it, and running a big organization."[93]

On Sunday, Rice said yes. The president had told friends he was not sure she would take the job, and was relieved when she agreed.

The following Saturday, Rice's friend David Manning, now the British ambassador to Washington, threw a black-tie surprise birthday party for Rice at his palatial residence on Massachusetts Avenue. Aunt Gee was there, and Gene Washington; Clara Rice came from California. Rice was presented upon her arrival with a red Oscar de la Renta gown. She changed in fifteen minutes and came downstairs to be greeted by the president. Sidney Blumenthal, a columnist for *Salon* and *The Guardian* and a former Clinton adviser, would later observe that she was behaving like Cinderella with her Prince Charming.[94] The next day Rice would be fifty years old, and she felt like a better chapter in her life was beginning.

CHAPTER 12

Madame Secretary

The State Department, 2005

Jim Wilkinson was tired of hearing about Stanford. Whenever he told the new secretary of state that she now had a monumental management job on her hands, it was always the same response: Stanford this, Stanford that, don't worry about it, I ran Stanford. It was six days after Bush's inauguration, Rice had just been sworn in, and she had brought with her a new team of advisers to reshape the administration's foreign policy in a second term. A huge array of challenges lay ahead in every part of the world, and there was little doubt of her mastery of the substance. But beyond the policy issues, Wilkinson understood that it was going to be his job to help rehabilitate Rice's image after the damaging years in the White House.

Wilkinson, who had followed Rice from the NSC to be her new senior adviser, had an aggressive hundred-day plan for her first months in office that charted every speech, trip, and interview with near-military precision. The fast-talking, thirty-five-year-old Wilkinson was an unlikely impresario for the elegant new secretary of state—he had grown up in Nacogdoches, Texas, as the son of a funeral director, and had waged many Republican battles as a Capitol Hill aide in the 1990s—but he had been Tommy Franks's spokesman during the Iraq War and understood the doubts about Rice in Washington. As one State Department official accurately summed up the perceptions of Rice's critics, "She's part of the unilateralist team that doesn't care about diplomacy, the State Department's irrelevant, Cheney and Rumsfeld run everything, our guy lost, Colin Powell lost, Condi's part of this neocon crowd that screwed Iraq up, she can't manage anything."[1]

Rice had just inherited the executive challenge of her life overseeing 15,500 employees in more than two hundred embassies and consulates around the world, and that was leaving aside the actual managing of American foreign policy itself. Wilkinson didn't see what any of that had to do with being provost of a private university, even one with 14,000 students and torturous faculty politics. Stanford had never had to reach out to an angry world after a preemptive war, but Rice kept insisting that her battles at Stanford had provided vital experience for her new job.

Rice's confirmation, though assured, had been rocky, and her two days of hearings before the Senate Foreign Relations Committee had served as a heated forum for members of both parties to vent about her performance as national security adviser and her role in the war. Rice had opened her testimony on January 18 with a statement that she thought made clear how much she was breaking from her past as a White House hawk—"the time for diplomacy is now"[2]—but her declarations of a coming renaissance in foreign relations were overshadowed by persistent questions about Iraq. The sharpest questions came from Barbara Boxer, a Democrat from California, who held up on a cardboard display some of Rice's past statements that Saddam Hussein was close to acquiring nuclear weapons. "I personally believe, this is my personal view, that your loyalty to the mission you were given, to sell this war, overwhelmed your respect for the truth," Boxer said.[3]

Boxer's berating tone angered Rice, and she showed a hint of the temper she had tried to keep under control since Stanford. "Senator, I have to say that I never, ever lost respect for the truth in the service of anything," Rice responded sharply. "It is not my nature. It is not my character. And I would hope that we can have this conversation and discuss what happened before, and what went on before and what I said, without impugning my credibility or my integrity."[4]

But Boxer and the other senators did not let up in their first opportunity to publicly grill Rice, who was no longer a White House aide protected by executive privilege from testifying to Congress. The hearing dragged on into the evening and spilled into the next day, when the committee voted 16–2 to send Rice's nomination for a full vote on the Senate floor, with Boxer and John Kerry voting no. But the committee did not actually send the nomination to the Senate floor until the following week. The delay was a symbolic but potent protest of Rice's role in the war, and it effectively meant that she would not be sworn in as planned shortly after the president was inaugurated on January 20. The Senate finally confirmed Rice on January 26 by a vote of 85–13, which represented the highest number of votes against a secretary of state nominee since 1825, when Henry Clay was confirmed in a vote of 27–14.[5]

Senate Democrats had used the occasion of the subsequent floor vote to denounce Rice as the architect of the administration's failures in Iraq, but some said they were hopeful about her promises of diplomacy and that Bush had a right to cabinet members of his choosing. "She does have the president's ear," said Senator Hillary Rodham Clinton, who voted to confirm Rice. Richard Lugar, the moderate Indiana Republican who was chairman of the Foreign Relations Committee, defended Rice as highly qualified for the job. "She's knowledgeable, she's smart, she's honorable," he said.[6]

Rice moved the next day into her jewel box of a suite on the top floor of the main State Department building, the uninspiring 1930s-era hulk on C Street just blocks from the White House in the Foggy Bottom neighborhood of Washington. In contrast to the drab, modern character of the building itself, the secretary of state's offices had been redone years earlier in the Federal Period style prevalent in the United States at the time of the State Department's founding in 1789. Rice would now receive her guests surrounded by a dazzling collection of eighteenth-century furniture and painting in an enormous ceremonial office, where Thomas Jefferson's grandfather clock stood at the doorway, but she would do her actual work in a much smaller adjoining office. There she displayed her footballs and football helmets and had a view out the windows of the Lincoln Memorial.

There was, to say the least, a lot of work to do: repair relations with the allies, stabilize Iraq in a year in which the country would hold its first free elections in half a century, move forward on a Middle East peace agreement, smooth frictions with Russia, and, most important, stop the nuclear threat from North Korea and Iran. Despite all the talk of a new era of diplomacy, the United States was at that moment at odds with Europe over how to persuade Iran to give up its suspected nuclear weapons program, and Rice's first order of business would be to seek a solution.

There was also the problem of having to deal with strains in relationships with China, India, Pakistan, and Sudan and with growing anti-American sentiment in Latin America, all of which had taken little of Rice's attention before. "I told her being secretary of state has nothing to do with being national security adviser," said a senior European diplomat. "The national security adviser has to be concerned about the topics that interest the president. On many important things, the president of the United States does not care, but the United States has to care. And therefore you have to care. At that time, the only concern was with Iraq, Iran, and the rest of the world didn't exist."[7]

Rice seized on the slogan "transformational diplomacy" to define her approach as secretary of state, which meant that her goal was to transform the world by pushing democracy wherever she went. She and the president were working off the same page, as they always had. George Bush had proclaimed in his second inaugural address that ending tyranny and spreading liberty around the globe was "the calling of our time," and because democracy choked off terrorism, America's "vital interests and our deepest beliefs are now one."[8] Bush's address was viewed as naive and arrogant by many of the allies in Europe, but it touched deep emotional chords in Rice, who had embraced so much of the president's idealism from the first term. "Transformational diplomacy" brought new definition and passion to her work, although the phrase and the ideal behind it would not survive reality two years into her tenure as secretary of state.

Rice turned for help to a group of old colleagues and friends, many of them from the administration of George H. W. Bush. Robert Zoellick, the onetime adviser to James Baker and the administration's trade envoy who had prepped Rice for her 9/11 Commission testimony, became Rice's number two, deputy secretary of state. Nicholas

Burns, a career foreign service officer who had worked with Rice on the Bush I National Security Council staff, became Rice's number three, undersecretary of state for political affairs. He would be her chief advocate for diplomacy with Iran. John Bellinger, Rice's legal adviser on the NSC who had been enraged by Cheney's secret dealings on torture, became her legal adviser at State. Philip Zelikow, Rice's co-author and colleague from the Bush I NSC, became her counselor and an increasingly vocal critic of American policy in Iraq. The spokesman she had brought with her from the NSC, Sean McCormack, worked with Wilkinson to put her in front of flattering backdrops and in warmer surroundings on her foreign trips, like a visit to a children's music school in Paris.

Rice rebuffed a lobbying campaign of the right wing to select John Bolton, the conservative intellectual and hard-liner on North Korea and Iran, as her top deputy. Instead she accepted Cheney's recommendation that Bolton go to the U.N., where, she told associates, he would implement policy, not make it. The result was that with a few exceptions, Rice had surrounded herself with internationalists, pragmatists, and even a closet Democrat or two. Conservatives were not entirely happy, but they held their fire because they thought that Rice was at heart probably one of them. Rice's power as secretary of state was cemented by another important decision by Bush: to make Rice's old deputy at the NSC, Steve Hadley, the new national security adviser. Smart and cautious but lawyerly and awkward in public, Hadley would generally be seen as continuing his role as Rice's deputy in the making of foreign policy.

Eight days into her new job, Rice embarked on the first phase of her effort to revive diplomacy, a week-long trip to Europe and the Middle East designed to set the tone that a fresh wind was blowing at State. "I'm going to go to ten countries in seven days or something like that," Rice joked to a group of State Department employees just before leaving. "I think they're not actually telling me. They don't want me to know."[9]

The goal of the trip was to ease the transatlantic rupture over the war in Iraq and a looming breach over Iran. As its logical centerpiece, Rice and her aides settled on her delivering a major speech in the heart of Paris. After the president's anger at Jacques Chirac and Powell's fights with Dominique de Villepin at the United Nations in the months leading up to the Iraq war in 2003, Rice's aides billed the event as if she were confronting the lions in their den.[10] It wasn't that far from the truth—Rice would be speaking at the Institute of Political Studies before a crowd of French intellectuals, hardly a receptive audience for a member of the Bush administration. But in her half hour speech on February 8, when she dressed more chicly than usual and delivered her remarks in the sober tone of a university lecture, Rice called on France and Europe to put aside their differences with the United States and together create a new Iraq and peace in the Middle East. "It is time to turn away from the disagreements of the past," Rice said. "It is time to open a new chapter in our alliance. America stands ready to work with Europe on our common agenda—and Europe must stand ready to work with America."[11]

The reaction was cautiously positive. Although Rice charmed her hosts with her style and her praise for France, enormous skepticism remained. "Condi's Great Game: To Seduce Paris," said the headline in the left-leaning daily *Libération*. The accompanying article noted that in her "pumps and navy blue suit accessorized with a belt and a large strand of pearls, she gave a speech in her own image: impeccable and soignée, seductive but without overdoing it."[12] Chirac, the man who had so angered Bush, kissed Rice's hand twice when she entered and left the Elysée Palace, and Michel Barnier, the French foreign minister, called her "Chère Condi" during a news conference.[13]

But the popular daily *France-Soir* ran a headline that asked "Can We Trust Rice?" and Jack Lang, the Socialist former culture minister, told France Inter Radio that while he recognized Rice's "charm and seduction," she was still the "Madame Hawk of yesterday" who had been "aggressive and fanatical" on Iraq.[14] The French were particularly disturbed by what they saw as Rice's ideological zeal on Iran, which the United States was accusing of fomenting terrorism and speeding up plans to produce a nuclear weapon.

At breakfast with six French intellectuals at the American ambassador's residence the day after her speech, Rice stunned some of the guests by branding Iran a "totalitarian state," a definition that did not take into account that Iran, unlike Saudi Arabia or Egypt, had an elected president and legislature. "She gave no proof that Iran was totalitarian, because she didn't have any," one of the guests, François Heisbourg of the Foundation for Strategic Research Paris, told *The New York Times* afterward. "It was scary. Unless there is some give and take on the American side we are heading for a real crisis."[15]

In fact, Rice was at that moment quietly moving the president toward a major shift in the administration's policy toward Tehran. She had arrived at this point after a three-year evolution and many ups and downs in her thinking, not least of which was Iraq, which effectively tied the administration's hands. Never again could the president—and Rice—rush to war without exhausting all diplomatic approaches first.

As national security adviser, Rice had started out as a skeptic that ties with Iran would ever improve. The United States had essentially frozen relations since the overthrow of the Shah and the 1979 hostage crisis that derailed Jimmy Carter's presidency, although at the end of the Clinton administration, Secretary of State Madeleine Albright had made some gestures to improve ties, including lifting small trade bans on pistachios and carpets. The efforts came to nothing, and the Bush administration took office with no desire to open relations.

But after the attacks of September 11, relations with Iran seemed on the brink of cooperation and possibly even friendship. Iran, which had never been a friend of the Taliban and had long been a rival of Afghanistan, supported the American war there in 2001. In 2003, Iran's leaders were hardly displeased, either, about Bush's ouster of Saddam Hussein, since Iran and Iraq had fought a bitter and bloody war in the 1980s for dominance in the Persian Gulf.

But a peace feeler from Iran later in 2003 was nonetheless rebuffed by the administration. It came in May in the form of a two-page proposal for a comprehensive dialogue with the United States on all issues, including Iran's nuclear program. The proposal was passed on by the Swiss ambassador in Tehran—Switzerland served as a diplomatic channel between the United States and Iraq—to the State Department, and some officials in the administration favored pursuing it to see if it was serious.[16] Others said they couldn't determine whether the proposal was from the Iranians or the Swiss, and Rice later said she never remembered seeing it.[17]

But it was in this period that Cheney and the administration's hawks were still heady over the victory in Baghdad and more interested in a policy that would topple the Tehran government rather than engaging it. By 2004, as Iraq deteriorated, fresh intelligence showed that Iran was stepping up its efforts to process uranium into nuclear weapons, the same evidence that Bush had cited as a cause for war in Iraq. Alarmed, the European allies came up with a plan to negotiate with Iran by offering it economic incentives in return for halting its nuclear program. To be credible, the plan needed the power of the United States behind it, but the Bush administration was skeptical and even hostile to the European ideas. Rice, though, had started to realize in her conversations with the Europeans and with her new team at the State Department that if the Europeans were to ever join in a tough policy of eventual sanctions or military force against Iran, they would have to be given latitude to try diplomacy first.

That was the state of play in late 2004 when a major blowup occurred between the United States and Europe over the European initiative. On October 15, envoys from Europe, Russia, Japan, and Canada met at the State Department with John Bolton, the very hawkish undersecretary of state for arms control, and informed him of plans for Britain, France, and Germany to open talks with the Tehran government. But Bolton could hardly disguise his disdain and brusquely said that he was highly skeptical that the plan would work or was even worth trying. Furious, the European envoys repaired to the office of Daniel Fried, the NSC's senior director for European and Eurasian affairs, to complain about Bolton's treatment, which one of them, employing diplomatic understatement, said "bordered on unacceptable."[18] Fried, a career diplomat who had served in the Clinton administration, was sympathetic. "They were on the ceiling," he recalled.[19] Fried went to Rice and told her it made no sense for the Europeans and Americans to be fighting among themselves when the real problem was trying to forge a common front on Iran. "This is nuts," he said.[20]

But Rice "was already there," Fried recalled.[21] Over the next months, as the administration remained skeptical about the European plan—although the White House said it would not oppose it—Rice worked on the president. Her goal was to have Bush throw U.S. support solidly behind the European negotiating track with Iran. "She thought, 'Look, we don't have to be in these talks, but the French,

Germans, and British are, and why wouldn't we support them?' " an adviser to Rice recalled. "They're our allies."[22] To bring Bush around to her thinking, Rice employed the subtle but persistent style that she had learned from experience might work. "She would push at him, and he would push back," the adviser said. "What was really happening was she was giving him a brief and he was thinking about it. But his style was to banter and push back and then see if you meant it. You know, 'That's not right, you don't mean that!' But she'd go back and back and back."[23] Eventually Rice persuaded Bush that if the United States was to repair relations with France, Germany, and the European Union, the way to get there was to be more supportive of their efforts on Iran.

Less than two weeks after Rice's first trip to Europe in February, she was back on the continent, this time with the president and with the Iran issue carefully worked out in advance so that Bush's sessions with European leaders would give him the comfort he needed to say yes. On February 21 over dinner in Brussels, the headquarters of the EU, Bush pressed Chirac to make sure that the two of them shared the same goal. Bush asked the French president bluntly if he wanted to make a deal with Iran that ensured it got nuclear weapons or if he wanted one that ensured it did not. "We can't let them have nuclear weapons," Chirac told Bush, in the recollection of the Rice adviser, who was at the dinner.[24] Bush, according to this official, replied, "If that's your view, then I can work with you."[25] (In 2007, Chirac let slip publicly that the world might be able to tolerate a nuclear-armed Iran, but it never became French policy.)

Two days later at a stop in Germany, Steve Hadley, the new national security adviser, took another crucial step to support the European negotiations by leaving open the possibility that Bush would consider offering economic incentives to dissuade Iran from pursuing its nuclear ambitions.[26] The step was critical because no European offer of economic help to Iran would be taken seriously if the United States opposed it and used its power to block the aid through sanctions. Within weeks, the United States and Europe finally had a deal: The administration assented to European wishes to let Europe offer modest economic incentives to Iran, and the Europeans assented to the administration's demands to take the negotiations to the tougher forum of the United Nations Security Council for possible sanctions if Iran rebuffed the offer.[27] The entire deal averted a transatlantic rift over Iran and opened the possibility of defusing the Iran crisis peacefully. The prospect for this strategy was doubtful, even in the minds of those who favored it, but it was the basic approach that kept Europe and the United States united well into 2007.

The 2005 shift in Iran strategy on Bush's European trip created major headlines, but Rice generated plenty of her own. On February 23, in an appearance before American troops in Wiesbaden, Germany, Rice wore a long, military-style black coat that blew open to reveal a skirt just above the knee and a pair of sexy, high-heeled black boots. The troops greeted Rice with raucous shouts of "We love you!"[28] while the rest of the world buzzed about the secretary of state's new "dominatrix" look. "Rice looked as though she was prepared to talk tough, knock heads and do a freeze-frame 'Matrix' jump kick if necessary," the fashion writer Robin Givhan observed two days later in *The Washington Post*, referring to Keanu Reeves and the long black coat that he wore in the action film *The Matrix*. "Who wouldn't give her ensemble a double take—all the while hoping not to rub her the wrong way?"[29]

Rice, who by this time was back in Washington, was both flattered and flustered by the new attention. "Why are these people writing all these stories about my boots?" she asked Wilkinson. Wilkinson, uncomfortable, said he didn't want to say. Rice, curious, pushed. Finally Wilkinson stated the obvious: "Condi, I don't know how to say this gently, but it's because men like those kind of boots—they think they're sexy." Rice, who was amused that Wilkinson felt this needed to be explained, whispered back, "*We know that.*"[30]

Two months in, Rice was finding that she liked the job. She was now "Madame Secretary" and more of a celebrity, with a new status and independence both inside and outside the administration. Although she and Bush still talked almost daily, she was not as tethered to the White House or the president's every need and demand. With Iran, she was beginning to push ahead on making policy instead of having to create a policy consensus among people who barely spoke to each other. "Condi likes to run things," said George Shultz.[31] It was in this period that Shultz heard one day from Bush how Rumsfeld now had to pay attention to Rice.[32] One White House official was startled to see Rice openly snap at Rumsfeld when the two started to disagree on an issue in a cabinet meeting. "Don, let's not go there," Rice said, brusquely cutting off the defense secretary.[33]

The new job also gave Rice the sense that she was no longer a transient in Washington. With four more years now ahead of her, she bought the apartment above hers at the Watergate and turned it into a new exercise and weight room, where a trainer would come twice a week, usually early Saturday and one evening. She casually dated—friends saw her with Raymond McGuire, an African-American Citibank executive in New York—but she continued to bring Gene Washington to White House dinners and official events. She went to Kennedy Center concerts and to dinner with her women friends, among them Ann Veneman, the executive director of UNICEF and former secretary of agriculture, and Harriet Miers, who had replaced Alberto Gonzales as the White House counsel.

Rice focused, too, on her music. Two years earlier, she had re-created her Stanford chamber group in Washington with four amateur string players, all lawyers by profession, and now she spent many of her Sunday afternoons in practice sessions with them at the Watergate. In 2003, the group had given a small concert at Rice's apartment, which attracted a bipartisan audience, including Miers, Federal Reserve chairman Alan Greenspan, and Supreme Court Justices Stephen Breyer and Ruth Bader Ginsburg.[34] The following year the group gave a concert at the British embassy for an audience of one hundred. As before, Rice found the music a way to escape from the anxieties of her day. "When you're playing there is only room for Brahms or Shostakovich," she later told Anthony Tommasini of *The New York Times*. "It's the time I'm most away from myself, and I treasure it."[35] The group often played one of Rice's favorite pieces, the intense and intricate Brahms Piano Quintet in F Minor, which Rice had earlier played with her group at Stanford. But Rice, showing a determination that seemed to border on arrogance given her amateur status, was determined to go further and master Brahms's Second Piano Concerto, one of the most dramatic and daunting challenges in the canon. It was as if she deliberately wanted to reach for something that would be beyond her grasp.

The spring moved quickly. In March, Bush announced his nomination of Bolton to the United Nations. On one level the choice repudiated the whole new climate of cooperation that Rice was seeking, since Bolton had not only opposed the Iran initiative but had once ridiculed the U.N. as useless and irrelevant. But after fending him off as her deputy, she accepted the White House demand that he go to the U.N., where he could be expected to follow Rice's orders. Rice understood as well that the man who had once said in the 1990s that ten stories could be lopped off the U.N. building and nothing would be missed might stir things up in a productive way. At the least, he would protect her right flank. When Rice's spokesman, Sean McCormack, was informed that he would have to sell Bolton with a straight face to the press, he burst out laughing.[36] Soon the expected denunciations of Bush's choice of Bolton came pouring in from around the world.

In April, Rice was in intense negotiations with Dov Weissglas, Ariel Sharon's chief of staff, a tough-talking, witty, and sometimes profane lawyer, about Sharon's plan to withdraw Israeli settlers and forces from Gaza and parts of the West Bank. Sharon had first floated the idea in late 2003, when he warned that if the Palestinians did not stop attacking Israelis he would simply "disengage" from dealing with them, withdraw the seven thousand Israeli settlers from Gaza, and wall off the area. The United States resisted the scheme at first, but then reversed course in 2004 and supported the plan only after extracting a promise from Sharon that he keep negotiating with Arafat and his people.

Sharon then began pressing the Bush administration to go still further in supporting his scheme, which was drawing opposition in Israel. His request was for the United States to provide political backing for two crucial long-term Israeli goals for a final Palestinian state. First, he wanted Bush to declare that in any final resolution of the Israeli-Palestinian issue, the Palestinians would have to agree that three major blocks of settlements in Jerusalem and the West Bank would end up in Israeli hands. In addition, the United States would recognize that Palestinian refugees and their descendants who had fled Israel in the 1940s would have a right to return to a new Palestinian state, but not to Israel itself.

Sharon's request set off one of the fiercest debates the administration had gone through on Israeli policy. Hard-liners allied with Cheney supported Sharon's request, but the State Department adamantly opposed it as prejudging the outcome of a future Israeli-Palestinian settlement. As Sharon and his aides learned of the rift in the administration over Sharon's request, his minister for immigrant absorption, Tzipi Livni, came to him and proposed that she travel to Washington to persuade Rice of Israel's cause. "So I went, and I saw how she was interested in the depth of the conflict, in finding a real process and doing what was right and just," Livni told Roger Cohen of *The New York Times* in 2007. "I had the opportunity to convince Rice, then national security adviser, and so make a contribution to the statement President Bush made soon after."[37]

Bush's statement "soon after," on April 14, 2004, said that any "just, fair and realistic framework" for Israel would mean that Palestinians would have to settle in their own state, not Israel. It was an enormous triumph for Sharon that so angered the Arabs that King Abdullah of Jordan canceled his visit to Washington two weeks later in protest. The statement also cemented the friendship between Rice and Livni, who would go on to become foreign minister and a close ally of Rice as secretary of state in negotiating future Israeli-Palestinian deals.

By the spring of 2005, Rice was spending considerable time working with Sharon and Weissglas on the actual details of the pullout. Her fear remained that without careful planning, Gaza would turn into a closed-off Palestinian prison and a breeding ground for radicalism. The actual withdrawal was due to begin in August, and Rice's diplomacy focused on getting Europeans and Arab leaders to make it go smoothly.

In May, a more immediate crisis loomed in Iraq as Rice tried to press the Shiite leaders in Baghdad to do more to quell the Sunni insurgency by reaching out more to Sunni leaders themselves. She sped to Baghdad on a fourteen-thousand-mile round-trip to reinforce the point that without more political flexibility, the Shiites could never hope to contain the Sunni rebellion.

In July, Rice closed an initial deal with India that would allow the country to secure international help to build nuclear reactors for its overwhelming domestic energy needs but allow it to keep its nuclear weapons. From the start of the administration, Bush had wanted to improve ties with New Delhi. His conservative advisers saw that a stronger India would serve as a political, economic, and military counterweight to China, and Bush had genuinely admired the entrepreneurial spirit of Indians he met in Texas while he was governor. The problem for U.S. policymakers was that India had long made clear that its number one priority from the West was civilian nuclear technology to build power plants for its booming economy. But American law forbade the sharing of such technology by any Western country as long as India possessed nuclear weapons. As secretary of state, Rice's goal was to close a deal allowing India to get the civilian technology but keep its nuclear arms, as long as it submitted to international controls and inspections of its civilian nuclear program. It was an excruciating negotiation led by Nicholas Burns, under Rice's direction. They had to make sure that India would agree to inspections to satisfy critics, who said the entire deal undermined the whole rationale for aiding countries that gave up nuclear arms—as first put forward under the Atoms for Peace program of President Dwight Eisenhower in the 1950s. India resisted even minimal steps to allow inspections until the very end.

Rice pushed hard, and thought she had lost any chance for an agreement on Sunday, July 17, after a difficult meeting at the Willard Hotel with K. Natwar Singh, the Indian external affairs minister. But the next morning she got up, called Zelikow at the crack of dawn, and told him that she was going to get the deal no matter what.[38] Rice then had breakfast with the Indian prime minister, Manmohan Singh, at Blair House, the official guesthouse across the street from the White House, where she told him that without Indian guarantees on inspections the deal would not be approved in Congress. Bush and Singh approved the agreement later the same day. Shyam Saran, the Indian foreign secretary, later said Rice's "tremendous effort and amount of energy" was critical to reaching the deal, but many details remained up in the air and there was a tortuous road ahead to approval in Congress.[39]

In August, as the Gaza withdrawal was underway, Rice looked back on her first seven months in the job with satisfaction and optimism. She had changed or refocused policies on Iran, Iraq, and India, and forged a genuine new partnership with Europe. She even had some grounds for claiming that democracy was advancing in troubled parts of the world. "This is a remarkable time," she said in an interview with *The New York Times* as she ticked off what she said were some of her accomplishments: the Iraqi election that past January, Afghan elections for their parliament, Egyptian contested elections for the first time, and the withdrawal of Syrian forces that past winter from Lebanon. "Something very dramatic is changing in the Middle East," she said. "And it is changing in the direction of—and I only say in the direction of—more open, more pluralistic, contested political environment." Bush's effort, and hers, in "pressing the case" for democratic change, she said, "I think has had a tremendous effect."[40] But nearly all of those accomplishments still had the potential to unravel and become more troublesome in the months ahead.

Less than two weeks later, on Monday, August 29, one of the deadliest storms in American history hit the Gulf Coast. At first it did not seem as catastrophic as had been feared. Hurricane Katrina had been downgraded to a Category 3 storm—from the most dangerous, a Category 5—by the time it made landfall in eastern Louisiana shortly after daybreak, and over the next hours its terrible eye swept east of New Orleans. The city seemed to have escaped the worst.

A day later, reality hit. The city's protective barrier of levees was breached and the muddy waters of Lake Pontchartrain engulfed New Orleans. Soon 80 percent of the city was underwater. New Orleans was ordered evacuated, but with nowhere to go, close to twenty thousand residents, most of them black and poor, took refuge in the Superdome. Another twenty thousand crowded into the city's Convention Center. Thousands were feared dead as food and water supplies dwindled. By Wednesday, August 31, Americans woke up to scenes of horror on their television sets that seemed straight from the Third World: bodies floating in floodwaters, people stranded on rooftops begging for rescue, looters running wild.[41]

That Wednesday afternoon, Rice left Washington for a vacation in New York. Soon after she arrived in the city, she worked on her backhand at the Indoor Tennis Club at Grand Central Station with Monica Seles, the tennis star, then met Gene Washington for dinner that evening. Afterward the two went to see the Broadway musical *Spamalot*. For Rice, it was the start of a pleasant break after months of record-breaking travel. But when the lights came on after the performance and audience members booed her, she knew that the trip was not going to turn out to be the respite she wanted.

The next morning, Thursday, September 1, as thousands of poor black refugees clamored for food and water inside the squalid Superdome, Rice went shopping at Ferragamo on Fifth Avenue for shoes. By the time she got back to the Palace Hotel in midtown Manhattan, Wilkinson, who was traveling with her, had found an item on the *Drudge Report* that made his heart sink:[42] The secretary of state had been spotted laughing it up the night before on Broadway while the Gulf Coast lay in tatters. "Theater goers in New York City's Great White Way were shocked to see the President's former National Security Advisor at the Monty Python farce last night—as the rest of the cabinet responds to Hurricane Katrina," the item reported.[43] That afternoon, more bad news for Rice appeared. The Web site Gawker.com reported that the secretary of state had just been seen spending thousands of dollars on new shoes at Ferragamo, an act that so reportedly outraged a fellow shopper that she went up to Rice and shouted, "How dare you shop for shoes while thousands are dying and homeless!" Rice later insisted that the encounter with the shopper never happened,[44] but the damage had been done. That afternoon she ended her vacation and headed back to Washington.

"By Thursday lunchtime, Thursday morning, I knew it wasn't sustainable," she later said, evidently meaning her trip to New York. "I knew I had to come back." When Rice called the president to inform him of her plans, she told him something that was just beginning to sink in at the White House, but was by now obvious to most Americans. "Mr. President, you have a race problem," Rice told Bush, as she recalled it. "Look at the screen."[45]

Rice later said that she had been slow to engage with the New Orleans crisis because she was thinking of herself solely as secretary of state—an official in charge of foreign disasters, not domestic ones. "I probably had not fully understood that I had also kind of gone into this category of national leader, or national figure, and that people expected me to be part of the solution for Katrina," she said. "I just didn't get it, frankly."[46] In Washington parlance, Rice was staying in her lane of traffic. But what she soon realized was that her new celebrity status and storybook life narrative required her to care about all the issues around her.

On Friday, Rice's first full day back in Washington, she spoke to Bruce Gordon, a former Verizon executive who had recently been selected as the new president of the NAACP. Rice had invited Gordon to lunch at the State Department several months earlier and the two had since struck up a friendly relationship. Now he told her what she already knew, that she and the White House had a huge race problem on their hands.[47] Rice called the president and arranged for Gordon and other black leaders to meet with Michael Chertoff, the homeland security secretary, in the West Wing the next day. In the meantime, Wilkinson was fighting with the White House over a trip he wanted Rice to make to Alabama, where Katrina had cut a wide swath of destruction across the state's Gulf Coast. The idea was for Rice to fly to her home state and express the sympathies of a native daughter—a first step in undoing the public relations problem of the shoe-shopping spree—but the White House refused to let her go ahead of the president's own trip to the region. Bush finally flew down for his first big damage-control trip on Friday, September 2, but he ended up doing even more damage to himself by standing at the Mobile airport at the side of Michael Brown, the disastrously hapless director of the Federal Emergency Management Agency, and declaring, "Brownie, you're doing a heck of a job."[48] That night, the rap star Kanye West gave voice to many African-Americans across the country when he declared on a live Katrina relief telethon that "George Bush doesn't care about black people."[49]

When Rice at last made her trip two days later to Alabama, to a black church outside Mobile, she launched into a vigorous defense of the White House's response, one of many she would make over the next months. "I don't believe for one minute that anybody allowed people to suffer because they were African-Americans, I just don't believe it," she told reporters at a community center in Bayou La Batre.[50] Suddenly, Rice was having to face the full nature of her public identity.

With the exception of her initial hiring as a tenure-track professor at Stanford, Rice had always denied that race was a factor in her success. Now she was beginning to come to terms with its significance in her life and in her public image. She was at the very least comfortable enough to use her racial identity for a political end, to defend the White House. It was a risky strategy, especially because people like Wilkinson were beginning to think she would have a political future after the Bush administration. But Rice, who knew how much her defense of Bush on race would antagonize blacks across the country, also felt she had no choice.

On September 12, when Bill O'Reilly of Fox News finally asked her bluntly, "Does it hurt your feelings when some anti-Bush people say that you're a shill for him and sold out your race?," Rice smiled in response. "Oh, come on," she said. "Why would I worry about something like that? Bill, the fact of the matter is, I've been black all my life. Nobody needs to help me how to be black."[51] The comment, a reprise of what she had said at Stanford when she was accused by blacks of selling out to the university administration, was always her last line of defense. Later, when she was asked why the White House had been slow to respond to the race crisis of Katrina, Rice came on less strong. "I don't know," she said. "I think when you're in a situation like that, there's so much going on and you're just trying to deal with the next thing, and maybe a little bit of the forest for the trees. But I can tell you that the president knew."[52] Rice went on to defend the president in a round of interviews during her week attending the United Nations General Assembly in New York.

There was good news for Rice later in September, when the administration announced that North Korea had agreed—in principle—to end its nuclear weapons program in exchange for security guarantees and economic benefits that would ensure its survival. The deal, announced on September 19 in Beijing, was a victory for Rice and the chief American negotiator, Christopher Hill, and their strategy of engaging in six-nation talks with North Korea that included Russia, China, Japan, and South Korea in addition to the United States. As in the case of Iran, it had been a slow, years-long process to get to that point. After Bush reprimanded Powell in early 2001 and shut off the possibility of U.S. talks with North Korea, the North Koreans admitted in October 2002 that they had a major weapons program, which presented the Bush administration with a crisis as it prepared to go to war with Iraq for the same reason. By early 2003 the administration finally agreed, under pressure from its allies in Asia, to talk to North Korea, and by that summer the United States was engaged in the six-nation talks. Rice had given strong support to the talks as secretary of state, not least because Iraq had taught her that if confrontation ever occurred with North Korea, she would have to show that every effort had been made to reach a diplomatic solution.[53] But she was still deeply skeptical that North Korea would actually implement the deal.

Her doubts seemed initially fulfilled the following day, September 20, when North Korea reneged on a part of the agreement and said that it wouldn't give up its nuclear weapons program until it got a civilian light-water nuclear reactor up front from the United States. Rice brushed it off, saying the administration would not get "hung up" on the snag,[54] but it was clear that she and the administration remained a long way from a solution. As negotiations churned on through the rest of the year, hard-liners in the administration, from Cheney to Bolton, held their fire, mostly because they assumed that in the end the six-party talks would fail.

The larger problem for Rice in the fall of 2005 was, as always, Baghdad. It had been a long, hard summer in Iraq—suicide car bombings, continued failures to train enough Iraqi security forces, and never-ending arguments between Sunnis and Shiites over how to share power in a unified government. But it had been a long, hard summer for the Bush administration in the United States, too. Cindy Sheehan, the mother of an American soldier slain in Iraq, had staged a protest and demanded to meet with the president for most of August outside Bush's Texas ranch. The president's refusal to see her while he spent days of his vacation mountain-biking had made him appear callous and helped inflame antiwar sentiment around the country. By September, the disastrous response to Katrina fed the view that the White House was incompetent, indifferent, and in over its head. All the bad news only reinforced the sense that the United States was sinking in Iraq and had no clear plan for how to win or bring the troops home.

Phil Zelikow, Rice's counselor at the State Department, had been writing her increasingly alarming memos on the descent into chaos in Iraq since the beginning of the year. Although Rice was continuing to keep an optimistic face in public, she was getting no such cheer from Zelikow in private. Rice had sent Zelikow to Iraq early in the year to assess what was happening, and he reported back to her in February 2005—only weeks after Rice and Bush had publicly exulted in the first free elections in Iraq in half a century—that Iraq was "a failed state."[55] In a memo in September after another trip to Iraq, Zelikow told Rice that there was a 70 percent chance of success in achieving a stable, democratic state in Iraq, which meant, he wrote, that there was a "30 percent chance of failure," including a "significant risk" of "catastrophic failure."[56] The United States was spread far too thin in Iraq, the memo said, and needed to do a far better job in securing the most volatile parts of the country so that reconstruction and reconciliation could take place. He did not specifically call for more troops, but he knew that more troops, or better-deployed troops, were needed.[57]

By October, Zelikow was even more disturbed. In near-daily conversations with Rice, he told her that there was no coherent strategy in Iraq.[58] Rumsfeld was passive, Zelikow said, and was determined to accelerate troop withdrawals and let the Iraqis sort out the problems on their own. Another problem, Zelikow told Rice, was that the White House was always looking for policy guidance from Baghdad, where Rumsfeld had dispatched General George Casey as the top U.S. commander after the Abu Ghraib scandal and Zalmay Khalilzad had just arrived as the new U.S. ambassador in June. But Casey and Khalilzad were handling day-to-day crises, Zelikow said, and couldn't set overall strategy from the field. They needed help from Washington, but where was Washington? In meeting after meeting, what was still functioning as Rice's old NSC Iraq Stabilization Group engaged in lengthy discussions about the crisis of the moment but little long-range thinking. As Zelikow later put it, "A PowerPoint presentation will be delivered. Much of the meeting will be consumed in hearing it. Questions will be asked about it." And then, he said, "the dogs bark and the caravan moves on."[59] Nothing was ever decided, and no one seemed in charge.

Privately, Rice shared many of Zelikow's views, although she later characterized her former co-author's language in the memos as "dramatic" and prone to hyperbole.[60] "I'm not saying I discounted what he was saying—I thought the analysis was very good," Rice said. "But Philip's penchant for blue language was something I knew firsthand."[61] Rice took no issue with Zelikow's judgment that the administration had a 30 percent chance of failure in Iraq, which she deemed "pretty good odds."[62] She also agreed that Rumsfeld's exit strategy was not an option.

On October 19, when Rice was called to testify about progress in Iraq before the Senate Foreign Relations Committee, she opened with a new articulation of the core strategy in Iraq, written by Zelikow and adapted from his memos. "Our political-military strategy has to be clear, hold and build," she declared. In other words, Rice said, the strategy was now for U.S. troops to clear out areas of insurgent control, hold and secure those areas with help from Iraqis, and then build a political consensus and durable Iraqi institutions. The slogan, which Zelikow came up with after he saw the successful "clear, hold and build" U.S. military operation in the violent northern Iraqi city of Tal Afar, was unassailable on the surface but was hardly a guide to greater success in other parts of Iraq. For one thing, the Tal Afar offensive had required so many American troops—five thousand—that it was difficult if not impossible to replicate elsewhere.[63] Both Rice and Zelikow knew that the United States did not have enough troops to "hold" cities and neighborhoods across the country. It was the beginning of the thinking in the administration that would eventually lead to a "surge" in troops in 2007 to try to spread stability in troubled parts of the country.

But because the slogan was a clear summary of military as well as political strategy, it infuriated Rumsfeld, who saw Rice as once again encroaching on his turf in areas she did not understand. She was mouthing a "bumper sticker," nothing more, he thought, and expecting the U.S. military to take responsibility for something the Pentagon was trying to get the Iraqis to do.[64] The U.S. military had to get its hands off the back of the Iraqi bicycle seat, Rumsfeld later told Bob Woodward. "We've got what, 263,000 Iraqi security forces?" Rumsfeld said. "I wanted them clearing. And then holding. And I didn't want the idea to be that it was just us."[65]

In her three and a half hours of testimony before the Senate, Rice was both conciliatory and combative, as she often was in public. But at the very end, she seemed to speak the most honestly when she offered a weary concession to Senator Barack Obama, the Democrat of Illinois, about the American plans to train Iraqi security forces and bring Iraq together. "I understand that, yes, it might not work," she told Obama after much of the hearing room had emptied out. "But every day we have to get up and work at our hardest to make it work."[66] It was an extraordinarily revealing moment, almost as if she were comfortable enough with Obama—another superstar African-American political figure with whom Rice was beginning to feel a certain chemistry—to show herself as fatalistic about her efforts compared with Rumsfeld, whose days were beginning to be seen as numbered in Washington. She at least seemed to convey the sense that success in Iraq was still a distant goal.

Two days later, Rice left for Birmingham, Alabama, and embarked on another step in her journey into her own past to find sources of strength and inspiration. More to the point, she was testing the environment for her future in public life. Wilkinson had made no secret that he wanted Rice to run for something someday—president or vice president or governor of California—and so he came up with the idea of inviting Rice's European counterparts to working dinners in places outside Washington, like Denver, Seattle, or San Francisco, where Rice could get exposure in important local television markets.[67] Rice countered that she really should go to her hometown, Birmingham, and invite her counterpart from Great Britain, the foreign minister, Jack Straw, an accomplished politician from Lancashire in northern England, with whom she had grown comfortable since the early days of the administration. The setting was in many ways a natural. Rice could invoke her past under segregation to make a larger point about the world she was trying to change and her vision that it was possible to see hope in the future even in the violence and cruelty of the present.

On October 21 at the University of Alabama at Tuscaloosa, the very same place where George Wallace had stood in the door and barred blacks from entering when Rice was eight years old, Rice gave what was the most idealistic—though perhaps calculated—speech of her life. It was certainly the most passionate, and laid bare more of her childhood than she had in public before. Any political consultant would have recognized it as a first step in offering up the story of her life as a rationale for public office. As her Aunts Gee and Connie and Uncle Alto listened in the audience, Rice told it well, evoking all the privileges, fears, and drama of her past.

> *I lived in Tuscaloosa, of course, when my father was the Dean of Students at Stillman College. But my hometown is just up Route 20 in Birmingham. And it's a place that I remember very fondly. It's a place of childhood toys and parties and really, in many ways, a secured childhood because I lived in a nice neighborhood where teachers and parents cared a great deal for the children and where we were all taught that we had every opportunity before us and that even if Birmingham had limited horizons for black kids, our parents didn't have limited horizons for us.*
>
> *And so we went to Jack and Jill and Tots and Teens and we took flute lessons and piano lessons and ballet lessons and swimming lessons and on Saturdays, French lessons. And our parents gave us a world that despite the world around us was one that was loving and caring and secure.*
>
> *But despite of my fond memories of Birmingham as a place where I was, as a child, secure, I also remember a place called "Bombingham"—where I witnessed the denial of democracy in America for so many years. It was, after all, the city of Bull Connor and the Ku Klux Klan, where blacks were haunted by rebel yells and terrorized by nightriders and accused of burning their own homes.*
>
> *And, of course, it was the city where my friend Denise McNair, and three other little girls, were blown up one Sunday morning while they were going to Sunday school at the Sixteenth Street Baptist Church. And it was a town where my father and his friends had to bear rifles at the top of the cul-de-sac in the community to keep nightriders out.*[68]

Rice then moved to her central point: The triumphant story of the American civil rights movement was a model for the kind of democracy and freedom that she and George Bush envisioned in the

Middle East. There had been skeptics in the past, and there were skeptics now, but Rice spoke with such intensity and fervor that if she was exploiting history and her own life to make a dubious political point—and there were people in Birmingham who thought that she was—it was clear that she believed in what she was saying. Like all politicians who believe in the validity of their own experience, Rice was presenting herself as more than an intellectual who had simply arrived at her views from her studies.

"Across the empire of Jim Crow, from upper Dixie to the lower Delta, the descendants of slaves shamed our nation with the power of righteousness, and redeemed America at last from its original sin of slavery," Rice said. "By resolving the contradiction at the heart of our democracy, America finally found its voice as a true champion of democracy beyond its shores." Even so, Rice went on, there were people who at one time "believed that blacks were unfit for democracy, somehow too childlike or too unready or too incapable of self-governing." Now there were the same voices arguing that people in the Middle East, "perhaps because of their color or their creed or their culture or even perhaps because of their religion, are somehow incapable of democracy." But it was "the very height of arrogance to believe that political liberty, and rights for women, and freedom of speech, and the rule of law, belong only to us." Rice concluded that "it is tyranny, not democracy, that has to be forced upon people at gunpoint."[69]

Rice spent the rest of the weekend in an odyssey through her past. With cameras and correspondents in tow, she visited the Brunetta C. Hill Elementary School, the first time she had been there since the age of eleven. When she saw her old band teacher, John Cantelow, who had been a block captain of the neighborhood patrols against night riders in that spring and summer of 1963, she hugged him and started crying. "She was a different kind of kid," Cantelow told the reporters traveling with Rice. "She was more mature than the others and very, very, very—how can I explain it, for a kid?—very focused."[70] Rice's old friend Carole Smitherman, the one who had waited outside for Rice to finish her piano lessons inside with Angelena, told reporters that Rice was an artist whose music "filled our streets."[71]

Questions about Rice's future followed her everywhere. "I don't want to run for office, but that doesn't mean some of you can't," she told a dozen children in Brunetta C. Hill School's library. On Saturday afternoon in Tuscaloosa, she was greeted with an explosion of cheers when she and Straw entered the field of Bryant-Denny Stadium at the Alabama–Tennessee football game for the ceremonial toss of the coin. Straw was astounded, not only by the crowds but by the terror that had been such a part of Rice's childhood. He recalled talking to her on the trip about gun control and could see that Rice was not a fan of it. "She said, 'Listen, had my dad not had access to firearms, our house might have been burned down or somebody might have been killed,' " Straw recalled.[72]

Rice returned to Washington and a president in the midst of twin political crises, the furor over the CIA leak investigation and the outing of an agency operative, Valerie Plame, as well as the storm over Bush's nomination of Rice's friend Harriet Miers to the Supreme Court. Bush had asked Rice what she thought about nominating the White House counsel to the Court, and Rice had told him she thought it was a good idea. She told him he would obviously have to make the argument that Miers's lack of judicial experience—she had never been a judge—was a positive because it would bring a person with a new kind of perspective to the bench. "Which I thought was completely sustainable," Rice later said.[73] But after weeks of raging criticism about Miers's qualifications—and anger from conservatives who questioned her ideology on abortion and other social issues—Miers withdrew as a nominee on October 27. "That was awful for me because Harriet and I are good friends," Rice later said.[74]

In November, Rice was back in the Middle East, brokering a deal on arrangements to facilitate the flow of goods into and out of Gaza following the Israeli withdrawal of forces and settlers the previous summer. The deal was essential to sustain the lives of Palestinians left in Gaza but also to meet Israeli concerns about arms and terrorists coming in. The negotiations took longer than expected, but Rice told both Sharon and Mahmoud Abbas, the Palestinian Authority president, that "we're going to get this done while I'm here."[75] On November 15, Rice led arduous all-night negotiations in her ninth-floor suite at the David Citadel Hotel to make it happen.

The marathon session was a big change for Rice, who as national security adviser had warned Powell so repeatedly during his miserable Middle East trip in the spring of 2002 to slow down. But this time she was willing to enmesh herself because of the urgent situation. Gaza, now entirely controlled by the Palestinians, desperately needed goods from the outside world. European and Arab leaders feared that cutting off Gaza would lead to instability and anger and strengthen the hand of the radical Islamist group Hamas in coming elections. But Rice still had to help Abbas and Palestinian moderates without undercutting Israeli security. In the end, the deal she negotiated gave Palestinians control over a crucial Gaza crossing, but with monitors from the European Union to make sure that arms and contraband could not get through. It was a victory, for her and the Middle East, but a short-lived one. By the end of the year, the narrow deal would begin to unravel as Hamas gained strength despite her best efforts to prop up the moderate Palestinians.

Rice's first year as secretary of state ended with another trip to Europe, this one for a NATO meeting to talk about sending more troops to Afghanistan. But in a case of bad timing for her, *The Washington Post* reported just before Rice's trip that the administration had set up a network of secret prisons for suspected terrorists around the world, many of them in Europe.[76] The story rekindled anger throughout the continent over the prisoners at Guantánamo and the American practice of rendition, the secret transfer of suspects to other countries, including those known to use torture.

Despite Rice's own misgivings about Guantánamo and the U.S. detention practices, she defended American policies wherever she went. "The United States does not permit, tolerate or condone torture under any circumstances," she told reporters before leaving on the trip, hoping to preempt the furor. "The United States does not transport and has not transported detainees from one country to another for the purpose of interrogation using torture."[77] Rice was on the defensive throughout the trip, but she was also annoyed about what she saw as European hypocrisy. The United States could not use European countries for transfers of prisoners without the countries' approval, and yet no one was coming forward in Europe to make that point.

"I used to talk to her a lot about the detainee policy," Jack Straw later recalled. But whenever he urged Rice to move the prisoners from Guantánamo or from the secret locations, she said, he recalled, "yes, she knew, but the problem was what to do with these people now." Rice was "trying to think of a way through" to an answer, he said.[78] In the end, Rice saw herself as standing up for a practice that she knew was hard to defend. The trip was an important milestone in her thinking that led to her decision to take on Cheney and push Bush to change the administration's policy the following year.

By the end of 2005, Rice had made an enormous impact on foreign policy and enhanced her own reputation as well. *Forbes* had her at the top of its list of the one hundred most powerful women in the world and she was the subject of a best-selling book, *Condi vs. Hillary*, by Dick Morris and Eileen McGann, that speculated on her possible future candidacy for president and a run against the former first lady, Hillary Rodham Clinton. Rice said the notion was absurd, but Wilkinson was not displeased.

CHAPTER 13

Hamas Won?

Washington, 2006

George Bush had begun to think that his secretary of state had gone native. Sometimes it seemed as if she had been absorbed into the great gray hulk of the State Department and transformed into someone he no longer knew. The national security adviser who had pushed so hard for war with Iraq was now in a Foggy Bottom swamp of diplomacy, talking all the time about—talking. And not only that, Rice was talking about talking to countries that Bush had been determined at the start of the first term not to speak to, like North Korea and Iran. Bush understood that diplomacy was now Rice's job, and to a large extent he shared her views that the United States could no longer be seen as the world's warmonger. But that did not stop him from goading her.

"You want me to sit down with Ahmadinejad?" Bush would tease Rice when she came over to meet with him in the Oval Office, referring to the radical Islamist who was Iran's president. "Kim Jong Il? Is he next?"[1] Rice laughed off the teasing and said no, she didn't expect the president to meet face-to-face with Ahmadinejad and especially not with Kim, the brutal, bizarre dictator of North Korea whom Bush said he loathed. But Bush kept it up, archly calling her "Madam Rice," as in, "Madam Rice, you're not coming in to tell me that we ought to change our position?"[2]

Rice enjoyed the needling, as she always had. It was how the president signaled affection and respect, but his pointed teasing also served to keep his top advisers a little bit on edge, which is exactly where the president wanted them. The year 2006, it turned out, was going to keep Rice on edge for months at a time.

On January 26, in a development that shocked both Rice and the White House, the radical Islamist party of Hamas won a landslide victory in Palestinian legislative elections over the moderate, secular leadership of President Mahmoud Abbas and the governing Fatah party. The outcome gave Hamas—considered a terrorist organization by the United States, Israel, and the European Union—the right to form a new government and determine the Palestinian political future. The earthquake reached far into Rice's office at the State Department, where her assumptions about "transformational diplomacy" were, at least for the moment, in ruins. She had supported the election as a way for Abbas to consolidate power and as a symbol of the new stirrings of democracy she promised in the Middle East. She had not expected the wrong party to win.

Rice had spent Wednesday, January 25, the day of the Palestinian voting, keeping track of election returns. The predictions were that Fatah would eke out a narrow victory and retain its hold on power. Exit polls of Palestinian voters throughout the day bore out that scenario, although by the time Rice left the office that evening there were warnings from State Department officials on the ground. Elizabeth Cheney, the vice president's daughter and a deputy assistant secretary of state who was in charge of promoting democracy in the Middle East, had come into Rice's office to deliver the news. "The numbers look like what we've been expecting, but our people out in the field are saying that it seems to them that Hamas might be doing better," Cheney said, in Rice's recollection.[3]

Rice took note but wasn't overly concerned and left for home and bed. The next morning, January 26, she was greeted with newspaper headlines, written as she had turned in the evening before, that summarized the situation as she had left it: Hamas had made a strong showing but Fatah appeared to have a narrow lead. Rice went upstairs to exercise and was on her elliptical trainer, watching the local news at about 5 A.M., when she saw a crawl of words across the bottom of the screen: "In wake of Hamas victory, Palestinian cabinet resigns."[4] The news was clearly the latest from the Middle East, where it was now the afternoon of January 26. Rice was perplexed. "I thought, 'Well, that's not right,' " she said.[5] She kept exercising, and the crawl continued. Finally she got off the elliptical trainer and called the State Department. "I said, 'What happened in the Palestinian elections?' And they said, 'Oh, Hamas won.' And I thought, '*Oh, my goodness, Hamas won?*' "[6] Rice called the chief State Department official on the ground in the Palestinian territories, but he was out and she had to leave a message. With that, she decided her most immediate course of action should be to get back on the elliptical trainer. "I thought, might as well finish exercising," Rice recalled. "It's going to be a really long day."[7]

That prediction, at least, was correct. Rice and the president spent the next many hours in a defensive crouch as they tried to put a positive spin on what they agreed was a disastrous turn of events. "So the Palestinians had an election yesterday, and the results of which remind me about the power of democracy," the president gamely offered at a White House news conference at 10:15 that morning, when he was assaulted by questions about the Hamas victory. "You see, when you give people the vote, you give people a chance to express themselves at the polls, and if they're unhappy with the status quo, they'll let you know."[8]

In retrospect, the election results would have been obvious to anyone who had more than a passing involvement in the Middle East. The first—and until January 2006, only—Palestinian legislative election was held in 1996 as part of the Oslo Accords that established the Palestinian Authority as an interim administrative organization in the West Bank and Gaza. Yasser Arafat's Fatah party won a majority of the seats. Over the years, as escalating violence prevented more elections, Fatah stayed in power and corruption ran rampant. A new era seemed possible after Arafat died in 2004 and Abbas was elected president in 2005, but Palestinians continued to view the long-serving Fatah administrators as entrenched and crooked. Hamas in the meantime established extensive networks of schools and hospitals that provided services that the Palestinian Authority did not. As a result, Hamas began winning local elections. Although the Bush administration supported Abbas—and poured hundreds of millions of dollars into the Palestinian Authority before the January 2006 election to help it meet its payroll, field security forces, and build schools and health clinics—it was not enough. Rice and her team at State had failed to appreciate the depth of hostility among ordinary Palestinians toward Abbas and Fatah.

Three days later, as Rice headed to London, she wearily acknowledged the obvious. "I've asked why nobody saw it coming," she told reporters, speaking of her beleaguered staff. "It does say something about us not having a good enough pulse."[9] She tried to put the loss in perspective, saying that even Hamas was "caught off guard" by the magnitude of victory, but it was an unusual admission of failure for her.[10]

She had no real choice because of the facts in front of her. Democracy, it seemed, was empowering the very forces—Islamic radicalism—that the United States was trying to tame. Israel had suggested to the United States that the Palestinian elections be postponed, or that Hamas be barred from participating on the grounds that it was a terrorist organization. In other elections in Northern Ireland and Bosnia, there had been requirements that the participating parties renounce violence. But the United States was so eager to have the election that it rejected those suggestions. "You ask yourself, are you going to support a policy of denying the Palestinians elections that had been promised to them at a certain point in time because people were fearful of the outcome?" Rice said.[11] There was no real alternative, she said, other than repressing the fury with totalitarian means. In the end she was philosophical about the results. "There is a huge transition going on in the Middle East, as a whole and in its parts," she said, referring to elections in Egypt and Lebanon that had put radical and terrorist groups in power. "The outcomes that we're seeing in any number of places, I will be the first to say, have a sense of unpredictability about them. That's the nature of big historic change."[12]

Years later, after the shock of the results had faded and Rice found herself dealing with a worsening set of problems created by Hamas in the Middle East, she was far less philosophical about the election. "I think there are plenty of things Fatah could have done to head off

Hamas, but not every problem is amenable to a U.S. solution," she said briskly. "That's one of the first things you have to realize. Not everything that goes wrong is America's fault."[13]

Another disaster struck less than a month later, this time again in Iraq. On February 22, a powerful bomb shattered the golden dome of one of the holiest sites in Shiite Islam, the Askariya shrine in the city of Samarra, some sixty miles north of Baghdad. The explosion, believed to be the work of Al Qaeda in Iraq, ignited a nationwide wave of sectarian violence. In retaliation, enraged Shiite militia members aimed rocket-propelled grenades and machine guns at Sunni mosques as Iraqi army soldiers stood helplessly by.[14] By the end of the day, mobs had struck or destroyed twenty-seven Sunni mosques in Baghdad and killed three imams and kidnapped a fourth.[15] Rice, who was in Saudi Arabia, called the bombing a "tragic incident" committed by those "who wish to tear the Iraqi people apart."[16] Her words were an accurate assessment of the goals of the bombers, and over the next year Rice would look back on the Samarra disaster as the start of a major downward spiral in Iraq. For her, it also created the sense that there was less and less she could do to salvage the administration's policy.

A week later, Rice was with Bush on a three-day visit to India, Pakistan, and Afghanistan that was relatively upbeat and a change from the anger that often greeted the president abroad. Rice spent five hours on the ground during a surprise stop in Kabul, where she disembarked from Air Force One in brilliant late winter sunshine with the snow-capped Hindu Kush in the background. It was Rice's third trip to the Afghan capital and Bush's first, and in both cases it was a long way from the Camp David war council meeting of September 15, 2001, when Rice had looked at the unfurled map of Afghanistan and thought of it as the place where great powers went to die. As compared with Iraq, Rice saw Afghanistan as a limited success, however precarious the country's future. Rice beamed as she helped cut the ribbon at the heavily fortified new American embassy in Kabul and as she shook the hand of Hamid Karzai, the American-installed Afghan president. Neither she nor Bush addressed the problem of growing violence in the country, a resurgent Taliban, or Afghanistan's reconstituted opium trade.

Rice's positive mood continued in New Delhi, where Bush and Manmohan Singh, the Indian prime minister, announced a final agreement on the Indian nuclear deal that Rice had hammered out in earlier form at Blair House the previous summer. The deal faced uncertain prospects for approval by the U.S. Congress and angry critics who said it would only encourage North Korea and Iran to pursue their own nuclear weapons, but for Rice and her chief negotiator, Nicholas Burns, it was, for the moment at least, a triumph. That night, March 2, Rice attended a state dinner in the outdoor gardens of New Delhi's Rashtrapati Bhawan, or President's House, once the home of the British viceroy, in a shimmering azure gown by Ralph Lauren. The next morning's *New York Times* illustrated the news of the Indian nuclear deal with a large front-page picture of Rice in her gown as the president, dressed in a tuxedo, gave her an admiring sideways glance.

Rice spent the rest of the month in the kind of travel that she had feared when she agreed to the job: a nine-day, 31,000-mile trip to Chile, Indonesia, and Australia. Rice went to Chile to attend the inauguration of Michelle Bachelet, the country's first woman president, but the stops in Indonesia and Australia were simply to show American support and shore up the countries' commitments to fighting terrorism. It was the sort of unremarkable trip that American secretaries of state took all the time and it resulted in far more time in the air than headlines. En route from South America to Asia, Rice's plane flew across the South Atlantic and made a refueling stop in the middle of the night in Africa, on a darkened, deserted runway in Namibia, and then another stop in Mauritius, where several of Rice's aides got on a bus and headed to the beach for a quick swim in the Indian Ocean.

As always, Rice had exercised the morning of the marathon trip in the hotel gym in Santiago, where she used the elliptical trainer and did jumping jacks in the same room as her traveling press corps. "I want to start by noting that I saw a number of people in the gym this morning, so people are getting into the spirit," she said in a briefing to reporters later that morning on her plane. Then she brightly added, to the irritation of the reporters who had slept in, "Those of you who weren't in the gym know who you were."[17] At her destination, Jakarta, she toured a Muslim school where she announced a new program to bring the characters of *Sesame Street* to Indonesian audiences, but before she shook hands with an actor in an Elmo costume, Rice, who was largely oblivious to the world of children, had to be quietly told who he was.[18]

Rice's travels for March were not yet over. In a reprise of her visit to Birmingham with Jack Straw the previous fall, she had accepted an invitation from Straw to go to the gritty town of Blackburn in Lancashire in northwest England, the heart of his constituency. But this trip turned out to be nothing like Rice's splashy return to Birmingham, and instead became a journey of mishaps and protests that reflected the troubles Rice and the administration were facing at home.

The trip began on Friday, March 31, when Straw had plans to take Rice to see a soccer match. But the team, the Blackburn Rovers, had changed the time of their game, and Straw ended up showing Rice around an empty stadium on a gray Friday, an opening metaphor for a trip that skidded rapidly downhill.[19] Later that same day, Rice headed to Liverpool for what she had hoped would be a meeting with Paul McCartney, the Beatle and Liverpool's famous son, but McCartney had been too busy to make it and Rice had to settle for a tour of the Liverpool Institute for the Performing Arts, where McCartney had once been a student. There she faced half a dozen students who stood at the school door with arms folded and black T-shirts that read "No torture. No compromise."[20] The following day 250 protesters ringed Blackburn's City Hall shouting "shame on you" as Rice and Straw arrived.[21]

But the lasting news of the trip was Rice's comment at a lecture organized by a British think tank, Chatham House, on March 31. In response to a question about what lessons she had learned from mistakes made over the past three years, Rice said at first that "if you are impervious to the lessons of the period that you've just been out of, you're really rather brain dead."[22] A short time later she said dismissively, as if lecturing a dull schoolchild, that she knew the Bush administration had made "tactical errors—thousands of them, I'm sure" in Iraq.[23] The comment generated headlines about Rice conceding mistakes in the war, and the next day she tried to spin her way out. "I meant it figuratively, not literally, all right?" she told reporters. "Let me be very clear about that. I wasn't sitting around counting."[24]

But by then the damage had been done with Rumsfeld, who once again saw Rice as stomping on his territory and criticizing him in the process. Four days later, when the defense secretary was asked about Rice's comment in a radio interview in North Dakota, he snapped back, "I don't know what she was talking about, to be perfectly honest."[25] Then he added for good measure: "If someone says, 'Well, that's a tactical mistake,' then I guess it's a lack of understanding, at least my understanding, of what warfare is about."[26]

From England, Rice and Straw headed for Iraq and a surprise visit to Baghdad, where Rice had an unpleasant order of business: getting rid of Ibrahim al-Jaafari, the Iraqi prime minister. Jaafari, a conservative Shiite, had become prime minister after the first set of Iraqi elections in January 2005 and had been renominated for the job after the most recent round of elections that December. By the time Rice was on her way to Baghdad in April 2006, Jaafari had failed to form a coalition government—he had no support among the Sunnis and Kurds—and had been unable to rein in the militias that had been fomenting violence across Iraq since the Samarra bombing two months earlier. Bush and Rice saw him as a weak and ineffective leader, although it is hard to know who could have brought the cauldron of Iraq under control at that point. Although they had been unhappy with Jaafari for a long time, they had effectively pulled the trigger in late March, when Zalmay Khalilzad, the American ambassador in Baghdad, told Shiite officials to pass on a "personal message" from Bush to Jaafari: The American president "doesn't want, doesn't support, doesn't accept" Jaafari as Iraq's prime minister.[27] The message leaked out, as the administration planned, and now Rice was going to deliver it directly to Jaafari himself.

It was not an easy trip by any account. On the flight from England, Straw was ill, so Rice gave him the foldout bed in her cabin while she stretched out on the floor in the corridor, not far from the burn bags that held classified information that needed to be destroyed. "It's an embarrassing moment, getting the bed," Straw later said.[28] When the two arrived in Baghdad, they were greeted by a torrential downpour that forced them to abandon plans to fly from the airport to the Green Zone by helicopter. Instead they had to be driven by an armored Suburban that got stuck in traffic for a half hour at a checkpoint. But they fared better than their entourage: Iraq was still so dangerous that Rice's staff and the accompanying press had to put on helmets and body armor and make the drive in tanklike vehicles called Rhinos. Jim Wilkinson, who was along on the trip, looked at the heavily padded group and could not resist a moment of sarcasm. "Don't worry, we're going to be greeted with flowers and sweets," he said, echoing a version of Cheney's infamous line that U.S. troops would be welcomed as "liberators."[29]

Later that day Rice and Straw met alone with Jaafari. It was one of the toughest meetings Rice ever had. A woman who had been transfixed by great power politics since Josef Korbel's lecture about the maneuverings of Stalin was now engaged in some huge power politics of her own. Although Rice was carrying out Bush's orders, she was nonetheless telling the acting leader of a sovereign country that he had to leave office. "Time to step aside," she bluntly told him, in one account of the conversation.[30] Rice told Jaafari that the Iraqis were frustrated, the Americans were frustrated, and Bush was frustrated. Straw backed her up, and afterward the two went out to face the press. When Rice was asked what would happen if she didn't see a government taking shape in five weeks, her answer was swift. "I'm not going to wait for five weeks," she replied.[31]

Although the visit initially seemed to have backfired—a top adviser to Jaafari told *The New York Times* on April 6 that Rice's pressure had only strengthened Jaafari's resolve to remain in the job and that she and Straw should not have come to Baghdad[32]—Jaafari finally bowed out on April 20. "I cannot accept being a barricade or looking like a barricade," he said in a late night television address in Iraq.[33] The next day the Shiite political bloc nominated a new functionary, Nuri Kamal al-Maliki, a little known ally of Jaafari who had fled Iraq when he was threatened with a death sentence under Saddam Hussein.

Five days later, on April 26, Rice was once again in Baghdad, this time with, of all people, Donald Rumsfeld. The two had been ordered there by Bush, who wanted them to put on a big display of American support for the new Iraqi prime minister and also to show that they themselves could work together after their many squabbles. Together Rice and Rumsfeld would assess the military and political operations in Iraq, Bush said, and then report back to him. "You both get to look at both parts of it and I can hear from you simultaneously," Bush told Rice, as reported by Bob Woodward.[34] Rumsfeld dutifully flew in overnight from Washington, arriving in Baghdad at dawn, while Rice's plane landed a few hours later from Ankara.

But a trip that was designed to at least superficially patch up the differences between Rice and Rumsfeld only publicly reinforced them. The two did speak together to Maliki, who told them that he saw his obvious challenges as easing tensions between Iraq's warring factions and fighting terrorism, and that he himself distrusted the Iraqi police. Rice, the daughter of Birmingham, at this point saw an opening to more personally connect with Maliki and responded that she, too, had feared the police as a child under Bull Connor.[35] But the previous year, she said, she had visited Birmingham and had met the black woman who was Connor's successor.[36] "And so these things can change," she said.[37] What she did not say was that the change in Alabama had taken decades, which was far more time than the United States had in Iraq.[38]

Whatever cooperation may have occurred between Rice and Rumsfeld in private was not apparent at a testy joint news conference at the American headquarters on the Tigris River later that day. Things got off to a rocky start when a reporter for Bloomberg News noted that Rumsfeld and Rice had to fly around Iraq in secret and then asked, "What does that say about prospects for restoring security and stability here?"[39] Security was Rumsfeld's responsibility, and Rice looked at the defense secretary to take the question, but he paused for several seconds of awkward silence as if steam were coming out of his ears. "I guess I don't think it says anything about it,' he answered tartly.[40] Gamely, Rice tried to smooth things over. "Obviously, the security situation will continue to take our attention and the attention of the Iraqis," she interjected. "But we've always said, and I feel it even more strongly today, that the terrorists are ultimately going to be defeated by a political process here."[41]

Rumsfeld's irritation was even more apparent moments later,

when a reporter asked him to comment on Rice's earlier statement in Britain about the "thousands" of tactical errors the United States had made in Iraq. "I said I hadn't seen it and I wasn't aware of what she meant," Rumsfeld replied with a tight smile. Then he turned to Rice. "But she's right here and you can ask her."[42] Rice cheerily launched into a reprise of her defense that she hadn't meant the comment literally, but Rumsfeld, whose main goal was still to withdraw U.S. troops from Iraq as quickly as possible, appeared bored and doodled as she spoke.[43]

Rice was finally back in Washington at the end of the month, free for a brief moment from Iraq but now facing a major problem on Iran. The European negotiations aimed at dissuading Iran from its nuclear ambitions—the ones Rice had persuaded the president to support the previous year—had failed. Iran was speeding ahead with its enrichment of uranium and presumably a nuclear bomb. In between her two April trips to Iraq, Rice had reached the conclusion that she would have to persuade the president to change his approach to Tehran once again, but this time in a far more significant way than in 2005. Rice's new plan, hatched with Steve Hadley and her aides at the State Department over the previous month, would reverse nearly three decades of American policy. She would have to ask Bush to do what the United States had not done in nearly three decades: agree to direct, broad-based negotiations with a country that had called for the destruction of Israel, and which Bush considered the world's number one sponsor of terrorism.

Rice had been wrestling with the problem since the previous winter, when the Europeans had opened negotiations and offered Iran economic incentives if it gave up its nuclear program but promised to support the United States on sanctions if Iran did not. The talks made no progress and a bad situation got worse in August when the militant Mahmoud Ahmadinejad was elected Iran's new president. By the early winter of 2006 the European talks had "crashed and burned," in the words of Nicholas Burns, the undersecretary of state and Rice's chief adviser on Iran.[44] Rice and her aides came up with the idea of bringing the Russians and Chinese into the negotiating circle to bolster pressure on Tehran for sanctions, but the Russians, who had major oil and gas investments in Iran that they did not want to jeopardize, were resistant to the idea. On March 30, Rice traveled to Berlin for what turned out to be a disastrous meeting with the Europeans on Iran, and on April 4 reported back to the president that the international coalition they had forged to face down Iran's nuclear threat was in danger of falling apart.[45] Iran was successfully exploiting divisions among the Europeans and Russians and among the Europeans themselves, Rice told Bush.[46]

"What I really needed to do was help the president understand why what we were doing wasn't going to work," Rice later said. "And that we could only build an international coalition against Iran if we had set out a policy that was reasonable on its own terms—and where if the Iranians didn't pick it up, it was the Iranians' fault, not our fault."[47]

Over Easter weekend, April 15 and 16, Rice sat at home at the Watergate and put together a plan. On paper, it consisted of a two-page outline of three tracks for the United States to follow: a threat of sanctions to be imposed by the United Nations Security Council, a set of what Rice called "bold" incentives for Iran to give up the production of all nuclear fuel, and a separate set of strategies for economic sanctions that could be imposed by the United States unilaterally if the Security Council failed to act.[48] To accompany the outline, Rice created her own color-coded calendar, running from May into June, which marked out a schedule for each track. The key to it was that Rice was willing to step up the concessions by making it explicit that the United States would join in direct talks with Iran if it stopped enriching uranium.

On Monday morning, May 8, over breakfast at the White House with the president and Hadley, Rice presented Bush with her plan. To illustrate her points, she showed them her chart, which Hadley immediately pronounced "brilliant, colorful and completely impenetrable."[49] A short time later, like a diligent student who had worked over the weekend for extra credit, Rice also showed her chart to Burns. "Who did this for you?" he asked, startled. "I did," she said proudly. "But who on our staff?" he pressed. "No, I did," Rice said again, explaining that she had asked an assistant for colored markers and monthly planners and then put it all together from her notes.[50]

Bush was intrigued by Rice's color-coded plan but still not convinced. He got closer to the idea at a National Security Council meeting on May 17, when Cheney agreed to the new approach, perhaps because the vice president liked the idea that if the plan failed, the United States could press its sanctions or even military options against Iran. In the short term, skeptics like Cheney saw that there didn't seem to be any other choice, particularly since the Europeans were not ready to ratchet up the pressure on Iran with sanctions unless the United States was ready to ratchet up the incentives. As the plan took shape, Bush consulted both Putin in Russia and Angela Merkel, the new chancellor of Germany, to make sure that they would support sanctions if the new negotiating approach failed.

On May 31, in a statement that had been edited by Bush, Rice finally announced the new policy. The United States would join the Europeans—that is, the so-called EU-3 countries of Britain, France, and Germany—in talks with Iran over its nuclear program, but only if Tehran suspended its uranium activities. As Rice put it at a morning news conference in the grandeur of the Benjamin Franklin Room at the top floor of the State Department: "To underscore our commitment to a diplomatic solution and to enhance the prospects for success, as soon as Iran fully and verifiably suspends its enrichment and reprocessing activities, the United States will come to the table with our EU-3 colleagues and meet with Iran's representatives."[51]

Rice made the announcement just before leaving for talks on Iran in Vienna, where the next day the Russians, Chinese, Europeans, and Americans agreed to suspend discussions of Security Council sanctions. Instead they offered a joint set of incentives aimed at persuading Tehran to come to the bargaining table. Iran quickly dismissed the offer. There was immediate criticism that Rice was setting up conditions that Tehran would never meet, and that the offer was only intended to prove Iranian intransigence and fail[52]—thereby paving the way for military action.

But Rice also got deserved high praise for smart diplomacy, and for getting the administration's hawks and diplomats to agree, however briefly, on an approach for Tehran. Determined that Iran would not turn into another failed war in Iraq, Rice had skillfully pushed the president in the way she knew how. "The president doesn't say, 'Well, I just don't think we should do it,' " Rice later said. "He just keeps asking questions. 'Well, what would it mean? How would we coordinate that?' Or, 'What if they said this? What if we did that?' And sometimes I didn't have the answers and I'd have to go back and look and think about it. Well, how would we choreograph it if, you know, the Iranians said, 'Yes, but.' Sometimes it was going back because I really hadn't thought through something. And that's why we have that kind of interaction."[53]

Rice's new reputation as an evenhanded negotiator willing to make concessions was undercut the following month in the Middle East. During the summer of 2006 Israel plunged into a chaotic two-front war in Lebanon and Gaza, and it produced the worst crisis Rice had yet faced as secretary of state. The fighting, between Israeli forces on one side and the Palestinians in Gaza and Hezbollah in Lebanon on the other, posed a familiar dilemma for her. Should she side with the administration's hawks and support Israel's military campaign, or with the Europeans and Arabs—and the rank and file at the State Department—who wanted to rein Israel in?

In this case Rice gave unwavering support to what she considered Israel's overwhelming security imperatives. The decision put her on the defensive in a conflict that left a thousand Lebanese dead, most of them civilians, and shattered much of the progress that Lebanon had made in putting itself back together since the end of a fifteen-year civil war in 1989. Rice's actions also subjected her to criticism that Cheney and his office were continuing to call the shots. In fact, she was acting much more on her own instincts and those of the president.

The troubles began on June 25, when eight Palestinian militants in Gaza, including members of Hamas, entered Israel through a secret tunnel and killed two Israeli soldiers, wounded three others, and kidnapped a nineteen-year-old corporal, Gilad Shalit.[54] Israel responded with attacks on Gaza and sent troops into the area from which they had painfully withdrawn the year before. While the attacks raged, the Lebanese radical Islamist and Iranian-backed party Hezbollah—seeing an opportunity with Israel tied down in Gaza—fired its own rockets into Israel, killing eight soldiers. Ehud Olmert, the prime minister who had replaced Ariel Sharon six months earlier, retaliated with a full naval blockade of Lebanon and a major bombing attack that put Beirut's international airport out of commission.[55] Hezbollah promptly fired more rockets, probably supplied by Iran, into Israel. By mid-July, less than three weeks after the young corporal had been kidnapped, the Middle East was in a full-scale conflict.

The fighting created an atmosphere of crisis at the G8 summit of industrialized democracies in St. Petersburg, Russia, where Tony Blair and Kofi Annan, the U.N. secretary general, proposed sending an international force to stop the fighting.[56] But the United States was skeptical about the effectiveness of any U.N. force and also about a cease-fire. The U.S. view was exposed for all the world to see when Bush was caught at a summit lunch on an open microphone complaining about Annan, who had been calling for a cessation of hostilities. Bush told Blair that he didn't like Annan's approach—"his attitude is basically ceasefire and everything else happens"—and that he felt like telling Annan to telephone President Bashar al-Assad of Syria, a key sponsor of Hezbollah along with Iran, "and make something happen."[57] If Syria would get "Hezbollah to stop doing this shit," Bush added, then "it's over."[58]

The presidential profanity created a minor ruckus, but it accurately reflected the administration's views that Hezbollah, not Israel, was to blame for the fighting. Now, while much of the world looked on at the killing in Lebanon in horror, Bush and the administration's hawks saw the crisis as an opportunity. Israel suddenly had an excuse to punish Hezbollah, the group that Richard Armitage, the deputy secretary of state under Colin Powell, had once called "the A Team of terrorists" in the Middle East, more threatening to the United States than Al Qaeda. The attacks on Hezbollah could also send a message to Hezbollah's patron Iran, which the administration saw as increasingly responsible for the roadside bombs that were killing Americans in Iraq.

By July 18, the United States and Israel had reached a consensus: Israel would pound Lebanon for another week to weaken Hezbollah's forces and then Rice would travel to the region and try to establish what the United States envisioned as a large and powerful international force to drive Hezbollah from southern Lebanon once and for all.[59] The awkwardness of the American position was that the United States would be seen as opposed to a cease-fire until Israel finished the job in Lebanon and as the civilian death toll continued to rise.

So for nearly a week, while Israel bombarded Lebanon, Rice stayed put in Washington, where she announced that the world was seeing "the birth pangs of a new Middle East,"[60] a statement widely derided as ignorant and naive. Criticism mounted about her foot-dragging, but Rice was adamant. "You were still in a situation in which the Israelis were trying to deal with Hezbollah operations that needed to be pushed back," she later said. "And just going in and saying, 'Everybody stop now,' " would be ineffective. "So why rush there and not be able to make it happen?' "[61]

On Sunday, July 23, Rice finally left for the Middle East. Her delay and the grim prospects for peace in the midst of the unchecked bloodshed were on display all over the world, including in a small corner of Birmingham she knew well. On that Sunday at Westminster Presbyterian, the Reverend Clyde Carter stood in the pulpit as Rice's father had decades earlier and asked the small congregation to pray for "this lady, this sister, this child of this church" as she headed off to the conflagration. Carter, whose wife, Eva, had been a devoted member of John Rice's youth group, described Condoleezza Rice's challenge more succinctly than had any talk show host in Washington that morning. "All of you know what she's having to do today?" Rev. Carter asked the assembled congregation. "Having to fly to the Middle East to put out a fire with a bucket of water!"[62]

Rev. Carter's words were borne out the following day, July 24, when Rice opened her trip with a surprise stop in Beirut to demonstrate American concern about the rising death toll in Lebanon. "I'm obviously right here because I'm deeply concerned about the Lebanese people," she said after her convoy of twenty SUVs had sped furiously on a zigzag course through the empty streets to avoid potential bombs and mortar attacks.[63] Rice met with the Lebanese prime minister, Fouad Siniora, and promised American aid, but she refused to support a cease-fire and she left the country with the Lebanese angry that she had come at all. Rice then met with the Israelis and Palestinians and on July 26 flew to Europe to try to work out an agreement to end the fighting with European and Arab envoys assembled in Rome. But again Rice refused to call for the immediate cease-fire that the others wanted.

In a stormy, hour-long debate with the group over the wording in a final communiqué from Rome, Rice argued for a "sustainable cease-fire." The others took that as code language for no cease-fire until Hezbollah was disbanded or disarmed—a practical impossibility. In despair, Siniora unleashed scathing denunciations of the West's inaction over Israel. "Is the value of human life less in Lebanon than that of citizens elsewhere?" he cried out, sounding almost Shakespearean. "Are we children of a lesser god? Is an Israeli teardrop worth more than a drop of Lebanese blood?"[64]

But Rice dug in and won the battle over the communiqué. In the end it called not for an "immediate cease-fire" but declared that the parties should "work immediately" for a cease-fire. "It doesn't do anyone any good to raise false hopes about something that's not going to happen," Rice said afterward, explaining her reasoning. "It's not going to happen. I did say to the group, 'When will we learn?' The fields of the Middle East are littered with broken cease-fires."[65] But Rice's victory came at a cost. In her refusal to yield to the impassioned calls for an immediate cease-fire, she had lost the larger public relations war.[66]

By then, she and Bush had begun to realize, belatedly, that Israel's devastating bombing campaign was not knocking out Hezbollah as they planned and was killing far too many Lebanese civilians. By July 29, Rice was back in Israel trying to hammer out a deal with Olmert for a cease-fire she had finally decided was necessary, but the next day disaster struck: An Israeli missile aimed at the town of Qana in southern Lebanon hit a residential apartment building, killing more than fifty civilians, many of them children. The youngest of the dead was ten months old.

Israel called it a mistake, but the U.N. Security Council expressed "extreme shock and distress" as scenes of dead children being pulled out of the wreckage dominated the international airwaves. Lebanon denounced the attack as a war crime and canceled talks that had been scheduled with Rice, but even before then, Rice and her aides huddled in her suite at the David Citadel Hotel on the edge of Jerusalem's Old City knew they had reached the end of their negotiations in the

Middle East. "Everybody agreed, you can't go to Beirut now," said Elliott Abrams, the neoconservative, pro-Israel aide traveling with Rice. "We kicked it around, and it was unanimous."[67] He described Rice as extremely dejected. "Had it not been for Qana, she would have brokered a cease-fire," Abrams insisted. "It would have been a fantastic achievement by any scale. It would have been great for the Lebanese government, because she was doing this, and great for Israel. And it was that damn misfired missile that stopped that."[68]

Rice confronted Olmert and asked him to suspend Israeli air strikes for forty-eight hours, and Olmert, after responding that Israel had warned Qana residents to evacuate, agreed.[69] But the American imprint was obvious when Adam Ereli, one of Rice's aides, announced the suspension, not the Israelis.[70] Rice headed home, exhausted and battered, to try to work out a solution to the crisis in the United Nations, but there was an almost poetic final humiliation after her complaints about the Middle East landscape of broken cease-fires: Israel resumed air strikes only twelve hours after it had suspended them.

Nearly two tumultuous weeks later, the U.N. Security Council finally brokered a cease-fire agreement that deployed thirty thousand Lebanese and U.N. troops in southern Lebanon and called for a phased withdrawal of Israeli troops from the region. John Bolton, the U.S. ambassador to the U.N., and Nicholas Burns, Rice's undersecretary for political affairs, had argued for days with negotiators from Paris, Beirut, Jerusalem, and the Arab League over the timing of the withdrawal of Israeli forces and whether there should be one U.N. resolution or two in the deal. In the end Rice had to fly up from Washington and help push through a final agreement late on Friday, August 11, that persuaded the Israelis that the force would be strong enough to keep Hezbollah from reoccupying southern Lebanon but assured the Lebanese that it would not have unchecked military powers.[71]

"Wednesday night John Bolton called and said, 'We had a really bad day up here, it's all split apart again,' " Rice recalled. "And I think it was Nick who said, 'It's like *Groundhog Day*.' You would think you'd have it negotiated, and the next day it's not there."[72] Reflecting back, she said the period was the most difficult she had yet experienced as secretary of state. "It was my most frustrating time because every time you thought you had it done, it would unravel, and I would have to keep finding different angles. At one point we might have two resolutions, that was to take care of some French concerns, but then that became a problem with the Israelis and the Lebanese who didn't want two resolutions, they wanted one. So then I had to go find some way to do a phased one-step resolution. It was constantly having a door closed, so let's find another door."[73]

Later that month, Rice had one of the sharpest confrontations with Dick Cheney that her aides had ever witnessed. This time it was over the issue that had plagued her trip to Europe in December 2005, the anger over the secret CIA prisons and the administration's practice of incarcerating people without trial at Guantánamo. Ever since the trip, Rice had been arguing more heatedly to Bush that the American position was no longer sustainable. The United States had concealed as many as one hundred Al Qaeda suspects in the CIA's secret prisons in Eastern Europe and Asia for five long years, and was continuing to hold some 450 people at Guantánamo Bay. The policy was killing the United States in Europe, Rice told Bush. She knew he wasn't overly concerned about what the Europeans thought, but the practical effect was that the Europeans were now less willing to cooperate with the United States on fighting terrorism.[74] Rice had plenty of company in her arguments with allies like Tony Blair, who had been pushing Bush in the same direction, and also Michael Hayden, the new director of the CIA, who was coming to the conclusion that he did not want to be in business as an international jailer.

But Cheney's ongoing counterargument, according to people familiar with it, was far more powerful to Bush: Holding suspected terrorists indefinitely in secret prisons and at Guantánamo might invite international criticism but was essential to avoiding another September 11. "If you set this up for him as, 'Mr. President, I need you to make the tough, unpopular decision which people will attack you for but is needed to defend this country,' it's catnip to him," said one administration official deeply involved in the debate.[75]

Rice's arguments suddenly took on new urgency on June 29, when the Supreme Court ruled 5–3 in *Hamdan v. Rumsfeld* that the military commissions the administration had created to try the Guantánamo detainees were illegal. The principal flaw, the Court said, was that the president had established them without authorization from Congress.[76] It was Cheney's secret directive back in November 2001 that had created the commissions in the first place, and the ruling was a major blow to him as well as a sweeping setback for the administration.

But rather than seeing the Supreme Court ruling as a defeat, Rice seized on it as an opportunity to step up her arguments to Bush. He would now have to create new commissions within the law, of course, but the larger issue, she told him, was that he could not hold the detainees in the secret prisons or at Guantánamo indefinitely.[77] While there was good reason to interrogate terrorism suspects over a long period of time, the administration was past the four-year mark and at a point of diminishing returns. And since they were holding some of those who had planned the 9/11 attacks, she said, didn't he want to bring them to trial on his watch, before the next president took office?[78]

The issue came to a head at a National Security Council meeting in mid-August. The session was in the Roosevelt Room rather than the Situation Room, which had been closed for renovations. Bush presided as usual, sitting in the middle of the long table, with Rice to his immediate left and Cheney to his immediate right. Assembled around the table were Rumsfeld, Hadley, Michael Hayden, the new White House chief of staff Josh Bolten, and John Negroponte, the director of national intelligence, which was the job overseeing all fifteen federal spy agencies that had been created as part of the reforms recommended by the 9/11 Commission in 2004.

Rice made the same pitch in front of everyone that she had been making for months in private to Bush. Although she directed her words at the president, everyone in the room could see that her words were also aimed at Cheney after nearly five years of being cut out of his secret maneuverings. The administration had to close the secret sites, Rice said forcefully. They were doing more harm than good. America was a nation of laws, and it was important for the United States to bring the issue to closure, both on foreign policy and moral grounds.[79]

When it was Cheney's turn to speak, he was equally forceful. He told the group that his first concern was that the detainees continued to have "intelligence value" because they were providing information about plots that might thwart future attacks.[80] Second, Cheney said, the United States had won cooperation on the prisons from other countries by assuring those countries that the prisons would be kept secret.[81] Revealing their existence, Cheney argued, would be seen as a betrayal of trust, and would make the countries less likely to cooperate with the United States on fighting terrorism in the future.[82]

Bush took it all in, made few comments, and did not, as usual, rule on the spot. But less than a month later, Rice effectively won the battle, if not the continuing war. In a speech in the East Room of the White House on the afternoon of September 6, the president announced the transfer of fourteen "high-profile terror suspects" held secretly by the CIA—including Khalid Sheikh Mohammed, the man accused of masterminding the September 11 attacks—to Guantánamo Bay.[83] He also urged Congress to authorize new military commissions to put terror suspects on trial. The commissions would replace those struck down as unconstitutional by the Supreme Court in June. The decision ended eighteen months of arguments between the State Department and the vice president's office, and years of disagreements between Rice and Cheney. Rumsfeld, who was close to Cheney but had been through the crucible of Abu Ghraib, seemed to people in the meetings to be on both sides of the issue.

The defense secretary's days were by then numbered, as Rice well knew. Although Bush had thought a number of times of replacing Rumsfeld, he had always rejected the idea as too disruptive in wartime, even when Andrew Card and others had pressed it upon him. Back in April 2006, Bush had asked a group of his closest aides over dinner at the White House for a show of hands on whether he should fire Rumsfeld. Rice, along with Card, Josh Bolten, and five other aides, voted yes, but Rove, Hadley, Dan Bartlett, and the president—the single vote that mattered—raised their hands no.[84] Bush felt a strong sense of loyalty to a man who had overseen Iraq and Afghanistan and who had tried to transform the military into a twenty-first-century institution. All the calls for Rumsfeld's ouster—particularly from a loud chorus of retired generals the previous spring who charged the defense secretary with incompetence and waging a war with insufficient troops—only stiffened Bush's resolve to keep him. The president hated to be seen as buckling under pressure.

But as the chaos in Iraq continued into the summer of 2006 and the midterm elections loomed, Bush began to change his mind. Baghdad had become more violent, not less, as U.S. commanders had handed over responsibilities to the Iraqi forces, which was undercutting Rumsfeld's central premise that the Iraqis could be trained and the Americans could go home.[85] The president's evolving view was obvious to anyone in a National Security Council meeting that August 17, when Bush had opened the session with a tough assessment that "things in the theater are not going well" and that there was a "lot of concern in the press and the public" about the situation.[86] "How do we make clear to people that we have a plan to defeat the enemy?" the president asked, according to notes from the meeting. "We need a clear way forward coming out of Labor Day."[87] Bush complained that instead of displaying firmness, the United States was "constantly adjusting tactics" and leaving an impression that the war was "not winnable."[88]

Rice was by then on vacation and not at the meeting, although her aides reported back to her what had transpired. Cheney was there, as were Rumsfeld, Hadley, Bolten, and General Peter Pace, the chairman of the Joint Chiefs of Staff. On the closed-circuit television were General George Casey, the top American commander in Iraq; General John Abizaid, the senior American commander in the Middle East; and Zalmay Khalilzad, the U.S. ambassador to Baghdad. Bush peppered the military leaders with questions: Could they quantify the progress, or lack of it, being made by Iraqi security forces? Were Iraqi forces killing the enemy when they shot at them? What about the training of Iraqi police? What about the pursuit of Al Qaeda in Iraq?[89]

Rumsfeld asked if there was anything the Baghdad embassy could do to force Maliki, the new prime minister, to make some political progress. "I have little leverage," Khalilzad complained.[90] Cheney interjected that whatever Maliki could do, he doubted that he could help with the larger problem of violence. "There's not even a clear consensus on who the bad guys are," the vice president said.[91]

Suddenly Bush began complaining that if Iraqis couldn't combat the enemy, the United States would have to step back in and help. "If the bicycle teeters, we have to put our hands back on," Bush said of the Iraqis. "We have to make damn sure they don't fail . . . we have to have enough military personnel."[92] The president's words were a direct challenge to Rumsfeld, who had long used the same metaphor to argue that the United States had to take its hands off the bicycle and let the Iraqis handle the security problem themselves. The upshot, according to one official at the meeting, was that Rumsfeld had "gotten the message—we're not on troop reduction autopilot anymore."[93]

By September, a White House rump group had formed to try to figure out what to do about Iraq as the midterm elections loomed and how to handle what was clearly going to be Rumsfeld's ouster. The rump group—Hadley, Bolten, Karl Rove, and Dan Bartlett, the president's counselor and communications chief—was taking its cues from Bush. The president had begun to have a series of conversations with Rumsfeld aimed at getting the defense secretary to step down, but he did not want to let Rumsfeld go if he could not find a good successor. "I've got to get comfortable with somebody," an administration official quoted Bush as saying that fall.[94]

Rice observed protocol and stayed away from the White House meetings on Rumsfeld's future, but after nearly six years of conflict with the defense secretary and her vote at the April dinner, no one needed to ask her opinion. "I knew her views," said the White House official. "It wasn't like we were taking votes on whether there was going to be a change. We knew that essentially the president had made up his mind."[95] Later, Rice emphatically said that she never spoke to Bush about the issue. "I never had a conversation with the president about Rumsfeld moving on," she said. "That would have been highly inappropriate. I wasn't going to talk to the president about one of my colleagues."[96]

But Rice did have a major hand in the change. She, along with Hadley, enthusiastically recommended to the president Rumsfeld's eventual replacement, Robert Gates. Rice knew and liked Gates from Bush I, when he had been her superior as deputy national security adviser under Brent Scowcroft—and an amused witness to her dressing down of Boris Yeltsin. "I told the president, 'We have to reach out to him,' " Rice recalled.[97] Like everyone at the White House, she knew that Bush needed to find someone he could work with before Rumsfeld would be gone.

Gates, who was at that moment the president of Texas A&M University, was in many ways Rumsfeld's antithesis. He had been shaped by the pragmatic foreign policy of the president's father, and had been critical in private about the administration's handling of Iraq.[98] Nearly two years before, he had turned down an offer from Bush to be the first director of national intelligence—Negroponte got the job—in part because Gates was reluctant to leave Texas A&M and return to Washington's cauldron. In 1987, Ronald Reagan had nominated Gates, then a top CIA official, to be the agency's director, but Gates withdrew in the face of senators' concerns that he had not been candid about his knowledge of the Iran-contra affair.[99] In 1991 he became CIA director under the first President Bush after former colleagues accused him during grueling confirmation hearings of skewing intelligence reporting on the Soviet Union to suit the Reagan White House.[100]

Rice spoke to Gates about taking the job, and although she did not say so directly in a later interview, she hinted that her conversations with him included discussions about the vice president's power and whether Gates would have a free hand in policy. "I think he wanted a little bit of a sense of, you know, how things were in the government," Rice said.[101] She was vague about when she actually spoke to Gates, saying it was "probably" days before he took the job, and that she was unsure what would come of their conversation. "In the final analysis I didn't know whether Gates would accept or the president would go through with it," Rice said.[102]

The Sunday before the election, Gates met secretly with the president at the ranch in Crawford, where both Bush and Gates apparently reached the comfort level they needed. Two days later, on November 7, the earthquake that the administration had feared finally occurred. American voters swept the Democrats back into power in the House and Senate in an overwhelming defeat for the administration. Bush called it a "thumping." Its first consequence was on November 8, when the president finally dismissed Rumsfeld. Only days before, Bush had said he would keep the defense secretary for the rest of the term, but now the president said the two had agreed "after a series of thoughtful conversations" that it was time for Rumsfeld to go.[103] The decision unleashed bitter complaints among Republicans who said the GOP might have won the election if Bush had been willing to announce the decision earlier.

For the president, the dismissal signaled his loss of confidence in his military team—not only Rumsfeld, but also Casey and Abizaid, who would both be replaced within months. Officials close to Bush said that he had finally realized he had to take more control of the war on which he had gambled his presidency, and that he could no longer simply cheer on his military commanders and assume they would do the right thing. "Suddenly he started asking questions, 'Why four brigades? Why five brigades? Why not eight brigades? Why not two brigades?' instead of 'Tell me what you need,' " recalled a former administration official. "He learned to ask, 'Why aren't we winning?' and not be satisfied when he was told by his generals, 'We are winning.' "[104]

For Rice, Rumsfeld's ouster removed one of her major headaches, although Cheney would remain a far more formidable adversary. But she now had a crucial new ally in Gates, and the assumption in Washington was that she was elated about Rumsfeld's departure. Rice, the careful victor, kept her true feelings to herself. She had always had a workable social relationship with the defense secretary. The two had lunch together on occasion, and Rumsfeld went to Rice's annual Christmas party to sing carols. Even Rice's closest staff members had never heard her bad-mouth him. "I didn't go around talking about Don Rumsfeld to anybody," Rice later said. "Look, Don was my colleague. And I know people find it hard to believe, but actually I like the man."[105]

In early December, less than a month after the election, Rice and the administration got another blast, this time from a powerful bipartisan ten-member panel, the Iraq Study Group. The panel had been created by Congress in March to assess the situation in Iraq and make recommendations for the future. In late 2005, when Rice had started to seriously worry about Rumsfeld's strategy in Iraq, she met with the people pushing for the creation of the panel, among them Representative Frank Wolf, a Virginia Republican worried about the administration's strategy in Iraq, and David Abshire, a veteran of past Republican administrations. Then she asked the president to give the group his blessing, and the president did.[106] "I encouraged him," Rice later said. "I thought it was a good idea. He was actually receptive."[107]

But Bush got more than he bargained for. After a tsunami of advance publicity, the commission of five Republicans and five Democrats announced at a packed news conference in Washington on December 6 that "the situation in Iraq is grave and deteriorating," and urged a complete overhaul of the president's strategy. The panel, led by James Baker and Lee Hamilton, a former Republican congressman and the director of the Woodrow Wilson International Center, called for the pullback of all American combat brigades over the next fifteen months and "a new diplomatic offensive" with Iraq's neighbors, specifically direct talks with Iran and Syria, to help build stability in the region. A day later, Bush pushed back so hard against the main recommendations that people close to Baker said the president was having a tantrum over being upstaged by the former secretary of state and his father's friend. But Rice, who had her own competitive relationship with Baker, had different views. "I thought it was bizarre and extreme to assume the president would take an outside study group and just kind of say, 'We're going to do all those things now,' " she said. "No, it had to fit into the context of the policies he wanted to pursue, that he thought were appropriate, that fit into certain regional policies."[108] As the president settled down and the months wore on, the White House would in fact follow many of the group's recommendations.

Gates was sworn in as defense secretary on December 18, and in his first days in office made the argument to the president that he should shut down Guantánamo as soon as possible and move the trials of terrorism suspects to the United States.[109] Rice joined Gates in recommending that Bush immediately close the prison—after all, the president had repeatedly said that he wanted to and just couldn't see a way to do it soon. But Attorney General Gonzales and Cheney's office strongly objected to moving the detainees to the United States, and Bush rejected Gates's and Rice's arguments, at least for the immediate future. The prison, housing some 385 suspects, stayed open.

As the year drew to a close, Bush moved toward reversing course in Iraq and authorizing a "surge" of forces to combat the insurgency. Rice gave strong public support to the idea, but in private she had only modest hopes that it would solve the administration's problems in Iraq. "She thinks it's worth a try," said one of her closest associates at the end of 2006. "Which is different than, 'It will work.' "[110] By then, Rice had decided to turn over the handling of Iraq to the man who would be her new number two after the first of the year, John Negroponte, who was moving into a spot left vacant after Robert Zoellick had resigned months earlier. Rice's associate described her as worn down and discouraged by the war. "I don't think that she has a strong view of the policy anymore," he said. "I think if we put a polygraph on her, she would say 'I can do very little as secretary of state to affect the outcome in Iraq.' "[111]

Instead, Rice turned her attention to another intractable problem, the Middle East. With only two years left in office, she had begun to think not only of Bush's legacy but her own. It was perhaps a sign of the hopelessness of Iraq that she now saw some hope in solving the conflict between the Israelis and Palestinians. Over Christmas vacation, she took home a stack of reports written by the State Department historian on previous American efforts to get a peace agreement in the Middle East, mostly to study the mistakes of the past. At the least, she had to make an effort after the shambles of Lebanon the previous summer, and try to pick up the pieces.

CONCLUSION

Rice started 2007 in a race with time. She had only two years left as secretary of state and she was desperate to make headway in the Middle East. Rice's goal was no less than an agreement between the Israelis and Palestinians on the creation of a Palestinian state, a breakthrough that would be treacherously difficult if not entirely out of reach. But Rice knew that she had to try to deliver some kind of result before the end of the term, even if it was only an attempt that failed. "She knows very well that if she doesn't do anything, she will be Iraq," a European diplomat who was a friend of hers observed.[1]

In January, Rice embarked on her new Middle East mission with a trip to Israel, the West Bank, Egypt, Jordan, Kuwait, Saudi Arabia, London, and Berlin. With Tzipi Livni, the Israeli foreign minister, she had decided to leave behind the interim arguments and recast the scope of her Middle East negotiations to focus on the big "final status" issues: the eventual boundaries of a Palestinian state, the future of Jerusalem, and the right of Palestinian refugees to return to the lands they lost at Israel's founding in 1948. On a second, discouraging trip to the Middle East in February, Rice noted that the parties had not talked about these issues in the previous six years, but that it now made sense to begin. "I'm committed to this," Rice told reporters in Jerusalem. "It takes hard work, it takes patience, it takes perseverance, it takes getting up, you know, after a bad day and trying to make a better day. And that's what I'm going to do."[2]

The lingering problem, of course, was what to do about Hamas, the victor in the parliamentary elections of 2006. A year and a half later, Hamas's rivalry with the Fatah party of Mahmoud Abbas had descended into a bloody civil war. Hamas easily took over the Gaza Strip in June, leaving Abbas, the beleaguered Palestinian president, in charge only of the West Bank. The new reality was captured when a masked Hamas gunman with an AK-47 sat at Abbas's abandoned desk in Gaza, picked up the phone, and announced: "Hello, Condoleezza Rice? You have me to deal with now."[3]

But she didn't. When the dust settled, Rice decided that there was no choice but to provide tens of millions of dollars in previously frozen aid directly to Abbas in a "West Bank first" strategy that left Hamas to fend for itself in Gaza. By August, Rice had made four trips to the Middle East and Bush had announced plans for her to lead a Middle East peace conference, excluding Hamas, in the fall—just the sort of parley that the president had rejected when Colin Powell had suggested the same idea five years before. But Bush was in a faster race with time than Rice, and with her continued prodding he was leaving the dwindling number of hawks in the administration behind. In June the president and Rice got help from Tony Blair, the British prime minister, who stepped down after ten years in office and accepted an appointment as a new Middle East envoy representing the "quartet" of world powers—the United States, the European Union, the United Nations, and Russia. Blair was expected to be a voice for compromise between Israel and the Palestinians on political and security issues and an ally of Rice in pushing the same agenda.

Midway through 2007, Rice's big success of the year was not in the Middle East but in North Korea. In February, negotiators for the United States and four other nations had reached a major deal in which North Korea agreed to close its main nuclear reactor in exchange for $400 million in fuel oil and aid. The Korean talks had been led by Christopher Hill, the assistant secretary of state for East Asia, but Rice had been unusually involved in his deliberations. In January, as the deal was coming together, she met with Hill in Berlin, where he presented her with the early elements of an agreement hammered out in lengthy sessions with his North Korean counterparts.[4] Rice liked what she saw and called Hadley in Washington and then the president. She pushed Bush as she had in the past to negotiate with a regime that he had declared he despised.[5]

"I said, 'This is a good deal,' " Rice recalled. "And, you know, 'We'll see if it holds.' "[6] Rice could look back on six tortured years of history with North Korea: Bush's rejection of talks in 2001, his acquiescence to them in 2003, the North Koreans' promise to end their nuclear program in 2005 and then their announcement of a successful nuclear test, to worldwide condemnation, in 2006. Through it all the six-party negotiations aimed at getting North Korea to give up its nuclear weapons had gone nowhere. Now Rice told the president that they needed to get Hill's deal as quickly as possible to the six-party table before the North Koreans changed their minds.[7] Bush agreed, and when the negotiations began in Beijing the following month, Rice was on the phone to Hill every day. "On the last day, Secretary Rice was up at 4:15 in the morning, calling me at 5:15 in the afternoon, to see how things were doing," Hill later told the House Foreign Affairs Committee.[8]

The deal may have been a breakthrough with North Korea, but it marked a breakdown in relations with the hawks who had once dominated the administration. The most outspoken of them was John Bolton, the former U.S. ambassador to the United Nations and the former chief of the State Department's arms control division, who went public on CNN and called the agreement "a very bad deal."[9] Even defenders of the agreement recognized its flaws—chiefly that it left for future negotiations the actual removal of North Korea's nuclear weapons and the fuel manufactured to produce them.[10]

Rice quickly pivoted from North Korea to try to put more pressure on Iran, which remained an intractable problem. The effort by the United States, Europe, Russia, and China to try to persuade the government in Tehran to abandon its nuclear ambitions showed no sign of success well into the second half of 2007. Every time the Bush administration tried to get the U.N. Security Council to issue another resolution and another set of economic sanctions, Russia and China balked.

The diplomatic stalemate led to a searching debate within the administration about what to do, as the hawks in Cheney's office threatened the possibility of future air strikes. The uproar led Mohamed ElBaradei, the director general of the International Atomic Energy Agency, to warn against what he called the "new crazies" pushing for the use of force.[11] Rice responded that she had "no idea" whom ElBaradei was referring to and insisted that American patience with diplomacy had not at all run out. "The president of the United States has made it clear that we are on a course that is a diplomatic course," she told reporters on June 1 on a trip to Madrid. "That policy is supported by all members of the cabinet, and by the vice president of the United States."[12] But it was obvious that although Rice had won the immediate battle for diplomacy first, the argument would continue through the life of the Bush presidency.

Rice had already come down on the side of talking to Iran as well as Syria on the future of Iraq—one of the Iraq Study Group's central recommendations. She had initially dismissed the idea out of hand. "That's not diplomacy, that's extortion," she told the Senate Foreign Relations Committee on January 11.[13] But a little more than two weeks later, Rice did an about-face, in large part out of frustration that nothing else was working, and said that the United States would in fact take part in talks with Iran and Syria. In May, at a regional conference on Iraq in Sharm el-Sheikh in Egypt, she met with the Syrian foreign minister, Walid al-Moallem, in the first significant contact between the United States and Damascus in two years. On the fringes of the Sharm conference, Ryan Crocker, the U.S. ambassador to Iraq, joined with David Satterfield, Rice's top adviser on Iraq, for an impromptu three-minute discussion with an Iranian deputy foreign minister.[14] But generally the talks came to nothing.

Rice's relationship with Putin, the Russian leader who had so buttressed her during those terrifying moments in the White House bunker on September 11, soured in 2007. The disagreement was over the very issue that Rice had discussed with Putin in Moscow during her first summer as national security adviser—the administration's plans to abandon the Antiballistic Missile Treaty. Although Putin had reacted relatively calmly when Bush made the announcement that the United States was pulling out of the treaty, Putin was threatened when the U.S. proceeded with plans to install a missile defense system in Europe. In April, Putin moved to suspend Russia's compliance with a treaty that limited conventional weapons in Europe and then appeared to compare the United States to the Third Reich during a speech on May 9 in Red Square.

On a visit to Moscow six days later, Rice, the Russia expert and protégé of Josef Korbel, had to argue that there was no "new Cold War," but she said she had raised the issue of tone in a meeting with Putin. "I have said while I am here that the rhetoric is not helpful," she told reporters.[15] To try to ease tensions, in July Bush invited Putin to the Bush family compound in Kennebunkport, Maine, where the Russian president went on a speedboat ride in the Atlantic and joined in a dinner of lobster and swordfish with Bush father and son, their wives, and, as always, Rice.[16]

Iraq continued to be Rice's biggest problem throughout 2007. In January the president announced a "surge" in American troop strength aimed at tamping down the violence and giving the Iraqi government breathing space to reconcile. But Republicans at home, who were facing reelection in 2008, began deserting the president as support for the war crumbled. Bush managed to hold off a stampede at least until September, when General David Petraeus, the new American commander in Iraq, went to Washington and recommended a withdrawal of 30,000 troops by the summer of 2008, which would put American troop strength at 130,000, the number before the surge. The administration in the meantime lost patience with yet another Iraqi prime minister, Nuri al-Maliki, who had failed like his predecessors to reach out to Sunni leaders and bring about a political reconciliation. In late August, Bush expressed "a certain level of frustration" with the Iraqi political process,[17] and Ryan Crocker went even further. The performance of Iraq's leaders was "extremely disappointing," he said, and the United States was not giving the Iraqis a "blank check."[18]

The political paralysis in Baghdad was making Rice more and more skeptical about the ability of the military to establish security on its own. More than four years into a war that the hawks had promised would be over in weeks, Rice now found herself in the same position as her old nemesis Rumsfeld. By May, even before Petraeus's recommendation, she was reported to be pushing on the inside for significant troop withdrawals in 2008.[19]

For Rice, Iraq would always be a bleeding wound. In 2007 it led once again to an exchange with Barbara Boxer, the Democratic senator from California. Reprising her sharp words during Rice's confirmation hearings, Boxer suggested that because Rice had no family in harm's way, she had paid no price in the war. "Who pays the price?" Boxer said. "I'm not going to pay a personal price. My kids are too old and my grandchild is too young. You're not going to pay a particular price, as I understand it, with an immediate family. So who pays the price? The American military and their families." [20]

Boxer was criticized for personalizing the debate, and the next day Rice responded that the comments were inappropriate. "I thought it was okay to be single," Rice told *The New York Times.* "I thought it was okay to not have children, and I thought you could still make good decisions on behalf of the country if you were single and didn't have children."[21] Rice's measured words hid the agitation she had felt at the rough hearing, where one reporter caught her pounding her clasped hands to her thigh, out of the senators' view.[22]

Rice was never especially self-reflective, but she was always optimistic, and in June 2007, when she was asked to assess how she had performed as national security adviser, she gave an odd answer. "I don't know," she said quietly. "I think I did okay."[23] The statement seemed utterly honest and devoid of spin, and did a lot to explain her frantic drive well into 2007 to try to get things right. Asked about mistakes she had made, she said, "I'm sure there's lots," but then said that she would worry about them when she was out of office. Rice expected to write her own book about her years in the administration, although she said she had kept no diary or taped recollections. "Do you really think I want to go home and write about what I did all day?" she asked.[24]

By mid-2007, with Bush's backing, Rice had redeemed her pledge from her confirmation hearing that "the time for diplomacy is now." In large part that was because she had to clean up in the second term the bitterness left from the wars of the first. But Rice did have some achievements she could call her own. She had reestablished a cooperative relationship with Europe in isolating Iran, made major progress in defusing the crisis over North Korea's nuclear program, and helped to rekindle the dialogue between the Israelis and Palestinians. Even though Iran remained a threat, it seemed possible that the foundation of economic and diplomatic pressure that Rice helped to build would be expanded by her successor, Republican or Democrat. Of course, her progress in stabilizing Iraq was limited at best.

With eighteen months left in office, it was still too early to come to definite conclusions about Rice's legacy. If she reached a deal on the Middle East and if North Korea moved further toward dismantling its nuclear weapons, Rice would be entitled to be judged a great success. If not, she would be seen as an interesting but minor secretary of state who did too little too late. Whatever the outcome, history would record that after 9/11 Rice presided over one of the most consequential periods of American foreign policy. The era was as significant as the fall of Vietnam and the opening of China under Henry Kissinger and the end of the Cold War under James Baker—two other Republican secretaries of state who had unchallenged latitude in making policy.

Rice did not have that kind of power in the first term, but she did in the second. The question was whether she would be able to harness that authority effectively in her remaining months in office. She may not have been an intellectual secretary of state like Kissinger or a master strategist like Baker, but she probably had more drive than either of them. The disciplined blaze of her life—from Birmingham to Denver to Stanford to Washington—suggested that she would throw everything she had into trying to triumph in the twilight of the Bush presidency. It was obvious from Rice's many metamorphoses that her real ideology was not idealism or realism or defending the citadels of freedom, although she displayed elements of all of them. Her real ideology was succeeding.

Given her determination, speculation remained about her political ambitions, and both Bushes participated in the game. In a revealing comment in late 2006, Laura Bush told *People* magazine that Rice would be a good candidate for president, but that she wasn't interested. "Probably because she is single, her parents are no longer living, she's an only child," Laura Bush said. "You need a very supportive family and supportive friends to have this job."[25] The president, as was his practice, addressed the issue by needling Rice. In a celebration of African-American History Month in the White House East Room in February 2007, Bush told the audience, including Rice, that he had welcomed Doris Kearns Goodwin, the author of *Team of Rivals*, about Lincoln's cabinet, the night before. "Abraham Lincoln surrounded himself with fine cabinet officers, all of whom wanted one thing—his job," Bush said. "Not so fast, Madame Secretary."[26]

Rice herself said it was only a matter of time before an African-American or a woman became president. She expressed admiration for Senator Barack Obama of Illinois, a Democratic candidate for president, noting that she had gotten to know him in his two years of service on the Senate Foreign Relations Committee. His candidacy, she said, showed that "we've come a long way in overcoming stereotypes, role stereotypes, about African Americans." She added: "I will say race is still a factor. When a person walks into a room, I still think people still see race. But it's less and less of a barrier to believing that that person can be your doctor or your lawyer or a professor in your university or the CEO of a company. And it will not be long, I think, before it's no longer a barrier to being president of the United States."[27]

In mid-2007, some friends said that Rice was still interested in a future gubernatorial race in California or that she would be tempted by an offer of the vice presidential spot on the GOP ticket. But Rice continued to say that she would return to Stanford, always her default position. She knew she would get a mixed reception there. The university administration would welcome her, but there likely would be protests from students and anger from many of the faculty about her years in the Bush White House and her tenure as provost. If Rice did go back to Stanford, few of her friends expected her to stay there for long.

Whatever Rice did, it would not be marking time. She was too ambitious for that, too caught up in the public life of the nation. She had revealed some of her thinking when she went to California in May with Alexander Downer, the Australian foreign minister, and spoke to a group of promising young black students at the Center for a New Generation, the program she had helped start when she was at Stanford. When an eighth grader, Kimmera Wilson, asked Rice what obstacles she had faced as an African-American woman in politics, Rice responded that she had been in the business so long that it didn't seem like there were many at all. But starting out, she said, there were two, one within others and one within herself.

"The obstacle within others is that they will tend to look at you and underestimate you just because of the color of your skin," Rice said.[28] The obstacle within herself, she said, was about setting limitations. Then she told the story yet again of how she had trained to be a concert pianist but had given it up to study the Soviet Union. "Now, my parents or teachers or others might have said, 'What in the world is a young black girl from Birmingham, Alabama, doing studying Russian?' " Rice recalled, not mentioning that that was close to how her parents did react. "But they didn't. They said, 'Oh, that's great. You want to study Russia.' "[29]

What that meant, Rice told the girl, was "not accepting a limitation on what I wanted to do and what I wanted to be. So don't ever let anybody set expectations for you of what you want to be and what you want to do. Those should be completely up to you, in line with your talents and how hard you are prepared to work. You can do anything that you want."[30]

Four months later, in a speech in September 2007 at a Christian elementary school in a minority neighborhood in Washington, Rice picked up the theme and spoke at length about her own life and how America rewards hard work with opportunity—the source, she said, of the nation's cohesion and optimism. "It is what has sustained Americans, whether the pioneers who managed to come over the Continental Divide in ways that I do not understand, or my ancestors who managed to go from three-fifths of a man in the Constitution to equal citizenship, to a point at which one of their descendants stands before you as the sixty-sixth secretary of state of the United States," Rice said. "It's that faith, that optimism, that belief, that is at the core of who we are."[31]

Rice's words, straight out of Titusville, were the testimony of a woman who understood how much her life told a story of America, and who had no intention of stepping off the world's stage.

ACKNOWLEDGMENTS

It is a pleasure to thank the many people who helped with this book. At Random House, my editor Kate Medina was an enthusiastic supporter from the very beginning and brought her elegant, intelligent eye to the manuscript. Robin Rolewicz was always there with the smart answer when I needed her, and Abigail Plesser helped out one hot week in August. I would also like to thank Gina Centrello, Tom Perry, Carol Poticny, and Steve Messina as well as my agent and friend, Amanda Urban, and my first editor at Random House, now at PublicAffairs, Peter Osnos.

I am of course indebted to Condoleezza Rice for her cooperation and the time she took in 2006 and 2007 for our interviews, and for her belief that talking to reporters is a good thing. I am indebted as well to her family, particularly Connie Ray in Birmingham and Clara Rice in Palo Alto, and Lativia Alston in Atlanta. Many thanks, also, to Rice's staff at the State Department, especially Brian Besanceney, Sean McCormack, Brian Gunderson, Jim Wilkinson, Ruth Elliott, Liz Lineberry, and Pam Stevens. At the White House, I am grateful for help from Dana Perino, Tony Snow, Dan Bartlett, Ed Gillespie, Scott McClellan, Gordon Johndroe, and Kate Starr.

More than 150 people opened their homes, offices, and memories to me as I reported this book across the country. They are far too numerous to list here, but in particular I would like to thank Odessa Woolfolk of the Birmingham Civil Rights Institute and Bob Corley at the University of Alabama at Birmingham; Mandy McCalla, Larry Horton, Chip Blacker, David Kennedy, Gerhard Casper, Jessica Rose, and Lisa and Andrew Cope at Stanford and in Palo Alto; and Haven Moses, Alan Gilbert, and my sister, Trine Bumiller, in Denver.

The New York Times gave me extended time away from the office to write this book, and I am grateful to my editors, Bill Keller, Jim Abramson, Phil Taubman, and, most recently, Dean Baquet. I am enormously thankful for my colleagues in the *Times*'s Washington bureau, who have made it such a congenial place to work, and whose reporting and expertise grace many of these pages. I would especially like to thank my old partners on the White House beat, David Sanger and Richard Stevenson. Michael Gordon provided invaluable guidance on the American military, Helene Cooper was helpful with her knowledge about Rice and the State Department, and Brent Staples was generous with his thoughts about race in America. Thanks also to Ron Skarzenski and Jan Harland.

I was fortunate to have such a fertile and stimulating home away from home at the Woodrow Wilson International Center, where I wrote much of this book. There I would like to thank Lee Hamilton, Michael Van Dusen, Philippa Strum, James Goldgeier, Lucy Jilka, Melaney Monreal, and my wise adviser, Robert Litwak. Patricia O'Toole, a fellow Wilson public policy scholar, was a guide in writing biography, and Janet Spikes ran one of the best libraries and research teams I have ever encountered.

I was equally fortunate to find a summer haven at the German Marshall Fund of the United States, where I completed this book in pleasant and convivial surroundings. There I am grateful to Craig Kennedy, Karen Donfried, John Glenn, Will Bohlen, board members David Ignatius and Robin West, and, not least, Zahid Hussein and Marc Hurtzel.

My research assistant at the Wilson center, Ariel Alexovich, transcribed many hours of interviews, chased after obscure information, pored over all of the Iraq books, and provided insight when she accompanied me on interviews with Condoleezza Rice. She allowed me to finish this book months earlier than I would have, and was unfailingly cheerful. Oliver Mains, my research assistant at the German Marshall Fund, was a great help at the end of the process.

The Bush administration and the Iraq War have been well documented by many authors who came before me, and their work was a vital resource for mine. I am indebted to Karen DeYoung of *The Washington Post*, whose biography of Colin Powell, *Soldier*, provided critical information about the first term and was a model to aspire to. Bob Woodward and his three books about the Bush White House, *Bush at War*, *Plan of Attack*, and *State of Denial*, were invaluable. In telling the story of Birmingham, I am indebted to Diane McWhorter and her book *Carry Me Home* as well as Taylor Branch's three-volume history of Martin Luther King and the American civil rights movement, particularly *Parting the Waters* and *Pillar of Fire*. I also greatly benefited from two other recent books about Rice, Marcus Mabry's *Twice as Good: Condoleezza Rice and Her Path to Power* and Glenn Kessler's *The Confidante: Condoleezza Rice and the Creation of the Bush Legacy*. Dale Russakoff, whose *Washington Post Magazine* article "Lessons of Might and Right" remains one of the best records of Rice's life in Birmingham, helped me navigate her hometown. Nicholas Lemann, whose *New Yorker* article about Rice, "Without a Doubt," remains one of the best records of her life ever, helped me with Stanford and the first Bush administration.

The idea for this book was born over an extended family dinner in Washington on the day after Thanksgiving in 2005, when Walter Isaacson, my onetime New York neighbor and longtime friend, informed me that it was time to write another book. I told him he was right, but I needed a subject. "Condoleezza Rice," he instantly said. A light flashed on, and I realized that I should have thought of it myself. I had always been fascinated by Rice, and I knew that the story of her life would take me through some of the most dramatic history of the last half century in the United States, including the tumultuous events I had covered for the *Times* from my first day on the White House beat—September 10, 2001. Walter has always been an incomparable source of story ideas, and I thank him and his wife, Cathy, one of my old partners in Troop 1511, as well as their daughter, Betsy, for their many years of camaraderie and support.

Many thanks as well to the friends who cheered along the way, especially Dan Yergin and Angela Stent, and Caroline Miller, who taught me how to travel cheaply through priceline.com. Aaron David Miller generously allowed me to read parts of his forthcoming book, *The Much Too Promised Land*, and gave me a great deal of help on the Middle East. Robert Draper provided some clues and good advice at the end. Geraldine Baum, as she has for more than three decades, kept me going, this time in phone calls from Paris that were always a great respite from the paragraph at hand.

I would also like to thank my family—my mother and stepfather, Gunhild and John Rose; my stepmother, Ruth Ann Bumiller; my mother-in-law, Etta Weisman; my two other sisters, Karen Johnson and Elken Maxwell; and my three stepbrothers, Stephen, Michael, and David Rose. Adela Gumahin, who is virtually a member of the family, deserves thanks as well. This is the first book I have written since the death of my father, Theodore Bumiller, but I feel he was here in spirit.

Last, I would like to thank my children, Madeleine and Teddy, for their good humor and cheer. I promise that never again will I spend an entire vacation locked up in a cottage with my laptop. Most of all, I want to thank my loving and patient husband, Steve, who stood aside, read and reread the entire manuscript, and made me laugh. This one is for him.

Elisabeth Bumiller

BIBLIOGRAPHY

Books

Albright, Madeleine, with Bill Woodward. *Madame Secretary.* New York: Miramax, 2003.

Baker, James A., III, with Thomas M. DeFrank. *The Politics of Diplomacy: Revolution, War and Peace, 1989–1992.* New York: G. P. Putnam's Sons, 1995.

Beschloss, Michael R., and Strobe Talbott. *At the Highest Levels: The Inside Story of the End of the Cold War.* Boston: Little, Brown, 1993.

Blackman, Ann. *Seasons of Her Life: A Biography of Madeleine Korbel Albright.* New York: Lisa Drew/Scribner, 1998.

Branch, Taylor. *Parting the Waters: America in the King Years 1954–63.* New York: Simon & Schuster, 1988.

———. *Pillar of Fire: America in the King Years 1963–65.* New York: Simon & Schuster, 1998.

Bremer, L. Paul. *My Year in Iraq: The Struggle to Build a Future of Hope.* New York: Simon & Schuster, 2006.

Bush, George, and Brent Scowcroft. *A World Transformed.* New York: Alfred A. Knopf, 1998.

Caldwell, H. M. *History of the Elyton Land Company and Birmingham, Alabama.* Birmingham: Self-published, 1892.

Chandrasekaran, Rajiv. *Imperial Life in the Emerald City: Inside Iraq's Green Zone.* New York: Alfred A. Knopf, 2006.

Clarke, Richard A. *Against All Enemies: Inside America's War on Terror.* New York: Free Press, 2004.

Connerly, Charles E. *The Most Segregated City in America.* Charlottesville: University of Virginia Press, 2005.

Davis, Angela. *Angela Davis: An Autobiography.* New York: Random House, 1974.

Department of Commerce. *Statistical Abstract of the United States, 1978.* Washington, D.C.: U.S. Government Printing Office, 1978.

DeYoung, Karen. *Soldier: The Life of Colin Powell.* New York: Alfred A. Knopf, 2006.

Dobbs, Michael. *Madeleine Albright: A Twentieth-Century Odyssey.* New York: Owl/Henry Holt, 1998.

Draper, Robert. *Dead Certain: The Presidency of George W. Bush.* New York: Free Press, 2007.

Eskew, Glenn T. *But for Birmingham: The Local and National Movements in the Civil Rights Struggle.* Chapel Hill: University of North Carolina Press, 1997.

Frum, David. *The Right Man: The Surprise Presidency of George W. Bush.* New York: Random House, 2003.

Garrow, David J. *Bearing the Cross: Martin Luther King Jr. and the Southern Christian Leadership Conference.* New York: William Morrow, 1986.

Gordon, Michael E., and Bernard E. Trainor. *Cobra II: The Inside Story of the Invasion and Occupation of Iraq.* New York: Pantheon, 2006.

Hamilton, Lee H., and Thomas H. Kean. *Without Precedent: The Inside Story of the 9/11 Commission.* New York: Alfred A. Knopf, 2006.

Leonard, Stephen J., and Thomas J. Noel. *Denver: From Mining Town to Metropolis.* Boulder: University Press of Colorado, 1990.

Mabry, Marcus. *Twice as Good: Condoleezza Rice and Her Path to Power.* New York: Modern Times, 2007.

Manis, Andrew M. *A Fire You Can't Put Out: The Civil Rights Life of Birmingham's Reverend Fred Shuttlesworth.* Tuscaloosa: University of Alabama Press, 1999.

Mann, James. *Rise of the Vulcans: The History of Bush's War Cabinet.* New York: Penguin, 2004.

McWhorter, Diane. *Carry Me Home: The Climactic Battle of the Civil Rights Revolution.* New York: Simon & Schuster, 2001.

Miller, Aaron David. *The Much Too Promised Land: America's Elusive Search for Arab-Israeli Peace.* New York: Bantam, 2008.

The 9/11 Commission Report: Final Report of the National Commission on Terrorist Attacks upon the United States. New York: W. W. Norton & Company, 2004.

Oberdorfer, Don. *The Turn: From the Cold War to a New Era: The United States and the Soviet Union, 1983–1990.* New York: Poseidon, 1991.

Packer, George. *The Assassins' Gate: America in Iraq.* New York: Farrar, Straus and Giroux, 2006.

Raines, Howell. *My Soul Is Rested: Movement Days in the Deep South Remembered.* New York: Penguin, 1983.

Rice, Condoleezza. *The Soviet Union and the Czechoslovak Army, 1948–1983: Uncertain Allegiance.* Princeton, N.J.: Princeton University Press, 1984.

Rice, Condoleezza, and Philip D. Zelikow. *Germany Unified and Europe Transformed: A Study in Statecraft.* Cambridge, Mass.: Harvard University Press, 1997.

Rothkopf, David. *Running the World: The Inside Story of the National Security Council and the Architects of American Power.* New York: PublicAffairs, 2006.

Suskind, Ron. *The Price of Loyalty: George W. Bush, the White House, and the Education of Paul O'Neill.* New York: Simon & Schuster Paperbacks, 2004.

Tenet, George, with Bill Harlow. *At the Center of the Storm: My Years at the CIA.* New York: HarperCollins, 2007.

Weill, Susan. "The Story Behind These Stories." In *Historic Titusville: People and Places.* Birmingham: University of Alabama at Birmingham, 2001.

Wiener, Jonathan M. *Social Origins of the New South: Alabama, 1860–1885.* Baton Rouge: Louisiana State University Press, 1978.

Woodward, Bob. *Bush at War.* New York: Simon & Schuster, 2002.

———. *Plan of Attack.* New York: Simon & Schuster, 2004.

———. *State of Denial: Bush at War, Part III.* New York: Simon & Schuster, 2006.

Congressional Hearings

Senate Select Committee on Intelligence. "Intelligence Reform Hearing." 108th Congress, 2nd sess., Aug. 18, 2004.

Senate Foreign Relations Committee. "Opening Remarks by Condoleezza Rice." 109th Congress, 1st sess., Jan. 18, 2005. State Department transcript, www.state.gov/secretary/rm/2005/40991.htm.

Independent Reports

"Bin Laden Determined to Strike in US," President's Daily Brief, Aug. 6, 2001. National Security Archive, www/gwu.edu/~nsarchiv/NSAEBB/NSAEBB116/pdb8-6-2001.pdf.

Blix, Hans. "Briefing to the United Nations Security Council," Feb. 14, 2003. www.un.org/Depts/unmovic/blix14Febasdel.htm.

———. "An Update on Inspection to the National Security Council," Jan. 27, 2003. www.un.org/Depts/unmovic/Bx27.htm.

International Committee of the Red Cross. "Report on the Treatment by the Coalition Forces of Prisoners of War and Other Protected Persons by the Geneva Conventions in Iraq During Arrest, Internment and Interrogation," Feb. 2004. www.globalsecurity.org/military/library/report/2004/icrc_report_iraq_feb2004.htm.

"The National Security Strategy of the United States of America," Sept. 2002. www.whitehouse.gov/nsc/nss.pdf.

Taguba, Major General Antonio M. "Investigation of the 800th Military Police Brigade" ("Taguba Report"), 2004. www.globalsecurity.org/intell/library/reports/2004/800-mp-bde.htm.

Public Remarks

Bush, George W. "President Bush Addresses the Nation," March 19, 2003, Washington, D.C. White House transcript, www.whitehouse.gov/news/releases/2003/03/20030319-17.html.

———. "President Bush Speaks to Reporters at Fort Hood, Texas," April 11, 2004, Fort Hood, Texas. White House transcript, www.whitehouse.gov/news/releases/2004/04/20040411.html.

———. "Statement by the President in His Address to the Nation," Sept. 11, 2001, Washington, D.C. White House transcript, www.whitehouse.gov/news/releases/2001/09/20010911-16.html.

———. "Transcript: Full Text of Bush's Private Exchange at G-8 Summit," July 7, 2006, St. Petersburg. *Washington Post* transcript, www.washingtonpost.com/wp-dyn/content/article/2006/07/17/AR2006071700402_pf.html.

Bush, George W., and Vicente Fox. "Remarks by President George W. Bush and President Vicente Fox of Mexico in Joint Press Conference," Feb. 16, 2001, San Cristóbal, Mexico. White House transcript, www.whitehouse.gov/news/releases/2001/02/20010216-3.html.

Bush, George W., and Kim Dae Jung. "Remarks by President Bush and President Kim Dae Jung of South Korea," March 7, 2001, Washington, D.C. White House transcript, www.whitehouse.gov/news/releases/2001/03/20010307-6.html.

Card, Andrew H., Jr. "Comments to Reporters," September 14, 2001, on board Air Force One. White House transcript.

Cheney, Dick. "Vice President Honors Veterans of Korean War," Aug. 29,

2002, San Antonio, Texas. White House transcript, www.whitehouse.gov/news/releases/2002/08/20020829-5.html.

Clarke, Richard A. "Testimony to the National Commission of Terrorist Attacks upon the United States," March 24, 2004, Washington, D.C. National Archives and Records Administration, www.9-11commission.gov/archive/hearing8/9-11Commission_Hearing_2004-03-24.pdf.

Corley, Robert G. "Class Lecture in a History of Birmingham Course," July 26, 2006, University of Alabama at Birmingham. Author present.

de Villepin, Dominique. "Remarks to the United Nations Security Council," March 9, 2003.

Johnson, Lyndon B. "Radio and Television Remarks upon Signing the Civil Rights Bill," July 2, 1964, Washington, D.C. lbjlib.utexas.edu/johnson/archives.hom/speeches.hom/640702.asp.

Kay, David. "Testimony to the National Commission on Terrorist Attacks upon the United States," Aug. 18, 2004, Washington, D.C. National Archives and Records Administration.

King, Martin Luther, Jr., "Eulogy for the Martyred Children," Sept. 18, 1963, Birmingham, Ala. Martin Luther King, Jr. Papers Project at Stanford University, www.stanford.edu/group/King/speeches/pub/Eulogy_for_the_martyred_children.html.

———. "I Have a Dream," Aug. 28, 1963, Washington, D.C., usinfo.state.gov/usa/infousa/facts/democrac/38.htm.

Noon, Rev. Thomas R. "Our 50th," unpublished history of Titusville and St. Paul Lutheran Church, Birmingham, Ala.

Powell, Colin. "Remarks by Secretary of State Colin Powell to the Pool," March 7, 2001, Washington, D.C. White House transcript, www.whitehouse.gov/news/releases/2001/03/20010307-3.html.

Rice, Condoleezza. "Briefing on Travel to Europe and the Middle East," July 21, 2006, Washington, D.C. State Department transcript, www.state.gov/secretary/rm/2006/69331.htm.

———. "Briefing to Reporters En Route to Rio de Janeiro," March 12, 2006, State Department transcript, www.state.gov/secretary/rm/2006/63024.htm.

———. "Commencement Address at Boston College," May 22, 2006, Boston. State Department transcript.

———. "National Security Advisor Holds Press Briefing," May 16, 2002, Washington, D.C. White House transcript. www.whitehouse.gov/news/releases/2002/05/20020516-13.html.

———. "Press Conference on Iran," May 31, 2006, Washington, D.C. State Department transcript, www.state.gov/secretary/rm/2006/67103.htm.

———. "Remarks at the National Press Club Newsmaker Luncheon," July 13, 2001, Washington, D.C. White House transcript, www.whitehouse.gov/news/releases/2001/07/20010713.html.

———. "Remarks with Jack Straw at Blackburn House," April 1, 2006. State Department transcript, www.state.gov/secretary/rm/2006/63980.htm.

———. "Remarks with United Kingdom Foreign Secretary Jack Straw," Birmingham, Ala., Oct. 22, 2005. State Department transcript, www.state.gov/secretary/rm/2005/55427.html.

———. "Remarks with United Kingdom Foreign Secretary Jack Straw at the Blackburn Institute's Frank A. Nix Lecture," Tuscaloosa, Ala., Oct. 21, 2005. State Department transcript, www.state.gov/secretary/rm/2005/55423.htm.

———. "Roundtable with Traveling Press," April 2, 2006, Baghdad. State Department transcript, www.state.gov/secretary/rm/2006/63994.htm.

———. "Testimony to the National Commission on Terrorist Attacks upon the United States," April 8, 2004, Washington, D.C. National Archives and Records Administration, www.9-11commission.gov/archive/hearing9/9-11Commission_Hearing_2004-04-08.pdf.

Rice, Condoleezza, and Donald Rumsfeld. "Joint Roundtable with Reporters," April 26, 2006, Baghdad. State Department transcript, www.state.gov/secretary/rm/2006/65317.htm.

Rumsfeld, Donald H. "Department of Defense News Briefing," October 9, 2001, Washington, D.C. Department of Defense transcript. www.defenselink.mil/transcripts/transcript.aspx?transcriptid=2034.

———. "Department of Defense News Briefing," April 11, 2003, Washington, D.C. Department of Defense transcript. www.defenselink.mil/transcripts/transcript.aspx?transcriptid=2367.

———. "Interview with Scott Hennen, WDAY Radio, Fargo, N.D.," April 4, 2006, Washington, D.C. Department of Defense transcript, www.defenselink.mil/transcripts/transcript.aspx?transcriptid=1225.

———. "Secretary Rumsfeld Roundtable with NATO Journalists," October 7, 2003, Colorado Springs, Colo. Department of Defense transcript. www.defenselink.mil/transcripts/transcript.aspx?transcriptid=3011.

Tenet, George. "Testimony to the National Commission on Terrorist Attacks upon the United States," March 24, 2004, Washington, D.C. National Archives and Records Administration, www.9-11commission.gov/archive/hearing8/9-11Commission_Hearing_2004-03-24.pdf.

Print and Broadcast Media

Newspapers: *The Birmingham News*, *Birmingham Post-Herald*, *Los Angeles Times*, *The New York Times*, *San Francisco Chronicle*, *San Jose Mercury*

News, The Stanford Daily, USA Today, The Virginian-Pilot, The Washington Post.

Magazines: *Columbia Magazine, Essence, Foreign Affairs, George, National Review, New York, The New Yorker, The New York Times Magazine, Newsweek, O, The Oprah Magazine, People, Vogue, The Washington Post Magazine, Washingtonian.*

Journals: *The American Historical Review, The American Interest, American Political Science Review, Soviet Studies, Stanford Report, World Politics.*

Online media: ESPN.com, Gawker.com.

Television/radio programs: CBS (*60 Minutes*), CNN (*Late Edition with Wolf Blitzer*), Fox News Channel (*The O'Reilly Factor*), NBC (*Meet the Press*), NPR.

Etc.

Bush, George W. "Text of a Letter from the President to Senators Hagel, Helms, Craig and Roberts," March 13, 2001. www.whitehouse.gov/news/releases/2001/03/20010314.html.

Clarke, Richard A. "NSC Memorandum for Condoleezza Rice," January 25, 2001. National Security Archives, www.gwu.edu/~nsarchiv/NSAEBB/NSAEBB147/clarke%20memo.pdf.

———. "Strategy for Eliminating the Threat from the Jihadist Networks of al Qida: Status and Prospects," January 25, 2001. National Security Archives, www.gwu.edu/~nsarchiv/NSAEBB/NSAEBB147/clarke%20 attachment.pdf.

"Concerns Regarding Equal Employment Opportunity for Women Faculty at Stanford University." Complaint filed with the United States Department of Labor, November 1998.

Manning, David. "Private Memorandum to Tony Blair," March 14, 2002. www.downingstreetmemo.com/manningtext.html.

Rycroft, Matthew. "Minutes of Prime Minister's Meeting," July 23, 2002. www.downingstreetmemo.com/memoplain.html.

NOTES

Introduction

1. Condoleezza Rice, author interview. Rice provided eight one-hour interviews with the author in 2006 and 2007 in Washington, D.C., for the purposes of this book. Material from those interviews is subsequently cited as "Rice interview." Two other lengthy Rice interviews with the author for *The New York Times* in December 2003 are specified as such.
2. Ibid.
3. Ibid.
4. Andrew H. Card, Jr., comments to reporters on Air Force One, Sept. 14, 2001.
5. Rice interview.
6. Ibid.
7. Ibid.
8. *The 9/11 Commission Report: Final Report of the National Commission on Terrorist Attacks upon the United States* (New York: W. W. Norton, 2004), p. 39.
9. Franklin Miller, author interview, Washington, D.C., Oct. 23, 2006.
10. *The 9/11 Commission Report*, pp. 39–40.
11. William Bushong, historian, White House Historical Association, author interview by telephone, Aug. 24, 2007.
12. *The 9/11 Commission Report*, pp. 40, 37.
13. Rice interview.

14. Barton Gellman and Jo Becker, "A Different Understanding with the President," *Washington Post*, June 24, 2007, p. A1.
15. *The 9/11 Commission Report*, p. 40.
16. Ibid.
17. Ibid.
18. Rice interview. Rice, Bush, and Cheney gave similar accounts to the 9/11 Commission about this initial phone call in which they said the president conveyed to the vice president his authorization to shoot down commercial aircraft. But others in the bunker that day who were taking notes, including Lynne Cheney, the vice president's wife, and I. Lewis Libby, then the vice president's chief of staff, did not note such a call. The 9/11 Commission said that there was no documentary evidence for such a call, although it pointed out that the sources were incomplete. The commission gave the matter intense scrutiny to determine whether the vice president might have authorized a shoot-down on his own. In the end, the commission's report came to no conclusion and simply related the differing accounts. The report did say that in most cases, the chain of command authorizing use of force runs from the president to the secretary of defense.
19. The account of Cheney's two shoot-down orders and subsequent conversation with the president in the bunker on Sept. 11, 2001, is drawn from *The 9/11 Commission Report*, pp. 40–41.
20. Ibid., p. 41.
21. Ibid.
22. Rice interview.
23. Ibid.
24. The account of the hijacked plane that was believed to be only five to ten miles out is drawn from *The 9/11 Commission Report*, p. 41.
25. Ibid.
26. Ibid.
27. Francis X. Clines, "Stunned Tourists, Gridlocked Streets, Fleeing and Fear," *New York Times*, Sept. 12, 2001, p. A20.
28. Ibid.
29. Maureen Dowd, "A Grave Silence," *New York Times*, Sept. 12, 2001, p. A27.
30. Rice interview.
31. Ibid.
32. Ibid.
33. Ibid.
34. Bob Woodward, *Bush at War* (New York: Simon & Schuster, 2002), p. 18.

35. Elisabeth Bumiller and David E. Sanger, "A Day of Terror: The President; A Somber Bush Says Terrorism Cannot Prevail," *New York Times*, Sept. 12, 2001, p. A1.
36. Ibid.
37. Ibid.
38. Woodward, *Bush at War*, p. 32.
39. Ibid., p. 30.
40. Ibid.
41. Ibid., p. 31.
42. George W. Bush, "Statement by the President in His Address to the Nation," Washington, D.C., Sept. 11, 2001, White House transcript, www.whitehouse.gov/news/releases/2001/09/20010911-16.html (accessed June 7, 2007).
43. Rice interview.
44. The account of the scene in the White House bunker after 11 P.M. on Sept. 11, 2001, is from a Rice interview.
45. Rice interview.
46. Ibid.
47. Ibid.
48. Ibid.
49. Ibid.
50. Ibid.
51. Ibid.
52. Ibid.
53. Ibid.
54. Ibid.
55. Condoleezza Rice, testimony to the National Commission on Terrorist Attacks upon the United States, April 8, 2004, www.9-11commission.gov/archive/hearing9/9-11Commission_Hearing_2004-04-08.pdf (accessed Aug. 21, 2007).
56. Rice interview.
57. Woodward, *Bush at War*, p. 270.
58. Stephen F. Hayes, *Cheney: The Untold Story of America's Most Powerful and Controversial Vice President* (New York: HarperCollins, 2007), pp. 346, 360.
59. Woodward, *Bush at War*, p. 270.
60. Rice interview.
61. Ibid.
62. Ibid.
63. Ibid.
64. Ibid.

65. Ibid.
66. Ibid.
67. Ibid.
68. Administration official, author interview.
69. Thom Shanker and David Sanger, "Gates Argued for Closing Guantánamo Prison," *New York Times,* March 23, 2007, p. A1.
70. Helene Cooper and David Sanger, "Strategy on Iran Stirs New Debate at White House," *New York Times,* June 16, 2007, p. A1.
71. Rice interview.
72. Ibid.
73. Andrew H. Card, Jr., author interview, McLean, Va., Nov. 13, 2006.
74. Miller interview.
75. Michael E. Gordon and General Bernard E. Trainor, *Cobra II: The Inside Story of the Invasion and Occupation of Iraq* (New York: Pantheon, 2006), p. 148.
76. George Shultz, author interview, Stanford, Calif., June 6, 2006.
77. Rice interview; administration official, author interview.
78. Rice interview.
79. David Kay, testimony to the Senate Select Committee on Intelligence, Aug. 18, 2004, www.intelligence.senate.gov/108835.pdf (accessed Aug. 21, 2007).
80. Card interview.
81. Ibid.
82. Ibid.
83. Neil A. Lewis, "Bush Adviser Backs Use of Race in College Admissions," *New York Times,* Jan. 18, 2003, p. A14.
84. Marcus Mabry, *Twice as Good: Condoleezza Rice and Her Path to Power* (New York: Modern Times, 2007), p. 280.
85. Rice interview.
86. Donna Brazile, author interview by telephone, Sept. 18, 2007.
87. Rice interview.
88. Ibid.
89. Rice friend, author interview.
90. Ibid.
91. Gerhard Casper interviews, Stanford, Calif., Aug. 14, 2006, and by telephone, Aug. 21, 2007.
92. Card interview.
93. Former White House official, author interview.
94. Jonathan Adelman, author interview, Denver, Colo., Dec. 7, 2006.
95. Rice interview.
96. A *Washington Post*–ABC News Poll in February 2007, www.washington

post.com/wp-srv/politics/polls/postpoll_022607.htm (accessed Sept. 19, 2007), found that 58 percent of respondents had a favorable opinion of Rice, a higher figure than for any other administration official. A *New York Times*–CBS News poll in October 2006, graphics.nytimes.com/packages/pdf/politics/20061010_poll_results.pdf (accessed Sept. 19, 2007), found that 44 percent of respondents had a favorable opinion of Rice, compared with 34 percent who had a favorable opinion of Bush, 20 percent who had a favorable opinion of Cheney, and 20 percent who had a favorable opinion of Rumsfeld.

Chapter 1: Twice as Good

1. Jonathan M. Wiener, *Social Origins of the New South: Alabama, 1860–1885* (Baton Rouge: Louisiana State University Press, 1978), p. 4.
2. Dean Spratlan, Union Springs historian, author interview by telephone, February 6, 2007.
3. The Twelfth Census of the United States, Bullock County, Ala., Sheet No. 11, June 8, 1990, James B. Hunter, enumerator.
4. Dean Spratlan, the Union Springs historian, was unable to locate a man with the first name of Alto in the census records of the time.
5. Rice interview.
6. Ibid.
7. Carolyn McKinstry, author interview, Birmingham, Ala., July 28, 2006.
8. Freeman Hrabowski, author interview, Baltimore, Md., July 12, 2006.
9. Nicholas Lemann, "Without a Doubt: Has Condoleezza Rice Changed George W. Bush, or Has He Changed Her?," *The New Yorker*, October 14, 2002, www.lexis.com/research/retrieve/frames?_m=68714fb05c31719b410c816fd8857163&csvc=bl&cform=bool&_fmtstr=FULL&docnum=1&_startdoc=1&wchp=dGLzVlz-zSkAb&_md5=83555fa5e8ae64b478b2e32f122652f8 (accessed Feb. 22, 2007).
10. Rice interview.
11. Ibid.
12. Ibid.
13. Genoa McPhatter, author interviews, Norfolk, Va., Oct. 18, 2006, and by telephone, Feb. 26, 2007.
14. Rice interview.
15. Ibid.
16. African-American Heritage of Bullock County, www.unionspringsalabama.com/aaheritage.htm (accessed Feb. 13, 2007).

17. Mattie Ray Bonds, author interview by telephone, July 27, 2006; Rice interview; McPhatter interview.
18. H. M. Caldwell, *History of the Elyton Land Company and Birmingham, Alabama* (Birmingham: Self-published, 1892), pp. 3–4, as quoted in Charles E. Connerly, *The Most Segregated City in America* (Charlottesville: University of Virginia Press, 2005), p. 18.
19. Diane McWhorter, *Carry Me Home: The Climactic Battle of the Civil Rights Revolution* (New York: Simon & Schuster, 2001), p. 31.
20. www.vulcanpark.org (accessed Feb. 13, 2007).
21. James Mann, *Rise of the Vulcans: The History of Bush's War Cabinet* (New York: Penguin, 2004), p. x.
22. Rice interview.
23. Ibid.
24. McPhatter interview.
25. Bonds interview.
26. McPhatter interview.
27. Ibid.
28. Ibid.
29. Ibid.
30. Richard Arrington, Jr., author interview, Birmingham, Ala., July 19, 2006.
31. Elaine Sciolino, "Bush's Foreign Policy Tutor: An Academic in the Public Eye," *New York Times*, June 16, 2000, p. A1.
32. Rice interview.
33. Rice family friend, author interview.
34. Ibid.
35. "Rice's Comments on Bush: 'Uncommonly Good Judgment,' " *New York Times*, Aug. 2, 2000, p. A20.
36. Ibid.
37. Rice interview.
38. Ibid.
39. Ibid.
40. McPhatter interview.
41. Harold Dennard, author interview, Birmingham, Ala., July 25, 2006. Dennard, a former member of John Rice's youth group, also provided a tour of the Rices' onetime home in the back of Westminster Presbyterian Church.
42. Ibid.
43. Rice interview.
44. Annye Marie Downing, author interview, Birmingham, Ala., July 21, 2006.

45. Ibid.
46. Lativia Alston, author interview by telephone, March 2, 2007.
47. McPhatter interview.
48. Susan Weill, "The Story Behind These Stories," in *Historic Titusville: People and Places*, a project of the Department of Communication Studies, University of Alabama at Birmingham, 2001.
49. Rev. Thomas R. Noon, "Our 50th," unpublished history of Titusville and St. Paul Lutheran Church, Birmingham, Ala.
50. Odessa Woolfolk, author interviews, Birmingham, Ala., July 19, and by telephone, Dec. 4, 2006.
51. J. Mason Davis, author interview, Birmingham, Ala., July 28, 2006.
52. Weill, *Historic Titusville: People and Places.*
53. Angela Davis, *Angela Davis: An Autobiography* (New York: Random House, 1974), pp. 104–5.
54. Glenn T. Eskew, *But for Birmingham: The Local and National Movements in the Civil Rights Struggle* (Chapel Hill: University of North Carolina Press, 1997), p. 53.
55. Woolfolk interview.
56. Jack Straw, author interview, Washington, D.C., Sept. 18, 2006.
57. Andrew Manis, *A Fire You Can't Put Out: The Civil Rights Life of Birmingham's Reverend Fred Shuttlesworth* (Tuscaloosa: University of Alabama Press, 2001), p. 151.
58. James T. Montgomery, author interview, Birmingham, Ala., July 21, 2006.
59. Celeste Mitchell King, author interview, Birmingham, Ala., July 19, 2006.
60. McPhatter interview.
61. Dale Russakoff, "Lessons of Might and Right," *Washington Post Magazine*, Sept. 9, 2001, p. W23.
62. Deborah Cheatham Carson, author interview, Birmingham, Ala., July 18, 2006.
63. Ibid.
64. Dale Russakoff, "Team Rice, Playing Away; Will State's Head Coach Miss Her First Kickoff?," *Washington Post*, Feb. 6, 2005, p. D1.
65. Carolyn Hunter, author interview, Birmingham, Ala., July 17, 2006.
66. Eva Carter, author interview, Birmingham, Ala., July 25, 2006.
67. Rice interview.
68. Carson interview.
69. Rice interview.
70. McPhatter interview.
71. Ibid.

72. Coit Blacker, author interview, Palo Alto, Calif., June 7, 2006.
73. Rice interview.
74. Ibid.
75. Mike Knepler, "Aunt G's Favorite Niece: Condoleezza Rice," *Virginian-Pilot* (Norfolk, Va.), March 6, 2002, p. E1.
76. Vanessa Hunter, author interview, Birmingham, Ala., July 17, 2006.
77. Elaine Sciolino, "The 43rd President: Woman in the News; Compulsion to Achieve—Condoleezza Rice," *New York Times*, Dec. 18, 2000, p. A1.
78. Rice interview.
79. Parnell Jones, author interview, Birmingham, Ala., July 24, 2006.
80. Carole Smitherman, author interview, Birmingham, Ala., July 25, 2006.
81. Ibid.
82. Rice interview.
83. Smitherman interview.
84. George Hunter III, author interview, Birmingham, Ala., July 18, 2006.
85. Vanessa Hunter interview.
86. Carolyn Hunter interview.
87. McPhatter interview.
88. Rice interview.
89. Ibid.
90. McPhatter interview.
91. Clara Rice, author interview, Palo Alto, Calif., Aug. 16, 2006.
92. Smitherman interview.
93. Connie Ray, author interviews, Birmingham, Ala., July 26, 2006, and by telephone, April 18, 2007.
94. Russakoff, "Lessons of Might and Right."
95. Danetta Thornton Owens, author interview, Birmingham, Ala., July 27, 2006.
96. Rice interview.
97. Woolfolk interview.
98. Connie Rice, author interview by telephone, Aug. 24, 2006.
99. Rice interview.
100. Ibid.
101. Ibid.
102. George Hunter III interview.
103. Ibid.
104. Ibid.
105. Eva Carter interview.

106. Ibid.
107. Rice interview.
108. Ibid.
109. Ibid.
110. Russakoff, "Lessons of Might and Right."
111. Rice interview.
112. Russakoff, "Lessons of Might and Right."
113. Rice interview.
114. Ibid.
115. Ibid.
116. Ibid.
117. Manis, pp. 306–9.
118. Rice interview.

Chapter 2: The Year of Terror

1. Manis, p. 147; McWhorter, p. 125. Manis quotes composite sources on the Judge Aaron incident, among them Ben Allen in Howell Raines, *My Soul Is Rested*, p. 153; and *Birmingham News*, Sept. 4, 1957. On the same incident, McWhorter quotes, among others, *Birmingham Post-Herald*, Oct. 8 and 30 and Nov. 6, 1957, and *Birmingham News*, Oct. 31 and Nov. 6, 1957.
2. McWhorter, p. 251.
3. Helen Shores Lee, author interview, Birmingham, Ala., July 27, 2006.
4. Taylor Branch, *Pillar of Fire: America in the King Years 1963–65* (New York: Simon & Schuster, 1998), p. 26.
5. Harrison E. Salisbury, "Fear and Hatred Grip Birmingham; Racial Tension Smoldering After Belated Sitdowns," *New York Times*, April 12, 1960, p. 1.
6. Ibid.
7. Branch, *Pillar of Fire*, p. 26.
8. Ibid., p. 24.
9. David J. Garrow, *Bearing the Cross: Martin Luther King Jr. and the Southern Christian Leadership Conference* (New York: William Morrow, 1986), pp. 227–29, in Manis, p. 332.
10. Fred Shuttlesworth, author interview, Cincinnati, Aug. 4, 2006.
11. McWhorter, p. 320; Manis, pp. 344–45. My account of Birmingham's 1963 run-off election for mayor also comes from Robert G. Corley's class lecture in his History of Birmingham course at the University of Alabama at Birmingham, July 26, 2006.
12. McWhorter, p. 331.
13. Ibid.

14. Montgomery interview.
15. Ibid.
16. Clara Rice interview.
17. Rice interview.
18. Ibid.
19. Shuttlesworth interview.
20. Ibid.
21. Ibid.
22. Taylor Branch, *Parting the Waters: America in the King Years 1954–63* (New York: Simon & Schuster, 1988), pp. 708–9.
23. McWhorter, p. 324.
24. Branch, *Parting the Waters*, p. 729.
25. Branch, *Pillar of Fire*, p. 47.
26. Ibid., p. 74.
27. Branch, *Parting the Waters*, p. 755.
28. Ibid.
29. McWhorter, p. 368.
30. Rice interview.
31. Hrabowski interview.
32. Rice interview.
33. McWhorter, p. 364.
34. Rice interview.
35. McWhorter, p. 366.
36. Branch, *Parting the Waters*, p. 756.
37. Ibid.
38. Ibid., p. 758.
39. Ibid., p. 759.
40. Ibid.
41. McKinstry interview.
42. Ibid.
43. Ibid.
44. McWhorter, p. 372.
45. Branch, *Parting the Waters*, p. 764.
46. Rice interview.
47. Claude Sitton, "Birmingham Jails 1,000 More Negroes," *New York Times*, May 7, 1963, p. 1.
48. Branch, *Parting the Waters*, p. 772.
49. Rice interview.
50. Ibid.
51. Hrabowski interview; George Hunter III interview.
52. McWhorter, p. 364.

53. Hrabowski interview.
54. Ibid.
55. Ibid.
56. Rice interview.
57. Ibid.
58. John Cantelow, author interviews, July 21, 2006, and Feb. 19, 2007.
59. Ann Reilly Dowd, "Is There Anything This Woman Can't Do?," *George*, June 2000, p. 90.
60. Cantelow interview.
61. Rice interview.
62. Ibid.
63. Branch, *Pillar of Fire*, p. 87.
64. Rice interview.
65. Ibid.
66. Ibid.
67. Martin Luther King, Jr., "I Have a Dream," August 28, 1963, Martin Luther King, Jr. Papers Project at Stanford University, www.stanford.edu/group/King/mlkpapers/ (accessed Aug. 21, 2007).
68. Rice interview.
69. Robert G. Corley, author interviews, Birmingham, Ala., July 23, 2006, and by telephone, Dec. 28, 2006.
70. McWhorter, p. 481.
71. Ibid., p. 499.
72. Ibid., p. 519.
73. McKinstry interview.
74. Ibid.
75. Rice interview.
76. Ibid.
77. Parnell Jones, author interview.
78. Abraham Woods, author interview, Birmingham, Ala., July 24, 2006.
79. McWhorter, p. 525.
80. Ibid.
81. John Herbers, "Negroes Pour Out into Streets in Shock and Anger at Bombing," *New York Times*, Sept. 16, 1963, p. 26.
82. McWhorter, p. 525.
83. Rice interview.
84. Chris McNair, author interview, Birmingham, Ala., July 17, 2006.
85. Maxine McNair, author interview, Birmingham, Ala., July 20, 2006.
86. McWhorter, p. 530.
87. Ibid.
88. Branch, *Parting the Waters*, p. 891.

89. Branch, *Pillar of Fire*, p. 139; *Parting the Waters*, p. 891.
90. Branch, *Parting the Waters*, p. 891.
91. Rice interview.
92. Marion Sterling, author interview, Birmingham, Ala., July 24, 2006.
93. John Herbers, "Funeral Is Held for Bomb Victims; Dr. King Delivers Tribute at Rites in Birmingham," *New York Times*, Sept. 19, 1963, p. 17.
94. Branch, *Parting the Waters*, p. 892.
95. Rice interview.
96. Ibid.
97. Branch, *Parting the Waters*, p. 892.
98. Martin Luther King, Jr., "Eulogy for the Martyred Children," Sept. 18, 1963, Martin Luther King, Jr. Papers Project at Stanford University, www.stanford.edu/group/King/speeches/pub/Eulogy_for_the_martyred_children.html (accessed Feb. 19, 2007).
99. Ibid.
100. Ibid.
101. Condoleezza Rice, remarks with United Kingdom Foreign Secretary Jack Straw, Kelly Ingram Park, Birmingham, Ala., Oct. 22, 2005, www.state.gov/secretary/rm/2005/55427.html (accessed Feb. 19, 2007).
102. Ibid.
103. Corley interview.
104. Montgomery interview.
105. McKinstry interview.
106. Rice interview.
107. Ibid.
108. President Lyndon B. Johnson's radio and television remarks upon signing the Civil Rights Bill, July 2, 1964, www.lbjlib.utexas.edu/johnson/archives.hom/speeches.hom/640702.asp (accessed Feb. 21, 2007).
109. Rice interview.
110. Ibid.
111. Ibid.
112. Russakoff, "Lessons of Might and Right."
113. Rice interview.
114. Ibid.
115. Ibid.
116. Russakoff, "Lessons of Might and Right."
117. Rice interview.
118. Haven Moses, author interview, Denver, Colo., Dec. 8, 2006.
119. Rice interview.
120. Ibid.

121. Ibid.
122. Ibid.
123. John Wesley Rice, Jr., résumé prepared in 1970, University of Denver, Penrose Library, Special Collections, biographical files, John Wesley Rice, Jr.

Chapter 3: Josef Korbel and the Power of Stalin

1. *Statistical Abstract of the United States, 1978*, U.S. Department of Commerce, Table No. 24, p. 24.
2. Therese M. Saracino, author interview, Denver, Colo., Dec. 7, 2006.
3. Ibid.
4. Ibid.
5. St. Mary's Academy, archives; Regina Drey, author interview, Denver, Dec. 6, 2006.
6. Oprah Winfrey, "Oprah Talks to Condoleezza Rice," *O, The Oprah Magazine*, Feb. 2002, www.accessmylibrary.com/coms2/summary_0286-24987993_ITM (accessed Feb. 21, 2007).
7. Rice interview.
8. Ibid.
9. Rice interview.
10. Stephen J. Leonard and Thomas J. Noel, *Denver: From Mining Town to Metropolis* (Boulder: University Press of Colorado, 1990), pp. 293, 376–80; Lisa Schiff, Denver Public Schools, author interview by telephone, Aug. 22, 2007.
11. Joy Gerity, author interview, Denver, Colo., Dec. 6, 2006.
12. Ibid.
13. Ibid.
14. "Campus Journal: From 'Not College Material' to Stanford's No. 2 Job," *New York Times*, June 23, 1993, p. B7.
15. Steven R. Weisman, "Rice Defends Bush's Race Record and Calls for Rebuilding Fairly," *New York Times*, Sept. 13, 2006, p. A24.
16. Rice interview.
17. Ibid.
18. Ibid.
19. Ibid.
20. Gerity interview.
21. Rice interview.
22. Ibid.
23. Ibid.
24. Ibid.
25. Ibid.

26. McPhatter interview.
27. Brooke Lea Foster, "The Real Condi Rice," *Washingtonian*, February 2007, p. 54.
28. Ibid.
29. Rice interview.
30. Ibid.
31. Ibid.
32. Ibid.
33. Isabel Wilkerson, "The Most Powerful Woman in the World: As National Security Adviser, Condoleezza Rice Has the Ear of the President. So Who Exactly Is This Daughter of 1960's Birmingham, and What Does She Bring to the Table?," *Essence*, Feb. 1, 2002, www.accessmylibrary.com/coms2/summary_0286-26647017_ITM (accessed Feb. 21, 2007).
34. Rice interview.
35. Ibid.
36. Ibid.
37. Ibid.
38. Ibid.
39. Robert Eckelberry, author interview by telephone, Aug. 21, 2007.
40. "Background: The Black Experience in America Seminar," publicity release, University of Denver Public Relations Office, University of Denver, Penrose Library, Special Collections, biographical files, John W. Rice, Jr.
41. Ibid.
42. Rice interview.
43. Ibid.
44. Julia Reed, "The President's Prodigy," *Vogue*, October 2001, p. 396.
45. Rice interview.
46. Winfrey, *O, The Oprah Magazine*.
47. Condoleezza Rice, author interview for *The New York Times*, Washington, D.C., Dec. 12, 2003.
48. Ibid.
49. Condoleezza Rice, "Commencement Address at Boston College, May 22, 2006," State Department transcript.
50. Rice interview.
51. Ibid.
52. Ibid.
53. Ibid.
54. Jay Nordlinger, "Star in Waiting," *National Review*, Aug. 30, 1999,

www.findarticles.com/p/articles/mi_m1282/is_16_51/ai_55432936 (accessed Feb. 22, 2007).

55. Rice interview.
56. Ibid.
57. Ibid.
58. Madeleine Albright, author interview, Washington, D.C., Jan. 23, 2007.
59. Condoleezza Rice, interview on NPR, June 2006.
60. Rice interview; Lemann, "Without a Doubt."
61. Rice, NPR interview.
62. Dowd, "Is There Anything This Woman Can't Do?"
63. Lemann, "Without a Doubt."
64. Terry Karl, author interviews by telephone, March 21 and Aug. 15 and 19, 2007.
65. Albright interview.
66. Rice interview.
67. Ann Blackman, *Seasons of Her Life: A Biography of Madeleine Korbel Albright* (New York: Lisa Drew/Scribner, 1998), p. 26.
68. Ibid., p. 43; Michael Dobbs, *Madeleine Albright: A Twentieth-Century Odyssey* (New York: Owl/Henry Holt, 1998), p. 49.
69. Blackman, p. 26; Dobbs, *Madeleine Albright*, p. 86.
70. Michael Dobbs, "Albright's Family Tragedy Comes to Light; Secretary Says She Didn't Know That 3 Grandparents Were Jewish Victims of Holocaust," *Washington Post*, Feb. 4, 1997, p. A1.
71. Dobbs, *Madeleine Albright*, p. 113.
72. Blackman, p. 95.
73. Ibid., p. 87; Dobbs, *Madeleine Albright*, p. 137.
74. Dobbs, *Madeleine Albright*, p. 120.
75. Israel Shenker, "Dr. Philip E. Mosely, Scholar of Soviet Affairs, Dead at 66," *New York Times*, Jan. 14, 1972, p. 36.
76. Dobbs, *Madeleine Albright*, p. 138.
77. Blackman, p. 100.
78. Ibid., p. 101.
79. Rice, NPR interview.
80. Rice interview.
81. Dobbs, *Madeleine Albright*, p. 41.
82. Blackman, p. 89.
83. Rice interview.
84. Alan Gilbert, author interview, Denver, Colo., Dec. 7, 2006.
85. Dobbs, *Madeleine Albright*, p. 87.

86. Blackman, p. 89.
87. Alan Gilbert interview.
88. Rice, NPR interview.
89. Albright interview.
90. Ibid.
91. Ibid.
92. Rice interview.
93. Ibid.
94. Mark L. von Hagen, "From 'Splendid Isolation' to 'Fruitful Cooperation': The Harriman Institute in the Post-Soviet Era," *Columbia,* Summer 1996, www.columbia.edu/cu/record/archives/vol22/vol22_iss1/Coop_Harriman_USSR.html (accessed Jan. 19, 2007).
95. Mark L. von Hagen, author interview, Jan. 23, 2007.
96. Catherine Kelleher, author interview, Bethesda, Md., Oct. 27, 2006.
97. Hedrick Smith, "Nixon, Brezhnev End Summit, Declare Week's Talks Moved World Nearer a Stable Peace," *New York Times*, June 25, 1973, p. 1.
98. Rice interview.
99. Elisabeth Bumiller and Richard W. Stevenson, "The Inauguration—The Ceremony: The Overview; Bush, at 2nd Inaugural, Says Spreading Liberty Is 'The Calling of Our Time,' " *New York Times*, Jan. 21, 2005, p. A1.
100. Rice interview.
101. Ibid.
102. George Brinkley, author interview by telephone, Jan. 18, 2007.
103. Ibid.
104. Ibid.
105. Rice interview.
106. Ibid.
107. Ibid.

Chapter 4: Football and the Strategy of War

1. Rice interview.
2. Carson interview.
3. Ibid.
4. Brinkley interview.
5. Ibid.
6. Ibid.
7. Ibid.
8. Ibid.
9. Rice interview.

10. Lemann, "Without a Doubt."
11. Michael Dobbs, "Josef Korbel's Enduring Foreign Policy Legacy," *Washington Post*, Dec. 28, 2000, p. A5.
12. Ibid.
13. Alan Gilbert interview.
14. Rice interview.
15. Alan Gilbert interview.
16. Ibid.
17. Rice interview.
18. Ibid.
19. Arthur Gilbert, author interview by telephone, Jan. 19, 2007.
20. Wayne Glass, author interview by telephone, Dec. 6, 2006.
21. Arthur Gilbert interview.
22. Glass interview.
23. Arthur Gilbert interview.
24. Jonathan Adelman, author interview, Denver, Colo., Dec. 7, 2006.
25. Cristann Gibson, author interview by telephone, Jan. 22, 2007.
26. Moses interview.
27. Ibid.
28. Mabry, p. 99.
29. Ibid., p. 101.
30. Rice interview.
31. Ibid.
32. Moses interview.
33. Ibid.
34. Rice interview.
35. Ibid.
36. Moses interview.
37. Ibid.
38. Ibid.
39. Rick Upchurch, author interview by telephone, Dec. 7, 2006.
40. Rice interview.
41. Gibson interview.
42. Joyce Moses, author interview by telephone, Feb. 9, 2007.
43. Ibid.
44. Gibson interview.
45. Rice interview.
46. Madeleine Albright with Bill Woodward, *Madame Secretary* (New York: Miramax, 2003), p. 80.
47. Rice interview.
48. Ibid.

49. Kelleher interview.
50. Ibid.; Adelman interview.
51. Rice interview.
52. Adelman interview.
53. Ibid.
54. Ibid.
55. Ibid.
56. Gary Hart, author interview by telephone, March 23, 2007.
57. Rice interview.
58. Ibid.
59. Albright, footnote no. 1 on p. 80.
60. Rice interview.
61. Ibid.
62. Adelman interview.
63. Kelleher interview.
64. Rice interview.
65. Kelleher interview.
66. Adelman interview.
67. Rice interview.
68. Adelman interview.
69. Ibid.
70. Ibid.
71. Blacker interview.

Chapter 5: She Tells Me Everything I Know About the Soviet Union

1. Rice interview.
2. Gloria Duffy, author interview, San Jose, Calif., Aug. 18, 2006.
3. Ibid.
4. Sidney Drell, author interview, Stanford, Calif., June 6, 2006.
5. Rice interview.
6. Ibid.
7. Condoleezza Rice, *The Soviet Union and the Czechoslovak Army, 1948–1983: Uncertain Allegiance* (Princeton, N.J.: Princeton University Press, 1984), p. 228.
8. Rice interview.
9. Cecilia Burciaga, author interview by telephone, Nov. 8, 2006.
10. Rice interview.
11. Rice, Blacker, and Burciaga interviews.
12. Rice interview.
13. Ibid.

14. Ibid.
15. Ibid.
16. Ibid.
17. "Concerns Regarding Equal Employment Opportunity for Women Faculty at Stanford University," complaint filed November 1998 with the United States Department of Labor; Letter from Paul N. "Pete" McCloskey, Jr., of counsel, Wagstaffe & Jellins, to James Henry, Esq., Gary Guff, Esq., U.S. Labor Department, Sept. 2, 1998; Michelle Levander, "U.S. Probes Stanford Promotion Policies," *San Jose Mercury News*, Feb. 2, 1999, p. 1A.
18. Rice interview.
19. Ibid.
20. Rose McDermott, author interview by telephone, March 8, 2007.
21. Rice interview.
22. McDermott interview.
23. Rice interview.
24. Donald Kennedy, author interview, Stanford, Calif., June 5, 2006.
25. Kori Schake, author interview, Washington, D.C., Nov. 21, 2006.
26. McDermott interview.
27. Jendayi Frazer, author interview, Washington, D.C., May 23, 2007.
28. Ibid.
29. Ibid.
30. Gene Washington, author interview by telephone, Sept. 14, 2007.
31. Hart interview.
32. Ibid.
33. David M. Kennedy, author interview, Stanford, Calif., Aug. 14, 2006.
34. Rice, *The Soviet Union and the Czechoslovak Army*, dedication page.
35. Ibid., p. 245.
36. Adam Garfinkle, "A Conversation with Condoleezza Rice," *American Interest*, Autumn 2005, pp. 47–57.
37. Joseph Kalvoda, review of Condoleezza Rice, *The Soviet Union and the Czechoslovak Army, 1948–1983: Uncertain Allegiance*, in *American Historical Review*, December 1985, p. 1236.
38. Christopher Jones, review of Condoleezza Rice, *The Soviet Union and the Czechoslovak Army, 1948–1983: Uncertain Allegiance*, in *Soviet Studies*, October 1986, pp. 602–4.
39. Ibid.
40. Dale R. Herspring, review of Condoleezza Rice, *The Soviet Union and the Czechoslovak Army, 1948–1983: Uncertain Allegiance*, in *American Political Science Review*, September 1985, pp. 904–5.
41. Rice interview.

42. Ibid.
43. Ibid.
44. Lemann, "Without a Doubt."
45. Randy Bean, author interviews, Palo Alto, Calif., Aug. 16, 2006, and by telephone, March 16, 2007.
46. Ibid.
47. Ibid.
48. Ibid.
49. Ibid.
50. Donald Kennedy interview.
51. Rice interview.
52. Ibid.
53. Ibid.
54. Ibid.; Marilyn Berger, "Reagan Dies at 93; Fostered Cold-War Might and Curbs on Government," *New York Times*, June 6, 2004, p. 1.
55. Rice interview.
56. Ibid.
57. Clara Rice interview.
58. Mary Bush, author interview, Bethesda, Md., Nov. 8, 2006.
59. Clara Rice interview.
60. Mabry, p. 110.
61. Ibid.
62. Rice interview.
63. Condoleezza Rice, "The Party, the Military, and Decision Authority in the Soviet Union," *World Politics*, October 1987, pp. 55–81.
64. Stanford faculty members, author interviews.
65. Rice interview.
66. Scott Sagan, author interview, Stanford, Calif., June 9, 2006.
67. Blacker interview.
68. Clara Rice interview.
69. Ibid.
70. Ibid.
71. Clara Rice interview.
72. Ibid.
73. Blacker interview.
74. Brent Scowcroft, author interview, Washington, D.C., Oct. 19, 2006.
75. Robert Blackwill, author interviews, Washington, D.C., Nov. 1 and Dec. 18, 2006, and Jan. 31, 2007.
76. R. Nicholas Burns, author interview, Washington, D.C., March 16, 2007.

77. Ibid.
78. Philip Zelikow and Condoleezza Rice, *Germany Unified and Europe Transformed: A Study in Statecraft* (Cambridge, Mass.: Harvard University Press, 1977), p. 20.
79. Rice interview.
80. Philip Zelikow, author interviews, Washington, D.C., Jan. 25, 2007, and Charlottesville, Va., Feb. 1, 2007.
81. George Bush and Brent Scowcroft, *A World Transformed* (New York: Alfred A. Knopf, 1998), pp. 13–14.
82. The account of the Kennebunkport meeting is drawn from Michael R. Beschloss and Strobe Talbott, *At the Highest Levels: The Inside Story of the End of the Cold War* (Boston: Little, Brown, 1993), pp. 21–23.
83. Card interview.
84. Scowcroft interview.
85. Bush and Scowcroft, p. 50.
86. Zelikow interviews; Bernard Weinraub, "Bush Unveils Aid Plan for Poland Linked to Recent Liberalization," *New York Times*, April 18, 1989, p. A1.
87. Rice interview.
88. Eva Carter interview.
89. Bush and Scowcroft, p. 143; Reed, "The President's Prodigy," p. 402; Felicity Barringer, "Smiling Soviet Leader Meets Bush and Proves Deft in Capital's Ways," *New York Times*, Sept. 13, 1989, p. A6.
90. Lemann, "Without a Doubt."
91. Scowcroft interview.
92. Zelikow and Rice, p. 107.
93. Ibid.
94. Ibid.
95. Ibid., pp. 125–26.
96. Ibid., p. 126.
97. Rice interview.
98. Zelikow and Rice, p. 160.
99. Rice interview.
100. Zelikow and Rice, pp. 208–9.
101. Ibid., p. 228; Serge Schmemann, "Upheaval in the East; Poles Are Promised Role in Talks on German Unity," *New York Times*, March 15, 1990, p. A12.
102. Don Oberdorfer, *The Turn: From the Cold War to a New Era: The United States and the Soviet Union, 1983–1990* (New York: Poseidon, 1991), p. 404.

103. James A. Baker III with Thomas M. DeFrank, *The Politics of Diplomacy: Revolution, War and Peace, 1989–1992* (New York: G. P. Putnam's Sons, 1995), p. 252.
104. Zelikow and Rice, p. 262.
105. Rice interview.
106. Zelikow and Rice, p. 266.
107. Bush and Scowcroft, p. 282.
108. Donnie Radcliffe and Roxanne Roberts, "On with the Sunshine Summit; At the White House, a Global Warming Trend," *Washington Post*, June 1, 1990, p. B1.
109. Ibid.
110. Rice interview.
111. Zelikow and Rice, p. 281.
112. Ibid., pp. 282–83.
113. Burns interview.
114. Marilyn Greene, "Summit Specialist Cold-Shouldered in San Francisco," *USA Today*, June 6, 1990, p. 2A.
115. James Gerstenzang, "Agent's Shoving of Black Bush Aide Probed," *Los Angeles Times*, June 7, 1990, p. A22.
116. Zelikow and Rice, p. 1.
117. Thomas L. Friedman, "Evolution in Europe; Four Allies Give Up Rights in Germany," *New York Times*, Sept. 13, 1990, p. A1.
118. Ibid.
119. Ibid.
120. Rice interview.
121. Burns interview.
122. Ibid.
123. Pete Wilson, author interview by telephone, March 23, 2007.
124. Ibid.
125. Burns interview.
126. Clara Rice interview.

Chapter 6: I Don't Do Committees

1. Karl interview.
2. Stanford News Service news release, "Back from D.C., Rice Offers Inside Look at U.S.-Soviet Relations," May 6, 1991, www.stanford.edu/dept/news/pr/91/910506Arc1394.html (accessed Sept. 20, 2007).
3. Shultz interview.
4. Ibid.
5. Ibid.
6. Steven Greenhouse, "Chevron to Spend $10 Billion to Seek Oil in

Kazakhstan," *New York Times*, May 19, 1992, p. A1; Neela Bannerjee and Mary Williams Walsh, "1 New Oil Company, 2 Corporate Cultures," *New York Times*, Oct. 17, 2000, p. C1.

7. Birgit Brauer, "Oil Begins Flowing Through Kazakh Pipeline," *New York Times*, March 27, 2001, p. W1.
8. Carla Marinucci, "Chevron Redubs Ship Named for Bush Aide; Condoleezza Rice Drew Too Much Attention," *San Francisco Chronicle*, May 5, 2001, p. A1.
9. Chevron Corporation, Marilyn Hutchison, executive assistant to Lydia Beebe, Chevron corporate secretary, telephone interview with Ariel Alexovich, March 8, 2007.
10. The dates of Rice's service on the J. P. Morgan International Council and the boards of Transamerica, Hewlett-Packard, and Charles Schwab are from SEC filings and information provided by the companies' corporate offices.
11. Rice's board fees are an estimate of what was standard compensation from the companies at the time.
12. Condoleezza Rice, 2000 Financial Disclosure Form, filed March 22, 2001, available at www.opensecrets.org/pfds/pfd2000/N99999990_00.pdf (accessed Aug. 23, 2007).
13. Blacker interview; Wilson interview.
14. Casper interview.
15. William Celis 3d, "Navy Settles a Fraud Case in Stanford Research Costs," *New York Times*, Oct. 19, 1994, p. A16.
16. Casper interview.
17. Blacker interview.
18. Casper interview.
19. Casper interview; Stanford faculty, author interviews.
20. Shultz interview.
21. Casper interview.
22. Ibid.
23. Timothy Warner, Stanford vice provost for budget and auxiliary management, author interview, Stanford, Calif., June 7, 2006.
24. Rice interview.
25. Warner interview.
26. Ibid.
27. Casper interview.
28. Warner interview.
29. Paul Brest, author interview by telephone, June 8, 2006, and interview, Palo Alto, Calif., Aug. 18, 2006.
30. Bean interview.

31. Brest interview.
32. Rice interview.
33. Casper interview.
34. Burciaga interview.
35. Ibid.
36. Joe Rodriguez, "What Was Stanford Thinking?," *San Jose Mercury News*, May 13, 1994, p. 11B.
37. Friend of Condoleezza Rice, author interview.
38. Katherine Corcoran, "Student Hunger Strike Is Over; Stanford Chicanos Make Some Gains," *San Jose Mercury News*, May 8, 1994, p. 1B.
39. Nora Elizabeth Villagran, "What They're Saying; Burciaga Layoff Has the University Community Abuzz," *San Jose Mercury News*, May 13, 1994, Peninsula Living, p. 4.
40. Burciaga interview.
41. Blacker interview.
42. Luis Fraga, author interview, Stanford, Calif., June 8, 2006.
43. Scott Pearson, author interview, Stanford, Calif., Aug. 17, 2006.
44. Walter Falcon, author interview, Stanford, Calif., June 5, 2006.
45. Carolyn Lougee Chappell, author interview, Stanford, Calif., Aug. 16, 2006.
46. Alison Schneider, "Stanford Revisits the Course That Set Off the Culture Wars," *Chronicle of Higher Education*, May 9, 1997, pp. 10–12.
47. Ibid.
48. Chappell interview.
49. Marsh McCall, author interview, Stanford, Calif., Aug. 14, 2006.
50. Ibid.
51. Cecilia Ridgeway, author interview, Palo Alto, Calif., Aug. 18, 2006.
52. "Concerns Regarding Equal Employment Opportunity for Women Faculty at Stanford," complaint filed with the United States Department of Labor.
53. Ridgeway interview.
54. Ibid.
55. American Association of University Professors Faculty Compensation Survey, 1997–1998, provided by John W. Curtis, director of research, American Association of University Professors, Washington, D.C.
56. Diane Manual, "Senators, Others Debate Status of Women Faculty," *Stanford Report*, May 20, 1998, news-service.stanford.edu/news/1998/may20/facsen520.html (accessed March 27, 2007).
57. Ibid.
58. Susan W. Schofield, Faculty Senate minutes from the May 14, 1998,

meeting, news-service.stanford.edu/news/1998/may20/minutes520 .html (accessed March 27, 2007).

59. Manual, *Stanford Report.*
60. Ibid.
61. Ibid.
62. Ibid.
63. Ibid.
64. Ibid.
65. Ibid.
66. Ibid.
67. Ibid.
68. Barbara Babcock, author interview, Stanford, Calif., June 8, 2006.
69. Ibid.
70. Michelle Levander, "U.S. Probes Stanford Promotion Policies," *San Jose Mercury News,* Feb. 2, 1999, p. 1A.
71. Ibid.
72. Colleen Crangle, author interview by telephone, Nov. 8, 2006.
73. Ibid.
74. McCloskey letter.
75. Lisa M. Krieger, "Discrimination Case: U.S. Department of Labor Is Resuming Its Investigation," *San Jose Mercury News,* Oct. 10, 2005, p. 1B.
76. Patricia P. Jones, vice provost for faculty development and diversity, Stanford University, author interview by telephone, March 2005; John Etchemendy, provost, Stanford University, letter to editor, "Women at Stanford," *Newsweek,* Jan. 20, 2003, p. 19.
77. "Tenure Rates Across Schools for Women and Men Assistant Professors Hired in Three Cohorts: 1975–1980, 1981–1986, 1987–1992," www.Stanford.edu/home/pics/chart1.grf (accessed Dec. 17, 2002); Patricia J. Jones, "Report on the Status of Women Faculty at Stanford," April 27, 2000, www.stanford.edu/home/administration/womenfaculty/html (accessed Dec. 17, 2002).
78. Rice interview.
79. Mann, p. 227.
80. George Barth, author interview, Stanford, Calif., Aug. 16, 2006.
81. Ibid.
82. Ibid.
83. Ibid.
84. Brest interview.
85. Ibid.

86. Mike Reynolds, author interview for *The New York Times*, by telephone, November 2003.
87. Condoleezza Rice, author interview for *The New York Times*, Washington, D.C., Dec. 12, 2003.
88. Ibid.
89. Dale Russakoff, "Team Rice, Playing Away; Will State's Head Coach Miss Her First Kickoff?," *Washington Post*, Feb. 6, 2005, p. D1.
90. George J. Tanber, interview of Condoleezza Rice for ESPN.com, Feb. 26, 2007, www.state.gov/secretary/rm/2007/feb/81110.htm (accessed March 3, 2007).
91. Russakoff, "Team Rice, Playing Away," *Washington Post*, Feb. 6, 2005, p. D1.
92. Susan Ford, author interviews, Woodside, Calif., Aug. 16, 2006, and by telephone, April 18, 2007.
93. Adam Kemezis and Marni Leff, "Rice to Step Down as Provost," *Stanford Daily* online, Dec. 11, 1998, daily.stanford.edu/article/1998/12/11/riceToStepDownAsProvost (accessed March 28, 2007).
94. James Robinson, " 'Velvet-Glove Forcefulness'; Six Years of Provostial Challenges and Achievements," *Stanford Report*, June 9, 1999 news-service.stanford.edu/news/1999/june9/rice-69.html (accessed March 28, 2007).
95. Shultz interview.
96. Stephen Krasner, author interview, Washington, D.C., March 26, 2007.
97. Rice interview.
98. Ibid.
99. Blacker interview.
100. Lemann, "Without a Doubt."
101. Bob Woodward, *State of Denial: Bush at War, Part III* (New York: Simon & Schuster, 2006), p. 6.
102. Shultz interview.
103. Mann, p. 249.
104. Elaine Sciolino, "The 2000 Campaign: The Advisor; Bush's Foreign Policy Tutor: An Academic in the Public Eye," *New York Times*, June 16, 2000, p. A1.
105. Rice interview.
106. Ibid.
107. Mann, p. 250.
108. Sciolino, "The 2000 Campaign."
109. Mann, p. 252.
110. Ibid., p. 251.

111. Frank Bruni, "Pressed by a Reporter, Bush Falls Short in World Affairs Quiz," *New York Times*, Nov. 5, 1999, p. A28.
112. "Does George W. Bush Know What It Takes to Be President?," George W. Bush interview with Andy Hiller, WHDH-TV, Boston, Nov. 3, 1999, www3.whdh.com/features/articles/hiller/22/ (accessed Aug. 22, 2007).
113. Bruni, "Pressed by a Reporter."
114. Rice interview.
115. Sciolino, "The 2000 Campaign."
116. Condoleezza Rice, "Promoting the National Interest," *Foreign Affairs*, January/February 2000, pp. 45–62.
117. Ibid.
118. Elisabeth Bumiller, David Sanger, and Richard W. Stevenson, "Bush Says Iraqis Will Want G.I.'s to Stay and Help," *New York Times*, Jan. 28, 2005, p. 1. Part of the quote is taken from an unpublished portion of an interview by Bumiller, Sanger, and Stevenson with Bush in the Oval Office on Jan. 27, 2005.
119. Richard A. Oppel Jr., with Frank Bruni, "The 43rd President: The White House Staff; Bush Adviser Gets National Security Post," *New York Times*, Dec. 18, 2000, p. A1.
120. Dowd, "Is There Anything This Woman Can't Do?," p. 88.
121. Clara Rice interview.
122. Mabry, p. 164.
123. Bean interview.
124. Ibid.

Chapter 7: Bin Laden Determined to Strike in US

1. "President George W. Bush's Inaugural Address," Jan. 20, 2001, White House transcript, www.whitehouse.gov/news/inaugural-address.html (accessed Sept. 20, 2007).
2. Rice interview.
3. "Condoleezza Rice Shares Feelings About the Inauguration and George W. Bush," NBC transcript, Jan. 20, 2001, www.lexis.com/research/retrieve/frames?_m=782256a4f6d1ff1467d7c416f7329c42&csvc=bl&cform=bool&_fmtstr=FULL&docnum=1&_startdoc=1&wchp=dGLbVtz-zSkAz&_md5=90d7b441d38956606c8a2a505065c298top (accessed April 18, 2007).
4. Ford interview.
5. Connie Ray interview.
6. *The 9/11 Commission Report*, pp. 235–36.
7. David Rothkopf, *Running the World: The Inside Story of the National*

Security Council and the Architects of Power (New York: PublicAffairs, 2006), p. 109.

8. Rice interview.
9. Elisabeth Bumiller, "A Partner in Shaping an Assertive Foreign Policy," *New York Times*, Jan. 7, 2004, p. A1.
10. Richard Armitage, author interview, Arlington, Va., May 21, 2007.
11. Roland Betts, author interview, New York City, Nov. 16, 2006.
12. Card interview.
13. Ibid.
14. Elisabeth Bumiller, "White House Letter; Black and White and Read by Precious Few," *New York Times*, Nov. 10, 2003, p. A19.
15. George Tenet with Bill Harlow, *At the Center of the Storm: My Years at the CIA* (New York: HarperCollins, 2007), p. 32.
16. Ibid.
17. Rice interview.
18. Former administration official, author interview.
19. Rice interview.
20. Ibid.
21. Ibid.
22. Jim Rutenberg and David E. Sanger, "Overhaul Moves White House Data Center into Modern Era," *New York Times*, Dec. 19, 2006, p. A26.
23. The account of the Israeli-Palestinian discussion at the January 30, 2001, National Security Council meeting is drawn from a Rice interview; Karen DeYoung, *Soldier: The Life of Colin Powell* (New York: Afred A. Knopf, 2006), pp. 314–17; and Ron Suskind, *The Price of Loyalty: George W. Bush, the White House, and the Education of Paul O'Neill* (New York: Simon & Schuster, 2004), pp. 70–75.
24. Rice interview.
25. Thomas E. Ricks, *Fiasco: The American Military Adventure in Iraq* (New York: Penguin Press, 2006), p. 6.
26. Ricks, p. 19; Kenneth Pollack, *The Threatening Storm: The Case for Invading Iraq* (New York: Random House, 2002), p. 93.
27. Frank Bruni and David E. Sanger, "From the Ranch, President-Elect Gazes Back and Looks to the Future," *New York Times*, Jan. 14, 2001, p. 1.
28. DeYoung, p. 315.
29. Ibid., p. 316.
30. Suskind, pp. 72–73; DeYoung, p. 316.
31. Suskind, p. 75.

32. Ibid.
33. Rice interview.
34. The account of the February 5, 2001, NSC meeting is drawn from DeYoung, pp. 316–17.
35. *The 9/11 Commission Report*, p. 200.
36. Richard A. Clarke, NSC memorandum for Condoleezza Rice, Jan. 25, 2001, National Security Archive, www.gwu.edu/~nsarchiv/NSAEBB/NSAEBB147/clarke%20memo.pdf (accessed April 12, 2007).
37. The Clarke paper, "Strategy for Eliminating the Threat from the Jihadist Networks of al Qida: Status and Prospects," was attached to his Jan. 25, 2001, memo to Rice and is also available through the National Security Archive at www.gwu.edu/~nsarchiv/NSAEBB/NSAEBB147/clarke%20attachment.pdf (accessed April 12, 2007).
38. Ibid.; Richard Clarke, author interview by telephone, April 25, 2007.
39. *The 9/11 Commission Report*, p. 201.
40. Condoleezza Rice, "9/11: For the Record," *Washington Post*, March 22, 2004, p. A21.
41. Rice interview.
42. *The 9/11 Commission Report*, p. 202.
43. Ibid.; also footnote 185 on p. 510.
44. Condoleezza Rice, testimony to the National Commission on Terrorist Attacks upon the United States, April 8, 2004, National Archives and Records Administration, www.9-11commission.gov/archive/hearing9/9-11Commission_Hearing_2004-04-08.pdf (accessed April 12, 2007).
45. Ibid.
46. Clarke interview.
47. Ibid.
48. Rice interview.
49. *The 9/11 Commission Report*, p. 200.
50. Ibid.
51. DeYoung, p. 317; James Dao with Steven Lee Myers, "Attack on Iraq: The Overview; U.S. and British Jets Strike Air-Defense Centers in Iraq," *New York Times*, Feb. 17, 2001, p. A1.
52. Rice interview.
53. The account of the Feb. 16, 2001, Mexico meeting is drawn from a Rice interview and DeYoung, p. 317.
54. Rice interview.
55. "Remarks by President George W. Bush and President Vicente Fox of

Mexico in Joint Press Conference," San Cristóbal, Mexico, Feb. 16, 2001, White House transcript, www.whitehouse.gov/news/releases/2001/02/20010216-3.html (accessed Sept. 20, 2007).

56. Rice interview.
57. Ibid.
58. Former administration official, author interview.
59. Steven Mufson, "Bush to Pick Up Clinton Talks on N. Korean Missiles," *Washington Post*, March 7, 2001, p. A20.
60. Ibid.
61. Rice interview.
62. Colin Powell, author interview by telephone, Oct. 26, 2006.
63. Rice interview.
64. "Remarks by Secretary of State Colin Powell to the Pool," March 7, 2001, White House transcript, www.whitehouse.gov/news/releases/2001/03/20010307-3.html (accessed Sept. 16, 2007).
65. "Remarks by President Bush and President Kim Dae Jung of South Korea," March 7, 2001, White House transcript, www.whitehouse.gov/news/releases/2001/03/20010307-6.html (accessed Sept. 16, 2007).
66. Doug Struck, "N. Korean Leader to Continue Sales of Missiles; A Conciliatory Kim Tells Europeans He Will Keep Promises, but Cannot Give Up 'Trade,' " *Washington Post*, May 5, 2001, p. A13.
67. Douglas Jehl and Andrew C. Revkin, "Bush, in Reversal, Won't Seek Cut in Emissions of Carbon Dioxide," *New York Times*, March 14, 2001, p. A1.
68. The March 13, 2001, telephone exchange between Rice and Powell on the Kyoto Protocol is from DeYoung, p. 327.
69. George W. Bush, "Text of a Letter from the President to Senators Hagel, Helms, Craig and Roberts," March 13, 2001, www.whitehouse.gov/news/releases/2001/03/20010314.html (accessed Sept. 16, 2007).
70. Rice interview.
71. Ibid.
72. Ibid.
73. DeYoung, p. 327.
74. Ibid., p. 328.
75. Rice interview.
76. DeYoung, p. 328.
77. Administration official, author interview.
78. Glass interview.
79. Rice interview.

80. Ibid.
81. Elisabeth Bumiller, "A Partner in Shaping an Assertive Foreign Policy," *New York Times*, Jan. 7, 2004, p. A1.
82. Rice interview.
83. Kevin Sack, "Ex-Klansman Is Found Guilty in '63 Bombing," *New York Times*, May 2, 2001, p. A1.
84. Kevin Sack, "Research Guided Jury Selection in Bombing Trial," *New York Times*, May 3, 2001, p. A12.
85. Rice interview.
86. Ibid.
87. Richard A. Clarke, *Against All Enemies: Inside America's War on Terror* (New York: Free Press, 2004), p. 236.
88. *The 9/11 Commission Report*, pp. 204, 255.
89. David Johnston and Eric Schmitt, "Uneven Response Seen to Terror Risk in Summer '01," *New York Times*, April 4, 2004, p. A1.
90. *The 9/11 Commission Report*, p. 204.
91. Ibid., p. 205.
92. Ibid.
93. Clarke, p. 234.
94. *The 9/11 Commission Report*, p. 205.
95. Ibid., p. 257.
96. Ibid., p. 259.
97. Johnston and Schmitt, "Uneven Response Seen to Terror Risk in Summer '01."
98. Ibid.
99. Rice interview.
100. Clarke, p. 236.
101. *The 9/11 Commission Report*, p. 258.
102. Ibid., p. 264.
103. Rice, testimony to the 9/11 Commission.
104. Ibid.
105. Card interview.
106. Tenet, pp. 150–51.
107. Tenet's version of his July 10, 2001, meeting with Rice is drawn from Tenet, pp. 151–53; George Tenet, interview with CBS *60 Minutes*, April 29, 2007, www.cbsnews.com/stories/2007/04/25/60minutes/main2728375.shtml?source=mostpop_story (accessed April 30, 2007); and Woodward, *State of Denial*, pp. 49, 51.
108. Tenet, pp. 143–44.
109. Rice interview.
110. Ibid.

111. Rice interview; *The 9/11 Commission Report*, p. 258.
112. Rice interview.
113. Tenet, p. 153.
114. Ibid.
115. George Tenet, testimony to the National Commission on Terrorist Attacks upon the United States, March 24, 2004, National Archives and Records Administration, www.9-11commission.gov/archive/hearing8/9-11Commission_Hearing_2004-03-24.pdf (accessed June 4, 2007).
116. Woodward, *State of Denial*, pp. 52, 80.
117. Rice interview; *The 9/11 Commission Report*, p. 211.
118. *The 9/11 Commission Report*, pp. 211–12.
119. Condoleezza Rice, "Remarks at the National Press Club Newsmaker Luncheon," White House transcript, July 13, 2001, www.whitehouse.gov/news/releases/2001/07/20010713.html (accessed June 4, 2007).
120. Ibid.
121. Jane Perlez, "Rice on Front Line in Foreign Policy Role," *New York Times*, Aug. 19, 2001, p. A10.
122. Daniel Fried, author interviews, Washington, D.C., April 13 and May 1, 2007.
123. Perlez, "Rice on Front Line in Foreign Policy Role," *New York Times*, Aug. 19, 2001, p. A10.
124. Martha Brant and Evan Thomas, with Christian Caryl in Moscow and Roy Gutman in Washington, "A Steely Southerner," *Newsweek*, Aug. 6, 2001, p. 28.
125. *The 9/11 Commission Report*, p. 260.
126. Tenet, p. 159.
127. David Johnston, Neil A. Lewis, and Don Van Natta Jr., "F.B.I. Inaction Blurred Picture Before Sept. 11," *New York Times*, May 27, 2002, p. A1.
128. Rice interview.
129. Rice, testimony to the 9/11 Commission.
130. Rice interview.
131. "Bin Laden Determined to Strike in US," President's Daily Brief, Aug. 6, 2001, National Security Archive, www.gwu.edu/~nsarchiv/NSAEBB/NSAEBB116/pdb8-6-2001.pdf (accessed April 15, 2007); Douglas Jehl and David E. Sanger, "Secret Briefing Said That Al Qaeda Was Active in U.S.," *New York Times*, April 11, 2004, p. A1.
132. *President's Daily Brief*, Aug. 6, 2001.

133. Ibid.
134. Jehl and Sanger, "Secret Briefing."
135. Rice interview.
136. George Bush, "President Bush Speaks to Reporters at Fort Hood, Texas," White House transcript, April 11, 2004, www.whitehouse.gov/news/releases/2004/04/20040411.html (accessed June 4, 2007).
137. Clarke, pp. 236–37.
138. *The 9/11 Commission Report*, p. 355.
139. Ibid., p. 272.
140. Ibid., p. 356.
141. Ibid., p. 212.
142. Rice, testimony to the 9/11 Commission.
143. *The 9/11 Commission Report*, p. 213.
144. Rice interview.
145. David Manning, author interview, Washington, D.C., Oct. 30, 2006.
146. Rice interview.

Chapter 8: After the Day of Terror

1. Woodward, *Bush at War*, p. 75.
2. Rice interview.
3. Ibid.
4. Woodward, *Bush at War*, p. 83.
5. Ibid.
6. *The 9/11 Commission Report*, p. 335.
7. Clarke, p. 32.
8. *The 9/11 Commission Report*, p. 335.
9. Woodward, *Bush at War*, p. 83.
10. Ibid.
11. Rice interview.
12. Woodward, *Bush at War*, p. 84.
13. Card interview.
14. Ibid.
15. Woodward, *Bush at War*, p. 85.
16. Ibid., p. 92; Rice interview.
17. *The 9/11 Commission Report*, p. 335.
18. Elisabeth Bumiller and David E. Sanger, "A Look Behind the Scenes, from White House Aides," *New York Times*, Oct. 9, 2001, p. B7.
19. Ibid.
20. Ibid.
21. Donald Rumsfeld and General Richard Myers, Department of Defense

news briefing, Oct. 9, 2001, Pentagon transcript, www.defenselink.mil/transcripts/transcript.aspx?transcriptid=2034 (accessed Aug. 22, 2007).

22. Woodward, *Bush at War*, p. 212.
23. Philip Shenon and David Johnston, "F.B.I. Agents Shift Antiterror Tactics; Orders Go Out to Pursue Leads to Try to Divert Any More Attacks," *New York Times*, Oct. 9, 2001, p. A1.
24. Sheryl Gay Stolberg and Alison Mitchell, "Letter Containing Anthrax Sent to U.S. Senate Leader," *New York Times*, Oct. 16, 2001, p. A1.
25. Elisabeth Bumiller and David E. Sanger, "Threat of Terrorism Is Shaping the Focus of Bush Presidency," Sept. 11, 2002, p. A1.
26. Ibid.
27. Ibid.
28. Rice interview.
29. Ibid.
30. Ibid.
31. R. W. Apple, "A Military Quagmire Remembered: Afghanistan as Vietnam," *New York Times*, Oct. 31, 2001, p. B1.
32. Thom Shanker, James Dao, Steven Lee Myers, and Eric Schmitt, "Conduct of War Is Redefined by Success of Special Forces," *New York Times*, Jan. 21, 2002, p. A1.
33. Woodward, *Bush at War*, p. 301.
34. DeYoung, p. 365.
35. Gellman and Becker, "A Different Understanding with the President."
36. Ibid.
37. Rice interview.
38. Ibid.
39. David E. Sanger, "Bush Offers Arms Talks to China as U.S. Pulls Out of ABM Treaty," *New York Times*, Dec. 14, 2001, p. A1.
40. David E. Sanger, "After ABM Treaty: New Freedom for U.S. in Different Kind of Arms," *New York Times*, Dec. 15, 2001, p. A8.
41. Woodward, *Plan of Attack*, pp. 53–54.
42. Ibid., p. 54.

Chapter 9: We Don't Want the Smoking Gun to Be a Mushroom Cloud

1. Michael Gerson, author interview by telephone, June 2007.
2. David Frum, *The Right Man: The Surprise Presidency of George W. Bush* (New York: Random House, 2003) p. 224.
3. Ibid., pp. 233–34.
4. Ibid., pp. 235–36.

5. Gerson interview; Matthew Scully, a White House speechwriter who was Gerson's subordinate, took credit for the phrase in an article in the September 2007 *Atlantic.*
6. Gerson interview.
7. Rice interview.
8. Ibid.
9. Ibid.
10. George W. Bush, "President Delivers State of the Union Address," Jan. 29, 2002, White House transcript, www.whitehouse.gov/news/releases/2002/01/20020129-11.html (accessed Aug. 23, 2002).
11. Elisabeth Bumiller, "Bush Says the U.S. Plans No Attack on North Korea," *New York Times,* Feb. 20, 2002, p. A1.
12. Gerson interview.
13. Betts interview.
14. Ibid.
15. Joel Brinkley, "Bomb Kills at Least 19 in Israel as Arabs Meet over Peace Plan," *New York Times,* March 28, 2002, p. A1.
16. David Brinkley and Serge Schmemann, "Sharon Calls Arafat an Enemy and Sends Tanks to Isolate Him at Headquarters in Ramallah," *New York Times,* March 29, 2002, p. A1.
17. Tom Clancy with General Tony Zinni (Ret.) and Tony Koltz, *Battle Ready* (New York: G. P. Putnam's Sons, 2004), p. 402.
18. DeYoung, p. 379.
19. Powell interview.
20. George W. Bush, "President to Send Secretary Powell to Middle East," April 4, 2002, White House transcript, www.whitehouse.gov/news/releases/2002/04/20020404-1.html (accessed Aug. 23, 2007).
21. Ibid.
22. Powell interview.
23. Ibid.
24. Ibid.
25. Administration official, author interview.
26. Administration official, author interview.
27. Card interview.
28. Former administration official, author interview.
29. Ibid.
30. Jacqueline Trescott, "High-Powered Duet for Arts Medalists: Yo-Yo Ma Teams With Condoleezza Rice," *Washington Post,* April 23, 2002, p. C1.
31. David Johnston, "F.B.I. Says Pre–Sept. 11 Call for Inquiry Got Little Notice," *New York Times,* May 9, 2002, p. A34.

32. Ibid.
33. David Johnston, "Pre-Attack Memo Cited Bin Laden," *New York Times*, May 15, 2002, p. A1.
34. David E. Sanger, "Bush Was Warned Bin Laden Wanted to Hijack Planes," *New York Times*, May 16, 2002, p. A1.
35. Condoleezza Rice, "National Security Advisor Holds Press Briefing," Washington, D.C., May 16, 2002, White House transcript, www.whitehouse.gov/news/releases/2002/05/20020516-13.html (accessed Sept. 20, 2007).
36. Ibid.
37. Elisabeth Bumiller, "Saudi Tells Bush U.S. Must Temper Backing of Israel," *New York Times*, April 26, 2002, p. A1.
38. DeYoung, pp. 385–86.
39. Ibid., p. 386.
40. Ibid.
41. Rice, author interview for *The New York Times*, Dec. 12, 2003.
42. Ibid.
43. Ibid.
44. Elisabeth Bumiller and David E. Sanger, "Bush Demands Arafat's Ouster Before U.S. Backs a New State; Israelis Welcome Tough Line," *New York Times*, June 25, 2002, p. A1.
45. Ibid.
46. Rice interview.
47. Ibid.
48. Ibid.
49. Ibid.
50. Ibid.
51. Ibid.
52. Bumiller and Sanger, "Bush Demands Arafat's Ouster."
53. David Manning, private memorandum to Tony Blair, March 14, 2002, www.downingstreetmemo.com/manningtext.html (accessed Oct. 25, 2006).
54. Ibid.
55. Rice interview.
56. Elisabeth Bumiller, "U.S. Must Act First to Battle Terror, Bush Tells Cadets," *New York Times*, June 2, 2002, p. A1.
57. Richard Haass, author interview, Washington, D.C., Oct. 19, 2006.
58. Ibid.
59. Ibid.
60. Matthew Rycroft, minutes of prime minister's meeting, July 23, 2002, www.downingstreetmemo.com/memoplain.html (accessed Oct. 25,

2006); background information about Dearlove's meetings in Washington and London from Oliver Mains, German Marshall Fund of the United States.

61. Rice interview.
62. Gordon and Trainor, p. 36.
63. Ibid., p. 50.
64. Ibid., p. 67.
65. Ibid., p. 68.
66. The account of Powell's Aug. 5, 2002, dinner with the president is drawn from a Powell interview; Woodward, *Plan of Attack*, pp. 150–51; DeYoung, pp. 401–02; and Gordon and Trainor, p. 71.
67. Powell interview.
68. Woodward, *Plan of Attack*, p. 151.
69. Powell interview.
70. Ibid.
71. Gordon and Trainor, p. 72.
72. Ricks, pp. 48–49.
73. Ibid.
74. Brent Scowcroft, "Don't Attack Saddam," *Wall Street Journal*, Aug. 15, 2002, www.opinionjournal.com/editorial/feature.html?id=110002133 (accessed Sept. 20, 2007).
75. Woodward, *Plan of Attack*, p. 160.
76. Ibid.
77. Ibid.
78. Senior European diplomat, author interview.
79. Woodward, *Plan of Attack*, p. 161.
80. Ibid.
81. Ibid.
82. "Vice President Speaks at VFW 103rd National Convention," Aug. 26, 2002, White House transcript, www.whitehouse.gov/news/releases/2002/08/20020826.html (accessed Aug. 23, 2007).
83. Ibid.
84. Rice interview.
85. Woodward, *Plan of Attack*, p. 164.
86. Rice interview.
87. Ibid.
88. Ibid.
89. Ibid.
90. "Vice President Honors Veterans of Korean War," Aug. 29, 2002, White House transcript, www.whitehouse.gov/news/releases/2002/08/20020829-5.html (accessed Aug. 23, 2007).

91. Woodward, *Plan of Attack*, pp. 167–68.
92. DeYoung, p. 409.
93. Elisabeth Bumiller, "Bush Aides Set Strategy to Sell Policy on Iraq," *New York Times*, Sept. 7, 2002, p. A1.
94. DeYoung, p. 410.
95. Condoleezza Rice, CNN, *Late Edition with Wolf Blitzer*, Sept. 8, 2002, transcripts.cnn.com/TRANSCRIPTS/0209/08/le.00.html (accessed June 17, 2007).
96. Sean McCormack, author interviews, May 9 and June 11, 2007.
97. Rice interview.
98. David Barstow, William J. Broad, and Jeff Gerth, "The Aluminum Tube Story: A Special Report—How White House Embraced Suspect Iraq Arms Intelligence," *New York Times*, Oct. 3, 2004, p. A1.
99. Ibid.
100. Ibid.; administration official, author interview.
101. Administration official, author interview.
102. "President's Remarks at the United Nations General Assembly," Sept. 12, 2002, White House transcript, www.whitehouse.gov/news/releases/2002/09/20020912-1.html (accessed Sept. 20, 2007).
103. Woodward, *Plan of Attack*, pp. 183–84.
104. DeYoung, pp. 409–10.
105. "The National Security Strategy of the United States of America," September 2002, www.whitehouse.gov/nsc/nss.pdf (accessed June 19, 2007).
106. Ibid.
107. David E. Sanger, "Beating Them to the Prewar," *New York Times*, Sept. 28, 2002, p. B7.
108. Ibid.
109. Tenet, p. 322.
110. Douglas Jehl, "Senators Assail C.I.A. Judgments on Iraq's Arms as Deeply Flawed," *New York Times*, July 10, 2004, p. A1.
111. Tenet, p. 323.
112. "President Bush Outlines Iraqi Threat," Oct. 7, 2002, White House transcript, www.whitehouse.gov/news/releases/2002/10/20021007-8.html (accessed Aug. 23, 2007).
113. "Review of the Pre–Iraqi War Activities of the Office of the Under Secretary of Defense for Policy," Inspector General, United States Department of Defense, released April 5, 2007, levin.senate.gov/newsroom/supporting/2007/SASC.DODIGFeithreport.040507.pdf (accessed Aug. 20, 2007); *The 9/11 Commission Report*, p. 66; R. Jeffrey

Smith, "Hussein's Prewar Ties to Al Qaeda Discounted," *Washington Post*, April 6, 2007, p. A1.

114. David E. Sanger, "Bush Sees 'Urgent Duty' to Pre-empt Attack by Iraq," *New York Times*, Oct. 8, 2002, p. A1.
115. Card interview.
116. Gordon and Trainor, p. 141.
117. Ibid.
118. Rice interview.
119. Ibid.
120. Manning interview.
121. "President Pleased with U.N. Vote," Nov. 8, 2002, White House transcript, www.whitehouse.gov/news/releases/2002/11/20021108-1.html (accessed Aug. 23, 2007).
122. John F. Burns and David E. Sanger, "Iraq Says Report to the U.N. Shows No Banned Arms," Dec. 8, 2002, p. 1.
123. Woodward, *Plan of Attack*, p. 249.
124. Ibid.
125. Ibid., p. 250.
126. Rice interview.
127. Ibid.
128. Ibid.

Chapter 10: No Way to Run a Railroad

1. Lawrence Wilkerson, author interview, Washington, D.C., Oct. 11, 2006.
2. DeYoung, pp. 439–40.
3. Wilkerson interview.
4. Ibid.
5. Ibid.
6. Elisabeth Bumiller, "War Public Relations Machine Is Put on Full Throttle," *New York Times*, Feb. 9, 2003, p. 17.
7. Steven R. Weisman, "Powell, in U.N. Speech, Presents Case to Show Iraq Has Not Disarmed," *New York Times*, Feb. 6, 2003, p. A1.
8. "U.S. Secretary of State Addresses the U.N. Security Council," Feb. 5, 2003, White House transcript, www.whitehouse.gov/news/releases/2003/02/20030205-1.html (accessed Aug. 23, 2007).
9. Douglas Jehl, "C.I.A. Chief Orders 'Curveball' Review," *New York Times*, April 8, 2005, p. A1.
10. Woodward, *Plan of Attack*, p. 254.
11. Ibid.

12. DeYoung, p. 429.
13. Ibid., p. 454.
14. Hans Blix, "An Update on Inspection to the National Security Council," Jan. 27, 2003, www.un.org/Depts/unmovic/Bx27.htm (accessed June 23, 2007).
15. Ibid.
16. Steven R. Weisman, "To White House, Inspector Is Now More a Dead End than a Guidepost," *New York Times*, March 2, 2003, p. 13.
17. Hans Blix, "Briefing to the United Nations Security Council," Feb. 14, 2003, U.N. transcript, www.un.org/Depts/unmovic/blix14Febasdel .htm (accessed June 22, 2007).
18. Weisman, "To White House."
19. Miller interview.
20. Gordon and Trainor, pp. 93–94, 96–97.
21. Woodward, *Plan of Attack*, p. 287.
22. Gordon and Trainor, p. 96.
23. Ibid., p. 77.
24. Woodward, *State of Denial*, p. 108.
25. Ibid., p. 109.
26. Miller interview.
27. Gordon and Trainor, p. 148.
28. Miller interview.
29. Ibid.
30. Woodward, *State of Denial*, p. 109.
31. Rice interview.
32. Ibid.
33. Ibid.
34. Ibid.
35. Gordon and Trainor, pp. 150–51.
36. Rajiv Chandrasekaran, *Imperial Life in the Emerald City: Inside Iraq's Green Zone* (New York: Alfred A. Knopf, 2006), pp. 28–29.
37. Miller interview.
38. Woodward, *Plan of Attack*, p. 281.
39. Gordon and Trainor, p. 160.
40. Chandrasekaran, p. 69.
41. Ibid.
42. Ibid.
43. Steven R. Weisman, "Patience Gone, Powell Adopts Hawkish Tone," *New York Times*, Jan. 28, 2003, p. A1.
44. Administration official, author interview.
45. DeYoung, p. 455.

46. Ibid.
47. Woodward, *Plan of Attack*, p. 345.
48. "Vice President Dick Cheney Discusses a Possible War with Iraq," *Meet the Press*, March 16, 2003, NBC News transcripts, w3.nexis.com/new/results/docview/docview.do?risb=21_T1944492531&format=GNBFI&sort=BOOLEAN&startDocNo=1&resultsUrlKey=29_T1944492534&cisb=22_T1944492533&treeMax=true&treeWidth=0&csi=157446&docNo=8 (accessed Aug. 23, 2007).
49. Woodward, *Plan of Attack*, p. 378.
50. Rice interview.
51. Woodward, *Plan of Attack*, p. 379.
52. Patrick E. Tyler, "U.S. and British Troops Push into Iraq as Missiles Strike Baghdad Compound," *New York Times*, March 21, 2003, p. A1.
53. Woodward, *Plan of Attack*, p. 379.
54. Rice interview.
55. Ibid.
56. Tenet, p. 393.
57. Ibid.
58. Elisabeth Bumiller and David Johnston, "Surprise Strike at Outset Leaves Urgent Mystery: Who Was Hit?," *New York Times*, March 21, 2003, p. A1; Gordon and Trainor, p. 170.
59. Ibid.
60. Rice interview.
61. Bumiller and Johnston, "Surprise Strike"; Gordon and Trainor, p. 174.
62. Woodward, *Plan of Attack*, p. 391.
63. Bumiller and Johnston, "Surprise Strike."
64. Ibid.
65. Rice interview.
66. Ibid.
67. Manning interview.
68. Bumiller and Johnston, "Surprise Strike"; Gordon and Trainor, p. 175.
69. George W. Bush, "President Bush Addresses the Nation," White House transcript, March 19, 2003, www.whitehouse.gov/news/releases/2003/03/20030319-17.html (accessed June 25, 2007).
70. Woodward, *Plan of Attack*, p. 398.
71. Gordon and Trainor, p. 177.
72. Steven Lee Myers, "U.S. Tanks Make Quick Strike into Baghdad," *New York Times*, April 6, 2003, p. A1.
73. Elisabeth Bumiller, David E. Sanger, and Richard W. Stevenson,

"How 3 Weeks of War Looked from the Oval Office," *New York Times*, April 14, 2003, p. A1.

74. "President Bush Meets with Prime Minister Blair in Northern Ireland," April 8, 2003, White House transcript, www.whitehouse.gov/news/releases/2003/04/20030408.html (accessed Aug. 23, 2007).
75. Elisabeth Bumiller, "The Women Behind Bush: They Promote and Defend, Nudge, Revere and Defer," *New York Times*, April 5, 2004.
76. Bumiller, "A Partner in Shaping."
77. Jeff Kojac, author interviews, Arlington, Va., Oct. 3 and 12, 2006.
78. Ibid.
79. Chandrasekaran, p. 40.
80. Ibid.
81. Donald Rumsfeld, Department of Defense news briefing, April 11, 2003, www.defenselink.mil/transcripts/transcript.aspx?transcriptid=2367 (accessed June 26, 2007).
82. Kojac interview.
83. Manning interview.
84. Ibid.
85. George Packer, *The Assassin's Gate: America in Iraq* (New York: Farrar, Straus and Giroux, 2005), p. 134.
86. Ibid.
87. Ibid.
88. Chandrasekaran, p. 40.
89. Rice interview.
90. DeYoung, p. 464.
91. Rice interview.
92. Ibid.
93. L. Paul Bremer, *My Year in Iraq: The Struggle to Build a Future of Hope* (New York: Simon & Schuster, 2006), p. 6.
94. L. Paul Bremer, "What We Got Right in Iraq," *Washington Post*, May 13, 2007, p. B1.
95. L. Paul Bremer, author interview, Bethesda, Md., May 10, 2007.
96. Rice interview.
97. Ibid.
98. Ibid.
99. Bremer interview.
100. Armitage interview.
101. Ibid.
102. Ibid.
103. Ibid.
104. Ibid.

105. Ibid.
106. Ibid.
107. Rice interview.
108. Powell interview.
109. DeYoung, p. 478.
110. Armitage interview.
111. Ibid.
112. Glenn Kessler and Peter Slevin, "Rice Fails to Repair Rifts, Officials Say; Cabinet Rivalries Complicate Her Role," *Washington Post*, Oct. 12, 2003, p. A1.
113. Armitage interview.
114. Bumiller, "A Partner in Shaping an Assertive Foreign Policy."
115. Richard W. Stevenson, "Back from Africa: Bush's Promises Will Be Watched," *New York Times*, July 14, 2004, p. A4.
116. Rice interview.
117. Sheryl Gay Stolberg, "Bush Requests $30 Billion to Fight AIDS," *New York Times*, May 31, 2007, p. A6.
118. Tenet, p. 459.
119. "Press Gaggle with Ari Fleischer and Dr. Condoleezza Rice," July 11, 2003, White House transcript, www.whitehouse.gov/news/releases/2003/07/20030711-7.html (accessed Aug. 24, 2007).
120. David E. Sanger and James Risen, "C.I.A. Chief Takes Blame in Assertion on Iraqi Uranium," *New York Times*, July 12, 2003, p. A1.
121. Administration official, author interview.
122. Rice interview.
123. Blackwill interview.
124. Woodward, *State of Denial*, p. 242.
125. Blackwill interview.
126. Ibid.
127. Ibid.
128. Ibid.
129. Ibid.
130. Bremer interview.
131. Ibid.
132. Ibid.
133. Blackwill interview.
134. Rice interview.
135. Ibid.
136. David E. Sanger, "White House to Overhaul Iraq and Afghan Missions," *New York Times*, Oct. 6, 2003, p. A1.

137. Donald Rumsfeld, roundtable with NATO journalists, Department of Defense transcript, www.defenselink.mil/transcripts/transcript.aspx?transcriptid=3011 (accessed June 28, 2007).
138. David E. Sanger and Thom Shanker, "Rumsfeld Quick to Dismiss Talk of Reduced Role in Iraq Policy," *New York Times*, Oct. 9, 2003, p. A1.
139. Rice interview.
140. Ibid.
141. Bremer, p. 245.
142. Bremer interview.
143. Administration official, author interview.
144. Card interview.
145. Ibid.
146. Fran Townsend, author interview, Washington, D.C., Nov. 7, 2006.
147. Ibid.
148. Bremer interview.
149. Ibid.
150. Ibid.
151. Bremer, p. 229.
152. Rice interview.
153. Ibid.
154. "President Discusses Trip to Iraq with Reporters," Nov. 27, 2003, White House transcript, www.whitehouse.gov/news/releases/2003/11/20031127-1.html (accessed Aug. 28, 2007).
155. Deborah Schoeneman, "Armani's Exchange . . . Condi's Slip . . . Forget the Alamo," *New York*, April 26, 2004, nymag.com/nymetro/news/people/columns/intelligencer/n_10245/ (accessed July 2, 2007).
156. Rice interview.
157. The author was one of those at the dinner who did not hear Rice say "My husb—"
158. Bremer, p. 252.
159. Clara Rice interview.
160. Ibid.

Chapter 11: Karl's Aide-de-Camp

1. Administration official, author interview.
2. Ibid.
3. James Risen, "Ex-Inspector Says C.I.A. Missed Disarray in Iraqi Arms Program," *New York Times*, Jan. 26, 2004, p. A1.
4. Ibid.

5. Ibid.
6. Bremer interview.
7. Ibid.
8. Dexter Filkins, "Iraqi Leadership Gains Agreement on Constitution," *New York Times*, March 1, 2004, p. A1.
9. Richard Clarke, interview with *60 Minutes*, March 21, 2004, CBS News transcript, www.cbsnews.com/stories/2004/03/19/60minutes/main607356.shtml (accessed Aug. 24, 2007).
10. Clarke, p. 236.
11. Clarke, p. 287.
12. Richard A. Clarke, testimony to the National Commission on Terrorist Attacks upon the United States, March 24, 2004, www.9-11commission.gov/archive/hearing8/9-11Commission_Hearing_2004-03-24.pdf (accessed July 4, 2007).
13. Thomas H. Kean and Lee H. Hamilton, *Without Precedent: The Inside Story of the 9/11 Commission* (New York: Alfred A. Knopf, 2006), p. 174.
14. Administration official, author interview.
15. Rice interview.
16. Ibid.
17. Ibid.
18. Condoleezza Rice, interview with *60 Minutes*, March 28, 2004, CBS News transcript, www.cbsnews.com/stories/2004/03/28/60minutes/main609074.shtml (accessed Aug. 24, 2007).
19. Rice interview.
20. Ed Bradley, interview with Condoleezza Rice for *60 Minutes*, March 28, 2004, CBS News transcript, www.cbsnews.com/stories/2004/03/28/60minutes/main609074.shtml (accessed Aug. 24, 2007).
21. Rice interview.
22. Jim Wilkinson, author interview, Washington, D.C., Oct. 13, 2006.
23. Ibid.
24. Ibid.
25. Kean and Hamilton, p. 178.
26. Alessandra Stanley, "Testimony Provides Breath of Racial Reality for TV," *New York Times*, April 9, 2004, p. A14.
27. Rice, testimony to the 9/11 Commission, April 8, 2004.
28. Ibid.
29. Ibid.
30. Richard Ben-Veniste, questions to Condoleezza Rice, 9/11 Commission hearing, April 8, 2004.

31. Rice, testimony to 9/11 Commission.
32. Timothy Roemer, questions to Condoleezza Rice, 9/11 Commission hearing, April 8, 2004.
33. Rice, testimony to 9/11 Commission.
34. Rice interview.
35. Ibid.
36. Kean and Hamilton, p. 182.
37. Major General Antonio M. Taguba, "Investigation of the 800th Military Police Brigade" ("Taguba Report"), 2004, www.globalsecurity.org/intell/library/reports/2004/800-mp-bde.htm (accessed Aug. 24, 2007).
38. Thom Shanker, "6 G.I.'s in Iraq Are Charged with Abuse of Prisoners," *New York Times*, March 20, 2004, p. 14.
39. Elisabeth Bumiller and Richard W. Stevenson, "Rumsfeld Chastised by President for His Handling of Iraq Scandal," *New York Times*, May 6, 2004, p. A1.
40. "President Bush, Jordanian King Discuss Iraq, Middle East," May 6, 2004, White House transcript, www.whitehouse.gov/news/releases/2004/05/20040506-9.html (accessed Aug. 24, 2007).
41. Donald Rumsfeld, testimony before the House Armed Services Committee, May 7, 2004, Pentagon transcript, www.defenselink.mil/speeches/speech.aspx?speechid=117 (accessed Aug. 24, 2007).
42. Elisabeth Bumiller, "In the Balance: Rumsfeld's Job," *New York Times*, May 8, 2004, p. A1.
43. Ibid.
44. Rice interview.
45. Administration official, author interview.
46. International Committee of the Red Cross, "Report on the Treatment by the Coalition Forces of Prisoners of War and Other Protected Persons by the Geneva Conventions in Iraq During Arrest, Internment and Interrogation," Feb. 2004, www.globalsecurity.org/military/library/report/2004/icrc_report_iraq_feb2004.htm (accessed Aug. 24, 2007).
47. Barton Gellman and Jo Becker, "The Unseen Path to Cruelty," *Washington Post*, June 25, 2007, p. A1; Dana Priest and R. Jeffrey Smith, "Memo Offered Justification for Use of Torture; Justice Dept. Gave Advice in 2002," *Washington Post*, June 8, 2004, p. A1; Neil A. Lewis and Eric Schmitt, "Lawyers Decided Bans on Torture Didn't Bind Bush," *New York Times*, June 8, 2004, p. A1.
48. Gellman and Becker, "The Unseen Path."
49. Ibid.

50. Ibid.
51. Ibid.
52. Dexter Filkins, "U.S. Transfers Power to Iraq 2 Days Early," *New York Times*, June 29, 2004, p. A1.
53. Eric Schmitt, "Insurgency and Able Government Prompted Transfer Decision," *New York Times*, June 29, 2004, p. A1.
54. Douglas Jehl, "Senators Assail C.I.A. Judgments on Iraq's Arms as Deeply Flawed," *New York Times*, July 10, 2004, p. A1.
55. 9/11 Commission Report, www.9-11commission.gov/report/911 Report_Exec.pdf (accessed July 6, 2007).
56. Ibid.
57. Zelikow interview.
58. Kay, testimony to the Senate Select Committee on Intelligence, Aug. 18, 2004.
59. Ibid.
60. Woodward, *State of Denial*, pp. 329–30.
61. Douglas Jehl, "U.S. Report Finds Iraqis Eliminated Illicit Arms in 90's," *New York Times*, Oct. 7, 2004, p. A1.
62. Glenn Kessler, "Rice Hitting the Road to Speak; National Security Adviser's Trips to Swing States Break Precedent," *Washington Post*, Oct. 20, 2004, p. A2.
63. Ibid.
64. Ibid.
65. Wilkinson interview.
66. James Glanz, William J. Broad, and David E. Sanger, "Huge Cache of Explosives Vanished from Site in Iraq," *New York Times*, Oct. 25, 2004, p. A1.
67. Ibid.
68. Ibid.
69. David E. Sanger, "Iraq Explosives Become Issue in Campaign," *New York Times*, Oct. 26, 2004, p. A1.
70. Ibid.
71. Jim Dwyer and David E. Sanger, "No Check of Bunker, Unit Commander Says," *New York Times*, Oct. 27, 2004, p. A17.
72. Eric Schmitt, "Soldier Tells of Destroying Some Arms," *New York Times*, Oct. 30, 2004, p. A12.
73. White House official, author interview.
74. Ibid.
75. Ibid.
76. Rice interview.
77. Ibid.

78. Ibid.
79. Ibid.
80. Ibid.
81. Ibid.
82. Ibid.
83. Elisabeth Bumiller, "Among Family and Friends, a Confident Bush Waits," *New York Times*, Nov. 3, 2004, p. P3.
84. Rice interview.
85. Bumiller, "Among Family and Friends."
86. Rice interview.
87. Ibid.
88. Woodward, *State of Denial*, p. 345.
89. Rice interview.
90. Bush friend, author interview.
91. Rice interview.
92. Ibid.
93. Ibid.
94. Sidney Blumenthal, "Delirious Rhetoric," *The Guardian*, Sept. 7, 2006, www.guardian.co.uk/commentisfree/story/0,,1866264,00.html (accessed Aug. 24, 2007).

Chapter 12: Madame Secretary

1. Administration official, author interview.
2. Condoleezza Rice, opening remarks to the Senate Foreign Relations Committee, Jan. 18, 2005, State Department transcript, www.state.gov/secretary/rm/2005/40991.htm (accessed July 8, 2007).
3. Steven R. Weisman and Joel Brinkley, "Rice Sees Iraq Training Progress but Offers No Schedule for Exit," *New York Times*, Jan. 19, 2005, p. A1.
4. Ibid.
5. Sheryl Gay Stolberg, "Rice Is Sworn In as Secretary After Senate Vote of 85 to 13," *New York Times*, Jan. 27, 2003, p. A3.
6. Ibid.
7. Senior European diplomat, author interview.
8. George W. Bush, "President Sworn-In to Second Term," 2005 Inaugural Address, Jan. 20, 2005, White House transcript, www.whitehouse.gov/news/releases/2005/01/20050120-1.html (accessed Aug. 24, 2007).
9. Condoleezza Rice, "Remarks at Town Hall meeting," Jan. 31, 2005, State Department transcript, www.state.gov/secretary/rm/2005/41414.htm (accessed Aug. 24, 2007).

10. Steven R. Weisman, "Secretary Rice, the New Globetrotter," *New York Times*, Feb. 7, 2005, p. A6.
11. Condoleezza Rice, "Remarks at the Institute d'Études Politiques de Paris—Sciences Po," Feb. 8, 2005, State Department transcript, www.state.gov/secretary/rm/2005/41973.htm (accessed Aug. 24, 2007).
12. Elaine Sciolino, "The French Are Charmed and Jarred by 'Chère Condi,'" *New York Times*, Feb. 10, 2006, p. A6.
13. Ibid.
14. Ibid.
15. Ibid.
16. Glenn Kessler, "In 2003, U.S. Spurned Iran's Offer of Dialogue," *Washington Post*, June 18, 2006, p. A16.
17. Glenn Kessler, "Rice Denies Seeing Iranian Proposal in '03; Remarks Add to Debate on Whether U.S. Missed Chance to Improve Ties with Tehran," *Washington Post*, Feb. 8, 2007, p. A18.
18. Steven R. Weisman, "U.S. Acquiesces in European Plan for Talks with Iran," *New York Times*, Oct. 16, 2004, p. A7.
19. Fried interview.
20. Ibid.
21. Ibid.
22. Administration official, author interview.
23. Ibid.
24. Ibid.
25. Ibid.
26. Elisabeth Bumiller, "Bush May Weigh Using Incentives to Dissuade Iran," *New York Times*, Feb. 24, 2005, p. A1.
27. David E. Sanger and Steven R. Weisman, "U.S. and Allies Agree on Steps in Iran Dispute," *New York Times*, March 11, 2005, p. A1.
28. Bumiller, "Bush May Weigh Using Incentives."
29. Robin Givhan, "Condoleezza Rice's Commanding Clothes," *Washington Post*, Feb. 25, 2005, p. C1.
30. Wilkinson interview.
31. Shultz interview.
32. Ibid.
33. Administration official, author interview.
34. Anthony Tommasini, "And on Piano, Madame Secretary," *New York Times*, April 9, 2006, section 2, p. 1.
35. Ibid.
36. Administration official, author interview.
37. Roger Cohen, "Her Jewish State," *New York Times Magazine*, July 8, 2007, p. 34.

38. Zelikow interview.
39. Glenn Kessler, *The Confidante: Condoleezza Rice and the Creation of the Bush Legacy* (New York: St. Martin's, 2007), p. 60.
40. Joel Brinkley and Steven R. Weisman, "Rice Urges Israel and Palestinians to Sustain Momentum," *New York Times*, Aug. 18, 2005, p. A8.
41. Robert D. McFadden and Ralph Blumenthal, "Bush Sees Long Recovery for New Orleans; 30,000 Troops in Largest U.S. Relief Effort," *New York Times*, Sept. 1, 2005, p. A1.
42. Mabry, p. 269.
43. As posted on Gawker.com. "Breaking: Condi Rice Spends Salary on Shoes," Gawker.com, Sept. 1, 2005, gawker.com/news/condoleezza-rice/breaking-condi-rice-spends-salary-on-shoes-123467.php (accessed July 10, 2005).
44. Mabry, p. 271.
45. Rice interview.
46. Ibid.
47. Administration official, author interview.
48. George W. Bush, "President Arrives in Alabama, Briefed on Hurricane Katrina," Sept. 2, 2005, White House transcript, www.whitehouse.gov/news/releases/2005/09/20050902-2.html (accessed Aug. 24, 2007).
49. Mabry, p. 274.
50. Condoleezza Rice, "Press Availability at the Bayou La Batre Community Center," Bayou La Batre, Ala., Sept. 4. 2005, State Department transcript, www.state.gov/secretary/rm/2005/52484.htm (accessed Sept. 20, 2007).
51. "Rice Talks to O'Reilly," Fox News transcript, Sept. 12, 2005, www.foxnews.com/story/0,2933,169421,00.html (accessed July 10, 2007).
52. Rice interview.
53. David E. Sanger, "Yes, Parallel Tracks to North, but Parallel Tracks Don't Meet," *New York Times*, Sept. 20, 2005, p. A6.
54. Steven R. Weisman, "U.S. Says North Korean Demand for Reactor Won't Derail Accord," *New York Times*, Sept. 21, 2005, p. A12.
55. Zelikow interview; Woodward, *State of Denial*, p. 388.
56. Zelikow interview; Woodward, *State of Denial*, p. 413.
57. Zelikow interview.
58. Zelikow's comments to Rice about Iraq in October 2005 are from Zelikow interviews with the author.
59. Zelikow interview.
60. Rice interview.
61. Ibid.

62. Ibid.
63. Elisabeth Bumiller, "Bush Defends His War Record, but Concedes Some Setbacks," *New York Times*, March 21, 2006, p. A8.
64. Woodward, *State of Denial*, p. 418.
65. Ibid.
66. Steven R. Weisman, "Rice, in Testy Hearing, Cites Progress in Iraq," *New York Times*, Oct. 20, 2005, p. A13.
67. Wilkinson interview.
68. Condoleezza Rice, "Remarks with United Kingdom Foreign Secretary Jack Straw at the Blackburn Institute's Frank A. Nix Lecture," University of Alabama, Tuscaloosa, Ala., Oct. 21, 2005, State Department transcript, www.state.gov/secretary/rm/2005/55423.htm (accessed July 13, 2007).
69. Ibid.
70. Steven R. Weisman, "On Trip to South, Rice Uses an Atypical Topic: Herself," *New York Times*, Oct. 24, 2005, p. A15.
71. Ibid.
72. Straw interview.
73. Rice interview.
74. Ibid.
75. Steven R. Weisman, "For Rice, Risky Dive into Mideast Storm," *New York Times*, Nov. 16, 2005, p. A1.
76. Dana Priest, "CIA Holds Terror Suspects in Secret Prisons; Debate Is Growing Within Agency About Legality and Morality of Overseas System Set Up After 9/11," *Washington Post*, Nov. 2, 2005, p. A1.
77. Condoleezza Rice, "Remarks Upon Her Departure for Europe," Dec. 5, 2005, State Department transcript, www.state.gov/secretary/rm/2005/57602.htm (accessed Aug. 24, 2007).
78. Straw interview.

Chapter 13: Hamas Won?

1. Administration official, author interview.
2. Ibid.
3. Rice interview.
4. Ibid.
5. Ibid.
6. Ibid.
7. Ibid.
8. "Press Conference of the President," Jan. 26, 2006, White House transcript, www.whitehouse.gov/news/releases/2006/01/20060126.html (accessed Sept. 20, 2007).

9. Steven R. Weisman, "Rice Admits U.S. Underestimated Hamas Strength," *New York Times*, Jan. 30, 2006, p. A1.
10. Ibid.
11. Ibid.
12. Ibid.
13. Rice interview.
14. Robert F. Worth, "Blast at Shiite Shrine Sets Off Sectarian Fury in Iraq," *New York Times*, Feb. 23, 2006, p. A1.
15. Ibid.
16. Condoleezza Rice, "Remarks with Saudi Foreign Minister Saud al-Faysal bin Abd al-Aziz Al Saud After Meeting," Riyadh, Saudi Arabia, Feb. 22, 2006, State Department transcript, www.state.gov/secretary/rm/2006/61910.htm (accessed Sept. 20, 2007).
17. Condoleezza Rice, "Briefing En Route Rio de Janeiro, Brazil," March 12, 2006, State Department transcript, www.state.gov/secretary/rm/2006/63024.htm (accessed July 24, 2007).
18. Steven R. Weisman, "Rice, in Indonesia, Supports Renewed Military Assistance," *New York Times*, March 15, 2006, p. A17.
19. Joel Brinkley, "Rice, in England, Concedes U.S. 'Tactical Errors' in Iraq," *New York Times*, April 1, 2006, p. A9.
20. Ibid.
21. Joel Brinkley, "Rice Finds British Muslims Want to Give Her an Earful," *New York Times*, April 2, 2006, p. 10.
22. Condoleezza Rice, "Remarks at BBC Today—Chatham House Lecture," Blackburn, England, March 31, 2006, State Department transcript, www.state.gov/secretary/rm/2006/63969.htm (accessed Sept. 20, 2007).
23. Ibid.
24. Condoleezza Rice, "Remarks with British Foreign Secretary Jack Straw at Blackburn Town Hall," Blackburn, England, April 1, 2006, State Department transcript, www.state.gov/secretary/rm/2006/63980.htm (accessed Sept. 20, 2007).
25. Donald Rumsfeld, interview with Scott Hennen, WDAY Radio, Fargo, N.D., April 4, 2006, Department of Defense transcript, www.defenselink.mil/transcripts/transcript.aspx?transcriptid=1225 (accessed July 17, 2007).
26. Ibid.
27. Edward Wong, "Bush Opposes Iraq's Premier, Shiites Report," *New York Times*, March 29, 2006, p. A1.
28. Straw interview.
29. Woodward, *State of Denial*, p. 458.

30. Ibid.
31. Condoleezza Rice, "Roundtable with Traveling Press," Baghdad, April 2, 2006, State Department transcript, www.state.gov/secretary/rm/2006/63994.htm (accessed July 18, 2007).
32. Kirk Semple, "Iraqi Says Visit by Two Diplomats Backfired," *New York Times*, April 6, 2006, p. A15.
33. Kirk Semple and Richard A. Oppel Jr., "Shiite Drops Bid to Keep His Post as Iraqi Premier," *New York Times*, April 21, 2006, p. A1.
34. Woodward, *State of Denial*, p. 461.
35. Ibid., p. 462.
36. Ibid.
37. Ibid.
38. Ibid.
39. Condoleezza Rice and Donald Rumsfeld, "Joint Roundtable with Reporters," Baghdad, April 26, 2006, State Department transcript, www.state.gov/secretary/rm/2006/65317.htm (accessed July 18, 2007).
40. Ibid.
41. Ibid.
42. Ibid.
43. Steven R. Weisman, "Rumsfeld Learns to Curb His Enthusiasm," *New York Times*, April 30, 2006, section 4, p. 3.
44. Burns interview.
45. Helene Cooper and David E. Sanger, "With a Talk over Lunch, a Shift in Bush's Iran Policy Took Root," *New York Times*, June 4, 2006, p. A1.
46. Ibid.
47. Rice interview.
48. Cooper and Sanger, "With a Talk over Lunch."
49. Ibid.
50. The account of Rice's color-coded chart and conversation about it with Burns is from a Burns interview.
51. Condoleezza Rice, "Press Conference on Iran," Washington, D.C., May 31, 2006, State Department transcript, www.state.gov/secretary/rm/2006/67103.htm (accessed July 19, 2007).
52. David E. Sanger, "Bush's Realization on Iran: No Good Choice Left Except Talks," *New York Times*, June 1, 2006, p. A8.
53. Rice interview.
54. Steven Erlanger, "Militants' Raid on Israel Raises Tension in Gaza," *New York Times*, June 26, 2006, p. A1.
55. Hassan M. Fattah and Steven Erlanger, "Israel Blockades Lebanon; Wide Strikes by Hezbollah," *New York Times*, July 14, 2006, p. A1.

56. Steven Erlanger and Jad Mouawad, "Diplomats Seek Foreign Patrols to Calm Mideast," *New York Times*, July 18, 2006, p. A1.
57. Ibid.
58. Transcript of George Bush's private remarks to Tony Blair at Group of Eight summit in St. Petersburg, Russia, July 17, 2006, *Washington Post*, www.washingtonpost.com/wp-dyn/content/article/2006/07/17/AR2006071700402_pf.html (accessed July 22, 2007).
59. Helene Cooper and Steven Erlanger, "U.S. Seen Waiting to Act on Israel; Strikes in Lebanon," *New York Times*, July 19, 2006, p. A1.
60. Condoleezza Rice, briefing on travel to Europe and the Middle East, Washington, D.C., July 21, 2006, State Department transcript, www.state.gov/secretary/rm/2006/69331.htm (accessed July 24, 2007).
61. Rice interview.
62. Rev. Clyde L. Carter, comments at Westminster Presbyterian Church, Birmingham, Ala., July 23, 2006.
63. Helene Cooper and Jad Mouawad, "In First Stop, Rice Confers with Leaders of Lebanon," *New York Times*, July 25, 2006, p. A13.
64. Craig S. Smith and Helene Cooper, "Cease-Fire Talks Stall as Fighting Rages on 2 Fronts," *New York Times*, July 27, 2006, p. A1.
65. Ibid.
66. Helene Cooper, "2 Steps Back: Rice's Careful Diplomacy Falters Under Renewed Assertiveness by the U.S.," *New York Times*, July 28, 2006, p. A12.
67. Elliott Abrams, author interview, Washington, D.C., May 23, 2007.
68. Ibid.
69. Helene Cooper, "Rice's Hurdles on Middle East Begin at Home," *New York Times*, Aug. 10, 2006, p. A1.
70. Helene Cooper, "From Carnage, a Concession," *New York Times*, July 31, 2006, p. A1.
71. Warren Hoge, Helene Cooper, and Thom Shanker, "U.S. Shift Kicked Off Frantic Diplomacy at U.N.," *New York Times*, August 14, 2006, p. A1.
72. Rice interview.
73. Ibid.
74. Administration official, author interview.
75. Ibid.
76. Linda Greenhouse, "Justices, 5–3, Broadly Reject Bush Plan to Try Detainees," *New York Times*, June 30, 2006, p. A1.
77. Administration official, author interview.
78. Ibid.

79. Dafna Linzer and Glenn Kessler, "Decision to Move Detainees Resolved Two-Year Debate Among Bush Advisers," *Washington Post*, Sept. 8, 2006, p. A1.
80. Administration official, author interview.
81. Ibid.
82. Ibid.
83. Sheryl Gay Stolberg, "President Moves 14 Held in Secret to Guantánamo," *New York Times*, Sept. 7, 2006, p. A1.
84. Robert Draper, *Dead Certain: The Presidency of George W. Bush* (New York: Free Press, 2007), p. 398.
85. Dexter Filkins, "Baghdad's Chaos Undercuts Tack Pursued by U.S.," *New York Times*, Aug. 6, 2006, p. 1.
86. Notes from National Security Council meeting, Aug. 17, 2006; administration official, author interview.
87. Ibid.
88. Ibid.
89. Ibid.
90. Ibid.
91. Ibid.
92. Ibid.
93. Administration official, author interview.
94. Administration official, author interview.
95. Ibid.
96. Rice interview.
97. Ibid.
98. Scott Shane, "Man in the News: Robert Michael Gates; Cautious Player from a Past Bush Team," *New York Times*, Nov. 9, 2006, p. A1.
99. Ibid.
100. Elaine Sciolino, "Slanting of Intelligence Becomes Issue for Nominee," *New York Times*, Sept. 19, 1991, p. A1.
101. Rice interview.
102. Ibid.
103. Sheryl Gay Stolberg and Jim Rutenberg, "Rumsfeld Resigns; Bush Vows 'To Find Common Ground'; Focus Is on Virginia," *New York Times*, Nov. 9, 2006, p. A1.
104. Former administration official, author interview.
105. Rice interview.
106. Ibid.
107. Ibid.
108. Ibid.

109. Thom Shanker and David E. Sanger, "New to Pentagon, Gates Argued for Closing Guantánamo," *New York Times*, March 23, 2007, p. A1.
110. Former administration official, author interview.
111. Ibid.

Conclusion

1. European diplomat, author interview.
2. Condoleezza Rice, "Roundtable with Print Journalists," Feb. 18, 2007, State Department transcript, www.state.gov/secretary/rm/2007/feb/80657.htm (accessed Aug. 28, 2007).
3. Steven Erlanger, "A Life of Unrest," *New York Times Magazine*, July 15, 2007, Section 6, p. 42.
4. David E. Sanger and Thom Shanker, "Rice Is Said to Have Speeded North Korea Deal," *New York Times*, Feb. 16, 2007, p. A3.
5. Rice interview.
6. Ibid.
7. Ibid.
8. Christopher Hill, briefing and hearing before the House Foreign Affairs Committee, Feb. 28, 2007, www.hcfa.house.gov/110/32548a.pdf (accessed Aug. 28, 2007).
9. John Bolton, interview with Wolf Blitzer, *The Situation Room*, Feb. 12, 2007, CNN transcript, transcripts.cnn.com/TRANSCRIPTS/0702/12/sitroom.02.html (accessed Aug. 28, 2007).
10. Jim Yardley and David E. Sanger, "In Shift, a Deal Is Being Weighed by North Korea," *New York Times*, Feb. 13, 2007, p. A1.
11. Mohamed ElBaradei, interview with Rob Broomby of the BBC, May 31, 2007, International Atomic Energy Agency transcript, www.iaea.org/NewsCenter/Transcripts/2007/bbc310507.html (accessed Aug. 28, 2007).
12. Condoleezza Rice, "Press Availability with Spanish Foreign Minister Miguel Moratinos," June 1, 2007, State Department transcript, www.state.gov/secretary/rm/2007/06/85907.htm (accessed Aug. 28, 2007).
13. Condoleezza Rice, testimony before the Senate Foreign Relations Committee, Jan. 11, 2007, State Department transcript, www.state.gov/secretary/rm/2007/78605.htm (accessed July 27, 2007).
14. Helene Cooper and Jon Elson, "U.S. Officials Meet Briefly with Iranians," *New York Times*, May 4, 2007, www.nytimes.com/2007/05/04/world/middleeast/05diplocnd.html?ex=1335931200&en=0191236f0b85993f&ei=5088&partner=rssnyt&emc=rss (accessed Aug. 29, 2007).

15. C. J. Chivers, "After Rice and Putin Meet, Russia Agrees to Soften Language," *New York Times*, May 16, 2007, p. A3.
16. Jim Rutenberg, "Putin Arrives in Kennebunkport for 2-Day Visit with the Bushes," *New York Times*, July 2, 2007, p. A8.
17. George W. Bush, news conference with Prime Minister Stephen Harper of Canada and President Felipe Calderón of Mexico, Aug. 21, 2007, White House transcript, www.whitehouse.gov/news/releases/2007/08/20070821–3.html (accessed Aug. 28, 2007).
18. Sheryl Gay Stolberg and Jim Rutenberg, "Bush Takes a Step Away from Maliki," *New York Times*, Aug. 22, 2007, p. A1.
19. David E. Sanger and David Cloud, "White House Is Said to Debate '08 Cut in Iraq Combat Forces by 50%," *New York Times*, May 26, 2007, p. A1.
20. Helene Cooper and Thom Shanker, "Passing Exchange Becomes Political Flashpoint Focused on Feminism," *New York Times*, Jan. 13, 2007, p. A8.
21. Ibid.
22. Dana Milbank, "The Secretary Vs. the Senators," *Washington Post*, Jan. 12, 2007, p. A1.
23. Rice interview.
24. Ibid.
25. "George & Laura Bush: The *People* Interview," *People*, Dec. 15, 2006, www.people.com/people/article/0,,20004374_2,00.html (accessed Sept. 20, 2007).
26. George W. Bush, comments on African American History Month, Feb. 12, 2007, White House transcript, www.whitehouse.gov/news/releases/2007/02/20070212-5.html (accessed Aug. 28, 2007).
27. Condoleezza Rice, interview on Fox News Sunday, Feb. 25, 2007, State Department transcript, www.state.gov/secretary/rm/2007/feb/81037.htm (accessed Aug. 28, 2007).
28. Condoleezza Rice, "Remarks with Australian Foreign Minister Alexander Downer at the Center for a New Generation," May 24, 2007, State Department transcript, www.state.gov/secretary/rm/2007/may/85484.htm (accessed Aug. 29, 2007).
29. Ibid.
30. Ibid.
31. Condoleezza Rice, "Remarks at Cornerstone School's 10th Anniversary Dinner," Sept. 17, 2007, State Department transcript, www.state.gov/secretary/rm/2007/09/92234.htm (accessed Sept. 22, 2007).

INDEX

ABOUT THE AUTHOR

ELISABETH BUMILLER, a Washington reporter for *The New York Times*, was a *Times* White House correspondent from September 10, 2001, to 2006. She is the author of *May You Be the Mother of a Hundred Sons: A Journey Among the Women of India* and *The Secrets of Mariko: A Year in the Life of a Japanese Woman and Her Family*. She wrote much of this book as a public policy scholar at the Woodrow Wilson International Center and as a transatlantic fellow at the German Marshall Fund of the United States. She lives in the Washington, D.C., area with her husband, Steven R. Weisman, and two children.

ABOUT THE TYPE

The text of this book was set in Janson, a misnamed typeface designed in about 1690 by Nicholas Kis, a Hungarian in Amsterdam. In 1919 the matrices became the property of the Stempel Foundry in Frankfurt. It is an old-style book face of excellent clarity and sharpness. Janson serifs are concave and splayed; the contrast between thick and thin strokes is marked.